The Legend of
Spring-heeled Jack

This is dedicated to my parents, Graham and Gloria,
for giving me the love, support and encouragement
to pursue dreams and monsters

The Legend of
Spring-heeled Jack

Victorian Urban Folklore
and Popular Cultures

Karl Bell

THE BOYDELL PRESS

First published 2012
The Boydell Press, Woodbridge
Paperback edition 2017

ISBN 978 1 84383 787 9 hardback
ISBN 978 1 78327 191 7 paperback

The Boydell Press is an imprint of Boydell & Brewer Ltd
PO Box 9, Woodbridge, Suffolk IP12 3DF, UK
and of Boydell & Brewer Inc.
668 Mt Hope Avenue, Rochester, NY 14620–2731, USA
website: www.boydellandbrewer.com

A CIP catalogue record for this book is available
from the British Library

The publisher has no responsibility for the continued existence or accuracy
of URLs for external or third-party internet websites referred to in this book,
and does not guarantee that any content on such websites is,
or will remain, accurate or appropriate

This publication is printed on acid-free paper

MIX
Paper from
responsible sources
FSC
www.fsc.org   FSC® C013056

Contents

Acknowledgements

Despite the generally solitary nature of historical research and writing, a book such as this never comes to fruition without the help and assistance of many others. Firstly I would like to thank Owen Davies for his continuing support for my research and his enthusiastic endorsement of this project. I am also grateful to Peter Mandler for his sharp and insightful critique of earlier drafts of several chapters; I can only hope that I have now addressed most of his concerns. I would like to acknowledge the financial support provided by the University of Portsmouth's Centre for European and International Studies Research as this enabled me to conduct some valuable research in the British Library. I must also thank my colleagues in the History department for continuing to accommodate my scholarly fascination with folklore and the fantastical.

There are an extremely small number of scholars working on Spring-heeled Jack at the moment but I would like to thank them for reaching out to welcome me into their ranks. Jacqueline Simpson generously shared her understanding of the legend whilst David Clarke and Mike Dash were both willing to offer me access to their recent or current work. I would also like to express my gratitude to Professor Bill Gray, director of the excellent Sussex Centre for Folklore, Fairy Tales and Fantasy. Bill kindly invited me to present a lecture on Spring-heeled Jack at the University of Chichester in 2010 and this helped inform my ideas for several chapters. I would also like to thank the commentators at academic conferences where I have presented papers on Spring-heeled Jack; they similarly made me reflect anew on both my evidence and interpretations.

I am especially grateful to Michael Middeke at Boydell and Brewer. Not only did he approach me about writing this book, but given that I was repeatedly caught between deadlines for this and another project he demonstrated great faith and understanding. I can only hope that the final product rewards his patience. In the later stages of its development I was also fortunate to work with Megan Milan and Anna Robinette; their efficiency and professionalism ensured the book's smooth progression from manuscript to publication. I must also thank Mark Vivian, the Picture Research Manager at the Mary Evans Picture Library. Not only did he help organise my acquisition of the right to use the image for the book cover, his subsequent provision of details relating to its exact dating helped clarify my understanding of Spring-heeled Jack's relation to early twentieth-century depictions of Dracula.

As ever, the biggest thanks have to be reserved for my wife and sons. Writing requires seclusion and time and these were necessarily paid for at the cost of sometimes benignly neglecting my responsibilities as a husband and father. For nearly two years Jo has graciously shared her husband with a vicious Victorian demon, not a claim most wives could (or would want to) make. My boys, Luca and Evan, were always there to restore my perspective, reminding me that monsters and the imagination are first and foremost to be played with and indulged, not dryly analysed. I am truly indebted to their unending provision of love, understanding, and strong coffee.

Introduction

Spring-heeled Jack leapt into the popular imagination on Tuesday 9th January 1838. This may seem like uncannily accurate dating for a cultural process, but it was the day on which *The Times* reported on an announcement made the day before by Sir John Cowen, the Lord Mayor of the City of London. Cowen had made public a letter from an anonymous 'Peckham resident' who wanted to bring news of a supposedly supernatural attacker to the attention of the authorities.[1] Since the previous autumn tales had been circulating among the villages that fringed south London, firstly of a phantom bull or bear, and then of a tall, dark, cloaked figure who pounced upon individuals, predominantly women. This strange, evolving character evaded capture through being fleet-footed and, according to rumour, almost superhumanly agile. Panic spread through the metropolis, with the press reporting tales of victims having their clothes sliced to shreds by the creature's claws, losing their wits, suffering convulsive fits or even dying of shock and fright.[2] Accounts came to describe a cloaked being with fiery eyes, who could vomit blue flames from its mouth, and whose sharp metal talons tore the flesh of its victims.

From January to March 1838 he occupied the columns of respectable metropolitan newspapers. Thereafter this urban legend left the capital to stalk the cities, towns and villages of England. From the 1840s to the 1870s Spring-heeled Jack was particularly active in the eastern and southern counties. In the 1880s and 1890s he gradually migrated into northern England and Wales. Newspaper reports on a supposed appearance in Everton, Liverpool, in 1904 have often been taken to mark the end of his activities, although rumours and associations with the name persisted into the 1930s. Emerging in the year that Victoria became queen, Spring-heeled Jack can make credible claim to being the first Victorian

---

[1] See *The Times*, 9th January 1838.
[2] See *Morning Chronicle*, 10th and 11th January 1838; *Morning Herald*, 10th January 1838; *The Times*, 11th January 1838; *The Examiner*, 14th January 1838; and *The Sun*, 20th January 1838.

urban legend.[3] Despite being a contemporary of Sweeney Todd and a shadowy predecessor to Jack the Ripper, he is, for more recent generations at least, the forgotten third member of this grim metropolitan triumvirate, finding himself completely eclipsed by the seemingly endless fascination with the Whitechapel murderer. Whilst originating as an urban legend, a modern expression of 'traditional' folkloric beliefs, he went on to become a penny serial character, the focus of theatrical plays, ballets and dioramas, and a nursery bogeyman to frighten children into obedience, before diffusing into Victorian culture to such a degree as to become an expression associated with swiftness, elusiveness or the inexplicable.

Although his legend faded, the Spring-heeled Jack trope survived to make sporadic revivals in twentieth-century popular culture. He took cinematic form in *The Curse of the Wraydons* (1946), a film based on an earlier Spring-heeled Jack play. The lead role was taken by Todd Slaughter, an actor associated with his portrayal of Sweeney Todd. Slaughter took the lead again in a 1950 play, *Spring-Heeled Jack, The Terror of Epping Forest*, which was staged at the Theatre Royal, Stratford. The eponymous hero of Philip Pullman's *Spring-heeled Jack* (1989) was the reimagined caped avenger of the late 1860s, saving orphaned waifs in a tale that both evokes and gently mocks the penny dreadful format. More recently he has been appropriated by the comic-book subculture, being the subject of a 2007 comic series by David Hitchcock and featuring in Warren Ellis' graphic novel, *Captain Swing and the Electrical Pirates of Cindery Island* (2011). Strongly alluded to in the 2011 series of BBC One crime drama *Luther*, his most notable return to the twenty-first-century popular cultural mainstream has been Mark Hodder's enjoyable, award-winning novel, *The Strange Affair of Spring-heeled Jack* (2010).[4]

These more recent reappearances are indicative of the fact that Spring-heeled Jack seems particularly well attuned to a current cultural trend for reinvented and reimagined Victoriana. This has spread beyond television adaptations of the works of familiar nineteenth-century novelists, beyond the neo-Victorian novels of Peter Ackroyd, Sarah Waters and Michael Faber, and on towards more overtly fantasised manifestations.[5] As indicated by Hodder's novel, this is

---

[3] Victorian society produced new urban legends as it underwent increasing urbanisation. Spring-heeled Jack beat Sweeney Todd into the popular imagination by at least nine years, the latter's penny serial origins in 'The String of Pearls: A Romance' appearing in Edward Lloyd's *The People's Periodical and Family Library* between November 1846 and March 1847.

[4] See *The Times*, 17th January 1950, p. 8. For Peter Terson's 1970 play, *Spring-heeled Jack*, see *The Times*, 26th August 1970, p. 6. The *Luther* episode first aired on 14th June 2011. Hodder's novel won the 2010 Philip K. Dick Award.

[5] See for example Ackroyd, *Dan Leno and the Limehouse Golem* (1995); Waters, *Tipping the Velvet* (1999); and Faber, *The Crimson Petal and the White* (2002).

perhaps best reflected in the science fiction subgenre of steampunk.[6] In recent decades Hollywood has also served up fantasised versions of both Victorian London and its monsters in *Bram Stoker's Dracula*, *From Hell* and *Sweeney Todd*. What this trend for a highly stylised Victoriana says about the longings and anxieties of our current historical moment is a subject that, alas, falls beyond the scope of this study.[7] Suffice to say that after a century of neglect the time seems to have come for Spring-heeled Jack to leap back onto the historical stage and back into the collective imagination, revived through our fantasised depictions of the period in which he first appeared.

Beyond aiding this revival, this study will do several things. Before outlining what they are, it is worth noting what this study deliberately avoids doing. The rather scant historiography on Spring-heeled Jack has tended to toy with the central questions that so vexed and intrigued Victorians: Who or what was Spring-heeled Jack? Where did he come from? These are *not* questions that this study seeks to answer, and it will only engage with them as aspects of larger issues. It makes no claim to solving or debunking the personal mystery of Spring-heeled Jack's identity. Steve Roud has recently asserted that 'the vast majority of [Spring-heeled Jack's] reported sightings and attacks never actually happened', and this study willingly progresses from an acceptance of that possibility.[8] Speculating on Spring-heeled Jack's historical 'truth' is of less interest and importance than what the fiction and the need for fabrication may reveal. As such, any delineating of 'real' and 'false' encounters will be largely coincidental.

My interest in Spring-heeled Jack is focused on the broader context of the legend and what it reveals about the nature of intersecting and overlapping popular cultures in this period. As Jeffrey Jerome Cohen has observed, each monster embodies dual narratives, 'one that describes how the monster came to be and another ... detailing what cultural use the monster serves.'[9] These dual concerns are at the heart of this study. It seeks to pin down and perform a historical autopsy on an urban folkloric figure renowned for, and even defined by, his elusiveness. At the same time an investigation of Spring-heeled Jack's cultural anatomy will necessitate grappling with the hybridity and operational dynamism of Victorian popular culture itself.

'Culture' is a notoriously difficult and slippery term, not least because the same word is used to mean so many different things at different times and across

---

[6] For a good overview of the steampunk subgenre see Vandermeer and Chambers, *The Steampunk Bible*.

[7] For some reflections on these issues see Arias and Pulham, *Haunting and Spectrality*; Hadley, *Neo-Victorian Fiction and Historical Narrative*; Heilmann and Llewellyn, *Neo-Victorians*; and Mitchell, *History and Cultural Memory*.

[8] Roud, *London Lore*, p. 149.

[9] Cohen, *Monster Theory*, p. 13.

different disciplines. The addition of 'popular' merely compounds the problem. Popular culture's association with 'the people' presents difficulties of definition and boundaries. Whilst the poor, the uneducated, the powerless or the subaltern classes all suggest helpful descriptions, they remain negative comparative formulations with 'elites' and merely act as substitute terms that do not necessarily help penetrate the conceptual obscurity of the 'popular'. As will be demonstrated through Spring-heeled Jack's legend, whilst the 'popular' has implicit links to the lower orders, it is frequently embraced by a broader social spectrum which stretches into the upper echelons of the middle classes too. These issues of how to determine the boundaries of inclusivity and exclusivity of popular culture, and the extent of porosity in such a notional boundary at any given time, form underlying concerns of the current study.[10]

In a recent, brisk jog through the historiography of cultural history Peter Burke has succinctly highlighted some of the fundamental and broad-ranging problems arising from the use of 'popular culture' as a framework for historical research. For a long time the application of dichotomous terms such as 'elite' and 'popular' encouraged a false assumption of cultural homogeneity amongst both groups.[11] This sense of homogeneity arose from the political agenda the term was serving. Used to support assertions of class consciousness and the creation and reaffirmation of social identities, it derived its consolidation through opposition to elite cultural influences and pressures.[12] Yet gender, age, race and locality are just the most obvious in a number of internally diverse and potentially divisive factors that prevented all of 'the people' sharing the same 'popular culture' or

[10]   For more on this see Williams, *Key Words*, p. 87; Gunn, *History and Cultural Theory*, pp. 54–81; Wilson, 'Popular Culture?', pp. 515–19; and Scribner, 'Is a History of Popular Culture Possible?', pp. 175–91.

[11]   See Burke, *What is Cultural History?* This two-tier dichotomous model is often associated with Burke's *Popular Culture in Early Modern Europe* (1978), although this text demonstrates that he was only too aware of its falsities and exemptions.

[12]   Historiographical engagement with popular culture had its forerunners in the nineteenth-century French historian Jules Michelet, and Annales historians such as Marc Bloc and Lucien Febvre, but it gained prominence as an area of (predominantly left-wing) historical study as a result of E. P. Thompson's *The Making of the English Working Class*. According to Thompson, popular culture did not only offer access to a 'history from below', it was a vital site and means of explanation for the formation of class consciousness. For these early historiographical developments see Thompson, *The Making of the English Working Class*; Hoggart, *The Uses of Literacy*; and Williams, *Culture and Society*. For a reflective overview see Sharpe, 'History from Below'. Building on this, historians of the 1970s and early 1980s began to analyse the lower classes as popular cultural consumers. See for example Malcolmson, *Popular Recreations in English Society*; Bailey, *Leisure and Class in Victorian England*; Cunningham, *Leisure in the Industrial Revolution*; Yeo, *Popular Culture and Class Conflict*; Storch, *Popular Culture and Custom*; Poole, *Popular Leisure and the Music Hall*; Bushaway, *By Rite*; and Golby and Purdue, *The Civilisation of the Crowd*. Such works generally perceived popular culture as a site of contestation.

experiencing the same cultural world. This has led historians to increasingly turn their attention to the heterogeneity of popular cultures, their interaction with one another and with 'elite' cultures.[13]

This was best encapsulated by Tim Harris' *Popular Culture in England, c.1500–1850.* Harris and his fellow contributors set out to problematise popular culture by illustrating its internal diversities. At the same time they argued that it was not sufficient 'just to look at different cultural spheres'.[14] Rather historians needed to examine the issue of interaction between those spheres, for in doing so they would be able to move beyond conceptual frameworks defined by two-tier cultural dichotomies such as elite and popular, urban and rural, literary and oral. Harris' problematisation of popular culture has necessarily led to a messier, more complex formulation.[15] The late 1990s were marked by criticisms of the attempt to contain cultures within a monolithic notion of the 'popular', since it risked concealing the fact that societies embody 'a multitude of overlapping and interpenetrating cultural systems, most of them subsocietal, transsocietal or both'.[16]

It has been suggested that the interrelation between 'elite' and 'popular' cultures was such that historians should dispense with using the two adjectives. One could equally say the same of the interaction between other supposed dichotomies such as oral and literary or metropolitan and provincial cultures. This cutting of the Gordian knot would seem to liberate the study of cultural interaction and transference up and down the social hierarchy and across geographical localities. Yet we need to temper this inclination towards a brutish conceptual vandalism which would tear down seemingly false divides; it is too easy a response to complex issues. As Peter Burke notes, 'The problem is that without these adjectives, the interactions between the learned and the popular become impossible to describe.'[17] Without a notion of interacting cultures we lose the dynamism that exists both within and between them, this vital energy becoming obscured as those recognisable differences collapse into a homogeneous cultural mulch. The idea of boundaries is good not because they mark dividing walls but because they facilitate a porous relationship where distinct cultures meet, enabling us to explore the exchanges and consequent hybridity that erode the

---

[13] Early-modern historians seem to have been more sensitive to this than modernists. See for example Reay, *Popular Cultures in England*; Harris, *Popular Culture in England*; and Mullan and Reid, *Eighteenth-Century Popular Culture.*

[14] See Harris, *Popular Culture in England*, pp. 26–7.

[15] This appreciation of nuance, diversity and interaction has created its own issues. For a succinct example linked to gendered cultures see Burke, *What is Cultural History?*, p. 27.

[16] Gunn, *History and Cultural Theory*, p. 80. See also Bonnell and Hunt, *Beyond the Cultural Turn*, and Dentith, *Society and Cultural Forms.*

[17] Burke, *What is Cultural History?*, p. 28.

notion of rigid demarcations. As this study's analysis of Spring-heeled Jack's cultural existence and movement illustrates, by rejecting hard dichotomies we do not necessarily have to surrender an appreciation of the important cultural differences through which we conceive the past.

Emma Griffin has argued that in the wake of these developments historians have tended to drift away from linking analysis of popular culture to larger historical concerns. In its original application, studies of popular culture provided a cultural dimension that interacted with, and had something to say about, broader social, economic and political trends, particularly as they related to class formation and identity. This, as Griffin rightly points out, has become lost.[18] As cultural historians have grown ever more adventurous, even arcane in their focus of study, so they have increasingly floated free from the socio-economic realities in which these cultural expressions existed. Griffin suggests that a renewed emphasis in this direction would help us regain perspective on the way power relations informed popular culture from outside. Equally, it would help us recognise how the formation of a notion of 'popular culture' played into power relations in the nineteenth century.[19] As Griffin notes, by failing to explore the 'structures of domination and subordination [which] affected the practice of popular culture', historians are creating 'studies of popular culture that are at best incomplete, and at worst misleading'.[20] The fault would seem to be that we have become too enamoured with the idea of popular cultures formed from within and employed as a form of collective agency. In doing so we have failed to rigorously engage with the broader issues of ownership of popular culture and the external forces that helped shape and conceive it. This study will address some of these failings, for Spring-heeled Jack provides not only a good model for exploring the contestation of cultural ownership but also clearly illustrates the necessity of an 'elite' engagement with popular culture for his legend to operate and thrive. However, in doing so it also suggests that Griffin may be calling for a reconnection with ideas that have subsequently evolved, for 'class', 'popular culture' and even notions of 'inside' and 'outside' no longer retain their former sense of coherence and solidity.

---

[18] See Griffin, 'Popular Culture in Industrialising England'.
[19] Of particular interest here is John Storey's *Inventing Popular Culture*. This provides a concise history of popular culture as an intellectual concept, a construct from 'above' as much as an organic expression from 'below'. As such, it reiterates how by applying the idea of 'popular culture' we naturalise into an observed historical context what in reality is a category formed by the observer. In this way the concept becomes the problem since the notion of 'popular culture' is informed by inherent assumptions, and our ways of thinking about it become bound by the very application of the term.
[20] Griffin, 'Popular Culture in Industrialising England', pp. 627 and 633.

This work also aims to further the diverse but intriguing engagements with popular culture, fictionality, belief and cultural practice that have been produced over the last decade or so. It shares resonances with, and perhaps some rather obvious debts to, Peter Bailey's excellent *Popular Culture and Performance in the Victorian City*. In many ways what follows articulates a sustained demonstration of Bailey's suggestion that 'the imaginary' can provide us with a useful means of access into a more developed appreciation of popular cultural dynamics.[21] In doing so it addresses the interactions and appropriations between different modes of popular cultural transmission whilst considering the struggle for interpretations which accompanied them. Like Bailey's focus on Ally Sloper and Champagne Charlie, this study's analysis revolves around another particular Victorian trickster anti-hero, although one who was a markedly different and darker creature than Bailey's more appealing characters. It similarly teases out the multiple symbolic significances of Spring-heeled Jack as he existed in a period marked by the coexistence of both older, customary practices and mentalities, and newer, commercialised forms of entertainment and mass culture.[22] Whilst Spring-heeled Jack did not necessarily fit neatly into the cultural 'circuits' and sense of knowingness which Bailey employs to dissect music hall entertainments, both of these ideas find a degree of significance and application in what follows.[23]

This study also draws upon ideas articulated in Michael Saler's recent work on modern enchantment and the 'ironic imagination'. Saler has used Sherlock

[21] Bailey, *Popular Culture and Performance*, p. 11.

[22] These approaches are largely derived from the eclectic influence of anthropological, sociological, semiotic and linguistic theories that were appropriated by the 'New Cultural History' of the 1980s and 1990s. These led to a shift of emphasis in the historical study of popular culture from simply being an arena for class struggle and identity formation to one focused on analysis and deciphering of symbolic meanings. The anthropologist Clifford Geertz's interpretative method of 'thick description' became a favoured blueprint for such analysis, though, as Robert Darnton found when he applied it to a historical context, this was not without its own methodological problems and critics. See Hunt, *The New Cultural History*. See also Geertz, *The Interpretation of Cultures*, pp. 3–30 and 412–53, and, for historians' engagement with his ideas and approaches, Shankman, 'The Thick and Thin', pp. 261–79; Goodman, 'History and Anthropology', pp. 783–804; Samuel, 'Reading the Signs', pp. 88–109; Biersack, 'Local Knowledge, Local History', pp. 72–96; and Waters, 'Signs of the Times', pp. 537–56. For Darnton see his *The Great Cat Massacre*, and Chartier, *Cultural History*, pp. 95–111.

[23] See Bailey, *Popular Culture and Performance*, pp. 128–50. The term 'mass culture' is not any easier to define than 'popular culture'. In an unsatisfying attempt to delineate the two Patricia Anderson rather vaguely described popular culture as 'any generally accessible, widely shared interest or activity ... of a majority of ordinary people', whereas 'mass culture' was defined by the involvement of a 'great many people' in 'any mass phenomenon'. See Anderson, *The Printed Image*, pp. 9–11. The cultural theorist John Fiske has dismissed the whole idea of mass culture as a false proposition. See Fiske, *Understanding Popular Culture*, pp. 23–4.

Holmes to illustrate a late- nineteenth-century cultural propensity for blurring the boundaries between the real and the fictional, concerns that are obviously pertinent to an examination of Spring-heeled Jack.[24]

Saler presents this blurring of Holmes' nature as a 'modern' enchantment, a yearning for the fantastical that has detached itself from traditional supernatural associations. Whilst Saler makes repeated claims for Holmes as one of the first characters to be treated in this way, Spring-heeled Jack had encapsulated these tensions and uncertainties decades before Conan Doyle penned his famous detective. As a 'fiction' that was said to prowl the streets of London, Spring-heeled Jack embodied this conflation of the fantastical and the mundane. What prevents him from being viewed as a modern enchantment in the Holmes model is the uncertainty and speculation about his being which hinted at persistent allusions to the supernatural. As will be demonstrated, Spring-heeled Jack was a culturally cantankerous Janus figure that looked forward to the 'modern' yet also trailed a long wake of traditional 'superstition' back into the past. Saler's work is also influential in the way he alludes to the 'synergistic effects' generated by the transference of fictional characters back and forth between text, stage and pictorial portrayals. He argues that such effects were increased and enhanced by the proliferation of mass-cultural media at the end of the nineteenth century. This study's interest in the generation and movement of Spring-heeled Jack's legend means that it necessarily draws upon similar notions of cultural transference, synergy and symbiosis. The fresh dimension that Spring-heeled Jack brings to this is the continuing importance of old media, particularly oral rumour, and the way emerging forms of new media had to both incorporate and contend with it in a way that is seen with hardly any other 'imaginary' characters one cares to think of. Beneath the dazzle of what Saler recognises as an emerging celebrity culture and all the immersive spectacle of fin-de-siècle entertainments was the quietly persistent thrum of a traditional oral culture with its own fantasies.

In recent years those two other key Victorian monsters, Sweeney Todd and Jack the Ripper, have increasingly gained credibility as the focus for serious

---

[24] Saler distinguishes between some who genuinely believed the fictional detective to be real and a larger group of 'ironic believers', people 'who were not so much willingly suspending their disbelief in a fictional character as willingly believing in him with the double-minded awareness that they were engaged in pretence'. Whilst having some issues with the neatly compartmentalised self-awareness suggested by this juggling act, it nevertheless moves us beyond simplistic views of belief or non-belief, encouraging the possibility that contemporary engagement with Spring-heeled Jack may have been marked by a knowing playfulness. See Saler, 'Clap if You Believe', p. 606. Saler's ideas on modernity's production of disenchanted enchantments have been developed in his 'Modernity and Enchantment: A Historiographic Review', and Landy and Saler, Re-enchantment of the World.

academic research, but Spring-heeled Jack has remained largely neglected.[25] Robert L. Mack's recent work on Sweeney Todd focuses predominantly on the urban legend's literary and theatrical manifestations, but he skilfully weaves these into broader cultural issues and anxieties from which the legend drew its strength and appeal.[26] Perhaps the closest parallels to this study's interest in exploring Victorian popular culture through a particular topic is seen in works on Jack the Ripper, arguably *the* figure who came to eclipse Spring-heeled Jack in the popular imagination. Academic engagement with the Ripper has not sought to contribute ever more baroque speculations to the many already amassed by self-styled 'ripperologists'; rather it tends to use the nature, text and context of the legend to explore more fundamental and wide-ranging issues, engaging with the Ripper 'event' and its legacy as a means of taking a depth sounding into Victorian society and culture. Of particular note here are Judith Walkowitz's fascinating *City of Dreadful Delight* and L. Perry Curtis' *Jack the Ripper and the London Press*. Whilst Walkowitz uses the Ripper to explore how her themes of feminist and

---

[25]   Spring-heeled Jack has a very threadbare historiography which is beset by elaboration, distortion and the misappropriation of contemporary sources which were themselves formulated on wisps of rumour and unsubstantiated assertions. Until recently there has been a notable lack of critical analysis. Earlier secondary sources tended to embellish a meagre skeleton of information. See Villiers, *Stand and Deliver*, pp. 238–52, and Dyall, 'Spring-heeled Jack'. Elliott O'Donnell's 1948 summary made an unverifiable addition to the legend by referring to an attack in the 1880s that, in true urban legend style, was said as having happened to an acquaintance of his childhood nurse. See O'Donnell, *Haunted Britain*, p. 75. The most credible work of recent years has been produced by Mike Dash. His lengthy and rigorous research into the legend has attempted to distinguish 'fact' from 'fakelore'. His greatest service in this respect has been the dissection of Peter Haining's *The Legend and Bizarre Crimes of Spring Heeled Jack* (1977). Prior to Dash's efforts Haining's work was the only substantial treatment of the legend. Dash's interrogation of the contemporary press has revealed Haining's book to be full of flaws and outright fabrications. Dash's close analysis of the primary material helped prune back some of the worst elaborations that had sprouted around the legend. In doing so he returned us to the way it was originally formulated in the press, namely a free-forming story replete with contradictions, gaps and guesses. See Dash, 'Spring-heeled Jack'. Dash's research has tended to focus on the minutiae of the legend's narrative. Whilst clearly sensitive to details and inconsistencies, he demonstrates little interest in (re)connecting the legend to the broader social and cultural context in which it was generated and sustained. This omission may be addressed in his forthcoming *Spring-heeled Jack: Sources and Interpretations*.

[26]   See Mack, *Wonderful and Surprising History of Sweeney Todd*. See also Crone, 'From Sawney Beane to Sweeney Todd'. Despite the fact that Spring-heeled Jack also took numerous popular literary incarnations in penny dreadfuls, comics and magazines, literary scholars have continued to neglect him. He received a very brief, descriptive chapter in Anglo, *Penny Dreadfuls*, pp. 68–73, and found sporadic mention in Springhall's *Youth, Popular Culture and Moral Panics*. He has remained conspicuously absent from more recent academic works where one might expect to have found mention of him. See for example Mighall, *A Geography of Victorian Gothic Fiction*, and Robinson, *Imagining London*.

sexual narratives were constructed and reinforced in late-nineteenth-century London, Perry Curtis examines the role of the late-Victorian media in formulating the Ripper mythos itself.[27] As with these works on the Ripper, this study situates Spring-heeled Jack in what Walkowitz nicely terms a 'dense cultural grid', those cultural webs in which his legend was formed and bound, and through which it was propagated and sustained.[28]

Sweeney Todd, Jack the Ripper and Spring-heeled Jack all thrived in a Victorian popular culture that was fascinated with violence, and awash with violent entertainments. This has been most skilfully explored in Rosalind Crone's recent work. In a similar vein to her work on Mr Punch, Spring-heeled Jack will also be considered as an expression of performative violence that blended the customary and the commercial. As Crone suggests, such displays possessed 'both subversive and conservative undertones', for even as they threatened to act as 'a kind of mini-revolution' they also tended to tip over into self-mockery on account of their artifice and excessiveness.[29] Mr Punch and Spring-heeled Jack both attracted cross-class interest and engagement, thereby muddying any simple affectation that these characters somehow 'belonged' solely to a plebeian culture. There are differences however. Crone argues that Punch was appropriated, tamed and made if not wholly then at least more respectable by a Victorian middle-class desire to transform him into a vehicle for bourgeois morality. Whilst sharing Mr Punch (and Ally Sloper's) mercurial evolution over time, Spring-heeled Jack was never tamed, for he remained the wild man of the urban (and rural) wilderness. Even when portrayed as a misunderstood costumed vigilante or, in his twilight years, as a nursery tale bogeyman, he still retained his fearful edges. Crone's work also raises some important questions that seem particularly pertinent to Spring-heeled Jack's function and durability in Victorian popular cultures. Considering violent entertainments as a safety valve that slackened a desire for actual violence, this study will necessarily reflect upon the issue of whether Spring-heeled Jack represented a controlled engagement with vicarious violence, the subversive articulation of a rebellious, imaginary icon or both.[30]

Medievalists and early-modern historians have long appreciated the interpretative insights to be gained from considering the cultural expression of monsters.[31] The modern period has been seen either to be deprived of similar

---

[27] See Walkowitz, *City of Dreadful Delight*, and Perry Curtis' *Jack the Ripper*. This developing body of academic Ripper scholarship is best summarised in Warwick and Willis, *Jack the Ripper*.

[28] Walkowitz, *City of Dreadful Delight*, p. 5.

[29] Crone, 'Mr and Mrs Punch', p. 1058.

[30] For more on these issues see Crone, *Violent Victorians*.

[31] See Williams, *Deformed Discourse*; Williams, *Monsters and Their Meanings*; and Lunger Knoppers and Landes, *Monstrous Bodies/Political Monstrosities*. For an overview see Asma, *On Monsters*.

fantastical beings or to have grown blasé about their existence. In a twenty-first-century popular culture both fascinated and saturated with vampires, zombies, aliens and serial killers, our monsters have perhaps become so ubiquitous as to no longer register as valuable – and powerful – cultural artefacts.[32] In the Victorian context Spring-heeled Jack is one of but a few characters that buck such a trend. With the exception of Dracula, the key figures in Andrew Smith's *Victorian Demons* attest to the essential if warped humanity of Victorian 'monsters'. Mr Hyde was the product of (suitably vague) scientific dabbling and a dark human psyche; an unfortunate like Joseph Merrick, the 'Elephant Man', was first a human sideshow freak and then a medical spectacle. For all his obvious depravities Jack the Ripper was just a man.[33] It is true that contemporary speculation and most official statements suggested Spring-heeled Jack was also nothing more than a man in disguise. What makes him stand apart from these others was the accepted *possibility*, at least amongst some Victorians, that he may have been something else, something supernatural or monstrous in a more traditional sense.

This study uses the mercurial nature of Spring-heeled Jack's cultural existence and ongoing transmogrification to consider the dynamic functioning of a multitude of popular cultures in Victorian society. Spring-heeled Jack is particularly suited to an exercise which focuses on the way those cultures coexisted, interacted, overlapped and diverged in this period. His cultural hybridity is indicated in the way he moved back and forth between oral rumours and press reports, a broader range of literary texts and theatrical forms, between the metropolis and the provinces, and industrial cities and rural villages. In such circumstances the idea of Spring-heeled Jack as a cultural 'text' necessarily oscillates between specific manifestations (penny dreadfuls for example) and the larger, more encompassing text of the legend which contained the entire cultural interplay of his various expressions. His constant reformulation as a cultural artefact meant Spring-heeled Jack became incorporated into the nineteenth century's transition from popular cultures located in custom and 'tradition' to a

---

[32] A 1961 article in *Flying Saucer Review* attempted to appropriate Spring-heeled Jack as a Victorian extraterrestrial. However misguided, and however much it said more about the emerging nature of a countercultural fringe of the time it was written than the period it was writing about, such an approach at least appreciated that this 'monster' possessed an evolving interpretative value. See Vyner, 'The Mystery of Springheel Jack'. See also Clarke, 'Bogeyman or Spaceman?', and Dash, 'Spring-heeled Jack', pp. 34–58.

[33] See Smith, *Victorian Demons*. For studies of nineteenth-century monstrosity see also Cavallaro, *The Gothic Vision*, pp. 171–206; Halberstam, *Skin Shows*; and Hurley, *The Gothic Body*. The Victorians' fascination with non-human monsters also found expression in the emergence of palaeontology and the popularity of fairy art. See for example Cadbury, *The Dinosaur Hunters*, and Bown, *Fairies in Nineteenth-Century Art*.

highly capitalised mass culture defined by the 'urbanization, commercialization, and nationalization of popular culture', although his mercurial nature problematises any clean, linear trajectory from the one to the other.[34] His traversing of our notions of 'high' and 'low' raises the intriguing dilemma of whether we should view him as a vehicle shuttling between cultures, or expand our interpretation of the 'popular' to be more inclusive of these particular 'elite' cultural interactions. As befits his prankster nature, Spring-heeled Jack's leaps back and forth across these perceived 'boundaries' simultaneously disrupt our neat cultural categorisations whilst offering us an appreciation of the operation of heterogeneous cultures in Victorian England. Spring-heeled Jack (temporarily) thrived in them all although ultimately, like the efforts of Victorian authorities and frightened local communities across the country, none of them ever permanently captured him.

Harris' text was formulated around some of the subdisciplinary domains through which historians engage with popular culture and, as Griffin suggests, we may have grown (too) comfortable working in these specialised areas of interest. Spring-heeled Jack's migration back and forth between ethnographic accounts and emerging forms of commercial entertainment, and his entanglement in a complex web of popular (and elite) cultures nicely illustrates why we need to resist this trend towards intra-cultural fragmentation. In our hunt for greater sophistication, and in our willingness to appreciate complexity and diversity, we threaten to immobilise the larger study of popular culture, for a persistent focusing on subcultural domains tends towards the negation of popular culture as representative of anything genuinely 'popular'. This study advances the view that we need to regain a sense of a popular cultural overview, one that must still recognise identifiably different domains within popular culture but no longer treat them as contained or static sites of cultural production and interpretation. In isolating and studying popular culture's sub- and transcultural constituents there has been an implicit interpretation of cultural frameworks such as class and gender as 'things' or 'sites' which clash, resist, respond, incorporate and adapt, thereby providing a particular collectivised perspective on broader cultural developments. Given his cross-cultural movements, a study of Spring-heeled Jack has to place greater significance on cultural energies than subcultural entities or spaces (as implied when we talk of different 'areas' of study). Whilst valuing such 'sites' as points of cultural generation and contact, the emphasis is on the dynamism generated through their intra-cultural transferences. In short, this

---

[34] Easton, *Disorder and Discipline*, p. 56. Patricia Anderson locates this transition from popular to mass culture in the period 1830–60, the height of Spring-heeled Jack's notoriety. See Anderson, *The Printed Image*, p. 1.

study is interested in the interaction between what it will term cultural 'nodes' and 'modes'.

The emphasis on overlapping component subcultures within popular culture has stripped away any sense of its internal homogenisation and has exposed what could be termed its various 'generators'. This metaphor should not imply a mechanistic or rigidly systematic understanding of cultures, something that naturally jars with cultural historians' inclination towards more fluid engagement with fields and discourses. Rather if we understand culture as signifying practices then these subcultural domains act as generators of signification. This study considers some of the generators or 'nodes' – gender, class, environment and locality – that seem most relevant to a study of Spring-heeled Jack. In this they are far from neutral, objective 'things', for all such nodal generators were animated and informed by the power relations at their core. Such relations lay behind questions as to why people told stories (as gossip, printed texts or performed plays) and how living in a city or a village, the capital or the provinces influenced reception and understandings of Spring-heeled Jack. The possible agendas and, more broadly, the acculturated assumptions behind the answer to these types of questions were part of what marked one type of generator from another, thereby causing the transmission of a trope like Spring-heeled Jack to be received and appropriated in different ways in different generative contexts. Peter Bailey probably put it more succinctly when he stated his own interest in exploring the 'processes of appropriation and exchange between cultural fractions [and] the reach of power and ideology.'[35]

In exploring Spring-heeled Jack's cultural mobility this study is less interested in the generators themselves than in the cultural energies they produced and the circulation of those energies back and forth, their transference along multiple paths of cultural transmission (or 'modes') and, within that, their translation. One of the reasons behind employing this terminology of 'nodes' and 'modes' is to shift focus away from over-familiar dichotomies such as urban and rural, oral and literary, popular and elite. A focus on locality as a nodal generator still allows for engagement with urban, rural, metropolitan and provincial contexts, yet it does so in a way that is not so closely bound to assumptions derived from a framework founded on oppositional differences. Similarly, by focusing on oral and literary modes of transmission the emphasis is less on their hierarchical relationship than on the differing ways in which they transmitted and translated Spring-heeled Jack. Due to his ambiguous nature this study necessarily muddies and softens the interaction between other dichotomies too, including the boundaries between text and context, subjectivity and objectivity, even 'reality' and representation. This extends to our ideas of the 'popular' and the

---

[35] Bailey, *Popular Culture and Performance*, p. 8.

'elite' too. In Spring-heeled Jack's case both 'popular' and 'elite' cultures existed in the field of cultural operation between these 'nodes' and 'modes', although if one were to use the term 'circuits' to link them then Spring-heeled Jack seems to have suffered from a number of faulty circuits with intermittent connections. Here 'popular' and 'elite' appear less as objective cultures and more as interpretative differentiations. When Spring-heeled Jack became a common trope shared by both cultures, their allusions to a sense of internalised coherence and integrity, and division from one another seem to be largely the product of rhetoric. As such, the notion of 'inside' and 'outside' popular cultures also becomes something of a discursive interpretation. In his own small way Spring-heeled Jack suggests that 'popular culture', broadly conceived, was not just an intellectual construction of social elites, but neither was it exclusively formed from 'within' as an expression of plebeian agency.[36]

Finally, this study's focus on an urban folkloric figure represents a response to Peter Burke's call for 'an age of co-operation' between historians and folklorists.[37] In using an urban legend as a rich signifier through which to gain interpretative insights into Victorian popular cultures, it contributes to a developing historiographical trend for engaging with folkloric and fairy-tale material.[38] To facilitate this the book is divided into three sections. Although the ordering of these sections possesses an identifiable chronological structure, proceeding from Spring-heeled Jack's genesis to his cultural decline, they do not develop in a linear fashion. The thematic concerns of the various sections necessarily require a degree of repeatedly cycling back to elements and incidents of Spring-heeled Jack's legend. In doing so the key concerns of each section and their individual chapters illustrate how the interpretative possibilities within particular events can be pulled apart to reflect different facets and insights depending on the altered analytical context in which they are considered. This allows us to unpack

---

[36] See Storey, *Inventing Popular Culture*, pp. 1–15.

[37] Burke, 'History and Folklore', p. 137. Despite the formation of the Folklore Society in 1878, academic historians have tended to perceive folkloric studies as lacking intellectually rigorous methodologies, and have been inclined to dismiss such efforts as antiquarian curiosities. See Burke, ibid., and Dorson, *The British Folklorists*. Like historians, twentieth-century folklorists were also surprisingly neglectful of Spring-heeled Jack. More recent works have started to address this omission. See for example Clarke, 'Unmasking Spring-heeled Jack'; Roud, *London Lore*, pp. 148–9; Westwood and Simpson, *The Lore of the Land*, pp. 480–1; Simpson, 'Research Note: "Spring-Heeled Jack"'; and Simpson and Roud, *A Dictionary of English Folklore*, pp. 340–1.

[38] For examples of historians' increasing engagement with folklore see Bell, *The Magical Imagination*; Handley, *Visions of an Unseen World*; Hopkin, 'Storytelling, Fairytales and Autobiography' and 'Legendary Places'; Davies, *The Haunted* and *Witchcraft, Magic and Culture*; and Hutton, 'The English Reformation and the Evidence of Folklore'. For a continuing literary emphasis on such topics see Harris, *Folklore and the Fantastic*, and Sumpter, *The Victorian Press and the Fairy Tale*.

the rich multiple meanings within deceptively simple and frequently sketchy accounts.

The first section outlines the chronological narrative of the legend before conducting a cultural historical autopsy on Spring-heeled Jack. Within his viscera we find a messy tangle of reality and fiction, past and present, fantasy and fear. Grafted onto a skeleton of older folkloric genealogies was an interwoven musculature of influences derived from plebeian theatre, cheap literature, contemporary anxieties about the local environment and personal safety, and class antagonisms. By examining how Spring-heeled Jack grew from local rumour to metropolitan press scare, to a migratory folkloric figure, this section introduces the study's key concern for the relationship between ethnographic accounts and his variety of popular cultural forms, especially in penny literature and the press. Whilst exploring Spring-heeled Jack's various cultural expressions, this study analyses the range of factors that enabled his appropriation into different cultures and facilitated his movement back and forth between them.[39]

The second section focuses on the variety of cultural functions served by Spring-heeled Jack across the Victorian period. Whilst exploring the ways his legend engaged with contemporary concerns about crime, urban space, gender, class and the evolving Victorian metropolis, it does not simply view different facets of his legend through these perceptual lenses. Rather it treats many of them as active 'nodal' components in the formation, articulation and perpetuation of that legend. For example, Spring-heeled Jack did not simply provide a vehicle for articulating gender and class relationships in this period; both actively informed the credibility (or not) of accounts relating to his appearances. As nodal factors, the survival and vitality of his legend were repeatedly dependent upon elite, preferably male, validation as much as 'popular' enthusiasm.

The third section of the book is based around a more overt investigation of the various popular cultural nodes and modes that generated and sustained Spring-heeled Jack's legend. As such, the focus shifts from his cultural functions to his cultural functioning, to an examination of his cultural dynamism. In short, it is an attempt to explore how popular cultures work and interrelate. It begins by exploring the importance of spatial localities as 'nodes' of popular cultural generation, arguing that a capacity to be appropriated into differing spaces and places was a significant factor in accounting for Spring-heeled Jack's durability across most of the Victorian period. It then focuses on his transmission and translation back and forth between oral, literary and visual modes. In focusing on this fluidity it uses Spring-heeled Jack to consider the relational nature of popular cultural energies in this period. In seeking to complicate our appreciation of the relationship between 'artefacts' constructed both 'within' and 'outside'

---

[39] Chartier, 'Culture as Appropriation', p. 236.

popular culture, this study engages with broader issues relating to the ownership of popular cultural tropes. This section concludes with an investigation of the various influences that came to impede Spring-heeled Jack's cultural functioning towards the end of the century, causing the dynamics that had sustained him throughout the Victorian period to falter, his hold on the popular imagination to weaken, and his cultural 'energies' to ebb and dissipate.

Therefore, this study uses the evolution, function and functioning of the Spring-heeled Jack legend to offer broader reflections upon the dynamics of Victorian popular cultures. In emphasising the mutability, mutuality and disconnection between various cultural nodes and modes within the context of the legend it questions hierarchical notions of dominance and subordination between differing popular cultures in this period, most obviously between its literary and oral dimensions. At the same time it seeks to go some way to reversing the historiographical tendency towards the fragmentation of popular cultures. Rather than reverting back to a unified, monolithic concept, this study's recognition of the relational interactions between the 'popular' and the 'elite', the metropolis and the provinces, and Spring-heeled Jack's oral, literary and visual formulations ultimately seeks to offer a richer understanding of the 'popular' in Victorian popular culture.

Part I

The Legend

1

The Legend of Spring-heeled Jack

Whilst the name of Spring-heeled Jack may be reasonably familiar, the story from which it originates is not so well known. The principal aim of this chapter is to set out a narrative of the legend's development from rural rumours around the fringes of south London in late 1837, through the metropolitan scare popularised in the press in early 1838, and then on to a migratory character of predominantly provincial folklore until his last sightings in the early years of the twentieth century. In doing so it aims to provide both a chronological framework of the legend's story arc and the raw material from which subsequent analysis will be drawn.

For historians, who by training and inclination are generally dependent upon written or visual sources for their information, a being that spent much of its life enveloped in oral rumour, gossip and conjecture is particularly hard to track. This is not to suggest a lack of primary sources. Given the diverse range of cultural forms that Spring-heeled Jack took in the nineteenth century there is a rich if somewhat scattered body of material that includes folklorist accounts, street ballads, several series of 'penny dreadful' stories (and illustrations), other literary texts which co-opted the character for their own use, journals, magazines, newspapers, comics, court accounts and published reminiscences by individuals reflecting back on the nineteenth century. There is certainly no shortage of newspaper coverage through which we can gain some access to Spring-heeled Jack's existence in a vibrant contemporary oral culture. That said, what follows cannot make claims to being a definitive, or necessarily even a comprehensive, account of his appearances. Such was the seeming ubiquity of this character that even if one were to undertake the herculean task of ferreting out every available newspaper account, one would still have to accept that this body of 'evidence' was just a glimpse of something far more widespread, a legend that only infrequently made its presence felt in print.

Spring-heeled Jack originated in September 1837, although his activities preceded his intriguing moniker by four months. As was often going to be the case, his name was only retrospectively applied by the press. At the time Barnes was still a village on the south-western fringe of London, and it was in this predominantly rural environment that rumours began to circulate of a ghost 'in the shape of a large white bull' which had 'attacked several persons, more particularly women, many of whom had suffered most severely from the fright.'[1] In January 1838 the London press began piecing together accounts of the peripatetic nature of the scare and the metamorphic entity at the heart of it, retrospectively tracking rumours of its progress through the autumn and winter of 1837 and into early 1838. Moving from Barnes to East Sheen, the white bull transformed into a white bear. Drawing closer to the capital, the 'ghost' changed from animal form to an 'unearthly visitant' at Richmond, and when he moved on to the 'quiet and retired villages of Ham and Petersham' he adopted 'the image of an imp of the "Evil One"'. After this he appeared in Kingston as an 'alleged supernatural visitant'. When he migrated north of the Thames, to Hampton Wick and Hampton Court, his appearance changed again, now being described as 'an unearthly warrior clad in armour of polished brass, with spring shoes and large claw gloves'. This anthropomorphic shift was retained around the metropolis, the claws becoming a marked feature of the 1838 attacks, the spring shoes perhaps the most enduring feature of the entire legend.[2]

He continued to appear in this armoured guise at Twickenham, Whitton, Hounslow and Isleworth. In the latter he was supposed to have attacked a local carpenter called Jones as he was returning home at about eleven at night through Cut-Throat Lane. The assailant, dressed 'in polished steel armour, with red shoes', met spirited opposition from Jones who was described as being 'a powerful man', and when he grappled with the 'ghost' two more came to its aid, tearing the carpenter's clothes 'into ribbons'.[3] Whilst reported without further comment, the idea that the 'ghost' had accomplices at hand who were similarly attired undoubtedly helped lead to the press' proposal that this 'ghost' was a malevolent prank conducted by a group rather than the actions of a single individual. Given to attacking women and scaring children, it was only when 'Jack' met resistance from an able-bodied man that his accomplices were revealed.

After Isleworth the 'ghost' made appearances at Heston, Drayton, Harlington and around the town of Uxbridge. Given the pattern of these appearances, the *Morning Chronicle* suggested that the 'ghost' then returned 'by the great Western Railway towards the metropolis', sightings being made in Hanwell, Brentford, Ealing, Acton, Hammersmith and Kensington. Retaining his armoured form and clearly not put off by the incident with Jones in Isleworth, he attacked a

---

[1] *Morning Herald*, 10th January 1838. It was not unusual for rural ghosts to be perceived as animal rather than anthropomorphic figures. Common bestial ghosts included dogs and hares. See Davies, *The Haunted*, pp. 34–8, and O'Donnell, *Animal Ghosts*.

[2] *Morning Chronicle*, 10th January 1838.

[3] Ibid. Villiers' later claim that an attack against Mary Stevens took place in 'Cut-Throat Lane' near Clapham Common seems to have been an appropriation of the place where Jones was attacked. The likelihood of two attacks in identically named lanes seems untenable. See Villiers, *Stand and Deliver*, p. 246.

blacksmith in Ealing, tearing 'his flesh with iron claws', whilst other accounts reported that he had torn 'the clothes from the backs of females'.[4] In late December and early January he was rumoured to have been in the neighbourhood of St John's Wood, 'clad in mail' and dressed 'as a bear'. At the same time 'the villain' was 'repeatedly seen in Lewisham and Blackheath' in south-eastern London. Suggesting that it was ahead of its metropolitan rivals in picking up on the story, as early as 28th December 1837 the *Morning Chronicle* had reported that 'some scoundrel, disguised in a bearskin, and wearing spring shoes, has been seen jumping to and fro before foot passengers in the neighbourhood of Lewisham, and has in one or two instances greatly alarmed females … He has been named "Steel Jack" by the inhabitants of Lewisham.'[5]

By this stage fear and rumour had the metropolitan population jumping at shadows, associating anything unusual or inexplicable with his name. In one incident 'the son of a respectable inhabitant of Old Brentford' had rushed up to a policeman in a state of alarm, informing the officer that he had seen 'the ghost'. When the policeman went to the indicated location 'he found the inspector on his white horse, awaiting the report of the sergeant of the section, totally unconscious of the alarm he had occasioned'.[6] Fabrications started to proliferate amidst the mounting clamour of reports. A supposed attack on a pie and muffin vendor in Hammersmith was later discredited, as was the assertion that 'one female was … frightened to death at the idea of meeting him'. Children claimed to have seen him 'dancing by moonlight on the palace-green' at the Royal Palace of Kensington, though this too was later disproved.[7]

Therefore, whilst Sir John Cowen's announcement on 8th January 1838 is generally seen to mark the start of a more publicised engagement with Spring-heeled Jack, it was not so much an introduction to events as the culmination of something that had already grown to such an extent that it could no longer be ignored by the authorities. It seems reasonable to presume that a single letter

---

[4] *The Times*, 9th January 1838.

[5] *Morning Chronicle*, 11th January 1838. For the scares in Greenwich and Lewisham in late December 1837 see 'Effects of Aristocratic Example', *Morning Chronicle*, 28th December 1837. One can see how the name 'Steel Jack' could derive from his armoured appearance but the Lewisham figure was not attired in this fashion. Although this local name did not find broader acceptance as media interest grew, this article suggests many of the other key components of Spring-heeled Jack's legend were in place by the end of December 1837. This included the spring shoes, the bestial allusions, the targeting of females and the notion that the whole endeavour was motivated by a wager.

[6] *Morning Chronicle*, 10th January 1838.

[7] Ibid. For more on these earlier accounts see also *The Times*, 9th and 11th January 1838; *Morning Herald*, 10th January 1838; *Morning Chronicle*, 11th January 1838; and *The Observer*, 14th January 1838. For a refutation of the Kensington Palace incident, cited in the *Morning Chronicle*, 11th January 1838, see *County Herald and Weekly Advertiser*, 20th January 1838.

about such a fantastical entity would have been unlikely to make it into the Mayor's public announcements. The real significance of Cowen's pronouncement was that it was reported in *The Times* the following day, marking the first of the emerging legend's transitions across cultures, from oral rumour to printed form. Whilst the *Morning Chronicle* had previously made mention of the 'Steel Jack' character who would evolve into Spring-heeled Jack, it was arguably the combined authority and respectability of the Lord Mayor and *The Times* that moved him into a different sphere of publicity.[8] Through Cowen granting the matter his attention and *The Times* making it known to the readers of the relatively expensive metropolitan press, the 'ghost' was introduced to social circles far above that of London's neighbourhood gossips.

The day before *The Times* report appeared Cowen had read before the journalists gathered at the Mansion House a letter from a 'Peckham resident' who wished to draw his attention to the existence of the ghost and the growing fear it was generating amongst residents of south London villages. Cowen, demonstrating little willingness to take immediate action, fell back on the excuse of jurisdiction, pompously announcing that since 'the terrible vision had not entered the city ... he could not take cognizance of its iniquities.'[9] Cowen believed the author of the letter was most likely a woman who had lost her senses as a result of this strange character, and with apparently mocking insincerity he asked her to furnish him with 'a description of the demon as would enable him to catch him.'[10]

From the point of view of London's broadsheet press, this oddity initially seemed to serve as just another example of lingering popular superstition and credulity, a common stance taken by respectable newspapers in a period that promoted 'the march of intellect'.[11] This indicates a certain misjudgement on the part of the authorities and journalists, a failure to appreciate the immediate vitality of a legend that was in the process of being born. Rather than being framed in terms of supernatural occurrences (and beliefs) that were safely confined to archaic folklore, Spring-heeled Jack was necessarily presented as news. If Cowen's announcement had been intended to expose the rumours to the ridicule of the press' readership it singularly backfired. Granted a degree of validity, even respectability, by the Mayor's attention to the matter and further enhanced by the authority of the printed medium, the reporting of the announcement opened the floodgates to a torrent of written correspondence from across

---

[8]   See *Morning Chronicle*, 28th December 1837.
[9]   The Lord Mayor of London was Head of the Corporation of London, and Mayor of the City of London, not the whole metropolis. Incumbents were appointed for the term of one year, Sir John Cowen holding this position 1837–38.
[10]   *The Times*, 9th January 1838.
[11]   For more on this see Rauch, *Useful Knowledge*.

the capital, each testifying to the activities of what was at this stage still being called the 'suburban ghost'. In one such letter an 'inhabitant of Stockwell' wrote to the Mayor to notify him (and, via publication in the press, a wider readership) that the culprit 'has frightened several persons in Stockwell, Brixton, Camberwell, and Vauxhall'. The writer then made unconfirmed assertions that some of these encounters had led to some victims dying of fright, an idea dismissed by a Mr Hobler on the grounds that the capital's press would have picked up on such sensational matters far earlier.[12] Yet the accounts kept coming in, some of them from sources that were granted credibility simply as a result of their social standing. Sometime in the week following the Mayor's announcement and its reporting in the press the daughter of Plutarch Dickinson Esq., of Plumer Villa, Dulwich, encountered a figure 'enveloped in a white sheet and blue fire' as she 'returned home ... from a party of friends'. This incident had left her 'nearly deprived of her senses, and ... lying in a very dangerous state' of health. Similarly, Timothy Marsh, a nine-year-old boy from Hammersmith, had been 'terribly frightened at the sight of a fellow dressed as a bear'.[13]

Although the menace initially was referred to in the second week of January as the 'suburban ghost', by 20th January the *Penny Satirist* was referring to him as 'Spring-heeled Jack'. Such a formulation seems to have come about in the preceding week for on the 14th January *The Examiner* had still been referring to him simply as 'the ghost'.[14] Newspapers' frequent use of quotation marks indicate an ironic rather than genuine engagement with the notion of Spring-heeled Jack as a supernatural entity. From early on they had promoted the view that the 'ghost' was 'a band of aristocrats, who, for a wager, has undertaken to personify a supernatural being'.[15] Whilst accounting for his apparent ubiquity across the capital, it also helped explain the diverse range of disguises worn in the many sightings. By 20th January *The Sun* was claiming that 'this gang of ghosts and hobgoblins' was a group of 'rascals ... connected with high families, and that bets to the amount of £5000 are at stake upon the success or failure of the abominable proceedings'. Without any apparent substantiation, the newspaper claimed the object of the wager was 'to destroy the lives of not less than 30 human beings!' It was prescribed that this should include 'eight old bachelors, ten old maids, and six ladies' maids, and as many servant girls as they can, by depriving them of their reason, and otherwise accelerating their deaths'.[16] On the same day, with

---

[12] *Morning Chronicle*, 11th January 1838.
[13] *The Sun*, 20th January 1838.
[14] The *West Kent Guardian* referred to this individual as 'Spring Jack' on 13th January 1838. Rather than arising from his peculiar means of propulsion, this nickname seems to relate to the way 'Spring Jack' leapt out at people and darted around the capital.
[15] *Morning Chronicle*, 10th January 1838.
[16] *The Sun*, 20th January 1838.

its tongue firmly in its cheek, the *Penny Satirist* suggested that the Bishop of London was responsible for the scare, using the ghost hoax to generate superstition that would urge people back to the pews.[17]

One newspaper's reference to 'the present crisis' which has 'excited so much terror and alarm in the vicinity of London' seems indicative of the fact that this was a genuine panic and not just another series of condescending reports about popular superstition. The main thrust of *The Sun's* report was to publicly promote the fact that 'a committee of gentlemen have spiritedly come forward for the purpose of raising a fund for securing these unfeeling wretches, alias "ghosts", and visiting them with that severe punishment which they so richly deserve'. The Lord Mayor was reported to be receiving 'subscriptions from ladies or gentlemen' and had already amassed '£35 towards the expenses of the prosecution'. Beyond the use of the press to promote this initiative, the committee had 'already circulated placards about the suburbs of London offering a reward of £10 for the apprehension of any of these heartless scoundrels'.[18]

Whether it was a provocative response to the Mayor's statement that he could not involve himself in matters outside the city or mere mischievousness in the face of these noble efforts by the committee, when Spring-heeled Jack made three reported appearances in February 1838 they did occur within London itself. More importantly, unlike the miasma of rumour and gossip that had swept through the capital's outskirts, granting an amorphous sense that the 'ghost' was everywhere, these incidents involved specific individuals in particular locations. By this time such accounts also had the attention of a watchful press and an anxious readership. The first incident occurred on the night of 20th February and has generally become the defining 'event' in the legend. This was enhanced by the lengthy testimony that the victim, Jane Alsop, and her family were willing to give to the Lambeth Street police office the next day. Here a magistrate daily obtained an account of reported crimes committed in the locality, and according to press reports the Alsop case was heard by both Mr Hardwick, the chief magistrate, and Mr Norton, the investigating magistrate. It was not just the detail of the testimony but also the Alsop family's willingness to come before a public court to admit to such that stood in marked contrast to the vague and unproven body of rumour that had circulated in the autumn and winter of the previous year. Journalists had had to hunt down supposed 'victims', and whenever they did, the individuals involved usually denied all knowledge or suggested it had not happened to them but somebody else.[19] The fact that the Alsops, a respectable middle-class family, were willing to risk derision to make their statement in

---

[17] *Penny Satirist*, 20th January 1838.
[18] *The Sun*, 20th January 1838.
[19] See *Morning Herald*, 10th January 1838.

the face of a press that was dismissing the accounts as the tales one might expect to hear from servant girls gave it a certain credibility.

Eighteen-year-old Jane Alsop recounted that she had been at home at Bearbinder Cottage, Bearbinder Lane, a location described as 'a very lonely spot between the villages of Bow and Old Ford'. Both her prosperous father and mother had been bedridden for several weeks with a 'rheumatic affection'. Also in the house that night were Jane's younger sister, Mary, and her older married sister who gave her name to the police as Mrs Harrison. The unusual level of detail offered by the Alsops, in terms of Spring-heeled Jack's appearance and mode of operation, makes the report worth quoting at length. On 22nd February the *Morning Chronicle* (along with several other metropolitan newspapers) ran the following account based on the testimony given at Lambeth Street the previous day:

> Miss Jane Alsop ... stated that, at about a quarter to nine o'clock on the preceding night [20th] she heard a violent ringing at the gate in front of the house, and, on going to the door to see what was the matter, she saw a man standing outside, of whom she inquired what was the matter, and requested he would not ring so loud. The person instantly replied that he was a policeman, and said 'For God's sake bring me a light, for we have caught Spring-heeled Jack here in the lane.' She returned into the house and brought a candle, and handed it to the person, who appeared enveloped in a large cloak, and whom she at first really believed to be a policeman. The instant she had done so, however, he threw off his outer garment, and applied the lighted candle to his breast, presented a most hideous and frightful appearance, and vomited forth a quantity of blue and white flame from his mouth, and his eyes resembled red balls of fire. From the hasty glance which her fright enabled her to get at his person, she observed that he wore a large helmet; and his dress, which appeared to fit him very tight, appeared to her to resemble white oil-skin. Without uttering a sentence, he darted at, and catching her, partly by her dress and the back part of her neck, placed her hand under one of his, and commenced tearing her gown with his claws, which she was certain were of some metallic substance. She screamed out as loud as she could for assistance, and by considerable exertion got away from him, and ran towards the house to get in. Her assailant, however, followed her and caught her on the steps leading to the hall door, when he again used considerable violence, tore her neck and arms with his claws, as well as a quantity of hair from her head; but she was at length rescued from his grasp by one of her sisters. Miss Alsop added that she had suffered considerably all night from the shock she had sustained, and was then in extreme pain both from the injury done to her arm and the wounds and scratches inflicted by the miscreant about her shoulders and neck by his claws or fangs.

Mary, Jane's younger sister, added that when she heard the screams 'she went to the door and saw a figure, as above described, ill using her sister. She was so alarmed at his appearance that she was afraid to approach or render any assistance.'

With Mr Alsop struggling to get out of bed and down the stairs, it fell to Jane's older sister to save her. Mrs Harrison, upon hearing the screams of both her younger sisters, 'ran to the door, and found the person before described in the act of dragging her sister Jane down the stone steps from the door with considerable violence'. Mrs Harrison grabbed hold of Jane 'and by some means or other, which she could scarcely describe, succeeded in getting her inside the door and closing it'. Describing Jane's condition, she reported that 'her sister's dress was nearly torn off her; both her combs dragged out of her head, as well as a quantity of her hair torn away'. Even after they had managed to shut Spring-heeled Jack outside he continued to knock at the front door, and 'it was only on their calling loudly for the police from the upper windows that he left the place'.[20]

The publicity garnered by reports of the Alsop attack stirred individuals to offer further financial reward for information leading to the detection and apprehension of the attacker. Mr Alsop had immediately offered ten guineas, and on 23rd February Sir Edward Codrington, a Member of Parliament, offered a further five pounds.[21] The Alsop case had roused public interest and indignation, and the subsequent investigation into it was covered by a number of newspapers. In fact, two investigations were conducted, one by Mr Young and Mr Guard, respectively the superintendent and an inspector of the Stepney-based K division of the police, the other by James Lea who was employed directly by the Lambeth Street police office. Lea reported his findings to the magistrate on 22nd February, claiming that 'he had no doubt that the person by whom the outrage had been committed had been in the neighbourhood for nearly a month past … and had, on one occasion, narrowly escaped apprehension'. Lea explained that 'a person, answering precisely his size and figure, had been frequently observed walking about the lanes and lonely places, enveloped in a large Spanish cloak, and was sometimes in the habit of carrying a small lantern about with him'.[22]

All three investigators took a similar stance in terms of agreeing that whilst Jane Alsop had been attacked, shock and fear had led her to mistakenly describe the appearance of her assailant. Dismissing the supernatural aura that accounts of Spring-heeled Jack generated in 1838, they described it as 'the result of a drunken frolic', disassociating it from 'the individual who was stated to have made his appearance in different outlets of the metropolis in so many different shapes'. Of course, this conclusion did not deny the existence of such an individual; it merely divorced it from being falsely associated with this particular case. Lea tried to explain away the white oilskin and helmet as Alsop's incorrect interpretation of the attacker's 'white shooting coat, and a cap with a peak in front', the suspect having supposedly 'been out shooting on the day in question'.[23] On 4th March *The Examiner* reported that two men called Payne and Millbank

[20] *Morning Chronicle*, 22nd February 1838.
[21] *Morning Chronicle*, 28th February 1838.
[22] *John Bull*, 25th February 1838.
[23] *Morning Chronicle*, 28th February 1838. See also *The Times*, 2nd and 3rd March 1838.

had 'undergone lengthened examinations' at the Lambeth Street office. Although they clearly were suspected of being Jane Alsop's assailants, there was not sufficient evidence to convict them, and 'the case was held over for further enquiry'. If the investigation was pursued further, its findings do not seem to have been newsworthy for the case disappeared from the press after this.

Yet the press interest stirred by the attack on Jane Alsop had been sufficient to overshadow how active Spring-heeled Jack was in the week that followed. He had certainly proved Mr Norton of the Lambeth Street police court wrong when the latter had declared that it was unlikely 'that the ghost would exhibit in the same neighbourhood for some time to come'.[24] In fact, with the audacity that came to define his character, Spring-heeled Jack made another appearance on 25th February, whilst the forces of law and order were still making investigations into the Alsop case. He had clearly not been deterred by his frustrated attack on the Alsop household. As in that previous attack he again deliberately roused the household to his presence by knocking on the door of 2 Turner Street. This residence, located near the Commercial Road, belonged to a Mr Ashworth and was not that far from the Alsop home in Bearbinder Lane. When Ashworth's servant answered the door, Spring-heeled Jack again cast aside his cloak to reveal 'a most hideous appearance'. Such were the servant's loud screams that Jack ran away, leaving the boy terrified but otherwise unmolested.[25]

Just three nights later, on 28th February, the day Lea gave a further report into the Alsop case, Spring-heeled Jack made his third attack in just over a week. Whilst Mr Hardwick of the Lambeth Street police office was still concluding the Alsop case, he was presented, on Tuesday 6th March, with Mr Scales and his sister Lucy's account of the attack. Eighteen-year-old Lucy Scales stated that around half past eight on the previous Wednesday night, she and her sister had just left the home of their brother, a butcher resident in Narrow Street, Limehouse, to return to their residence in Week's Place, also in Limehouse. As they walked down Green Dragon Alley, 'they observed some person standing in an angle in the passage ... enveloped in a large cloak'. As Lucy, who was walking ahead of her sister, drew closer to the figure 'he spurted a quantity of blue flame right in her face, which deprived her of her sight, and so alarmed her that she instantly dropped to the ground, and was seized by violent fits, which continued for several hours'. Lucy informed Hardwick that she had initially thought the figure was a woman since it seemed to be wearing a bonnet, but in the quick glimpse she caught before the attack she saw it was a 'tall and thin' man. Lucy's brother had heard the screams, but by the time he reached his two sisters, Lucy in the grips of a fit and being cradled by her sister, the attacker had fled. Lucy

---

[24] *The Examiner*, 25th February 1838.
[25] *Morning Herald*, 27th February 1838.

assured the court that her sister could provide a more detailed description since she had escaped assault and had more opportunity to observe the assailant. Unfortunately, her sister had not been present 'when the officer called, else she would have attended' with her siblings.[26] Given the absence of this vital witness, Mr Scales gave Hardwick a second-hand account of what she had told him once they managed to get Lucy back to his house. She too had described the attacker as tall and thin, possessing a 'gentlemanly appearance'. She had noticed he held a small lamp and that, as Lucy approached him, he had cast open the large cloak in which he was wrapped, 'exhibited the lamp, and puffed a quantity of flame from his mouth'. Lucy instantly collapsed, and her sister was momentarily dazzled by the flash of light in the darkness and covered her eyes before going to Lucy's aid. She had informed her brother that 'the individual did not utter a word, nor did he attempt to lay hands on them, but walked away in an instant'.[27]

The attack against Lucy Scales has generally been eclipsed by the Alsop case and certainly does not appear to have stirred a similar degree of media interest. Most newspapers carried only brief summaries. There was probably a class dimension to this, the Scales sisters being associated with their brother's trade as a butcher, but equally there were gendered issues that further undermined the credibility of the account too.[28] From the newspapers' perspective there was also a lack of sustained, dramatic content in the incident. Although Lucy had collapsed in response to the fireball blown into her face, there was no subsequent mention of burns, the real damage being done by a fit brought on by shock. Furthermore, rather than persisting with the attack against a clearly vulnerable young woman, Spring-heeled Jack had simply walked away.

Despite this lack of press interest, Lea, the officer who had investigated the Alsop attack, was also assigned to investigate the Scales case. Whilst kept busy by two cases associated with Spring-heeled Jack, he clearly refused to accept popular gossip that would suggest he was searching for a supernatural being in east London. He investigated the alley where the attack on Lucy Scales had taken place, noting its ideal design for observing approaching pedestrians. He had also attended an experiment conducted at the London Hospital that seemed to confirm that the police were not faced with a fire-breathing demon but an inventive human prankster who had devised a way of producing fireballs, most likely as a result of 'blowing through a tube in which spirits of wine, sulphur, and another ingredient were deposited and ignited'. Whilst this may account for

---

[26] *Morning Post*, 7th March 1838.

[27] *Morning Chronicle*, 8th March 1838.

[28] These issues will be considered further in Chapters 3 and 4. For examples of the reports see *Bell's Life in London*, 11th March 1838, and *Leeds Mercury*, 24th March 1838.

the strange headgear noted by both Jane Alsop and Lucy Scales, it would seem that in the first case the candle given by Alsop had served as the ignition (hence the delayed attack), whilst the bull's eye lantern had provided the flame in the second. The shared fire-breathing element led Hardwick, the chief magistrate, to conclude that 'these disgraceful outrages were committed by the same individual, and not by several'.[29] Such a conclusion suggests that the initial deduction presented in January, that a gang of pranksters was donning a variety of disguises as part of a malicious wager, had started to fade by late February when Spring-heeled Jack's appearance and mode of operation had become more fixed.

Despite the *Morning Post*'s clear attempt to not make public a recipe for a fire-breathing solution, imitators began to appear. On 2nd March the *Morning Herald* reported on how in a very public act a man had entered the White Lion pub in Vere Street, announced to the landlady that he was Spring-heeled Jack, then pulled out a club and attempted to strike her with it. In late March Charles Grenville, described as 'a tall, ill-favoured young man', was 'charged with having frightened a number of women and children nearly into fits, by imitating the silly and dangerous pranks of Spring-heeled Jack' in Kentish Town. Grenville, a local man 'considered of weak mind, but perfectly harmless', had donned 'a huge mask (painted blue and bright at the lips)' as 'a bit of fun'. The magistrate agreed, dismissing the case with a warning to Grenville not to do it again.[30]

Eighteen-year-old James Painter was arrested for his attack on Mrs Ann Amsinck in Kilburn on 31st March. At eight in the evening Mrs Amsinck had been walking with a friend near the house in which Painter was employed as a footman. She had been suddenly 'seized by a most ghostly looking figure, habited in a white sheet, and wearing a hideous mask, from which depended a long beard'. This attack did not go as planned as the women recognised the young man's voice, and when he fled they gave pursuit. Mrs Amsinck took the case to court and Painter, after a dressing down from Mr Rawlinson, the magistrate, was fined £4.[31] Such pranks added to the mercurial legend, keeping Spring-heeled Jack's name in the press and the public imagination, although he was never hamstrung by suspicions of genuinely being any of the arrested individuals. With an adaptability that would prove vital to his durable existence throughout the nineteenth century, accounts continued to appear. Spring-heeled

---

[29] *Morning Post*, 7th March 1838. One newspaper reported that '"Spring-heeled Jack", or some fool who assumes the character' was charged at Lambeth Street police court for the attack on Lucy Scales. It is unclear from the brief account of the case whether an actual individual was charged or the blame was just placed on Spring-heeled Jack. See *Leeds Mercury*, 24th March 1838.

[30] *The Examiner*, 25th March 1838. The *Morning Post*, 20th March 1838, gave the culprit's name as Daniel Granville, indicative of the fact that press accounts of the legend are far from consistent, even in terms of the names of hoaxers brought to court.

[31] *Morning Post*, 4th April 1838.

Jack seemed to have gained sufficient hold over the popular imagination that the appearance of imitators before magistrates could be accommodated. Those who were caught were deemed to be merely misguided mortals. The real Spring-heeled Jack was always somewhere else, eluding capture.

Reports continued to seep into the press of the shocking effects encounters with Spring-heeled Jack or his various imitators could have upon his victims. At five o'clock in the morning of Saturday 10th March a thirteen-year-old servant boy in the employment of Mr Priest, a poulterer, had been busy attaching a horse to his master's cart in Westmoreland Mews in London's West End. When he turned from his labours he was startled to find two tall men wrapped in cloaks standing in front of him, their arms outstretched and their faces coloured red. His instant assumption was that they were 'members of the "Spring-heeled Jack" family'. Such was his fright that the boy gave a loud scream for help before collapsing to the ground. Assistance arrived within minutes but by then the scary figures had disappeared and the boy was discovered in 'a state of insensibility' from which he was very slow to recover.[32]

From the spring of 1838 accounts of Spring-heeled Jack's appearances began to move beyond the capital. On 14th April *The Times* reported an appearance on the Sussex coast, the fiend having apparently surrendered his anthropomorphic shape as he left the city and reverted to his bestial form once again. Appearing before a gardener 'in the shape of a bear or other four-footed animal', he gave a growl before pursuing the terrified man. Eventually, the beast 'scaled [a] wall, and made his exit'.[33] As stories proliferated, so the idea that Spring-heeled Jack was a single individual began to strain beyond the point of credibility. On 19th May the *Leeds Mercury* reported that Spring-heeled Jack had made his way up to Whitby on the north-east coast. Again, he had appeared in 'the shape of a bear'. In a rare exception to accounts outside London after early 1838, this Spring-heeled Jack was said to possess claws which had left his female victim's face 'much injured and disfigured'.[34] Yet by the 26th May he was said to be responsible for having deprived fourteen-year-old Thomas Worth of his senses in the village of Carshalton, Surrey, a few days earlier. Whilst on his way to work at six in the morning, Worth had suddenly been leapt upon by a 'scoundrel in some awful disguise', and the encounter had left him 'bereft of reason'. Although it was possible that the same Spring-heeled Jack had hurried from the north-east to the southern counties, the feasibility of this was somewhat undermined by the Surrey account suggesting that he had been conducting his 'mischievous pranks' around Carshalton for a 'few weeks'. The *Morning Post* logically assumed that

---

[32] *Morning Post*, 13th March 1838, p. 7.
[33] *The Times*, 14th April 1838.
[34] *Leeds Mercury*, 19th May 1838.

the attack on the boy had been the actions of an 'individual who has been personating the character of "Spring-heeled Jack"'.[35] By June the legend seems to have spread nationwide, the *Bristol Mercury* reporting that 'Spring-heeled Jack, having left London and its neighbourhood, is now visiting the more distant parts of the country. This mischievous personage seems endowed with ubiquity, for, according to the county press, he was last week, at the same time, in most of the boroughs, villages, and cities in England.'[36]

The press continued to record encounters throughout the middle of the century, adding to the sense of the legend's perambulation around the country. Generally, Spring-heeled Jack would materialise in random 'episodes' which were given a sense of coherence through press reportage, then revert back to a background haze of oral rumour, fear and speculation. Mike Dash has suggested that this period of Spring-heeled Jack's career was rather vague and therefore not worthy of trawling the local newspapers for evidence.[37] However, an investigation of some key regional titles indicates there was a fairly steady stream of reports scattered across the country throughout the 1840s–60s. Given that I have managed to find accounts relating to Manchester, Norwich and Portsmouth, three specific cities studied in a completely different research context, it seems safe to state that this legend possessed a lively afterlife beyond its brief metropolitan notoriety in 1838.

This apparent ubiquity also suggests that press coverage remained under-representative of the true extent to which tales of encounters and sightings were circulating in many localities in this period. Spring-heeled Jack was sustained more by rumour than press coverage, and beyond newspaper reportage there were assertions (generally made after the date in question) that he had been seen in Chichester and the Home Counties in the 1840s, in the Midlands in the 1850s, and Middlesex in 1863.[38] Such accounts tend to lack precise dates and adhere to a familiar narrative format of surprised and frightened women encountering a leaping figure at night to whom they allocate the name 'Spring-heeled Jack'. In an attempt to limit the accruals that arose from this retrospective application, the following focuses on incidences which were at least given a degree of substance by press reports from the time in which they supposedly occurred.

In February 1841 Spring-heeled Jack appeared in Bristol, attacking a fourteen-year-old girl called Ellen Hurd. Her assailant, described as 'a tall man, dressed in a rough great coat', threatened her and then used a pair of scissors to 'cut off the whole of the hair at the back part of her head'. The local press reported this as

---

35   *Morning Post*, 26th May 1838, p. 7.
36   *Bristol Mercury*, 2nd June 1838.
37   Dash, *Spring-heeled Jack*, p. 15.
38   Simpson and Roud, *Dictionary of English Folklore*, p. 340.

'one of the freaks of the unmanly ruffian who, under the name of "Spring-heeled Jack", has been lurking about in bye-places lately'.[39] By April he was supposedly back in London, terrorising the King's Road in Camden, targeting females but hiding when men approached. He was described as 'a tall man, or brute, enveloped in a large blue cloak, with glasses of a dark colour over his eyes, which gave him a most awful appearance'. He was said to assault his female victims 'in the most shameful and indelicate manner', taking 'indecent liberties' with them.[40] Veiled through a language of early-Victorian prudery, these are perhaps the first hints of possible sexual assaults. In October he was seen around Tottenham and Edmonton, and had apparently returned to breathing fire as in 1838. One account claimed he was seen 'emitting fire from his mouth and flinging it about as he runs away'. When chased by a policeman in Tottenham, Spring-heeled Jack fled, 'throwing fire in the road with both hands'. The officer retrieved a piece of wood covered in 'a phosphoric substance', but the perpetrator escaped into a nearby graveyard. A couple of nights later he harassed the home of a gardener called Burnett, who lived near Bruce Castle, Tottenham. The man was awoken by his cottage door 'being suddenly burst open'. Catching sight of Spring-heeled Jack, Burnett was about to pursue him when his family began screaming that they had 'heard someone on top of the house'.[41]

In 1842 he was not only seen but briefly captured in the town of Eye, Suffolk. The regional press suggested a gang again, for it referred to the disturbances caused by the 'nocturnal visits of Spring-heel Jack and his friends'. When one of their number was captured by 'a party of gentleman' responding to a call for the police, he pleaded to be released, claiming 'my character is forever ruined'. Locked in the station house, he soon disappeared; the *Ipswich Journal* recorded that by 'some chemical process' he had transformed into 'a spirit' and thereby escaped his cell. Two of his accomplices 'were brought up on a suspicion of being concerned with Jack' and 'after a suitable admonition [were] dismissed'.[42]

In 1845 Spring-heeled Jack returned to the capital again, appearing in Hanwell and Ealing, though these may not have been genuine appearances. In February a butcher, Richard Bradford, appeared before the Brentford petty sessions charged with frightening women in that locality by impersonating Spring-heeled Jack. Bradford's defence was that he had donned female attire to make himself a target, hoping to draw Spring-heeled Jack out so that he might capture him. Given that he was arrested wearing 'a gown, shawl, and other accoutrements', there may have

---

[39]   *Bristol Mercury*, 13th February 1841. See also *Bristol Mercury*, 7th August 1841.
[40]   *The Era*, 11th April 1841. See also *The Examiner*, 11th April 1841, and *Musical Opinion and Music Trade Review*, October 1896, p. 14.
[41]   See *The Times*, 23rd October 1841, and *Freeman's Journal and Daily Commercial Advertiser*, 26th October 1841.
[42]   *Ipswich Journal*, 2nd April 1842.

been some truth to this. With none of the frightened women appearing at the hearing, Bradford was reprimanded and then discharged.[43] In the autumn of 1845 Spring-heeled Jack was rumoured to be active near Yarmouth in Norfolk. In September an inquest heard a case of mistaken identity arising from the fear he had generated in the locality, the tragic result being that a fifty-year-old man called Purdy had been set upon and beaten by a young man called Henry Noble. Purdy subsequently died, although a coroner later cleared Noble of any guilt in his death.[44] Peter Haining claimed that not only did Spring-heeled Jack make an appearance in Jacob's Island in London on 12th November 1845 but, for the first time, committed a murder. In this encounter he supposedly breathed fire into the face of Maria Davis, a young prostitute, before hurling her from a bridge into the mud below, where she subsequently drowned. Despite the colourful drama and apparent precision of such an account, this incident does not appear to be corroborated by contemporary evidence. If a death could have been attributed to Spring-heeled Jack then one would have expected the story to have been snapped up by the more sensational newspapers at least. This does not appear to have been the case, and, as Dash's careful research indicates, the incident probably has to be viewed as a later fabrication until sources can suggest otherwise.[45]

In 1847 Spring-heeled Jack's name was associated with a court case in Teignmouth, Devonshire. During the winter he had taken to scaring, pestering and molesting women. In fact, this turned out to be an imitator case. Captain Finch, a resident of Shaldon, a retired army officer of sixty and a man alleged to be in very poor health, was brought before Mr Tucker, the local magistrate. The case had been brought by a female servant of Miss Morgan who 'had been twice assaulted in January between nine and ten at night, by a man disguised in a skin coat having the appearance of a bullock's hide, skull-cap, horns and mask'. These attacks caused the woman to suffer from 'serious fits'. The press played on the case's explicit class dimension, setting up the word of a 'highly respectable' army officer against one who 'belonged to the humblest rank'. Despite his poor physical match to such an athletic figure, Finch was eventually found guilty.[46] Unlike most of his provincial perambulations, this one drew a considerable degree of attention from a broad range of regional newspapers.[47] This diverse coverage hints at the way an 'appearance' of Spring-heeled Jack in one part of

[43]   See *Newcastle Courant*, 14th February 1845, and also *Age and Argus*, 8th February 1845.
[44]   See *Illustrated London News*, 27th September 1845, p. 203, and also O'Donnell, *Haunted Britain*, pp. 74–5.
[45]   Haining, *Legend and Bizarre Crimes*, p. 85. For a refutation of this supposed incident see Dash, *Spring-heeled Jack*, pp. 32–3.
[46]   *Lady's Newspaper*, 3rd April 1847.
[47]   See *Daily News*, 29th March 1847; *Northern Star*, 3rd April 1847; *Bell's Life in London*, 4th April 1847; and *Hampshire Telegraph*, 10th April 1847.

the country was circulated around others, thereby helping to transmit his name around the nation in a seemingly haphazard fashion. As such, Spring-heeled Jack's legend had no geographical centre, and was formulated less at the site of the 'event' than in the more diffused imagined community fostered by a developing nineteenth-century print culture.[48]

As suggested above, Spring-heeled Jack's legend was fed by deliberate hoaxing but also through cases of mistaken identity. In January 1849 several newspapers ran the story of how a butcher from Tynemouth who had missed his train from Newcastle had leapt onto it as it passed by. Clinging to the outside of the train for several miles, he eventually 'gained the footboard of the carriage, and, rearing himself up, his white, panic-stricken countenance presented itself, in contrast to the blackness of the night, against the glass of the door'. Upon seeing this unexpected figure outside the train, the startled guard had thought it was Spring-heeled Jack. Once the guard realised the man was not the legendary phantom but a hapless passenger, he pulled him inside.[49]

In 1850 Spring-heeled Jack was associated with a ghost around Wakefield. He was given diabolical associations by rumours that claimed he had left a lingering smell of brimstone in his wake. Granting this visitation a further supernatural tone, it was reported that people had resorted to laying the ghost by 'exorcisms, coupled with the plenteous sprinkling of holy water'. This was credited with driving him out of Wakefield, but he soon reappeared on nearby East Moor. Local inhabitants of that region were reported to 'have been alarmed by this half monster, half man, walking the ground "midst the pale glimpses of the moon, making night hideous"'. One man claimed he had observed 'the goblin trotting at an unearthly speed', and, with further allusions to the diabolical, asserted that the creature had left a '"cloven hoof" … mark on the ground'.[50] Around the winter of 1852–53 Spring-heeled Jack was seen in Norwich, Norfolk. His appearance does not seem to have made the local press but it was recorded in a street ballad of the period. This claimed that every night for a week the streets of the city had been thronged with hundreds of people keen to catch a glimpse of him. According to the ballad, speculation as to Spring-heeled Jack's origin was rife, with some claiming to have seen him 'descend from the sky', whilst others thought he had risen from the ground. As usual, when the police tried to trap him in the

[48] See Anderson, *Imagined Communities*.
[49] See *Lloyd's Weekly Newspaper*, 14th January 1849, and *Trewman's Exeter Flying Post*, 18th January 1849.
[50] *Manchester Times*, 18th May 1850.

Chapelfield area of the city, Spring-heeled Jack escaped by leaping away, mocking the constables who were unable to match his pace and dexterity.[51]

In terms of press reportage, the 1860s represented something of a lull in contemporary accounts. Rather with the historical distance of several decades, one begins to see a mid-Victorian reflection on the early manifestations of the legend. A generation after the events, a number of accounts from this period helped consolidate the idea that Henry de La Poer Beresford, the Marquis of Waterford, may have been either the original Spring-heeled Jack or the leader of the band of aristocrats who had brought terror to the capital in 1838. This appears to have been based on little more than the bad reputation of an aristocratic hellraiser. Contemporary newspapers such as *The Examiner* had reported on his bouts of public drunkenness, gambling and vandalism, including his most notorious deeds in Melton Mowbray in 1837, when he painted parts of the town red and then broke an associate out of the town gaol.[52] After the wild adventures of his youth Waterford had settled down to a life of aristocratic respectability. The fact that Spring-heeled Jack and the Marquis were not one and the same (at least after 1838) appears to have been proven by the fact that the monster continued to make appearances long after the man had died.[53] Yet the association persisted and was hardening into 'fact' by the time E. Cobham Brewer included an entry on Spring-heeled Jack in the 1911 edition of his *Reader's Handbook of Famous Names in Fiction*. The entry began with the claim that the 'marquis of Waterford, in the early part of the nineteenth century, used to amuse himself by springing on travellers unawares, to terrify them' and added that 'from time to time others have followed his silly example'.[54]

---

[51] Norfolk Heritage Centre, 'Pranks of the Ghost'. It was suggested in the late 1890s that this was a hoax perpetrated 'upon the credulity of the public by means of a magic lantern, or some device for producing an optical illusion'. See *Norfolk and Norwich Notes and Queries*, 5th November 1898, p. 411.

[52] See *The Examiner*, 22nd May 1836, and 16th April, 18th June, 2nd, 8th and 16th July 1837. See also Augustus Sala, 'Shows', p. 276.

[53] See *Manchester Times*, 1st August 1868. Haining is particularly at fault in embellishing the Marquis of Waterford association with outright fictions. When Spring-heeled Jack frightened the servant at 2 Turner Street on 25th February 1838, Haining asserts that the boy caught a glimpse of the assailant's cloak which was embroidered with 'an ornate crest' with a 'W' set 'in gold filigree'. See Haining, *Legend and Bizarre Crimes*, p. 52, and also Dash, *Spring-heeled Jack*, p. 32. This incident received scant mention in the metropolitan press and this supposed detail is not supported by any contemporary account that survives. If the Marquis of Waterford went to the effort of making such an elaborate disguise (including possibly a mask, helmet, suit, fire-breathing apparatus and even spring-heeled boots) it seems unlikely that he would then don a cloak that effectively had his name on it.

[54] Brewer, *Reader's Handbook*, p.1038.

Spring-heeled Jack may have appeared in Portsmouth in the 1860s. In his reminiscences about the town F. J. Proctor recounted how 'a tremendous scare was caused by a dare-devil called "Springheel Jack", who had strong springs fixed to the soles of his boots and always popped up in uncanny places to the consternation of women and children'. He claimed to have watched Spring-heeled Jack's 'ghostly pantomime' as he leapt 'over tombs on a starry midnight', describing the figure as an 'ogre' dressed in white. Proctor observed that 'like a rolling snowball pushed down a hill and gathering size, the tale of this apparition increased as it travelled', though 'ultimately it got too hot for "Springheel Jack", so he suddenly disappeared in the flesh'. Despite this, his reputation was said to have lingered in the town. One has to be a little wary of taking such an account at face value, for these were the recollections of a local man writing in the 1920s. Proctor did not locate this Portsmouth appearance in a specific year, and one has to question how far such an 'eyewitness' account was influenced by memory and the passage of time.[55]

The 1860s marked further cultural shifts in the legend. In June 1863 a play, *Spring-heeled Jack; or, a Felon's Wrong*, was produced at the Grecian Theatre, London.[56] This was followed by W. Traver's more successful 1868 play, *Spring-Heeled Jack; The Terror of London*, a piece given extra credence by its assertion that this 'extraordinary drama' was 'founded on facts'.[57] Traver's play had adopted the title of a successful penny dreadful serial with the same name that had been running since at least the year before, suggesting the playwright was seeking to profit from another popular cultural expression of the Spring-heeled Jack legend. Given the gap of thirty years since the scare of 1838, this serialised story had been able to reinvent Spring-heeled Jack. Rather than being portrayed as a monster who terrorised the innocent, he was now reimagined as an oddly costumed hero who flouted the law but upheld justice and punished the wicked, becoming, in effect, a Victorian prototype for the costumed superheroes of the twentieth century. Conflating many of the original details from the earlier press accounts, this new Spring-heeled Jack wore 'a repulsive-looking mask ... and a pair of gloves made of the hide of some animal, at the tips of the fingers of which were nails tapering to a point at the end and very long'. He also possessed a reversible cloak, worn as black when wishing to conceal himself in shadows, white when confronting his enemies, the latter presumably to encourage the idea that he was a ghost. In one encounter in which he seeks to terrify a bullying drunk, his appearance becomes even more startling, for his 'head and body glowed with a blue, phosphorescent fire, from the back of which hung, in graceful folds, a long

[55] Proctor, *Reminiscences of Old Portsmouth*, pp. 26–7.
[56] *Reynolds's Newspaper*, 28th June 1863.
[57] *The Era*, 30th August 1868, and 20th June 1880.

striped cloak, like a tiger skin'.[58]

Despite this literary change of persona, in 'real' folkloric accounts of the 1870s Spring-heeled Jack continued in his traditional role of frightening prankster. The 1870s marked something of a late renaissance for the legend, for it witnessed a revival in accounts and regained something of the media interest it had possessed in 1838. In February 1872 *The Courant* reported on the 'Edinburgh Ghost', linking it by name to Spring-heeled Jack. Seen in the western part of the city, this association had arisen from the way the 'ghost' was said to possess 'remarkable agility'. According to rumour, the ghost had 'bounded the canal at a leap' and thought 'nothing of vaulting over a cab or pretty high wall'. The ghost scared a wine merchant's delivery boy who fled, leaving his basket of goods. When he returned he found some of the alcohol he had been transporting had gone. Ten days later it was reported that Spring-heeled Jack had moved from Holyrood to Leith where he had surprised two girls. One ran away but the other was 'so overcome that she fell to the ground in a faint'.[59] These Scottish accounts appear to represent relatively rare excursions across the border.

By October his name was being associated with the 'Peckham ghost', although the 'Spring-heeled Jack' moniker was applied by the press rather than locals.[60] Unlike many previous accounts which had frequently involved people wrapped in white sheets, there were considerable similarities between this local manifestation and earlier descriptions of Spring-heeled Jack. People noted the ghost's unusual height (often accorded to the wearing of spring-heeled boots) and the fact that, when pursued by a gang of navvies, it leapt a six-foot fence. One witness, at first faced with the thought of having to defend himself with an umbrella against the 'ghost', was fortunate enough to be able to simply observe it as it leapt away. The onlooker asserted that it had 'spring-heeled or india-rubber soled boots, for no man living could leap so lightly, and ... fly across the ground in the manner he did last night'.[61] It is worth noting that he did not actually see such contraptions but rather presented the idea as the only logical explanation, an assertion repeated in numerous accounts since 1838. Given that this observation was made three weeks into the Peckham 'visitations', the press associations with Spring-heeled Jack may have already been influencing such interpretations. In late November a man called Joseph Munday was arrested for these disturbances, and whilst rumours of further appearances were supposedly made, local press interest died down in early December, seemingly content that the guilty

---

58   *Spring-heel'd Jack: The Terror of London* (1867), pp. 3–4 and 23.
59   See *Glasgow Herald*, 5th and 15th February 1872.
60   See *News of the World*, 17th November 1872; *Illustrated Police News*, 28th December 1872; and *Camberwell and Peckham Times*, 19th and 26th October, 2nd, 9th, 16th, 23rd and 30th November, and 7th December 1872.
61   *Camberwell and Peckham Times*, 9th November 1872.

culprit had been caught. Munday, a 'middle-stature fellow, brawny built' and forty-three years old, did not really fit the description of the tall, athletic figure described by previous witnesses, but when he was bound to find a surety of £10 to be on good behaviour for the next six months it seemed to put an end to Spring-heeled Jack's appearances in Peckham.[62] This retrospective application of Spring-heeled Jack's name to 'ghosts' by contemporary metropolitan newspapers or through later local folkloric accounts was also seen in Sheffield in April and May 1873. Initially referred to as the 'Park Ghost', this local manifestation also acquired the 'Spring-heeled Jack' name on account of its apparent athleticism and ability to leap walls.[63]

The sheer audacity of Spring-heeled Jack's new focus of interest in 1877 garnered him renewed media attention. Rather than attacking pedestrians in urban streets or country lanes, he now started to target military establishments, the first of which was the Aldershot army camp in Hampshire. In March and April rumours circulated that the sentry guards in the more remote posts had been harassed by a ghost during the previous winter, and the spring had brought a renewed spate of attacks. As the *Preston Guardian* reported, 'The course pursued is generally to stalk the sentry – one who is posted on some lonely spot, such as the magazine, being chosen as the victim – and then suddenly to leap upon his back, attempt to disarm him, and in the confusion caused ... the attacking party effects his escape.' In response, it was reported that sentries had been doubled and had taken to loading their weapons with live ammunition.[64] Newspapers from opposite ends of the spectrum, the respectable *Times* and the wildly sensational *Illustrated Police News*, both recorded the incidents whereby frightened soldiers were slapped in the face as Spring-heeled Jack leapt over their heads, the latter title carrying a depiction of an attack by ethereal ghosts. When the soldiers fired at him, their shots proved ineffective, doing much to re-establish an aura of supernatural power that had drained away over the years. Despite this, *The Times* took the level-headed approach that it was most likely a soldier who had smuggled the disguise onto the base.[65] The *Illustrated Police News* claimed the ghost, who 'the soldiers irreverently styled "Spring-heeled Jack"', returned in late

---

[62] See *Camberwell and Peckham Times*, 30th November and 7th December 1872. It is interesting to note that the *Illustrated Police News*, never one to shy away from a sensational story, did not pick it up until after this episode had run its course, only reporting on it on 28th December 1872. When it did, it ran an image of a cart driver being frightened by a capering, rather comical figure in white.

[63] For contemporary reports see *Sheffield Daily Telegraph*, 23rd and 31st May 1873; *Sheffield and Rotherham Independent*, 23rd, 24th and 26th May 1873. For a good analysis of the Sheffield appearances see Clarke, 'Unmasking Spring-heeled Jack'.

[64] *Preston Guardian*, 28th April 1877, and *Illustrated Police News*, same date.

[65] *The Times*, 28th April 1877. See also Golicz, *Spring-heeled Jack*.

summer, a story that was not reported by other metropolitan newspapers. As if having gained in confidence from the April attacks, Spring-heeled Jack was now said to 'climb the sentry box, and pass his hand (which is arranged to feel as cold and clammy as that of a corpse) over the face of the sentinel'. He was supposedly seen on the night of Friday 31st August at the powder magazine in the North Camp, where he 'nearly frightened the sentry out of his wits, by slapping his face with his death-like hand' before he 'disappeared, hopping and bounding into the mist'.[66]

If harassing the British army was not enough, in November 1877 the *Illustrated Police News* ran a picture of Spring-heeled Jack being sighted and shot at on Newport Arch, a Roman ruin in Newport, Lincolnshire. It claimed that the figure, dressed in animal skins with horns or ears, was shot at as he ran across the rooftops, the hides appearing to make him bulletproof, for he eluded injury and capture once again. Despite such a sensational appearance, the story does not seem to have been repeated in either the regional or metropolitan press, and one has to consider the extent to which the paper had realised putting Spring-heeled Jack on the illustrated cover made for improved sales.[67] This may also explain why another weekly penny serial, purportedly penned by George Augustus Sala, and appearing in the *Boy's Standard* in 1878–79, generated enough profitable interest to run for forty-eight instalments.

In October 1878 the *Hampshire Telegraph* claimed the Aldershot army camp had 'again been honoured by a visit from that evil goblin known as "Spring-heel Jack", a celebrity, by the way, not altogether unknown to Portsmouth fame'. The army's failure to stop him the previous year led the newspaper to note that 'his little pleasantries of last year are being repeated with increased hardihood for the amusement of sentries on isolated posts'. Again, he was 'fired upon more than once … but as would become an orthodox ghost, has always escaped scatheless, while … civil and military police have tried night after night in vain to capture him'.[68] Suspicion turned towards the idea of it being a prank by an officer on the base. Orders were issued that sentries were 'on no account to fire their rifles at any one who does not answer their challenge' for fear that they would hit the 'ghost'. This oddly counterproductive order provided a source of mirth for some of the comical papers.[69]

The Times' belief that the Aldershot 'ghost' had been a soldier appeared to be justified by the fact that when the 3rd Battalion, 60th Rifles, previously stationed at Aldershot, moved to Colchester in 1878 Spring-heeled Jack followed them. It

---

66   *Illustrated Police News*, 8th September 1877.
67   Ibid., 3rd November 1877.
68   *Hampshire Telegraph*, 9th October 1878.
69   *Funny Folks*, 26th October 1878.

was reported that the 'principal scene of his operations is the Abbey field, where he has visited several lonely sentries, all of whom he has frightened, and two so seriously that they are now under treatment in the garrison hospital, it being feared that the mind of one is completely unhinged'. With rumours circulating in the locality of the camp, the provincial newspapers picked up the story from late October, and in November reported that 'as a superfluous military preparation, the sentinels have been doubled'.[70] This actually brought results, for in December 1878 the prankster's invulnerability to injury finally ran out as a sentry eventually succeeded in bayoneting him in the leg. He was revealed to be a subaltern officer.[71] As with the original appearances in London, the *Ipswich Journal* suggested that these pranks were performed by a group of officers, and that this individual who had been unfortunate enough to get himself captured was merely one among many 'military Spring-heel Jacks'.[72]

These well-publicised activities in Essex in December were swiftly followed in the same month by Spring-heeled Jack rumours circulating around Bury, in the neighbouring county of Suffolk. This short hop across county boundaries was fairly unusual as Spring-heeled Jack accounts tended to manifest in locations scattered across the country. In this case the relatively short journey from Colchester to Bury may have been facilitated by local and regional oral networks as much as by the press which disseminated rumours to a wider audience. The rumours in Bury in late December were tracked to a porter at the Suffolk General Hospital who claimed to have been walking alone one night when he encountered 'a tall figure clothed apparently in a black and white hairy skin, which enveloped its head, and reached to the ground'. When the porter prepared to throw a stone at the figure, it 'glided away amongst the adjacent trees'. When interrogated by a regional newspaper, the porter asserted that what he had seen was a man in disguise although his description of the figure's movements did not necessarily support such an interpretation.[73]

Press reports continued to trickle in throughout the 1880s and 1890s but there was a notable decline in encounters, and these two decades seemed to mark a fundamental alteration in the legend, a sense that the energy that had sustained it in the popular imagination was draining away. This was illustrated in a number of ways. In September 1881 the *Illustrated Police News* ran an article that lamented the nature of modern ghosts and expressed a nostalgic fondness for their more traditional forebears who had performed a moral service in exposing

---

[70]   *Bristol Mercury*, 31st October 1878, and *Reynolds's Newspaper*, 10th November 1878.
[71]   See *Bristol Mercury*, 31st October 1878; *Leeds Mercury*, 31st October 1878; *Hampshire Telegraph*, 2nd November 1878; *Reynolds's Newspaper*, 10th November 1878; and *Lloyd's Weekly Newspaper*, 29th December 1878.
[72]   *Ipswich Journal*, 21st December 1878.
[73]   *Bury and Norwich Post*, 24th December 1878, p. 4.

criminals or revealing 'guilt-hidden treasure'. Spring-heeled Jack was mentioned by name, being described as 'the most vulgar and unromantic ghost imaginable'.[74] The following year the *Daily News* compared him unfavourably with 'old well-established ghosts' such as 'the headless cavalier [and] the blue lady', entities of 'venerable antiquity' against which he appeared to be nothing more than 'a mere vulgar ruffian, fond of horse-play'.[75] At the same time there was a nostalgic reformulation of his earlier pranks in London. With time having blunted the edge of terror, those frightening months began to be viewed as an intriguing curiosity from writers' youths. As was often the case with retrospection, elaborations and alterations crept in, his claws in one account being replaced by 'a monomaniacal propensity to … gash [his victims] with a fine-edged, silver-handled knife'.[76]

Indicative of ongoing changes, an account from Richmond in 1884 declared the locality was being disturbed by 'a ghost of the "Spring-heeled Jack" type', suggesting he was shifting from being an individual to a category of ghost, a marked loss of specificity that was going to become a feature of the legend in the late nineteenth century. The association with the name seems to have arisen from the swiftness with which this 'figure clad in white' had outpaced a horse. The witnesses, a Mr John Bradley and his servant, pursued the figure up Reeth Road but 'the mode of its progression caused considerable uneasiness to the observers', and it eventually disappeared 'towards the West Field'.[77] In some contexts Spring-heeled Jack underwent a shift from being a figure of fear to a figure of fun. In 1878 *Funny Folks* had printed a comic-strip cartoon of Spring-heeled Jack at Aldershot, depicting him being repelled by soldiers brandishing umbrella bayonets because they were not allowed to use their rifles.[78] This trend continued on stage. In January 1887 Spring-heeled Jack was a character in *Jack and the Beanstalk*, a pantomime running at the Grand Theatre, Birmingham. His appropriation into such a context seemed to signal that his days of genuine terror had come, or were swiftly coming, to an end.[79]

Added to this, the 1880s and 1890s saw an increase in the number of hoaxers and imitators being captured; each revelation of a man in a costume seemed to whittle away at the supernatural mystique that had previously surrounded Spring-heeled Jack's name. When he made an appearance 'between New-cross and Rotherhithe' in August 1882, the press automatically assumed it was the work of a hoaxer. The *Daily News* reported that 'some witless joker' was

---

74   *Illustrated Police News*, 17th September 1881.
75   *Daily News*, 22nd August 1882.
76   See for example Horne, 'The Great Fairs and Markets of Europe', p. 180; *All the Year Round*, 9th August 1884, pp. 345–50; and *Lloyd's Weekly Newspaper*, 25th February 1900.
77   *Northern Echo*, 1st August 1884.
78   *Funny Folks*, 26th October 1878.
79   *The Era*, 1st January 1887. See also 22nd and 29th January 1887.

attempting to scare women and children, although the paper recorded that 'the arrival of some male passengers scared him away before serious mischief was done'.[80] A similar tone informed an account of Spring-heeled Jack's appearance in Darlington in 1884. Claiming it was part of a more general 'visit to various towns in the North', a regional newspaper then did its utmost to suggest the 'ghost' was yet another irresponsible human prankster in disguise. In this case it could not be proved, for he appears to have avoided capture.[81] Others were not so fortunate. Writing in 1907 William Jaggard recalled that in Warwickshire in the 1880s 'a youth, in ghostly disguise of mask and long white sheet' would leap out from behind hedges to terrorise women and children in country lanes, his leaps aided by 'powerful and noiseless springs' attached to his shoes. After a number of such scares, locals made a concerted effort to capture him. When they did so this 'Spring-heeled Jack' was revealed to be 'the son of a local coal merchant, a youth not overburdened with common sense'.[82] In Clewer, near Windsor, in 1885 a hoaxer leapt onto a policeman's back and knocked him down in the street. The policeman attempted to grapple his attacker but he made his escape. Chased by the police, the athletic young man was eventually captured and, after a night in the station cell, received a stern dressing down before the magistrate.[83] Even fictional stories involving Spring-heeled Jack started to focus not on a supernatural monster but the eventual capture of an impersonator.[84]

The late 1880s saw a cluster of accounts in Wales. In January 1886 what was described as a 'Welsh Spring-heel Jack' was reported to be 'causing the utmost excitement and alarm' in the district between Wrexham and Exlusham. Alongside the more familiar accounts of women and children left suffering from shock, the *Cheshire Observer* reported that even the workers in the nearby collieries were reluctant to travel to and from work alone when it was dark. As if to indicate that Spring-heeled Jack was persisting into a changing world, he was said to have appeared in front of the horse-drawn tram that ran between Wrexham and Rhos. Such comments reiterated that his days of leaping stage coaches now seemed increasingly remote.[85] In February 1888 he was reported to be in North Wales, causing 'a terrible scare all along the North Carnarvonshire coast'. The enterprising promoters of a local bazaar at Portmandoe seemed to have realised an opportunity to cash in on this Welsh appearance and got the

---

[80] *Daily News*, 22nd August 1882.
[81] *North-Eastern Daily Gazette*, 28th January 1884.
[82] *Notes and Queries*, 10th Series, 18th May 1907, p. 395.
[83] *Ipswich Journal*, 24th January 1885.
[84] See for example *Young Folks Paper*, 25th August 1888, p. 126. This story appears to be a shortened, largely plagiarised copy of Lewis Hough's 'Catching a Tar' which appeared in the *Union Jack*, 30th March 1882, p. 407.
[85] *Cheshire Observer*, 16th January 1886, p. 2.

town crier 'to announce that Spring-heel Jack had been caught, and would be on exhibition from five to ten each night'. This had the desired effect of drawing crowds, although they were probably somewhat disappointed to find themselves watching a performance of 'a young man dressed as Spring-heel Jack'. Yet whilst reporting this promotional prank, the press also recognised the seriousness of the local scare, with both women and workmen being left 'terror-stricken', and one lady in particular rendered 'seriously ill from fright and shock'.[86]

Spring-heeled Jack may have made an appearance in Everton in autumn 1888, but that season in that particular year belonged to Jack the Ripper, and all attention was focused on Whitechapel; if he did appear in Liverpool it does not seem to have made it into the press.[87] Whilst weakened by the various developments outlined above, from the autumn of 1888 the aging Spring-heeled Jack was forever eclipsed by the newer, more sensational figure of Jack the Ripper. Spring-heeled Jack's name remained on people's tongues into the early 1890s but now he was more often associated with the debate surrounding the damaging moral influence that his cheap penny fiction serials inflicted upon juveniles.[88] Even as the folkloric demon faded, this stronger association with penny dreadfuls pushed him further into the realm of a literary fiction, causing obfuscation of his increasingly muted existence as a 'real' entity. The fear was no longer that one would suffer physical harm as a result of a real encounter, but rather mental and moral corruption from reading trashy stories filled with violence and anti-authoritarian messages in which the 'hero' frequently fought and mocked policemen. At the same time the name 'Spring-heeled Jack' became more diffused as common criminals and showmen, particularly acrobats, began to appropriate the catchy moniker.[89]

Despite these developments, his name still retained some vestigial power to prompt fear in local communities. On Tuesday 18th August 1891 there was a mobbing of a 'Spring-heeled Jack' by an 'excited crowd' in the Market Square in Galashiels in the Scottish borders. Sustained rumours about his appearances at night in the Gala Park district had stoked the local community to a point of anxious tension. A local crowd had gathered in the square to watch the town

---

[86] *Bristol Mercury*, 4th February 1888.

[87] See Whittington-Egan, *Liverpool Colonnade*, pp. 139–40.

[88] See for example 'The Influence of the Penny Dreadful', *Saturday Review*, 20th October 1888, p. 458; *Daily News*, 19th July 1890, p. 4; 'The Literature of Rascaldom', *Pall Mall Gazette*, 21st July 1890; *Quarterly Review*, July 1890, pp. 150–3; 'A Literary Causerie', *The Speaker*, 26th July 1890, pp. 104–5; and *Scots Observer*, 2nd August 1890, p. 267. See also Ackland, 'Elementary Education and the Decay of Literature'.

[89] See for example accounts about 'Spring-heeled Jack, or the Demon Jumper', in *The Era*, 15th November 1890 and 31st January 1891. For a criminal known as Spring-heeled Jack see *Northern Echo*, 7th December 1893.

band, and when what one paper described as a 'peculiarly-dressed female' entered the square, the crowd somewhat irrationally presumed her to be 'Spring-heeled Jack' and set upon her. The *Dundee Courier and Argus* reported that the woman had to be removed to the town's police office for her own protection.[90]

Spring-heeled Jack made an early migration beyond the shores of the British mainland in September 1891 when he was associated with a scare in St Peter Port, Guernsey. Four youths were caught pretending to be Spring-heeled Jack in the suburbs of the town, three of whom were sons of high-ranking army officers. Their social standing did not stop them from receiving sentences that required either the payment of a fine or up to one month's imprisonment.[91] Later, in October 1897 *The Star*, a Guernsey newspaper, suggested that Spring-heeled Jack pranks had started once again. Again, it was believed some 'senseless young men have been scaring timid persons at night in the neighbourhood of Collings road, the Couture'. They were said to be dressed in black and white clothing and were 'furnished with springs which enabled them to leap considerable distances'. As with many later cases of hoaxing, what had started as speculation about Spring-heeled Jack's seemingly abnormal movements and leaps had become the actual means by which pranksters could mimic such feats. Groups of men had banded together to hunt these 'Spring-heeled Jacks', and on the evening of 26th October they had spotted and pursued one. One of the pursuers had brought the 'Spring-heeled Jack' down by hitting him with a heavy stone, and the group had then set upon him, inflicting such a beating that the newspaper described him as having been left 'half dead'.[92]

Spring-heeled Jack made a late appearance in Neath, South Wales, in 1898. For several weeks in early November he had been scaring young women, had chased two servant girls, and had adopted the unsettling practice of 'tapping at ... kitchen windows, making unearthly cries, and leaping over garden walls'. In one attack he told his victim he would let her go if she stopped screaming and proved true to his word. Interestingly, she made no mention of his appearance, only that when she saw him again he simply 'raised his hat'. Yet this late manifestation was not always so gentlemanly. On Sunday 13th November he viciously attacked a servant girl. Around 10.15 pm she had gone

> into the scullery, which [was] just outside the door of the kitchen, to get a utensil of some sort ... she was suddenly pounced on from behind, her dress was ripped open, and her face blackened and scratched. The girl screamed and fainted ... Mr Newton [her employer], hearing her cries, came downstairs, and found her lying unconscious in the yard.

---

[90] *Dundee Courier and Argus*, 20th August 1891.
[91] See *Daily News*, 16th September 1891, p. 3, and *Birmingham Daily Post*, 19th September 1891, p. 7.
[92] See St Peter Port's *The Star*, 28th October 1897, and also 2nd November 1897.

The girl regained consciousness but 'remained hysterical throughout the whole of the night'.[93]

1904 saw both the publication of Alfred Burrage's (writing as 'Charlton Lea') new serial, *The Spring-heeled Jack Library*, and some of the last accounts of Spring-heeled Jack sightings. Indicative of his declining status in the popular imagination by the early twentieth century, Burrage's serial ran for only twelve instalments before ending. If this illustrated a waning of his commercial appeal, so September 1904 is often taken to mark his last overtly public appearance in Britain. In a rather muddled event that was retrospectively given shape and form by the application of the 'Spring-heeled Jack' name, he was supposedly seen bounding down William Henry Street in Everton during several nights. The *News of the World* reported that 'crowds of people assemble nightly' to catch a glimpse of him but 'only a few have done so yet'. In an account from much later in the century it was claimed that in a final encore he 'was seen to jump clean over the terrace houses from Stitt Street to Haigh Street, and then hop back across the slate roofs to Salisbury Street, after which he was never seen again.'[94]

This last statement was untrue. Just a few months later, in November 1904, his name was associated with the hunt for a ghost in Kent, although as had become the increasing trend by the turn of the century, the press referred to a Spring-heeled Jack 'type' rather than a particular individual.[95] Rumours of his name and appearances lingered up to the Second World War. A newspaper account from 1957 claimed that in the early twentieth century he had been known to mug Manchester weavers for food on their way to work in the morning.[96] Even when he had become abstracted into a more generic bogeyman to scare children into obedience, the power evoked by his name still generated fear amongst children for several generations. Jacqueline Simpson and Steve Roud have claimed that such beliefs remained 'fairly widespread among children up to the First World War', whilst the work of Sandy Hobbs and David Cornwell has indicated that Spring-heeled Jack's name was still known to Glaswegian children into the mid-late 1930s.[97]

Rumours continued around Sheffield until the First World War, and later there were supposed appearances in Warrington in 1920, and Bradford in September

[93]   *Western Mail*, 15th November 1898.
[94]   *News of the World*, 25th September 1904. See also *Liverpool Daily Post*, 25th January 1967, and *Liverpool Echo*, 19th May 1967, for the deconstruction of this 'Spring-heeled Jack' appearance.
[95]   See *Daily Mirror*, 19th November 1904, p. 3.
[96]   *Gorton and Openshaw Reporter*, 27th December 1957.
[97]   See Simpson and Roud, *Dictionary of English Folklore*, pp. 340–1, and Hobbs and Cornwell, 'Hunting the Monster with Iron Teeth', pp. 127–9.

1926.[98] In Bradford a ghostly white figure was seen around Grafton Street for several nights, and whilst not labelled 'Spring-heeled Jack', there were tacit associations made through the ghost being tall and dexterous, possessing 'a fleetness of foot comparable ... to that of an Olympic champion'. Like Spring-heeled Jack, he also took to the rooftops to evade capture.[99] A final scare in Campbeltown, a herring port in Scotland, in December 1937 was perhaps the most faithful re-enactment of all the key ingredients of the Victorian legend. Fearful inhabitants consciously associated the 'apparition' with Spring-heeled Jack by claiming he had mimicked the latter's leaping ability by 'attaching mechanisms to his feet'. The story was picked up by the *Daily Mirror* and unfolded along now familiar lines. Women were left shocked and faint by nocturnal appearances, whilst men and youths banded together in armed groups to patrol the streets of the town in search of 'the ghost'. The miscreant's ability to appear in a number of places simultaneously also encouraged locals to resort to the press interpretation of a century earlier, namely that there were a number of pranksters involved in this mischief.[100]

This period was also marked by Spring-heeled Jack's emigration from Britain as he transformed into a migratory legend that was disseminated and appropriated into different cultures around the world. As with the myriad accounts within Victorian Britain, it is obviously more credible to assume that this was an adapted folkloric motif rather than an individual Victorian monster making its lonely way around the globe. The most faithful foreign homage to the Victorian original came with the 'Black Flash' appearances in Provincetown, Cape Cod, Massachusetts between 1938 and 1945. This strangely familiar character was similarly tall, dressed in black, possessed 'eyes like balls of flame' and was equally capable of huge leaps. In one account it was even said to have spat fire at a teenager.[101] Having achieved his liberation from the confines of British culture by becoming a generalised folkloric type, Spring-heeled Jack's interaction with other world cultures meant he could only ever be a variant of the individual who had been forged in the context of the Victorian popular imagination. Whilst spawning an international progeny, Spring-heeled Jack, as an English Victorian, can be said to have aptly died in the early decades of the twentieth century.

[98] The Warrington incident is mentioned in Fields, *Lancashire Magic and Mystery*, p. 11. For the Sheffield rumours see Clarke, 'Unmasking Spring-heeled Jack', pp. 32–4.
[99] See *Bradford Daily Telegraph*, 11th September 1926.
[100] See *Daily Mirror*, 6th December 1937.
[101] See Dash, *Spring-heeled Jack*, pp. 26–8. See also Cahill, *New England's Mad and Mysterious Men*, pp. 23–9.

2

The Cultural Anatomy of a Legend

Spring-heeled Jack was a 'new' legend who also had identifiable links to earlier cultural influences. It was this rich hybridity that prevented him from merely being a nineteenth-century version of a pre-existing migratory motif. Although wholly original, Spring-heeled Jack's originality was located in the gestalt derived from his opulent cultural compilation. In many ways Spring-heeled Jack was not so much born as evolved, his legend defined by a transformative, acquisitive nature that left him in a state of constant gestation. Whilst this may sound like a convoluted way of saying it was made up as it went along, the legend's construction was not random. A potent blend of cultural components and narrative contours cumulatively informed the providence of the legend, and this chapter seeks to delineate some of the threads within that rich cultural tangle. Therefore, whilst dealing with a popular phenomenon that was marked by its fluidity, this chapter situates Spring-heeled Jack as a product of the period in which he first appeared.

As is often the case with cultural history, it is far easier to identify than explain the direct correlation between Spring-heeled Jack's contemporary cultural influences. What follows is an exploration of what appears to be the most pertinent social and cultural factors which cohered to create a sense of substance and depth from which something original was spawned. This chapter is structured around some fundamental questions about Spring-heeled Jack's emergence in 1837–38. Firstly, why did he appear when and where he did? Why did he appear as he did? Why did he act as he did? Finally, why did his legend persist beyond the initial 1838 scare? In considering the construction and semiotics of early-Victorian monstrosity this and subsequent chapters are influenced by what Jeffrey Jerome Cohen has termed 'monster theory'.[1] Whilst this involves interpreting cultures based on the monsters they produce, in the context of this chapter this will also involve reading a monster from the culture in which it was formed.

---

[1] For more on 'monster theory' see Cohen, *Monster Theory*, especially pp. 3–25.

Why did Spring-heeled Jack appear when and where he did?

There are obvious teleological pitfalls in viewing Spring-heeled Jack simply as an 'inevitable' product of the historical context in which he first appeared, but they should not deflect us from appreciating its conduciveness to monster making. Whether one considers its social, economic, political or cultural dimensions, the 1830s was a turbulent decade of seething tension and gnawing anxieties. If the issue of Catholic rights in 1828–29 had not sufficiently captured the popular imagination, the bruised resentment of lower-class political reformers who felt betrayed after the failure of the 1832 Reform Act did. The memory of the Swing riots was still fresh in rural communities, especially in southern and eastern England, and the implementation of the harsher regime set out by the Poor Law Amendment Act of 1834 articulated vocal reaction from the Anti-Poor Law movement. At the time of Spring-heeled Jack's first appearances the Chartist movement was fermenting, ready to make its entrance in 1838. Several historians have identified the 1820s and 1830s as a crucial period in the shift from the direct action of eighteenth-century 'mob' riots to new forms of collective but essentially peaceful demonstrations of strength. In such a context it is possible to read Spring-heeled Jack as a vestigial manifestation of older forms of popular protest.[2] In terms of developing industrialisation and urbanisation, there was a growing sense amongst more astute contemporaries that England was on the cusp of a modern age. Personifying this upheaval, 1837–38 was marked by the death of William IV and the ascent to the throne of Victoria, her youth and gender generally being embraced as a sign of refreshing vitality rather than fearful expectation.

Added to these issues was a shift towards a more disciplined and regulated society. The divergence between elite and popular cultural activities that had become increasingly noticeable from the later seventeenth century entered an altered relationship in this period. Rather than merely seeking distance from popular cultural forms and expressions, the social elite, particularly its more sober bourgeois elements, sought to assert some control over popular culture, enhancing a sense of nascent class difference, at least in vague terms of 'them' and 'us'. This desire to tame popular culture was made explicit in terms of laws which banned blood sports and fairs, in the development of a professional metropolitan police force from 1829 (followed in rural areas from 1839), in the efforts of temperance societies for moral reform, and the founding of mechanics institutes directed towards rational leisure and self-improvement. In terms of manners

[2] See for example Rogers, *Crowds, Culture, and Politics*, pp. 248–74, and Tilly, *Popular Contention in Great Britain*, pp. 240–393. For overviews of this period see Hilton, *A Mad, Bad, and Dangerous People?*, pp. 573–627, and Royle, *Modern Britain*.

and cultural attitudes, much of the constraint or restraint that was articulated through the culture of decorum, self-control and self-improvement that we identify with Victorian Britain was put into place prior to the young princess' ascension to the throne.[3] Such was the sense of upheaval and change that the 1830s was even marked by a popular millenarianism and a vogue for prophecies. Yet the existence of a tense and potentially volatile context does not itself explain the appearance of Spring-heeled Jack. It provided the circumstances in which the potential for myth making and mass panics can be situated and entertained, but not a justification. Cultural responses are not necessarily immediate or causally linear in their operation, and we are therefore required to engage with particular aspects of culture in the late 1830s to appreciate Spring-heeled Jack's origins.

A sensational culture is often associated with the 1860s, when the phrase frequently prefixed the words 'novel', 'journalism' and 'play'. Yet elements of such a culture were already evident in the late-Regency period. Above all else, sensation hungered for the new, a yearning reflected in many contemporary street ballads which deplored the popular enthusiasm for hoaxes, 'humbugs' and scams. Given the disproportionate influence of the metropolitan press in the 1830s, it was significantly easier to generate a media sensation in London than in the provinces.[4] A voracious metropolitan press was hungry for engaging snippets of news from the provinces to fill its column inches, and in 1837–38 this helped draw Spring-heeled Jack's evolving story towards London. This was aided by the fact that within this culture of sensation was a propensity for violence, theatricality and spectacle. These proclivities found expression in penny gaff melodrama, Newgate flash sheets and the public hangings they related to, and even the street shows of Mr Punch, the homicidal glove-puppet. Rosalind Crone has demonstrated how Punch's brutality in the early nineteenth century contrasted to his role in eighteenth-century marionette shows. Whilst Regency audiences had been fairly comfortable with the knockabout violence of the shows, Victorians came to express concern about the violent scenes, their underlying messages, and audiences' positive responses to both.[5] Concurrent with this was the introduction of a fairly consistent cast of fellow puppets, including Punch's wife, Judy, a constable, a hangman and the devil, all of which arguably represented figures of authority. Robert Leach has viewed Punch's aggressive behaviour as a resistance to social constraints, one that has obvious resonance in a period marked

---

[3] See Wilson, *Making of Victorian Values*; Emsley, *Crime and Society in England*; Langford, *Englishness Identified*; Golby and Purdue, *Civilisation of the Crowd*; Gatrell, *The Hanging Tree*; Morgan, *Manners, Morals and Class in England*; and Mason, *Making of Victorian Sexuality*.

[4] Diamond, *Victorian Sensation*, p. 2.

[5] Crone, 'Mr and Mrs Punch', p. 1070. Like Spring-heeled Jack, Punch was familiar to a broad range of social classes and age groups in Regency London. See ibid., p. 1064.

by the multi-pronged campaign to curb or shape popular culture.[6] Whilst Spring-heeled Jack's antics could be simply interpreted in a similar way, even down to his sharing of Punch's disturbing strain of misogyny, there is cause for hesitancy. Crone has convincingly argued that Punch prompted both subversive and conservative readings, his rejection of authority being undone by his comically excessive behaviour.[7] As will be considered in a later chapter, whilst it is easy to formulate Spring-heeled Jack as an anti-authoritarian rogue, he also had the potential to be a highly controlling figure, especially regarding women and children.

There was also a popular taste, amongst the better educated as much as plebeians, for the pleasure of manufactured terror. E. J. Clery has argued that indulging in 'artificial terror' had become 'an industry' from the 1790s, spearheaded by the first wave of gothic novels.[8] For those who lacked the money or literacy to engage with Horace Walpole, Anne Radcliffe, Matthew Lewis or, in its final first gasp, Mary Shelley, there were many small publishers and hack writers who were willing to oblige by shamelessly plagiarising those works for the lower classes. This frequently involved butchering them down to chapbook-length tales that retained only the ghosts and deaths.[9] If the pleasures to be gained from sadistic violence, sexual menace, the macabre and the supernatural had grown a little jaded through overfamiliarity, then the move beyond the safe realm of fiction was the next appealing sensation. Spring-heeled Jack was very much informed by a gothic sensibility for he embodied the dual menace of criminality and supernatural 'superstitions', a simultaneous threat to both the dominant moral and intellectual hegemonic beliefs of a period which was supposedly witnessing the 'march of intellect'. His appearance and actions played to a gothic inclination for 'exceptional figures ... the preternatural intrusions of ghosts and demons ... and extreme experiences'.[10] Linked to conventions of gothic villainy, and thus potentially familiar, his threat was intensified by his transgressing of the boundary between fiction and reality. Harboured amidst a haze of rumour he did not so much break through from one to the other as disturbingly blur the boundaries between the two. At the same time that a popular culture of sensation flirted with fear, it was also fascinated with the monstrous and the aberrant, a centuries-old aspect of commercialised popular culture but one that was to reach a notorious peak in the Victorian freak show.[11]

6   Leach, *Punch and Judy Show*, pp. 54–5.
7   Crone, 'Mr and Mrs Punch', p. 1058.
8   Clery, 'Pleasure of Terror', p. 165. See also Carroll, *Philosophy of Horror*.
9   Clery, *Rise of Supernatural Fiction*, pp. 143–4.
10   Garrett, *Gothic Reflections*, p. 3.
11   See Durbach, *Spectacle of Deformity*; Tromp, *Victorian Freaks*; and Garland Thomson, *Freakery*.

In a period marked by a trend towards increasing and intensified control the monstrous represented the appealingly uncontrolled, a trait best represented by the way Spring-heeled Jack's heterogeneous shifting between beast, ghost and devil tacitly opposed notions of a more stable homogeneity.

Despite first appearing in rural Barnes, Spring-heeled Jack's initial moniker, the 'suburban ghost', indicated his trajectory towards the urban centre. Whilst a literature of terror may have titillated and thrilled, the developing urban environment was a genuine realm of unease. In the larger urban centres Georgian optimism about the civilising qualities of cities was starting to turn to the doubts and apprehension of the Victorian era. Cholera had ravaged English cities in 1830–31 and prompted a dawning awareness of urban poverty and public health dangers. Unlike any other city of the 1830s, including expanding northern industrial towns, London was unusually large, giving one the sense of being enclosed within a chaotic, man-made environment. As Friedrich Engels noted, 'The very turmoil of the streets has something repulsive, something against which human nature rebels.'[12]

Such an environment stimulated an instinct, if not for the gothic then at least the strange. Around the mid nineteenth century Henry Mayhew recorded London shore-workers' urban folkloric beliefs that wild pigs lived in the sewers of Hampstead.[13] London's contemporary commentators such as Dickens and the social investigators of the 1840s did much to help construct the image of a dark, mysterious 'other' London, and Spring-heeled Jack's repeated emergence from the shadows granted him the role of herald to this hidden metropolis. Voicing cultural fears and desires, and articulating issues of instability, suppression and transgression, the urban gothic acted as a perceptual interface between grim realities and overt fantasies. Gothic tropes bled from literary fictions into official and journalistic reports on the sanitary, living and working conditions of the poor, particularly in London, providing a ready-made framework of images and emotional responses to draw from. This was a gothic modern city, labyrinthine, dark, secretive and dangerous, in terms of both crime and disease. The language if not the description was often heightened for effect, though it rarely strayed into the overtly supernatural.[14] As Thomas Wright noted, whilst criminals conducted their deeds within the nocturnal city, they were considered

[12] Engels, *Condition of the Working Class*, p. 68. For changing attitudes towards the city see Robinson, *Imagining London*, pp. 1–19, and Dentith, *Society and Cultural Forms*, pp. 103–27.

[13] Mayhew, *London Labour and the London Poor*, vol. 2, p. 154. See also Boyle, *Black Swine in the Sewers*.

[14] See Kay, *Moral and Physical Condition of the Working Class*; Engels, *Condition of the Working Class*; and Tropp, *Images of Fear*, pp. 75–87.

'the most attractive feature of the night life of cities', for they 'afford much food for reflection, both to the philosophically and sensationally inclined'.[15]

Yet, as was his contrary nature, Spring-heeled Jack did not appear in London's most notorious locales, places such as the St Giles rookery, Seven Dials, or Whitechapel.[16] Darkest England was not located in the quiet, respectable suburbs where he performed his antics and assaults. Writing in 1858 James Augustus St John noted that the supernatural was more likely to appear at the metropolitan fringe rather than in its already fantasised dark centre. Dismissing the idea that superstition was the preserve of the rural dweller, he declared, 'A slight acquaintance with the inhabitants of London must speedily dissipate this idea. On the outskirts of our prodigious city, where the sheen of its gas-lamps mingles with the light of the glow-worm in the fields, beliefs as ancient as the world still prevail in unimpaired force.'[17]

The various locations claimed as the site of Spring-heeled Jack's origin were not random. Perceived as a ghost, several accounts suggest his local origins lay in superstitious associations with haunted or at least morally tainted locations. Elliott O'Donnell claimed that Spring-heeled Jack's first appearance near Barnes Common automatically linked him to a place that at that time 'bore none too good a character, on account of the numerous robberies and assaults that frequently took place there ... A peculiarly atrocious crime was perpetrated in a house bordering on the Common, whilst on the Common itself there were numerous supposed suicides.'[18] Likewise, Elizabeth Villiers made much of what she mistakenly assumed to be his first appearance in Cut-Throat Lane near Clapham Common in 1838. She noted how the Common 'was looked upon with superstitious fear by all who lived near', whilst locals believed 'more than one grim happening had given baptism to Cut-Throat Lane'. As such, some people believed Spring-heeled Jack 'was not flesh and blood but a haunting spirit born of the evil associations of Cut-Throat Lane, since from that lane he never went far'.[19] In some cases his later perambulations in 1838 tapped into a pre-existing psychogeography of supernatural associations. His appearance in Hammersmith resonated with the local disquiet caused by the 'Hammersmith Ghost' in 1804. In such ways this newly energised creation charged itself by connecting to emotive signifiers retained in the collective memory and imagination, the supernatural histories of the capital acting as a dynamo that granted him the force to ultimately leap out into the provinces.

---

[15] Wright, *Great Unwashed*, pp. 199–200.
[16] See Shore, 'Mean Streets', pp. 151–64.
[17] Augustus St John, *Education of the People*, p. 32.
[18] O'Donnell, *Haunted Britain*, p. 73.
[19] Villiers, *Stand and Deliver*, pp. 238–9 and 247.

There are undoubtedly functionalist interpretations suggested by Spring-heeled Jack's emergence and migration in 1837–38. Given the tensions and pressures of the late 1830s, it would be all too easy to consider him as what Charles Mackay termed one of those 'seasons of excitement and restlessness, when ... whole communities suddenly fix their minds upon one object, and go mad in its pursuit'.[20] The reaction of the press and public may seem hysterically disproportionate to the appearance of a ghost, although there was an understandable reason for this; unlike more conventional ghosts that tended to intersect but not interact with the living, Spring-heeled Jack demonstrated a more predatory quality. Yet as an explanation, mass hysteria is prone to concealing more than it reveals, obscuring the complexities of any given cultural moment through resort to a reductionist (and, at least implicitly, dismissive) explanation.[21] The mass panic interpretation dissolves the legend of Spring-heeled Jack into a collective narrative spun from misinterpretations mixed with the misappropriation of more mundane assaults. This study rejects such reductive interpretations, holding to the notion that there is undoubtedly greater value in exploring the dialectical intercourse between realities and fantasies that the legend offers. In seeking to explore the expansive nature of the legend and what it suggests about Victorian popular cultures, it seems inappropriate if not wholly wasteful to narrow it to a single functional interpretation, a view that would necessarily demand highlighting certain aspects at the neglect of others.

Why did he appear as he did?

Spring-heeled Jack's appearance derived from a popular imagination still steeped in traditional folklore (though not necessarily a purely oral one) of ghosts and demonology. As Walter Scott observed in his *Letters on Demonology and Witchcraft* in 1830, the appearances of an apparition 'fall like the seeds of the husbandman, into fertile and prepared soil, and are usually followed by a plentiful crop of superstitious figments'.[22] Spring-heeled Jack sprouted from this lush field of the popular imagination which desired and willingly accommodated the fantastical in a way that middle-class commentators and especially sceptical

---

[20] Mackay, *Extraordinary Popular Delusions and the Madness of Crowds*, p. xv. Although Mackay was sufficiently attuned to the contemporary popular cultural pulse of the metropolis to appreciate the voguish sayings on its streets in 1841, he appears to make no direct mention of Spring-heeled Jack as a recent 'popular delusion'.

[21] Mackay's *Extraordinary Popular Delusions* reiterated an essentialist approach which advocated the unchanging nature of group behaviours over the centuries. See Melville Logan, 'Popularity of Popular Delusions', pp. 213–41.

[22] Scott, *Letters on Demonology and Witchcraft*, p. 48.

journalists were unwilling to do. Whilst his talons, fire-breathing and seemingly inhuman leaps could have all been produced by materials and means of the period, they clearly helped generate a supernatural aura, suggesting the persistent strength of these diabolical signifiers in the popular imagination. If one were to believe that the 1838 appearances were the result of a malevolent prank conducted by a group of young gentlemen, then these features were probably consciously intended to contribute to such a diabolical image.

His initial incarnations, shifting mercurially from ghost, to bear, to devil, all played to long-established supernatural folkloric tropes: the mischievous and often malevolent Puck of fairy lore; the ability of witches and their imps to transform back and forth between animal and human or demon form; the hybrid animal-human-monster depictions of the horned and hoofed devil himself, folklore's ultimate trickster.[23] Importantly, it was this fusion of supernatural allusions that made such a powerful impact, for he was not merely a ghost, a beast (incongruously a bear) or a devil but potentially all three. Unlike the eighteenth century which had seen an elitist response of mockery or muted neglect towards the supernatural, the dawning of the Victorian period witnessed an ardent attraction to the supernatural. A fascination with ghost stories, fairy tales and mesmerism was embellished by the mid-century attraction of spiritualist séances and the fin-de-siècle appeal of parapsychology, hypnotism, clairvoyance and ritual occultism. Within that heady mix were delineations between what was deemed a traditional body of supernatural 'superstition' located in the uneducated lower classes, and what would emerge as more respectable, 'modern' forms of supernaturalism, such as spiritualism, which attempted to distance themselves from the former by resort to a scientific lexicon of forces, fluids and powers. Such ideas and practices were engaged in along a spectrum that ranged from conscious scepticism, through ironic titillation, to earnest belief. In doing so the supernatural and the paranormal retained appealing dimensions of the unknown and the inexplicable in an age marked by the colonising instincts of materialist and positivist interpretations of the world. Although contested, the

---

[23] Later literary portrayals embellished him with hooves, horns, claws and even bat-like wings. This will be explored in more detail in Chapter 7. A later journal even associated Spring-heeled Jack with Hermes, messenger of the Greek gods. See Fitzgerald, 'Robin Goodfellow and Tom Thumb', p. 311. For the portrayal and popularity of the fairy in Victorian visual and literary cultures see Sumpter, *Victorian Press and the Fairy Tale*; Bown, *Fairies in Nineteenth-Century Art*; Silver, *Strange and Secret Peoples*; and Zipes, *Victorian Fairy Tales*.

existence of the supernatural provocatively disrupted the laws governing received notions of the natural order.[24]

Spring-heeled Jack's transformation from phantasmal bull, to white bear, to anthropomorphic demon was also engendered by his transition from the rural to urban environment. Whilst rural ghosts could be bestial or human in appearance, urban ghosts were nearly always anthropomorphic. Spring-heeled Jack's metamorphosis arose from these pre-existing cultural expectations about ghosts which prevented him from retaining a bestial form if he were to remain credible as he entered the London suburbs. In accounts of rural folkloric belief witches could also assume animal form, most commonly a hare, whilst in 1716 Richard Boulton recorded how the devil could appear 'in divers shapes', including men, ghosts and animals.[25] Owen Davies has argued that in this period this is how most animal ghosts were viewed. Fusing the phantasmal with the demonic, such entities were presented as being unusually large, even headless, often eerily white or, in their most familiar form, as black dogs, possessing the large or fiery eyes that some victims granted to Spring-heeled Jack.[26] He was never simply a ghost or devil but alluded to aspects of both. Given this, there appears some credibility to Mike Dash's claim that Spring-heeled Jack's other guises were viewed as merely deceptive concealments of his true demonic nature. Such views help explain why it was the devilish figure that eventually dominated as the definitive image amidst the mass of rumours.[27]

As a London ghost Spring-heeled Jack was not as incongruous as one may first assume. In a cultural centre as large and old as London there was naturally a well-established tradition of popular ghosts, the most famous of which was probably the Cock Lane Ghost of 1762. This hoax was based around an unseen poltergeist rather than an apparition, but the news of its sensational antics had spread through the capital via the same potent blend of oral rumour and press reports that later perpetuated Spring-heeled Jack. In doing so it similarly engaged the attention of Londoners from across the social hierarchy. The Hammersmith Ghost of 1804 bore more obvious affinities with Spring-heeled Jack. On the night of 3rd January 1804 Thomas Milward, a bricklayer, was shot dead by Francis Smith, an excise officer who thought he was a ghost. This unfortunate

---

[24] Bown, Burdett and Thurschwell, *Victorian Supernatural*, p. 1. For the changing engagement with the supernatural in the eighteenth and nineteenth centuries see McCorristine, *Spectres of the Self*; Handley, *Visions of an Unseen World*; Davies, *The Haunted*; Smajic, *Ghost-Seers, Detectives, and Spiritualists*; Smith, *Ghost Story*; Melechi, *Servants of the Supernatural*; and Pearsall, *The Table-Rappers*.

[25] Boulton, *Compleat History of Magick*, vol. 1, p. 46.

[26] Davies, *The Haunted*, p. 35. For the tradition of shape-shifting ghosts see pp. 36–8.

[27] Dash, 'Spring-Heeled Jack', p. 51. See also Thomas, *Religion and the Decline of Magic*, pp. 589–90.

incident was the culmination of a month of rumours about a ghost haunting the neighbourhood, with gossip suggesting it was the spirit of a local man who had committed suicide by cutting his throat the previous year. As a predecessor to Spring-heeled Jack's shape-shifting image, the Hammersmith Ghost was said to have sometimes dressed in a white sheet, at other times in animal skins. Similarly, encounters had led to supposed cases of people being left traumatised with shock and even frightened to death. Given this consternation, patrols of young men had nightly taken to the streets to hunt for it. It was Milward's misfortune that in this fearful environment his white work clothes led frightened locals to mistake him for the ghost. Smith and a companion had been drinking in the White Hart pub, and in a fit of drunken bravado took it upon themselves to hunt the ghost with a gun. When Smith sighted Milward he called out to the builder to identify himself. When Milward did not respond and kept advancing, Smith shot and killed him.[28]

Just as one account of Spring-heeled Jack bred others, so just over a week after the Hammersmith 'ghost' scare the St James Park Ghost appeared. Accounts were granted a little more credibility than usual, for they came from a soldier of the Coldstream Guard who claimed to have seen the ghost of a headless woman in the park in the dead of night. The soldier was hospitalised with shock, and a few nights later he was joined by a second serviceman who witnessed the apparition and subsequently suffered a fit. As with the Mayor's announcement of the letter from a Peckham resident in 1838, so in 1804 *The Times* was willing to publish a declaration by one of the soldiers. Whilst the paper did not assert the reality of the ghost, it was nevertheless complicit in providing him with a public forum for expressing his opinion. Unlike the usual white-shrouded ghost, the St James Park Ghost's appearance was quite distinctive, for despite a haziness to parts of its figure it was 'dressed in a red striped gown with red spots between each stripe'.[29]

Perhaps most pertinent was a case in 1832. Rather than being a simple ghost, rumours referred to a clawed 'monster' which assaulted women and scaled walls. Another account claimed he wore armour and was engaged in 'a wager to strip

---

[28] See Davies, *The Haunted*, pp. 21–2.
[29] *The Times*, 16th January 1804. It was later claimed it had been a hoax perpetrated by the use of a phantasmagoria, a piece of technology very much in vogue in the first decade of the nineteenth century. See *The Times*, 17th and 24th January 1804, and also *Morning Chronicle*, 21st January 1804.

the clothes off a certain number of females in a certain time'.[30] Such a character, if real, clearly referred back to the London 'monster' of the 1790s and anticipated Spring-heeled Jack's appearance six years later. Doubtless there were many such incidents and stories circulating in the capital that did not make it into the press. Rather than seeking to suggest a linear trajectory from the Hammersmith Ghost to the formation of Spring-heeled Jack in early 1838, it seems a more realistic proposition that they merely reflected a propensity to believe in ghosts and a willingness to articulate such tropes as explanations amongst the metropolitan population. As such, they were emblematic of the supernatural context in which Spring-heeled Jack thrived, not direct antecedents. Similarly, accounts that claimed Spring-heeled Jack had scared people to death also conformed to an existing tradition of ghost narratives. It was not unknown for inquests to record death by fright as a valid explanation in some cases, and, as seen with the soldiers who encountered the St James Park Ghost, the shock of a confrontation with the spectral could result in extreme and violent physical responses. In December 1830 George Gillett had been tried at the Old Bailey for the manslaughter of Mary Steers on account of his having deliberately impersonated a ghost. Gillett had dressed up in a white sheet and gave the octogenarian such a fright that she became ill and never recovered, dying a fortnight later.[31]

Whilst all this could be read as reflecting the 'survivalist' character of folklore, a view which plays to the hegemonic narrative successfully promoted by advocates of progress in the nineteenth century, it seems more appropriate to read it as the transformation of such tropes and mentalities. Despite having forebears, Spring-heeled Jack was a modern creation. Described as tall, thin and even 'gentlemanly', his tight-fitting white clothes beneath a dark cloak marked him as something different to more familiar accounts of shroud-wrapped specters. Such an appearance granted him a knowing theatricality that rendered his encounters a performance as much as a manifestation. His appearance in London in 1837–38 challenged the perceptions of antiquarians and folklorists who viewed such accounts as insights into lingering 'superstition' and pre-industrial cultural mentalities that were believed to be in slow but terminal decline in a 'modern' age. Spring-heeled Jack bucked this trend, for he reflected contemporary concerns, and it was his contemporaneousness that gave his urban

---

[30] See Roud, *London Lore*, p. 146. Roud also draws parallels with early Spring-heeled Jack encounters but unfortunately he does not provide a citation for his quote about this 'monster'. Later, in August 1834, rumours spread of a ghost in St Giles Church, London. This turned out to be another case of mistaken identity, the 'ghost' being a grieving mother who kept a vigil at her recently deceased son's grave for fear that his corpse would be stolen by bodysnatchers. See *The Times*, 23rd August 1834.

[31] See *The Times*, 18th December 1830, and 10th January 1831. See also Davies, *The Haunted*, pp. 184–5.

legend such power. Unlike most ghosts, Spring-heeled Jack did not haunt a fixed location but migrated around the city, acquiring a sense of apparent purposelessness that became identified as a quality of the modern ghost.[32] He was in many ways the epitome of such entities, for unlike the ghosts of the medieval and early-modern period he served no obvious moral or social purpose such as exposing crimes or offering insights into the future. He was merely a vicious jester engaged in his own solipsistic joke.

The 1830s and 1840s were marked by an intensified sense of approaching millenarian crisis, the expectation of imminent and perhaps dramatic social and political change. Popular culture was permeated with prophetic imagery and even apocalyptic rhetoric, a trend that had been aroused by the French Revolution and dampened only in intensity rather than ubiquity due to the persistent uncertainty derived from a sense of modernisation.[33] The early nineteenth century had witnessed the appearance of millenarian cult leaders such as John Wroe, Richard Brothers and Joanna Southcott, whilst talk of divine retribution was still evident in response to the cholera outbreak of 1832 or extreme natural disasters such as earthquakes. These millennarian tensions found one of their most memorable expression mere weeks after Spring-heeled Jack had left London for the provinces, for in May 1838 William Courtenay's self-proclamation as the messiah resulted in what became known as the Battle of Bossenden Wood in Kent. Popular millenarianism was underpinned by the utterances of clergymen (both Anglicans and more evangelical nonconformist groups such as the Primitive Methodists) and by a popular print culture of prophetic chapbooks. In terms of popular religion, violent storms were still indicative of God's anger, whilst angels fought an invisible war with demons for possession of human souls.[34] Popular millenarianism did not necessarily require the appearance of the devil as an indicator of the end of days, but in the heightened rhetoric which attended contemporary millenarian hysteria, people did still make claims that the devil had been seen.[35] It would be overburdening the Spring-heeled Jack scare to claim it was a muted form of secularised millenarianism, but one cannot dismiss the obvious allusions to the diabolical in his appearance.

---

[32] In Stith Thompson's folkloric motif index Spring-heeled Jack best matches up to folkloric trope motif E261, 'Wandering ghost makes attack', usually attacking travellers at night. See Thompson, *The Folktale*, p. 257.

[33] Harrison, *Early Victorian Britain*, p. 131.

[34] See Wolffe, 'Judging the Nation', pp. 292–6, and Reay, *Last Rising of the Agricultural Labourers*. See also Wells, 'English Society and Revolutionary Politics'; Fulford, *Romanticism and Millenarianism*; Thompson, *Making of the English Working Class*, pp. 127–30 and 419–31; and Harrison, *Second Coming*.

[35] See for example Bell, 'The Humbugg of the World at an End', p. 454.

The idea of the biblical Satan as a physical individual had been declining in the popular imagination since at least the late seventeenth century. Increasingly, he became a remote supernatural influence, not directly manifesting but rather acting as a puppet-master behind witches and misleading apparitions, acting through others, most obviously in cases of bodily possession and exorcism.[36] However, the devil also existed in oral folklore, contemporary street ballads and other forms of cheap literature, and here accounts suggest he was more likely to physically manifest. Conforming to two predominant narratives, he was variously an instrument of retribution and/or an arch-trickster. Print culture's appropriation of the devil for satirical and comic effect, particularly from the eighteenth century, helped dilute his diabolical power, and early-nineteenth-century street ballads even portrayed him as a comic figure being brutally beaten by gruff working-class folk.[37] This contrasted sharply with folkloric accounts which explained local typography by alluding to the devil as a being of immense power, strength and (in some cases) size. As late as 1867 two Lancashire folklorists could claim, 'The power of the devil [and] his personal appearance ... must still be numbered among the articles of our popular faith.'[38] Spring-heeled Jack's more overtly theatrical aspects such as fire-breathing did not fit neatly

[36] See Davies, *The Haunted*, pp. 109–10. This idea of demonic forces working through deceptive spirits continued into the second half of the nineteenth century when the evangelically-minded lambasted the growing popularity of spiritualist séances as updated and fashionable snares of Satan. They claimed the apparent ease of interaction with spirits (possibly angelic or demonic rather than the souls of humans) pointed to an imminent resurgence of Satan prior to a final confrontation. See for example Yates, 'Essay on Superstition' (1853).

[37] See examples in the Madden Ballad Collection, Cambridge University Library, including 'The Devil Disguises Himself for Fun', 'The Devil on His Ramble', 'The Devil and Little Mike', and 'The Devil and the Lawyer'. The devil's greatest nineteenth-century literary reworking as Mephistopheles in Goethe's *Faust* probably came too late to have influenced initial ideas of Spring-heeled Jack. Whilst the first part of Goethe's work was published in 1808, the second was only completed in 1832. Goethe was promoted by Thomas Carlyle, via his translations and also in his *Sartor Resartus* (1834), but it is hard to judge how far this would have percolated into the popular imagination by early 1838. Spring-heeled Jack's later depictions in penny serials arguably owe a greater debt to a Mephistophelian imagery and theatricality. A more pertinent textual source relating to Spring-heeled Jack may have been Charles Sedley's *Asmodeus; or, The Devil in London: A Sketch* (1808). In the vein of Spring-heeled Jack, Asmodeus is a devil who describes himself as a 'wandering spirit' who is compelled to roam the earth for one hundred years, and who possesses the ability to inhabit whatever mortal form he wishes. See Sedley, pp. 25 and 27. He takes Tom Hazard, a new-found companion, to Kensington Garden, a location where Spring-heeled Jack was later said to appear, and when Hazard agrees to become Asmodeus' student 'they mounted in the air, gently hovering over the heads of the gay crowd that filled the park' (p. 32). Sedley's urban devil was revived in Edward Bulwer Lytton, *Asmodeus at Large* (1833).

[38] Harland and Wilkinson, *Lancashire Folklore*, p. 81. See also pp. 82–92.

into these folkloric images, but clearly alluded to hellish associations with fire and brimstone.

The Enlightenment and romanticism had both served to free Satan from traditional biblical conceptualisations, and as a result in the late eighteenth and early nineteenth centuries the devil became a more amorphous signifier than in previous periods.[39] Although it was not overtly articulated in the 1838 scare, Spring-heeled Jack can be seen to embody a popular romanticist notion of the devil. Often seen as a reaction to the rationalism of the Enlightenment, romanticism's development from the mid eighteenth century emphasised emotion and imagination, a solipsistic individualism and a propensity for the supernatural, the sublime and the grotesque. For many romantics the devil stood in heroic resistance to repressive authority and the tyranny of convention, a notion of the political poseur rather than a genuine theological interpretation. Here the devil became conceptualised as the romantic hero, one who was 'alone against the world, self-assertive … powerful'.[40] Spring-heeled Jack resonated with this notion of the rebellious individual in a society increasingly bound by legislation and its enforcement agencies. Despite the devil having become depersonified and appropriated for satirical or political purposes, Spring-heeled Jack's associations with the diabolical still retained genuine power in the popular imagination in the late 1830s. Nor was it merely a residual power, for such accounts stoked fears afresh. The Times reported accounts that spoke of him as a 'devil' with neither irony nor embarrassment, and in March 1838 Figaro in London reported, 'By his claws and hideous appearance some have supposed him to be the devil himself.' The Penny Satirist took a less sombre tone towards the notion of Spring-heeled Jack as a devil. In a skit involving a hunt for 'The Ghost', Spring-heeled Jack sings, 'I came from Pandemonium, If they lay me I'll go back; Meanwhile around the town I'll jump, Spring-heeled Jack.' Mocking the millenarian impulses of the period his song went on to claim that people were swiftly abandoning 'their scientific airs' and turning back to prayer.[41]

Why did Spring-heeled Jack act as he did?

Spring-heeled Jack was firmly located in a long tradition of customary disguise, mischief, intimidation and violence. His first appearances coincided with a

---

[39] See Burton Russell, Mephistopheles, p. 169. See also Muchembled, History of the Devil, especially pp. 167–217.

[40] Burton Russell, Mephistopheles, p. 175. See also p. 176. Romanticism did not offer a coherent view on the heroic devil; it tended to suggest a deliberate attempt to provoke rather than offering any clearly structured intellectual or theological position.

[41] See The Times, 9th January 1838, p. 4; Figaro in London, 10th March 1838; and Penny Satirist, 27th January 1838, p. 2. See also Penny Satirist, 20th January 1838.

period in which such practices were coming under sustained assault from moral reformers, educators and legal statutes.[42] Mumming had traditionally involved men and women swapping clothes to visit houses at New Year. Masked mummers had performed songs or even folk plays to convey good wishes for the season in return for refreshment from those upon whom they called. By the nineteenth century the entertainment and even the goodwill were disappearing as men and boys blackened their faces, donned disguises and turned up at people's doorsteps to beg for (and given their disguise, possibly coerce) drink or some other form of largesse. The degree of intimidation behind such performances arguably increased as the idea of communal obligation to such performers declined over the course of the century.[43] Therefore, a custom that had previously served as a means of confirming local communal solidarity had, by the 1860s and 1870s, witnessed a transformation in its meaning and certainly its reception. Localised customary traditions such as the 'Whipping Toms' in Leicester and the mischief makers who built dams in Exeter on Lawless Day involved people temporarily seizing control of parts of towns and enforcing rituals whereby largesse was granted or punishments inflicted on pedestrians. In nineteenth-century Norwich there was a more benevolent custom surrounding the mysterious Jack Valentine, a figure (usually an adult member of the household) who would knock on doors on 14th February and leave gifts for its inhabitants.[44] In Shetland the invented tradition of Up-Helly-Aa involved groups of disguised men participating in a winter celebration. Having evolved from more spontaneous acts of disorder such as setting fire to tar barrels, from the 1870s it involved the burning of a replica Viking longship. Unlike the ongoing randomness of Spring-heeled Jack's appearances, reformers such as the Total Abstinence Society had successfully managed to confine it to a particular time (the last Thursday in January) and place (Lerwick), thereby channelling customary unruliness into a set 'tradition'.[45]

As in encounters with Spring-heeled Jack, these carnivalesque forms of local customary culture relied upon theatricality and performance, and frequently involved the appropriation and transformation of the mundane so that urban streets became impromptu theatres. The election of a Lord of Misrule in carnival

[42] For the attack on customary practices see Golby and Purdue, *Civilisation of the Crowd*, pp. 41–87; Bushaway, *By Rite*, pp. 238–79; and Beckett, 'Lewes Gunpowder Plot Celebrations', p. 487.

[43] See Storch, *Popular Culture and Custom*, p. 2. For a Bradford case in which this custom led to an assault by a mummer who was refused drink or money see *Leeds Mercury*, 3rd January 1868. The collection of largesse during the mummers' plays was usually undertaken by the performer who played 'Johny Jack or Devil Doubt'. See Pettitt, 'Here Comes I, Jack Straw', p. 7.

[44] See Madders, *Original Sketch of How They Keep St. Valentine's Eve in Norwich*; Smith, 'Jack Valentine in Norfolk'; and Robinson, 'Jack Valentine'. See also Bushaway, *By Rite*, pp. 178–80.

[45] See Gailey, 'The Nature of Tradition', p. 155. See also Brown, *Up-helly-aa*.

and other customary inversions or suspensions of the social order not only mocked the powerful but elevated the lowly. In creating customary figureheads and bestowing upon them a temporary leadership, the common individual's rising up from amongst the crowd was often marked by a ritualistic dressing up.[46] As Spring-heeled Jack came to demonstrate, this act of concealment and empowerment marked such figures as different and granted them the freedom to defy or usurp social convention.

The early nineteenth century had witnessed more assertive, destructive figure-heads in imaginary 'folkloric' leaders such as General (Ned) Ludd in the 1810s and Captain Swing in the early 1830s. Like Spring-heeled Jack, these characters thrived on rumour and official speculation, the accumulation of which gave them a sense of possessing both uncanny ubiquity and elusiveness in the popular imagination. In doing so it granted them a phantasmal presence not unlike the 'suburban ghost' himself.[47] Here the customary trickster had turned from conducting mischievous pranks to articulating socio-economic protest through the smashing of knitting frames and the burning of hayricks. Depending on one's perspective, such actions reaffirmed 'popular' trickster figures as roguish outlaws or dangerous criminals. Like mummers, it was not unknown for Swing rioters to visit farmers' homes to assert their demands, these actions acquiring a strong element of intimidation when they resorted to the simplest of disguises, namely blackening their faces.[48] Spring-heeled Jack's actions in 1837–38 established a new customary tradition that subsequent imitators paid homage to throughout the rest of the century. Yet an important distinction between Spring-heeled Jack and other 'traditional' or invented customary practices was that his appearances were not linked to localised places, regular seasonal customs or identifiable grudges. In keeping with his rather anarchic character, such appearances were highly random, sporadic and migratory.

Once he migrated into London from its outskirts Spring-heeled Jack fitted neatly into a long tradition of metropolitan hellraisers, 'monsters' and street roisters. He had distant antecedents in the early-eighteenth-century Mohocks,

[46] This was seen in rural harvest home celebrations, but also in industrial trades with the dressing up of a senior apprentice as 'Old Clem' in honour of St Clement, patron saint of blacksmiths and anchor-makers. See Bushaway, *By Rite*, pp. 185–6.

[47] Recent work has demonstrated an appreciation of the phantasmagoric nature of Captain Swing, including his threat to spill from rural areas into urban ones, again a fear that reflects Spring-heeled Jack's migration. See Griffin, 'Swing, Swing Redivivus or Something After Swing?', pp. 459–97, and Jones, 'Finding Captain Swing', pp. 429–58. For General Ludd see Navickas, 'The Search for "General Ludd"', and Simms, 'Ned Ludd's Mummer's Play'. Other than the devil himself, supernatural tricksters such as Will o' the Wisp were believed to lure people to their doom by misleading them. See Simpson and Roud, *Dictionary of English Folklore*, p. 391.

[48] Pettitt, 'Here Comes I, Jack Straw', p. 14.

a vicious gang of aristocratic thugs who callously wounded men and sexually assaulted women. The association was not lost on early-Victorian journalists. In 1844 *Lloyd's Weekly London Newspaper* condemned 'those facetious gentlemen – adherents of "Spring heeled Jack" – who, in their cups, like their predecessors, the Mohocks, wittingly disturbed the nocturnal quiet of families, and thought it good manly sport to terrify women and children'.[49] More significantly, his first appearance stands equidistant between two notorious metropolitan fiends, the 'London Monster' of 1788–90 and Jack the Ripper in 1888. As it did for both predecessor and successor, the contemporary press played a key role in simultaneously promoting and constructing the immediate scare and the legend that its publicity subsequently fostered. Like press reports of John Cowen's announcement at the Mansion House in January 1838, John Julius Angerstein had promoted hunts for the London Monster through posters, with the result that the fear and excitement of the early months of 1838 resonated with what Jan Bondeson grandiosely refers to as 'the Monster-mania' of 1790. Both the London Monster and Spring-heeled Jack escalated their attacks from harassment to grappling and wounding. Demonstrating a similar modus operandi to Spring-heeled Jack, the London Monster had pursued and attacked women in the streets, usually cutting their clothes and wounding them, often by stabbing them in the buttocks. Just as some newspapers in 1838 suggested there was a gang of Spring-heeled Jacks operating in London, so following the trial of Rhynwick Williams, the man accused of being the London Monster, it was rumoured that 'a group of "Men-Monsters" were wounding women in the streets'.[50] Perhaps most pertinent to the subsequent formation of Spring-heeled Jack was the rumour that the London Monster was 'an evil spirit, who could make himself invisible to evade detection ... [and] who could change his appearance at will'.[51]

Beyond this, and arguably more important than distant historical predecessors, was a popular fascination with criminality. The sensationalisation of criminality was nothing new when Spring-heeled Jack appeared, even if his particular form and actions offered intriguing novelties. Indicative of the way rogues had long been capable of traversing popular cultural forms, in 1724, the year of his execution, the notorious prison-breaker Jack Sheppard had been

---

[49] *Lloyd's Weekly London Newspaper*, 9th June 1844. For more on the Mohocks see Guthrie, 'No Truth or Very Little in the Whole Story?'; Statt, 'The Case of the Mohocks'; and, for a longer perspective, McDaniel, 'Some Greek, Roman and English Tityretus', especially pp. 59–64. For changing narratives of violence see Crone, 'Mr and Mrs Punch'; Wiener, *Men of Blood*, and also his 'Alice Arden to Bill Sykes'.

[50] See Clark, *Women's Silence*, p. 117. See also McCreery, 'Moral Panic in Eighteenth-Century London?', and Bondeson, *London Monster*. For Williams' trial see www.oldbaileyonline.org/, reference number t17901208-54.

[51] Bondeson, *London Monster*, p. 64.

assured a posthumous existence through the appearance of engravings depicting his daring escapes, three plays and two books which helped fictionalise his life.[52] John Marriott has suggested that this popular fascination with criminality waxed and waned in response to contemporary fears and pressures, and that following a swell of enthusiasm in the 1720s and 1730s (a period which also witnessed the hanging of Dick Turpin), by the 1770s the popularity of such publications had ebbed. Significantly for the emergence of Spring-heeled Jack, this popular interest in criminality returned in the 1830s when the socio-economic and political tensions outlined earlier emerged once more.[53] This fascination was rooted in its articulation of fears about social instability but also in the way it provided a cathartic sense of security through ending the criminal's narrative at the gallows, thereby transforming real lives into morality plays. Largely bucking the trends suggested by Marriott, the *Newgate Calendar's* sensational and moralised biographies of criminals had so captured the popular imagination that it was rarely out of print after its first publication in 1773. This was supplemented by flash sheet ballads that were printed to accompany public executions, the most popular of which sold hundreds of thousands of copies. The London-based printing entrepreneur James Catnach made his wealth and dubious reputation with the publication of this gallows literature which gave potted, frequently fictionalised accounts of criminals' lives, confessions and final lamentations.[54]

Of considerably greater sophistication was the emergence of what became termed the 'Newgate novel' in the 1830s. Having precedents in the success of Walter Scott's romanticising of outlaw characters, Edward Bulwer-Lytton's *Paul Clifford* (1830) and *Eugene Aram* (1832), and William Harrison Ainsworth's *Rookwood* (1834) and *Jack Sheppard* (1839) are frequently identified as the key culprits in a reimagining of eighteenth-century rogues and criminals.[55] In part these works can be read as a reaction to the 'silver fork' fiction that had dominated in the period between 1815 and 1830. Rather than narratives that focused on the lives of the wealthy, the Newgate novels romanticised the bold commoner and the outsider who set themselves against the tyranny of propriety and lawful obedience. The themes of these novels, especially Ainsworth's treatment of Dick Turpin in *Rookwood* (1834), percolated down to cheaper levels of literature and

[52] See Brewer, *Pleasures of the Imagination*, pp. 435–6.
[53] Marriott, 'Spatiality of the Poor in Eighteenth-Century London', pp. 131–2.
[54] For flash ballads and execution literature see Gatrell, *Hanging Tree*, pp. 109–96, and Hindley, *Curiosities of Street Literature*, pp. 159–237. For James Catnach see Hindley, *Life and Times of James Catnach*.
[55] See John, *Cult Criminals*, and Hollingsworth, *Newgate Novel*. For the way eighteenth-century criminal fiction addressed some of the concerns of later gothic fiction see Moore, *Con Men and Cutpurses*, pp. ix–xxiv.

helped prompt a subsequent glut of highwayman 'penny bloods'. Targeting a wider, more adult readership than the later 'penny dreadfuls', such works fused thrilling adventures and violence into a historical criminal narrative that frequently alluded to earlier gothic settings such as dungeons and castles. In 1836 their most notorious publisher, Edward Lloyd, produced the *History and Lives of the Most Notorious Highwaymen, Footpads ... and Robbers of Every Description*. Charles Mackay's *Extraordinary Popular Delusions and the Madness of Crowds* (1841) contained a chapter on the 'Popular Admiration of Great Thieves' in which he condemned the influence of such literature. Articulating a claim that was also levelled at contemporary penny gaff theatres and later penny dreadful serials, he suggested such literature was prone to creating thieves from young readers and theatre-goers who were keen to emulate a life of romanticised criminality.[56] Given the absence of any hard or even consistent information regarding Spring-heeled Jack's nature and intentions, the contemporary cheap literary fad for highwaymen likely influenced interpretations that led to him being viewed as a bizarre variant on the gentleman of the road. At the same time his ability to elude and make fools of the law enforcement agencies of the day also resonated with the most popular aspects of Jack Sheppard's story, not his tawdry burglaries but his daring escapes from some of London's most notorious prisons.

However, as with many of the other cultural tropes and narrative influences which informed his construction, Spring-heeled Jack did not neatly conform to the fictionalised criminal. Ainsworth's novels romanticised Jack Sheppard and Dick Turpin into likeable rogues and folkloric heroes. Devoid of the temporal gap and fictional boundaries which fostered such romanticising, Spring-heeled Jack's earliest appearances firmly depicted him as a malicious villain. It took the distancing of another generation before his fictional image of the 1860s came to overlap with the roguish but chivalrous highwayman of popular myth, the man whose code of honour ensured he was selective in his choice of victims. Furthermore, given the notoriety and publicity he received in the press, Spring-

---

[56]   See Mackay, *Extraordinary Popular Delusions*, pp. 632–46. See also Springhall, *Youth, Popular Culture and Moral Panics*. Mackay's fears seemed to have been proven in 1840 when *The Times* reported that the murder of Lord William Russell by one of his valets, B. F. Courvoisier, had been inspired by the latter's attendance at a stage production of Ainsworth's *Jack Sheppard*. In response, future adaptations of Ainsworth's novel were not permitted and existing productions discouraged. The adaptation viewed by Courvoisier had been produced by James T. Haines, a playwright credited by Haining with creating a play about Spring-heeled Jack in 1840. See Stephens, *Censorship of English Drama*, especially pp. 61–77, and for the Haining assertion, *Legend and Bizarre Crimes*, p. 114. As will be explained in Chapter 7, I have been unable to locate any evidence indicating the veracity of Haining's claim.

heeled Jack's avoidance of the gallows obviously denied his criminal narrative its expected moralised conclusion.[57]

This equally applied to his debt to melodramatic narratives which found expression across many forms of popular cultural entertainment, including gothic chapbooks, the penny blood that appropriated and replaced them, unlicensed theatres and the even cheaper penny gaffs. Indicative of the elements that most appealed to the popular imagination (and which swiftly rose to the surface in accounts of Spring-heeled Jack), these theatres typically shortened well-known dramas, cutting out everything except the violence and the appearances of ghosts.[58] In one literary depiction of penny gaffs, a single performance managed to squeeze 'three ghostesses, four murders, two castles burnt to the ground, and a comic dance' into little more than half an hour's entertainment.[59] Popular melodrama drew upon a heady blend of tragedy, crime, sentimental romance and even gothic horror, and this rich cocktail made it a cultural form inclined towards dramatic excess, exaggerated emotion, dialogue and action.[60] Its tropes of the hapless (female) victim and despicable yet engagingly theatrical villain certainly informed the contours of narrative accounts of Spring-heeled Jack's early appearances.

Part of melodrama's appeal lay in its presentation of a simplistic Manichean world view, pitching moral, honest, but poor or powerless protagonists against evil, corrupt, and powerful villains. As part of its fictional simplification of the world melodrama employed identifiable signifiers to indicate the moral nature of particular characters, with the early-Victorian villain's black clothing acting

[57] In this there was a fictional precedent in the highwayman Captain Macheath in John Gay's *The Beggar's Opera* (1728). Macheath's cheating the hangman had driven critics to claim that such fiction was an incentive to a life of crime.

[58] Booth, *English Melodrama*, p. 55. For the popularity of ghosts and the supernatural in plebeian theatre see Mayhew, *London Labour and the London Poor*, vol. 1, p. 15.

[59] Springhall, *Youth, Popular Culture and Moral Panics*, p. 25. Like Spring-heeled Jack, penny gaff theatre had a 'guerrilla' relationship with urban spaces, temporarily appropriating empty shops and vacant warehouses in which to stage performances. Springhall calculates that in 1838 there were between 80 and 100 penny gaffs in London, mostly in the East End, nightly performing to an estimated 24,000 people in total. See ibid., p. 18. For an indication of the powerful visual appeal of melodramatic theatrical bills from this period see Wright, *Some Habits and Customs*, p. 155.

[60] Ledger, *Dickens and the Popular Radical Imagination*, p. 156. After the 1843 Theatre Regulation Act only licensed West End theatres could perform spoken melodramas. Whilst penny gaffs resorted to mime and silent pantomime to accommodate this legal restriction, it would not have prevented understanding by an audience that was adept at picking up meanings and subtexts from woodcuts at the head of street ballads, the depiction of monstrous animal-human hybrids in satirical broadsides, or violent puppet shows. As Ledger notes, melodrama depended more upon the 'theatrical semiotics of gesture' than spoken dialogue. See ibid., p. 7.

as a sartorial shorthand for his villainy.[61] In gothic melodrama the villain often had his face darkened with burnt cork (usually to imply a Mediterranean origin) and was 'strangely costumed' in boots, cloak and even gauntlets, an image which resonates with Londoners' accounts of Spring-heeled Jack as a dark, cloaked figure.[62] There were subgenres of melodrama, ranging from the more moderate forms of romantic or domestic melodramas through to the extremes of gothic melodrama, and even 'monster melodrama', its aim simply being to excite audience emotions by frightening them.[63] In gothic melodrama the villain's intense energies, excessive theatricality and sadistic nature pushed him towards a diabolical caricature, his innate evil being the mechanism that drove the plot forward.[64] These qualities made him a powerful, dramatic presence and certainly the most interesting of melodrama's stock types of characters, but it also firmly designated him a sensational fiction rather than a real human being. Accounts of Spring-heeled Jack seem to echo the heightened narrative of a gothic melodrama that had spilled beyond the bounds of the stage and into the streets. It has been claimed that nineteenth-century melodramatic villains were 'types struggling to become individuals', an ambition that resonates with Spring-heeled Jack's cultural trajectory in early 1838.[65]

Regardless of the particular subgenre, the melodramatic villain was usually socially superior to those he sought to harm. Although familiar from gothic novels, the predatory aristocrat who seduced and ruined young lower-class women was also a key stage villain of the early nineteenth century. So ingrained was this stereotyping that Montagu Slater claimed that whenever an aristocratic figure walked on stage in London theatres in the 1830s and 1840s he was immediately identified as the villain of the piece and greeted with howls from the audience.[66] This trope derived from melodrama's development within a tradition of popular radicalism that promoted democracy and decried aristocratic corruption and privilege. Radical publications such as the *Poor Man's Guardian* (1831–35) naturally demonised the aristocracy as a symbolic 'other' to a moralised, sentimentalised self-image of radicals as the voice of the common people. In radicals' mythologising of the remote past the aristocracy were linked to the Norman conquerors who had been depriving freeborn (Anglo-Saxon)

---

[61] See Walkowitz, *City of Dreadful Delight*, pp. 86–7; Taylor, *Players and Performances*, p. 122; and Booth, *English Melodrama*, pp. 18–20.

[62] See Booth, *English Melodrama*, p. 68.

[63] Disher, *Blood and Thunder*, p. 80.

[64] See John, *Dickens's Villains*, pp. 51–2.

[65] Ibid., p. 49.

[66] Ibid., p. 64. See also Clark, 'Politics of Seduction in English Popular Culture'. For aristocratic rakes and libertinism see Mackie, *Rakes, Highwaymen, and Pirates*; Kelly, 'Riots, Revelries, and Rumor'; and Kramnick, 'Rochester and the History of Sexuality'.

Englishmen of their rights and freedoms ever since 1066. This popular aspect of melodramatic theatre was very quickly incorporated into the formation of Spring-heeled Jack's legend. On the very day *The Times* reported on the Mayor's statement about Spring-heeled Jack it included the Peckham resident's suggestion that it was the result of a bet amongst individuals belonging to 'the higher ranks of life' to appear in various guises with the aim of frightening people. Conforming to familiar stereotypes of the gentry's callous and predatory nature towards lower-class women, within a week another paper was claiming that the wager now involved killing six women.[67] Spring-heeled Jack, however, did not simply conform to melodramatic convention. His accounts had a theatrical villain but lacked heroes and happy endings. Spring-heeled Jack's elusiveness in 1837–38 denied the satisfying catharsis that would have come with his capture and punishment. Rather than being vanquished, Spring-heeled Jack seemed to take it upon himself to leave London and spread his particular brand of mischief elsewhere.[68] As such, his accounts, whilst often articulated through the tropes and vocabulary of the melodramatic, were denied the reassuring conventions of melodrama, namely that the engagement with villainy would result in its ultimate defeat by virtue.

In addition to the crude, class-based moralised divisions evident in melodramatic theatre, there was also a range of printed publications which sought to present the aristocracy as depraved, predatory and inhuman. Since the French revolutionary wars radicals, pamphleteers, essayists and balladeers had drawn upon melodramatic conventions to voice their protests. One particular form of radical print culture that cultivated the popular imagining of bizarre man-monsters was the mock showman's handbill, a familiar satirical device employed in early-nineteenth-century broadside ballads. This took more developed form in William Hone's satirical *The Political Showman* (1821). Hone's frequent collaborator, George Cruickshank, provided a frontispiece depicting an image of the Beast from the Book of Revelations. Alluding once again to the devil and tapping into contemporary pre-millenarian ideas, the Beast had frequently been invoked in printed satire during the political and religious turmoil of the mid seventeenth century and had been revived in the early nineteenth century to help demonise Napoleon.[69] *The Political Showman* depicted a human menagerie

---

[67] See *The Times*, 9th January 1838, p. 4, and *The Examiner*, 14th January 1838, p. 27. Despite this crude class delineation melodrama was far from being a purely working-class cultural form. For the promotion of middle-class ideological values through melodramatic conventions see Springhall, *Youth, Popular Culture and Moral Panics*, pp. 33–4.

[68] See John, *Dickens's Villains*, especially pp. 48–69. See also Baer, *Theatre and Disorder*, and Brooks, *Melodramatic Imagination*.

[69] See for example, Madden Ballad Collection, Cambridge University Library, 'The Prophecy'. See also Wood, *Radical Satire and Print Culture*, pp. 39–40 and 83.

in which politicians were human-animal hybrids which were paraded before the reader, their distorted portrayals dehumanising the powerful into fantasised symbols of a corrupt and profligate other.[70]

This fusion of the monstrous and the aristocratic had also found contemporary expression in John Polidori's Lord Ruthven in *The Vampyre: A Tale* (1819). This was followed by melodramas and operas such as J. R. Planche's *The Vampire; or the Bride of the Isles* (1820) so that by 1838 the trope of the aristocratic vampire was becoming established in the collective imagination.[71] Spring-heeled Jack owed a degree of kinship to the literary vampires of the 1820s and 1830s. Like them he was perceived as male, possibly aristocratic, and certainly predatory, all of which can be read as a continuation of villainous motifs from the first wave of gothic literature. Spring-heeled Jack's association with such figures was made easier by the fact that in the first half of the nineteenth century vampires assaulted (and killed) but had not yet developed those later defining aspects of their mythos such as the infection and transmutation of victims into vampires.[72]

Individuality and Sustainability

Unlike the hundreds of other rural ghosts existing in local folklore and circulating in oral culture at the time, Spring-heeled Jack was adopted and transformed into something else. This begs the question, what was so special about him? The explanation for his initial sustainability in the popular imagination seems dependent upon three factors. Firstly, the entity that became Spring-heeled Jack progressed along a fairly unique register of depictions. This was not a scale of credibility so much as one of imaginative power and appeal, each being arguably more potent in the collective imagination than the last. A beast-man was more affecting than a bull, an armoured man more so than a man in skins, a devil more than a ghost. At the same time each step was a move towards greater individualisation, thereby separating him from his more conventional spectral peers. Rather than the familiar portrayal of the shroud-clad ghost, he became armoured, acquired tangibility in his metallic claws and his capacity to run and leap, whilst his monstrous fire-breathing apotheosis granted him even greater 'weight' and specificity. Based on rumour and speculation, such a complex series

---

[70]   Ibid., p. 183. For an example see Norfolk Heritage Centre, 'Menagerie of Wild Animals'. Since the medieval and early modern period the popular imagination had associated hybridity with portents of 'wrongness'. See Wilson, *Signs and Portents*.

[71]   See Frayling, *Vampyres*, p. 62.

[72]   Warwick, 'Vampires and Empire', p. 203. Links between Spring-heeled Jack and vampires were consciously developed in the 1890s following the success of Bram Stoker's *Dracula*. See Chapter 8.

of metamorphoses was going to be nigh on impossible to duplicate, granting him a rather individual genesis.

Secondly, this transformation from anonymous ghost to an identifiable individual was facilitated by the press reportage of early 1838. This formed the imagined public space in which wildly conflicting ideas and descriptions circulated and ultimately coalesced. Vital to this process was the third factor, the emotive name that both distinguished him and informed his subsequent longevity. 'Jack' was a traditional expression of the everyman hero, the anonymous individual, or the wily trickster in popular printed literature, ballads and folktales, and 'Spring-heeled Jack' fitted comfortably into this established tradition. Elizabeth Villiers suggested he was called Jack 'for lack of another name', but it was an extremely popular name for penny fiction protagonists in the 1830s. The application of this name therefore tapped into a rich, pre-existing association with daring protagonists and escapades in classic chapbook tales. Spring-heeled Jack's activities resonated with these fantastical narratives whilst having the added potency of relocating them into a modern urban setting. Several commentators noted how Spring-heeled Jack's leaping led them to 'confuse him with the owner of the seven-leagued boots' and that his tale had credibility in the minds of fearful children because 'Jack the Giant Killer and the Seven League Boots [were] some of the things they accepted as veritable history'. In oral culture Jack was also a popular English folk customary name for personifications and embodiments of ideas such as 'Jack in the Green', 'Jack o' Lent' and 'Jack o' Lantern'.[73]

The acquisition of the name 'Spring-heeled Jack' marked an important individualising shift from his initial title, the 'suburban ghost', a generic moniker defined merely by locality. Despite their illogical and incongruous nature, wildly diverse accounts of a white bull, a bear, an armoured figure, an imp, devil, goblin, ghost or human prankster were all held together by a single name. Like the coining of 'Jack the Ripper' fifty years later, it enabled a coherent narrative to be formed from a series of seemingly disconnected attacks and encounters. It was this coherence and the sense of purpose it fostered (even if it could not be fathomed) that granted Spring-heeled Jack his initial residence in the popular imagination.[74] Whilst journalistic accounts attempted to assert an authoritative interpretation of Spring-heeled Jack in 1838, his remained a diffused, cumulatively constructed narrative which defied a singular, controlling authorship. Even if we accept the idea that his initial appearances were nothing more than a prank

---

[73] See *Notes and Queries*, 10th Series, 30th March 1907, p. 256, and Knights, *Norfolk Stories*, p. 8. For the popular use of the name 'Jack' in folklore see Simpson and Roud, *Dictionary of English Folklore*, pp. 196–9.

[74] As has been observed with regard to the Ripper, assuming Spring-heeled Jack was a single individual enabled the press to speculate on his purpose when they had little reliable factual information to deliver. See Oldridge, 'Casting the Spell of Terror'.

by a number of young men, the phenomenon that grew from this was clearly not a matter of conscious design. As will be examined in a later chapter, for much of the rest of the century he was sustained by the synergy between different cultural forms and modes of expression, acquiring the ability to shuttle back and forth across a myriad of Victorian cultures and media. Anchored by his intriguing name, this process fostered a sense of both ubiquity and longevity.

Spring-heeled Jack was constructed from the interwoven strands of pre-existing narrative tropes and familiar motifs that were close to hand in the popular culture of the late 1830s. What animated him in the collective imagination was a seemingly paradoxical tension between resonances with, and significantly individualised differences from, those existing cultural trends. The affinities allowed him to have recognisable points of cultural familiarity and identification, but it was the differences and their unusual combination that made him appealing to a sensation-hungry public. His greatest potency lay in his blurring and transgression of the boundaries of the real and the imaginary. Both lent powerful aspects to the dynamic. Unleashed from the safe constraints of the book, play or oral folktale, his existence in reality made him credible, tangible and all the more scary for it. Yet such was his fantastical allure that the mundane became enchanted through his links to a realm that was normally accessed through fiction, legends, myths and nightmares. This fusion implicitly questioned the certainties of reality, its content and its boundaries. Yet whilst this chapter has suggested some of the cultural filaments that informed his construction, we must accept that Spring-heeled Jack possessed no solid core beneath them. If, as Cohen claims, 'the monstrous body is pure culture' then its skin is impenetrable.[75] Whilst providing a rich signifier upon which we can read its multiple and mercurial surface meanings like a palimpsest, we have to accept that Spring-heeled Jack will remain a cipher. This is not to concede analytical defeat, but rather to work with the nature of the beast. Much of his appeal, for historians and the Victorians themselves, resides in his openness to interpretation. Our monsters are to be feared, perhaps even desired, but if they were ever to become truly known to us then they would become diminished, thereby surrendering their hold over our imaginations.

---

[75] Cohen, *Monster Theory*, p. 4.

Part II

Cultural Functions

3

Spring-heeled Jack, Crime and the Reform of Customary Culture

When Spring-heeled Jack has been remembered at all it is as a curious footnote in the history of nineteenth-century crime, and this chapter approaches its various concerns from this perspective. Spring-heeled Jack intersected but never clearly correlated with contemporary notions of criminality. Whilst accounts firmly indicate Spring-heeled Jack was male, the rumours that he was a malevolent aristocratic prankster contradicted more conventional views that most criminals were lower-class men motivated by poverty. Given his peripatetic nature, Spring-heeled Jack was not associated with any of the capital's perceived criminal localities. Despite multiple appearances around London he appears to have studiously avoided the most infamous metropolitan localities of the time, namely 'the Westminster rookery known as Devil's Acre ... St Giles ... the Saffron Hill and Field Lane areas of Holborn ... to the north of the City, an area comprising parts of Whitecross Street, Golden Lane, and Grub Street ... and ... the eastern nexus of parts of Whitechapel, Spitalfields, Bethnal Green and Shoreditch.'[1] Since he roamed freely through a diverse range of neighbourhoods, from quiet rural suburbs, to poorer districts like Limehouse, to respectable ones like Kensington and Richmond, it was hard to portray him as a product of a particular criminal (or criminalised) environment.

Furthermore, Spring-heeled Jack was dependent upon being seen, upon drawing attention to himself, and his overt theatricality clearly ran counter to more mundane criminality that emphasised concealment. Nor were his motivations typical. Assaults were commonly fuelled by alcohol or verbal provocation that built to physical violence, yet with the possible exception of the attack on Jane Alsop, neither was known to have motivated Spring-heeled Jack's seemingly random attacks. In fact, the deliberate construction of his varied disguises and the possible efforts undertaken to make spring-heeled boots all suggested his 'crimes' involved a thorough degree of premeditation. These very obvious divergences

---

[1] Shore, 'Mean Streets', p. 153.

from 'normal' criminal practices clearly contributed to his distinguishing individuality within the popular imagination.[2]

This chapter begins with a brief consideration of the (often retrospectively
applied) criminal associations made with Spring-heeled Jack, particularly as
a new type of highwayman. It then engages in an exploration of the gendered
nature of his crimes. Predominantly focusing on his activities around London
between 1838 and 1845, it explores contemporary issues relating to the street
as a gendered space, how his assaults on women were fitted into rape narratives
informed by press reporting, and how such accounts presented competing conceptions of masculinity. Finally, it reflects on the ways in which Spring-heeled
Jack was embroiled in the struggles between a persistent, popular customary
culture and the rise of a public culture of self-restraint and surveillance. In such
circumstances Spring-heeled Jack had the potential to articulate both radical
and conservative interpretations. Appropriated by both sides in the struggle for
popular culture, Spring-heeled Jack played to vicarious fantasies of rebellion
whilst also acting as an influential means by which to encourage conformity to a
bourgeois emphasis on self-discipline and constraint.

Defining Spring-heeled Jack's Criminality

Spring-heeled Jack was conceived as several types of criminal in the popular
imagination. The earliest portrayals in the press depicted him as a highly
elaborate mugger or a malevolent, irresponsible prankster. Once imitators began
to mimic him their association with sexual assault and rape added another
criminal dimension to his character. Retrospective interpretations tended to
become more favourable. Many came to cast him as an unusual highwayman,
this owing less to his actions in London in 1838 and more to the masked rogue
image of his literary portrayals from the late 1860s onwards. Such views seemed
to subsequently colour misremembered reminiscences and secondary accounts.[3]
By the 1830s real highwaymen had vanished from the roads around London
and were being increasingly viewed with a nostalgia that smoothed over some
of the harsher realities, leaving only the legend behind. The publication of *Paul
Clifford* by Edward Bulwer-Lytton in 1830 and the gothic romance *Rookwood*
by William Harrison Ainsworth in 1834 did much to further the highwayman's

---

[2] For the changing nature of crime and violence in this period see Smith, 'Violent Crime and the
Public Weal'; Wood, *Violence and Crime*; D'Cruze, *Everyday Violence* and *Crimes of Outrage*; King,
Crime, Justice and Discretion; Landau, *Law, Crime and English Society*; and Linebaugh, *London
Hanged*. For a historiographical overview see Emsley and Knafla, *Crime History and Histories of
Crime*.
[3] For a good example of this see Villiers, *Stand and Deliver*.

journey into romanticised fiction, works that remained tethered to historical reality by the thinnest of facts.[4] In these fantasised reinventions of the highwayman one sees the promotion of an emerging contemporary emphasis on restrained male violence. These 'knights of the road' were presented as eighteenth-century examples of men who asserted themselves through a blend of threat and charm, but who did not have to resort to violence itself. If Ainsworth's novels (and their underlying messages) remained inaccessible on account of illiteracy, similar legendary accounts of these criminal folk heroes were promoted through street ballads, chapbooks and the ever popular *Newgate Calendar*.

Spring-heeled Jack's later literary reinvention conformed to this cult of the folkloric robber-hero that went back via Dick Turpin to at least Robin Hood, promoting the notion that criminality and the use of violence was justified by serving a sense of popular justice. Like Jack Sheppard, Spring-heeled Jack's dexterous escapades and escapes made fools of the authorities, again suggesting that accounts of his actions may have both built upon and updated existing narrative blueprints. Similarly, the highwayman association arguably furnished certain narrative tropes, particularly Spring-heeled Jack's alleged attacks on coaches.[5] Yet as was often the case with Spring-heeled Jack, it required a certain period of forgetting and subsequent reinvention to recreate him as a new type of heroic rogue. The physical (and psychological) harm inflicted upon his victims in 1838 did not fit with the romanticised ideal of gentleman highwaymen, for whilst he possessed their daring audacity he certainly lacked their supposed civility.

As if to emphasise Spring-heeled Jack's trumping of the standard highwayman motif, the anonymous author of the 1878 *Spring-heeled Jack: The Terror of London* included a completely superfluous scene in which he confronts such a character. The reader is informed that the heroic highwayman had 'eschewed the orthodox scarlet' clothing, an indication that Spring-heeled Jack's scarlet costume owed something to this tradition as much as to any diabolical allusion. Spring-heeled Jack confronts the highwayman by leaping over his head, the distraction inadvertently causing him to save the robber's intended victims. The highwayman calmly puts a bullet through the top of Spring-heeled Jack's mask, expecting to kill him. Merely grazed, Spring-heeled Jack gives 'another shriek more supernatural than the first', and the highwayman's nerve finally breaks. He races away on his horse, convinced that since his bullet had not killed 'the

---

[4]   Clive Emsley has claimed that eighteenth-century criminals such as Dick Turpin and Jack Sheppard 'reached the apex of their mythical appeal' in Ainsworth's novels, their romanticised depiction a marked contrast to Dickens' more threatening portrayal of criminality and brutish masculinity in Bill Sykes in *Oliver Twist*. See Emsley, *Hard Men*, p. 31. See also Spraggs, *Outlaws and Highwaymen*, and Sharpe, *Dick Turpin*.
[5]   See for example Villiers, *Stand and Deliver*, pp. 243 and 247.

uncanny-looking being', he was dealing with 'an enemy possessing ... extraordinary if not unearthly attributes'.[6]

If not specifically a highwayman, then the idea that Spring-heeled Jack was a robber was also the result of later accruals to a legend frequently constructed in retrospect. In 1838 there were only unsubstantiated assertions by the likes of Thomas Lott who declared Spring-heeled Jack was 'some determined thief' who by his disguise and performance sought to incapacitate household servants long enough for him to 'obtain and escape with his booty on easy terms'. Lott's views about the vulnerability of private property seem somewhat misplaced, for whilst several encounters occurred on the doorsteps of houses, none ever involved Spring-heeled Jack crossing the threshold.[7] As a reflective article in the *Manchester Times* in 1868 asserted, he 'was no robber ... he never assaulted anybody for the purpose of stealing'. In 1884 *All the Year Round* similarly stressed that he never took 'a single coin from his victims, even when fright had rendered them an easy prey'.[8]

However, by the turn of the twentieth century the idea of Spring-heeled Jack as a unique robber had started to develop. In February 1900 *Lloyd's Weekly Newspaper* claimed that in 1838 Spring-heeled Jack

> had taken to robbery, and Mr Clinch, a banker and moneylender, was robbed by him at five o'clock in the afternoon of seven hundred pounds in gold and notes in the Tottenham Court Road, 'Jack' escaping by a series of marvelous leaps and bounds that carried him over all obstacles. On Feb. 26 complaints were received at all the Metropolitan courts of outrages and robberies committed by 'The Terror of London' the night before.

Such claims do not appear to have been supported by press accounts from 1838. Yet even here he was presented in the legendary tradition of the defender of popular justice, the paper claiming 'only wealthy persons were robbed'.[9] As will be suggested below, these links to the folkloric robber-hero played to a certain radicalism in the popular imagination's perception of Spring-heeled Jack.

From a more official perspective magistrates may have found some difficulty in matching Spring-heeled Jack's bizarre activities and their consequences to legally defined crimes. Whilst developing laws on assault were directed towards the body, catering for physical and sexual violence, they seemed less able to accommodate mental assaults and the frequently cited loss of wits arising from

[6] See Anon., *Spring-heeled Jack*, pp. 91–3.
[7] *Morning Chronicle*, 11th January 1838. See the Alsop attack, *The Times*, 22nd February 1838, and also the attack on the Burnett household in Tottenham in October 1841 in *The Times*, 23rd October 1841.
[8] See *Manchester Times*, 1st August 1868, and *All the Year Round*, 9th August 1884, p. 346.
[9] *Lloyd's Weekly Newspaper*, 25th February 1900.

Spring-heeled Jack's attacks.[10] Merely frightening somebody, even to the point of mental imbalance, appears to have been treated as nothing more than an immoral prank by a cowardly man against a defenceless woman. Approaching Spring-heeled Jack from a judicial perspective, magistrates had to filter claims about demons, fire-breathing and ghosts through a legal framework. This gave little scope for flirting with popular rumours about the supernatural. If the press was sometimes willing to fuel speculation about Spring-heeled Jack (see Chapter 7) the magistracy represented what happened to enchantment when it had to be orientated and organised through prosaic regulation. Despite all the sensationalised accounts of people being frightened to death, when offenders were captured and brought before magistrates they typically received a stern dressing down and/or a relatively small fine. In March 1838 Charles Grenville was 'charged with having frightened a number of women and children nearly into fits, by imitating the silly and dangerous pranks of Spring-heeled Jack'. Yet when Grenville explained that 'it was only a bit of fun, that's all; I meant no harm', the magistrate, Mr Rawlinson, seems to have agreed. Describing Grenville as being of 'weak mind, but perfectly harmless' he discharged the impersonator with a warning not to repeat such foolish actions again.[11] With nobody physically harmed, and with local knowledge of the prisoner, the magistrate saw fit to play down the drama and not punish a misjudged prank.

The issue was less clear cut with Richard Bradford in the 1845 Brentford case. On the evening of 26th January, between the hours of eight and nine, Spring-heeled Jack was sighted in Boston Lane, between Brentford and Hanwell. When Constable Denton went to the location he found Bradford 'dressed in women's clothes, over his own dress, and carrying with him a stable pitchfork, which it is supposed he raised above his head to form the imaginary horns which have created such great alarm'. Bradford was arrested and the next day presented to the local magistrate at Hanwell. At the crowded petty sessions hearing that followed 'the gown, shawl, bonnet, and apron, and also the pitchfork, and a stick which the prisoner had in his other hand, were produced'. Bradford argued he had donned such garb as a disguise so as to lure Spring-heeled Jack into attacking him so that he could then be captured. The case against Bradford being an imitator was weakened by the fact that none of those who had been frightened by Spring-heeled Jack were present 'although they had promised to attend'. Like Grenville, Bradford was discharged with 'a suitable admonition ... as to his future conduct'.[12] Press accounts did not specify whether the magistrate's concern was

---

[10]   Following the formation of the Metropolitan Police in 1829 there were a glut of laws directed at legislating against violent and unruly behaviours. See Wiener, *Reconstructing the Criminal*, especially pp. 14–91.

[11]   *The Examiner*, 25th March 1838.

[12]   *Age and Argus*, 8th February 1845.

with Bradford's dressing up in imitation of Spring-heeled Jack or his vigilante efforts to capture such a person.

However, where there were clearer indications of physical assault, magistrates responded accordingly. In March 1838 an imitator called Priest, a blacksmith, was found guilty of a number of attacks on 'respectable females in the neighbourhood of Islington'. These had involved him taking 'indecent liberties with them'. Here the legal transgression, suggestive as it was of attempted sexual assault, was considerably greater than a misjudged 'prank'. This was reflected in the corresponding punishment. The magistrate, Mr Rogers, freely 'regretted … that the pillory was done away with, as [Priest] deserved severe punishment'. In lieu of this, he had to content himself with sentencing Priest to 'three months … hard labour at the House of Correction'.[13] Therefore, whilst Spring-heeled Jack may have been associated with many crimes in the popular imagination, in the eyes of the law he lacked the coherent individuality that he was frequently granted in press reports. He was never just one legendary figure, but many mundane 'criminals'; sometimes a foolish prankster in need of a rebuke, at others a sex offender who required far tougher punishment.

Gender and Urban Space

Spring-heeled Jack attacked men and women but there was clearly a predilection towards female victims. This disproportionate threat was presented in an anonymous letter to *The Times* in January 1838; alluding to the nature of the wager behind the attacks, it declared 'the bet is that the monster shall kill six women in some given time'.[14] This obvious bias will be used to explore Spring-heeled Jack's role in linking crime, the control of urban space and gender perceptions.

Nineteenth-century urban popular culture was predominantly outdoors and street based in nature. Streets were sites for socialising, exchanging gossip, playing, courting and fighting, for men and women alike. Yet gendered notions did play a part, for whilst public spaces were not permanently masculine, they became increasingly so after nightfall. After dark social conventions meant female spatial movement became more constrained, with certain urban spaces becoming effectively moralised and sexualised, especially alleyways and courts that led off from main thoroughfares. Contemporary press reports suggested that the 'majority of indecent assaults and rapes … were perpetuated as the woman occupied public areas and tangential spaces, such as alleyways', the latter

---

[13]   *Surrey and Middlesex Standard*, 3rd March 1838.
[14]   *The Times*, 11th January 1838.

commonly associated with prostitutes.[15] Navigating the urban street therefore required sensitivity to moralised communal configurations of space, for not only was there the threat of sexual assault, but also, if passing too close to a particular locality, the danger that a woman could be misconstrued as having solicited the attack merely by being in that location.[16] This was indicated in Spring-heeled Jack's attack on Lucy Scales in Green Dragon Alley, Limehouse, on 28th February 1838. Similarly, in Camden in 1841 his favoured locale for attacks was believed to be College Grove, a narrow, 'dark and badly paved turning' which led onto Camden High Street.[17] Spring-heeled Jack's repeated utilising of the concealed nature of these particular aspects of the urban terrain reiterated that the tributaries away from the main street were marked sites of potential danger and moral ambiguity. The underlying message was that if a woman was not in such a place she would not be vulnerable to attack, thus shifting the onus of responsibility from attacker to victim.

In response to this difficult negotiating of urban spaces, the legend of Spring-heeled Jack quickly formulated a familiar narrative trope that was repeatedly promoted in press accounts, namely that women no longer dared leave the domestic sphere unaccompanied. On 10th January 1838 the *Morning Chronicle* reported that 'no respectable female has since left house after dark without a male companion'. Similarly, *The Times* announced that such was the level of fear generated in Lewisham and Blackheath in early January that 'women and children durst not stir out of their houses after dark'.[18] A few days later *The Examiner* reported that 'the females of Hammersmith and its vicinity feared to walk abroad after nightfall, in consequence of the molestations of a ghost or monster to which they were exposed'.[19] Following the attack on Jane Alsop in February a letter addressed to Mr Hardwick, the Lambeth Street office magistrate, declared, 'The alarm which the outrage has created at the east end of the metropolis is considerable, so much so that females are afraid to move a yard from their dwellings after dusk, unless they are very well protected.'[20]

Newspapers may merely have been reflecting contemporary views, but the frequent repetition appeared to actively promote the expected response in future encounters. Press accounts seemed to implicitly indicate acceptable patterns of behaviour and respectable public conduct, suggesting that women were adapting their own behaviours by avoiding the streets at night. The implication of Spring-heeled Jack's seemingly random attacks was that the greatest danger arose not

---

[15] Jones, 'She Resisted with all her Might', p. 110.
[16] See Walkowitz, 'Narratives of Sexual Danger', pp. 187–8.
[17] *The Era*, 11th April 1841.
[18] *The Times*, 11th January 1838.
[19] *The Examiner*, 14th January 1838.
[20] *Morning Chronicle*, 28th February 1838.

from what a woman did or did not do, or even where she did or did not go, but simply from the fact that she was a woman. Press reports that advertised (and encouraged) restriction on female movement about the city can be read as a conservative appropriation of Spring-heeled Jack's activities for their own moralising or disciplining purposes. Whilst it was most likely intended as a piece of humour, the *Penny Satirist*'s depiction of Spring-heeled Jack terrorising women on a heath in March 1838 explicitly made this point. Apparently naked except for cloak, boots and a visored helmet, he was portrayed reaching out for two fleeing women with his clawed hands. In the accompanying text the women cry 'Murder!', whilst Spring-heeled Jack spouts a misogynistic, moralising rant:

> I have seen your wickedness! I know all your naughty doings! ... I have heard all your gossiping tales and slanderous anecdotes! Now is the day of retribution! I am the spirit of judgement! ... I come to hold the reins of sin, and check the course of immorality! It is the sinner only that fears! The good I harm not! The innocent will kiss my hands, and play with my talons; but the wicked heart I will tear out.[21]

In this instance, Spring-heeled Jack had been appropriated as a vehicle for evangelical (male) conservatism.

Most newspapers from the late 1830s onwards expressed moral outrage at Spring-heeled Jack's assaults on women, with no explicit indication that they had been culpable in the attack. What was frightening about Spring-heeled Jack was that he attacked, perhaps even targeted, those who may have made every effort to remain invisible as they passed through the streets. This did not stop female victims being compelled to contribute to notions of their victimhood. Spring-heeled Jack was not necessarily a sex attacker, for he attacked and tore the clothes from men as well as women, without any suggestion of either sexual motive or, indeed, sexual assault.[22] Yet whatever his intentions, contemporary female accounts often adopted or adapted the narrative conventions of such assaults. Again, it was the press that was influential in promoting a format that conveyed conventions which could then be circulated through oral culture. In the 1820s it 'began to publicize the frequent indecent assaults on respectable women in London streets', encouraging the belief that women who walked unaccompanied at night were at great risk, a notion reiterated and reinforced by accounts of

---

[21] *Penny Satirist*, 10th March 1838. The infrequent moralising of the late 1830s and early 1840s had become more sustained by the 1880s when concerns about threatening female sexuality and outcries against prostitution had grown louder and shriller. See Walkowitz, *City of Dreadful Delight*.

[22] See for example the attack on a blacksmith in *The Times*, 9th January 1838, and an assault on a carpenter in the *Morning Chronicle*, 10th January 1838. The same cannot be said for some imitators who clearly donned the Spring-heeled Jack guise to sexually harass and possibly assault female victims.

Spring-heeled Jack.[23] Metropolitan newspapers granted considerable space to criminal court reporting, but by claiming sexual assaults were "too disgusting to relate" rendered rape all the more frightening: it became a nameless, shadowy horror'.[24] Rather the press employed obscure euphemisms such as 'committed the outrage', a term that was sufficiently vague as to leave the imagination free to invent the most dreadful speculations.

In Camden in 1841 accounts claimed that Spring-heeled Jack 'assaults his helpless victim in the most shameful and indelicate manner'. In one incident, a 'lady' was attacked 'a few paces from St. Pancras workhouse' and her assailant started to take 'the most indecent liberties with her'. In this case his victim 'made great resistance' and managed to escape into the nearby Elephant and Castle pub 'in the most agitated state'. Having explained 'the brutal way in which she had been treated', she was escorted home by one of the pub's patrons. A later victim, a young girl called Cope, was less fortunate and, indicative of the press's vague allusions to rape, she was consequently described as being left 'in a very bad state of health'. Mixing the vague with the particular, *The Era* claimed:

> The miscreant jumps from his hiding place, and stretching out his arms under his cloak, makes that article of clothing have the appearance of a huge pair of black wings, which completely blocks up the thoroughfare. He then envelopes the frightened female in the folds of his cloak and commits the most disgusting assaults upon her.[25]

However, readings of such accounts are complicated by the fact that the term 'outrage' did not have fixed implications and could simply suggest moral condemnation of Spring-heeled Jack's deeds. Whilst there was no evidence of sexual assault upon Jane Alsop, a number of newspapers entitled their reports 'Outrage against a young woman'. Likewise, the attack on fourteen-year-old Ellen Hurd in Bristol in 1841 was reported under the title 'Disgraceful Outrage', more a statement of moral shock than an indication of sexual assault.[26]

Although sexual harassment and assault were far from uncommon, many women were reluctant to take the issue to court.[27] Female victims were aware that a trial would involve their character and respectability being judged as much as the offender's actions, and the law was only liable to protect a woman if she conformed to the signifiers of victimhood. This in itself was no easy feat, for

---

[23] Clark, *Women's Silence*, p. 117.

[24] Ibid., p. 112.

[25] *The Era*, 11th April 1841.

[26] See for example *The Times*, 22nd February 1838; *John Bull* and *The Examiner*, 25th February 1838; *Morning Chronicle*, 28th February 1838; and *The Times*, 2nd March 1838. For the Ellen Hurd article see *Bristol Mercury*, 13th February 1841.

[27] For details about rape prosecutions and convictions in this period see Wiener, *Men of Blood*, pp. 86–7.

defendants were constrained by the social convention that respectable women did not openly talk about sex (or rape) in public. Given this, one can see why some sordid encounters may have been fantasised into attacks by Spring-heeled Jack. Due to public interest in such a bizarre entity, women may have been freer to narrate an account of awkward events when invoking the name of a character whose nature and being were ontologically ambiguous.[28] Conversely, this purportedly supernatural being and his strange, disturbing attacks could be reconfigured into culturally recognisable and acceptable ways of thinking by reference to more mundane violence.[29] As Anna Clark has noted, when women wrote out their own accounts of sexual assaults they 'almost invariably adopted a tone of melodramatic romance … of innocent maidens who always faint when ravished', thus avoiding 'the necessity of describing a confusing and painful experience'.[30]

Press reports frequently alluded to victims' extreme responses to encounters with Spring-heeled Jack. Whilst some fainted, the press recorded that many collapsed in fits or lost their mental faculties, his attacks being psychological as much as sexual assaults. The Lord Mayor's first letter from a Peckham resident recounted the response of a servant girl who, upon answering the door bell, found Spring-heeled Jack standing before her in the 'dreadful figure [of] a spectre'. The press reported that the girl 'immediately swooned, and has never from that moment been in her senses, but, on seeing any man, screams out most violently "Take him away!"' Two other 'ladies' who had lost their senses were 'not expected to recover' and would likely 'become burdens to their families'.[31] This swiftly became an established narrative trope in accounts of Spring-heeled Jack. A contributor to *The Times* on 11th January 1838 reported on both physical and mental assaults, claiming that 'several young women had really been frightened

---

[28] This was a potentially risky manoeuvre. Stevenson has argued that 'feminine "ingenuity" was associated with deceit', any indication of which was liable to discredit a female complainant's testimony. See Stevenson, 'Ingenuities of the Female Mind', p. 94.
[29] For similar knowing narrative testimony see Gaskill, 'Witches and Witnesses', and also his 'Reporting Murder'.
[30] Clark, *Women's Silence*, pp. 81–2.
[31] *The Times*, 9th January 1838. See also *Morning Chronicle*, 11th January 1838. It was this supposed female susceptibility to hysteria that led the Lord Mayor to express the view that the 'Peckham resident' who had first brought the matter to his attention was female. Despite the author referring to himself as 'he', Cowen felt the letter 'which was written in a very beautiful hand, was the production of a lady'. The Lord Mayor went so far as to suppose the author to be one of seven ladies who 'the unmanly villain' had deprived of their senses. The association with mental trauma implicitly discredited the value of her account. See *The Times*, 9th January 1838. Cowen's slur conflated a number of long associations between feminine irrationality, mental vulnerability and the supernatural. For the early-modern context see Stephens, *Demon Lovers*; Willis, *Malevolent Nurture*; and Roper, *Oedipus and the Devil*.

into fits – dangerous fits and some … had been severely wounded by a sort of claws the miscreant wore on his hands'. With something of a comic tone, the *Penny Satirist* recorded that '[a] servant girl in Kensington … has been so powerfully affected that her person has swelled so enormously that her mistress has dismissed her as unfit for household work'.[32] Spring-heeled Jack allegedly appeared before three 'ladies' in Blackheath one evening in 1838, although the specific date was not given. In response to seeing the 'monster' which was said to possess 'a phosphoric lustre … tremendous long ears, horns and tail like those of a bullock', one woman 'fell down in a fit, and the other two had resort to that potent weapon in the female armoury, a good scream'. This summoned a policeman to their aid, but 'the apparition threw itself over his head and disappeared on the heath'. Later, near Woolwich, a girl fell into a fit when confronted by a figure breathing 'blue flame … from his mouth'.[33]

The press' message about Spring-heeled Jack's threat to women's supposedly more fragile mental health was best demonstrated by the Ellen Hurd case in Bristol in 1841. The *Bristol Mercury* reported that this 'exceedingly delicate and neat-looking girl' possessed a 'vacant expression of countenance [which] denoted that her mental faculties were not in a healthy state'. This, the *Bristol Mercury* reported, was a result of the trauma suffered in an earlier attack by Spring-heeled Jack in Park Street, Bristol. It claimed that prior to the attack she had been 'in full possession of her intellectual powers', but after the assault in which she had had her hair cut off, Hurd was left so 'dreadfully terrified by the outrage as to become deranged, and after remaining at home for some time in a state of much danger, she was admitted an inmate of the lunatic ward of St. Peter's Hospital'.[34]

Since expected modesty hampered free expression in court, rape narratives generally required one of two formulations, the frequent use of which suggest women were familiar with the accepted tropes in such cases; either the woman would fight back with all her strength, resisting to the point of exhaustion, or she would be rendered passive and unaware by fainting. Invoking such ideas helped ensure that respectability could be retained even if chastity had been stolen. Beyond these set narrative expectations were symbolic indicators that were also influential if women were to construct and retain their victimhood and, by extension, their respectability. Class, often defined by fathers or other male relatives, was a basic influence, a 'lady' being more likely to garner sympathy than a lowly 'woman'. Prior to the assault the victim should have acted with due modesty and reserve, but during the attack she needed to have struggled and

---

[32] *Penny Satirist*, 20th January 1838.
[33] *All the Year Round*, 9th August 1884, pp. 348–9. For other victims reduced to fits see *Leeds Mercury*, 19th May 1838, and *Bell's Life in London*, 4th April 1847.
[34] *Bristol Mercury*, 7th August 1841.

resisted vociferously. Afterwards there needed to be a clear indication of injuries received, and the assault needed to be made known to others, preferably figures of authority, as soon as possible. To explore this it is worth comparing the Jane Alsop and Lucy Scales attacks. Occurring just eight days apart in late February 1838, the details as they were reported at the Lambeth Street police office and subsequently in the press indicate the complicated semiotics of assault and victimhood.

Treating the bizarre and unprovoked assault as akin to attempted rape, Jane Alsop did everything required to participate in the portrayal of her victimhood and thereby protect her respectability. It was this that demanded that she present herself before the Lambeth Street police office the very next day, for despite the association with Spring-heeled Jack the incident had to be swiftly reported. Jane's case was undoubtedly bolstered by the Alsops' social respectability, their collective appearance before the magistrate and her family's public corroboration of her testimony. Her case was further aided by the fact that the struggle against Spring-heeled Jack had occurred on the doorstep of the Alsop household. Jane had been attacked in front of the family home, not in the street, and prior to the assault she had done nothing but compliantly respond to the man's request for a candle. Joanne Jones has argued that indicators of 'struggle, physical injury, emotional distress … were woven into the newspapers' narrative of sexual crimes as supporting evidence of the victim's accusation' and this was clearly seen in Jane Alsop's case.[35] Press reports reiterated that Jane had acted appropriately throughout the encounter, for she had 'screamed out as loud as she could for assistance', and by 'considerable exertion' she had briefly escaped Spring-heeled Jack's clutches before he attacked her again. Jane's torn attire, the fact that she had 'suffered considerably all night from the shock', the obvious injuries to her arm, and the numerous 'wounds and scratches inflicted by the miscreant about her shoulders and neck' (presumably still visible when she appeared before the

[35] Jones, 'She Resisted with all her Might', p. 108. Villiers provided a questionable account of an attack upon Mary Stevens near Clapham Common in 1838 (no precise date given) in which the sexual harassment element is more explicit. Villiers recorded that when Stevens was terrified by a tall figure leaping out at her as she passed an alleyway 'she would have sunk on the ground, but strong arms caught her and held her prisoner. She felt a man's lips on her face, deliberately he kissed her, then with a loud laugh let her go, and leaping extraordinarily high, vanished into the night as mysteriously as he had come.' However, 'no great weight was attached to the recital' since she 'had been alone [and] there were no witnesses to prove whether she had exaggerated what had occurred'. People suspected elements of her account were fantasised, Spring-heeled Jack's huge leaps being dismissed as 'the highly coloured version of a simple incident which a hysterical woman might be expected to give', whilst 'the kisses might have existed in [her] imagination'. See Villiers, *Stand and Deliver*, pp. 241–2, 243 and 248.

magistrate the next morning) all served as testimony to not just the viciousness of the attack but also her spirited struggle against her assailant.[36]

Yet despite this almost perfect testimony, her account was not without criticisms. These were implicitly linked back to notions about the weakness of the female mind. Whilst all three investigators agreed that 'a violent outrage ... had been committed' as described by Jane and her sisters, 'they thought that in her fright the young lady had much mistaken the appearance of her assailant.'[37] Mr Hardwick, the magistrate, declared that he could not conceive why Jane Alsop would have given such 'a melodramatic or exaggerated description of her assailant' even though it had been corroborated by her sisters. Lea, the court's investigating officer, was certain she had mistaken a shooting coat and cap for the bizarre headgear and oilskin she claimed her attacker wore. This may say more about Lea's stolid pragmatism than anything else, but it at least hints at a sense that Jane's testimony was less than totally secure, that the fantastical depiction she had conjured was suspected of being the result of a temporarily overwrought mind.

Leaving aside the obvious class aspect (this will be considered in the next chapter), Lucy Scales' case was more precarious from the start. Firstly, it was informed by a number of gendered issues only hinted at in the Alsop attack. Lucy was attacked in the street, near the entrance to Green Dragon Alley, in the evening. Although accompanied by her younger sister, two young females without a male escort on the street at night were vulnerable to being misconstrued as prostitutes. Furthermore, they were in a transitional limbo between the 'patriarchal' protection of their brother's home (there was no mention of a father in this case, the brother adopting the patriarchal role to the point where he spoke on his younger sister's behalf at the police office) and their own abode. The implicit suggestion was that Lucy's presence in the street after dark constructed a situation which potentially invited attack. The 'rules' as to how to conduct oneself in the street were largely a product of the second half of the nineteenth century when numerous etiquette books were published, many

---

[36] *Morning Chronicle*, 22nd February 1838.

[37] *Morning Chronicle*, 28th February 1838. James Lea's investigation into the Alsop attack led to two suspects being brought before the Lambeth Street police office on Wednesday 28th February; Mr Payne, a master bricklayer, and Mr Millbank, a carpenter. A local wheelwright, James Smith, testified to Millbank being in a belligerent (and apparently drunken) mood on the evening of the assault. According to Smith, as he passed the two men Millbank challenged him by saying, 'What have you to say to Spring Jack?' Despite Smith's willingness to testify against them, ultimately the case appears to have foundered on a lack of anything more than circumstantial evidence, assertion and counter-assertion. See *The Times*, 2nd March 1838, and *The Examiner*, 4th March 1838.

containing sections on female deportment in the streets.[38] In 1838 these codes of behaviour for navigating public spaces had yet to be written.

Whereas Jane Alsop struggled, Lucy's account illustrated an alternative narrative trope. When Spring-heeled Jack spat blue flame at her face, 'she instantly dropped to the ground, and was seized with violent fits, which continued for several hours'. This was perhaps a third response to attack, albeit not a conscious one. Between active resistance (as in the Alsop case) and passive fainting there was the abrupt and involuntary loss of control which again rendered a person devoid of volition, effectively protecting her from being cognisant as surely as if she had become unconscious. Mr Scales, a butcher, had swiftly responded to his sisters' screams and on finding Lucy on the ground had quickly returned her home. The only thing he and a second arrival on the scene, a person described as 'a respectable female', could confirm was that Lucy was found having a fit. Unlike the Alsop case, there were no physical injuries, no sign of struggle, no attacker and no corroborating evidence. The other witness, Lucy's sister, had been some way behind her and was then supposedly dazzled by the burst of flame. Worse yet, unlike Jane who had the visible support of her family, Lucy's sister failed to attend the Lambeth Street office. Compared to Jane Alsop's encounter there was just the word of a young lower-class woman who had suffered a fit in the street at night. Perhaps aware of this, Mr Scales produced a certificate signed by Charles Pritchel, a surgeon resident at 18 Cock Hill who confirmed that he had visited Lucy on the night of Wednesday 28th February and found her to be 'suffering from hysterics and great agitation, in all probability the result of fright'.[39] The doctor's written verification was an obvious example of the power of the respectable, male medical practitioner employing his professional authority to bolster a testimony that was otherwise quite precarious.

Whilst the circumstances of the encounter did not particularly encourage a sympathetic hearing, Lucy's account was further weakened by being expressed in terms of an overexcited female imagination. Whether intentional or not, the grounds for such an interpretation were laid by her brother. He reported to the magistrate that 'it was not a little singular that one of his sisters had been reading in a newspaper, a few minutes before they left his house, the account under the head of this office, of Spring-heeled Jack, when he remarked that it was not likely that this personage would come to his neighbourhood, from the fact of there being so many butchers residing in it'. Mr Scales had observed that 'the account, so far from alarming his sister, appeared to have a different effect'. The insinuation was that this article was playing on his sister's mind, and that the encounter just 'a few minutes after his sisters had left his house' was in all

[38] Nead, *Victorian Babylon*, p. 72.
[39] *Morning Chronicle*, 8th March 1838.

likelihood nothing more than a fantasy arising from her excited mental state.[40] Given this apparently flawed position, the press may have been less willing to champion Scales' case and certainly devoted less coverage to the incident than the Alsop attack.[41]

Struggles for Popular Culture

Spring-heeled Jack offered a particular and peculiar way of articulating contemporary issues behind the struggle for popular culture. The period in which he appeared was witnessing the development of an increasingly restrictive society. Following the relatively laissez-faire attitudes of the Georgians, the 1820s and 1830s marked the start of a protracted attempt to tame popular culture.[42] 'Taming' tends to encourage a view of popular culture as an object that was shaped from 'outside' and gradually whittled away into something more acceptable to those above. It is probably more appropriate to view it as the site of an ongoing power struggle between the dominant and the subordinate. Whilst the former used both legal coercion and consensual persuasion, the latter's tactics included a rearguard action defined by adaptation, evasion, resistance and the surrender of redundant cultural practices to better ensure the survival of others. Within this struggle was the dynamic playing out of the question as to the extent to which popular culture possessed its own agency and volition, and how far it was shaped by external power structures exerting political, cultural and economic influences.

Spring-heeled Jack's earliest attacks occurred within a broader but increasingly contested culture of violence. Whilst popular cultural entertainments such as bare-knuckle boxing, dog fighting, bull baiting and cock throwing embodied a high level of actual violence, other forms such as penny gaffs theatres and the aptly named 'penny bloods' indulged a vicarious longing for imagined and performed violence. As upper- and middle-class involvement in most of these events declined it became easier to associate what were deemed uncivilised practices with plebeian culture, particularly those in the poorest, least reputable districts of expanding cities.[43] In opposition to these popular cultural forms and the responses they provoked in their audiences was an emerging bourgeois

---

[40] Ibid.

[41] See *Bell's Life in London*, 11th March 1838.

[42] See Griffin, *England's Revelry*; Golby and Purdue, *Civilisation of the Crowd*; and Bushaway, *By Rite*.

[43] See Crone, *Violent Victorians*. For other cultures of violence in this period see Shoemaker, 'Male Honour'; Wiener, 'Alice Arden to Bill Sykes'; and Cockburn, 'Patterns of Violence in English Society'.

ideal of self-control and self-restraint, one that prized self-discipline as indicative of both a 'civilised' individual and society.[44] These values were given voice through numerous avenues, most obviously by way of the newspaper, sermon and classroom. The promotion of these qualities, especially as they were related to masculine behaviours, can be read as an attempt to internalise what some scholars, most notably Michel Foucault, have seen as the nineteenth century's general shift towards a more institutionalised, disciplinary society.[45] More recently, Martin Wiener has asserted that 'the decades after 1820 saw a heightened concern with unregulated human power, both personal and collective. The advancing individualism of the age had a dark, anarchic side that few failed to sense.'[46] This anarchic individualism found its most marked contemporary personification in the startling appearance and bizarre, unfathomable actions of Spring-heeled Jack.

Writing of Spring-heeled Jack's predecessor, the 'London Monster', Jan Bondeson has noted how his 'over-the-top "stagy" appearance … and his abusive and violent behaviour' must have caused Londoners to imagine 'Mr Punch had jumped down from his stage at Bartholomew Fair and headed towards the West End'.[47] In the late 1830s this mantle of the archetypal figure of anarchic male violence was assumed by Spring-heeled Jack. His apparent spontaneity and release from the normal bounds of moral and legal prescript embodied the spirit of the carnivalesque, as did his excessiveness in terms of both multiplicity of forms and disguises, and his numerous, energetic 'performances'. Whilst there appear to have been very real consequences to his actions, at least according to the vibrant field of gossip and rumour in which his legend circulated, Spring-heeled Jack enacted a highly individualised and dangerous form of street theatre. In doing so he disrupted perceived 'norms' relating to the nature and ownership of urban spaces, and civic and gender relations. When demons and ghosts were reported to be running amok in the streets of London, the modern, secular, disenchanted world truly appeared to have turned upside down. Spring-heeled Jack's nocturnal antics made him a genuine lord of misrule.[48]

For those who appreciated the resonances, Spring-heeled Jack appeared to be a lodestone that drew associations with traditional customary practices, or else provided a new focus onto which those ritualised behaviours could be projected in the modern age. In this context Spring-heeled Jack gives credence

---

[44] Smith, 'Violent Crime and the Public Weal', p. 191.
[45] See Foucault, *Discipline and Punish*.
[46] Wiener, *Reconstructing the Criminal*, p. 11.
[47] Bondeson, *London Monster*, p. 12.
[48] For more on the carnivalesque in earlier popular culture see Billig, *Laughter and Ridicule*; Castle, *Masquerade and Civilization*; and Bakhtin, *Rabelais and His World*. For more on the Lords of Misrule see Hutton, *Rise and Fall of Merry England*, p. 91.

to Peter Bailey's claim that Victorian popular culture 'can be understood as a performance culture no less than those of early modern or "traditional" societies'. Particularly pertinent in this case is Bailey's further observation that, unlike the more ritualistic customs of 'traditional' societies, those in the nineteenth century tended to be more 'improvisatory and individualized'.[49]

In an increasingly restrictive surveillance society one might have expected the popularity and durability of Spring-heeled Jack's legend to reside in his articulating an anti-authoritarian sentiment. With speculation and uncertainty surrounding his motives, Spring-heeled Jack was a rebel potentially open to appropriation by any number of causes. Evolving 'modern' notions of civilised and self-restrained masculinity certainly jarred with customary behaviours which had revelled in a far more robust and boisterous expression of maleness.[50] By means of deliberately public demonstrations, Spring-heeled Jack wilfully denied a hegemonic, consensual pressure towards self-discipline, and implicitly opposed the reconstituting of masculinity on the basis of self-control. Even as the broader popular culture of which he was a part was being compromised and pressured, he stood as a symbol of masculine obstinacy, an anarchic and increasingly anachronistic personification of customary behaviours that would not be tamed, let alone controlled. In this capacity he was one of the more visible signs of popular cultural resistance in a struggle that was defined less by entrenched 'fronts' and more by a roving guerrilla campaign by both reformers and their opponents.[51] As seen with his numerous imitators throughout the Victorian period, there were those who willingly responded to his example. Reflecting on Spring-heeled Jack in 1884, *All the Year Round* noted how his actions and notoriety had 'had the effect of making many silly young men emulous to enact the ruffian' with the result that 'cowardly assaults on women were reported in various parts of the metropolis, under the impression … that it was all a "lark"'.[52]

It is uncertain how far plebeian communities would have picked up on details reported in the press which demonstrated that Spring-heeled Jack had cunningly found ways to work around or within the developing system of policing. For example, *The Times* reported that James Lea, the investigator for the Lambeth Street magistrates, had recognised that Spring-heeled Jack's attacks occurred 'between 8 and 9 o'clock, the time at which the police change'. The perpetrator clearly knew the police shift patterns and operated accordingly, their work structure at least partially determining the time of night at which Spring-

---

[49] See Bailey, *Popular Culture and Performance*, p. 11. See also Griffin, 'Affecting Violence'.

[50] Wiener, *Men of Blood*, p. 6.

[51] For an example of a rather different expression of this struggle see Rude, 'Against Innovation?'

[52] *All the Year Round*, 9th August 1884, p. 349.

heeled Jack was likely to strike.[53] Although it would certainly not have been the intention of the press to promote such a view, the details contributed to the idea that Spring-heeled Jack was an individual who an increasing surveillance culture could not stop. Through knowledge or cunning he had detected the system's loopholes and operated accordingly. In doing so he implicitly championed the notion that people did not necessarily have to change their behaviours, and that there were points of weaknesses within the forces that were being applied to popular cultural reform in this period.

That said, it is perhaps a little too easy to romanticise Spring-heeled Jack as an icon of popular customary rebellion. Although we are largely dependent upon 'elite' sources of information such as press reports, the overwhelming evidence would suggest that the plebeian potential to vicariously align themselves with him, to cock a snook at a society monitored by the police, employers, workhouse officials, government health boards and teachers, was rarely actualised. A petty session case at Bicester on 4th October 1861 appears to have been more an exception than the rule. The accused, William, Mary and Charles Robinson, had been charged with setting fire to a hayrick on Reverend H. J. De Salis' farm in Fringford. Following this act of arson, two pieces of paper were delivered to De Salis. One stated:

> Don't Blame your Foreman no longer for he his Inocent as A child unborn, For I done the deed and my name is spring Heel Jack. Catch me if you can. Don't Blame him no more for if you do you Blame the wrong man I am sure and I fear none of your Police finding me out you see that.[54]

A police search of William Robinson's house led to the discovery of writing paper that matched that sent to Reverend De Salis, whilst a prayer book and account book contained handwriting that matched those on the letter. Clearly no criminal masterminds, the Robinsons had set fire to the hayrick whilst James Stone, a policeman who had been guarding the rick-yard, was in the Robinsons' home. Stone was not so busy being plied with refreshments as not to notice that both William and Mary had left the house.[55] This burning of hayricks and the Robinsons' clumsy attempt to employ Spring-heeled Jack as a shield for their actions have obvious resonance with the protest activities of the Swing rioters in the early 1830s, including their apportioning of such symbolic protest

[53] *The Times*, 23rd February 1838. The attack on Lucy Scales also took place at about half past eight in the evening.

[54] *Jackson's Oxford Journal*, 12th October 1861. This deliberate attempt to scapegoat Spring-heeled Jack should not be associated with the fact that by the 1880s and 1890s his name became a popular moniker for many a common criminal, none of whom were ever realistically considered to be *the* Spring-heeled Jack.

[55] Ibid.

to an imaginary folkloric figure. Yet unlike Captain Swing, or General Ludd before him, Spring-heeled Jack could not be presented as a leader of a 'popular' movement or as a man of the people, for he clearly preyed upon plebeian communities themselves.

As will be explored in a later chapter, this did not mean that Spring-heeled Jack could not be appropriated by local communities. One of his principal functions in this context was to help those communities construct a sense of themselves by way of a shared external threat. His most common application was as the focus of communal ghost hunts, a popular tradition that persisted into the mid nineteenth century in urban environments. As with numerous other ghost scares these hunts for Spring-heeled Jack can be read as predominantly plebeian spatial assertions and reclamations that enabled disruption to the 'official' ordering of the streets. This had more ritualistic, mundane customary equivalents in such nineteenth-century practices as 'Riding the Black Lad' in Manchester, but the communal allusion to the supernatural seemed to give greater reason to transgress the bounds of accepted public decorum. Importantly, as with other ghost hunts, the appearance and search for Spring-heeled Jack represented a spontaneous and potentially volatile communal performance as enthusiastic crowds surged unpredictably around the streets, pulled hither and thither by a ferment of rumour and 'sightings'. These intrinsic qualities meant the initiative and agency was with the community, whereas the authorities, and especially the police who sought to restore order, were forced into a reactive and responsive position that temporarily suggested a loss of control.[56]

Throughout the Victorian period Spring-heeled Jack's appearances showed communities were constantly inclined to take matters into their own hands by resorting to older communal practices of self-protection. As one contributor to *The Times* put it in January 1838, 'There ought to be a stop put to this, but the police, I am afraid, are frightened at him also.'[57] During Spring-heeled Jack's appearances in the King's Road, Camden, in April 1841, it was reported that if the police failed to catch him 'the husbands of several females he has assaulted … will take the law into their own hands, and cool his brutal propensities by ducking him in the [nearby] canal'.[58] In such cases there was an inherent lack of faith in the police force and even an unwillingness to acknowledge their authority

---

[56] For more on this customary ritual see Wood, 'Pedlar of Swaffham', pp. 180–4, and Steinberg, 'Riding of the Black Lad'. These points are developed further in Chapter 6.

[57] *The Times*, 11th January 1838.

[58] *The Era*, 11th April 1841.

in being able to control the streets.[59] Ever since their advent nine years before the Spring-heeled Jack scare, the Metropolitan Police had met with plebeian hostility. Working-class communities long resented the intrusion of the 'blue plague' which was seen as the most explicitly coercive agency in the struggle for popular cultural reform. Attacks upon policemen became an endemic, if increasingly sporadic, element of plebeian resistance and frustration.[60]

The press gave little evidence of direct physical confrontations between Spring-heeled Jack and the police, for he generally remained too elusive and the police too sluggish in their responses. In a few imitator cases such as that perpetrated by Charles Grenville in Kentish Town, the police were actively seeking and, indeed, waiting for him to appear. Later, in Clewer in 1885, another imitator assaulted a policeman by leaping onto the officer's back. In contrast to the disapproving tone with which newspapers reported the incident, the plebeian culture of struggles with (and assaults on) policemen meant it is unlikely that this attack would have even registered as a crime in the popular imagination.[61] It is not surprising to find that contemporary press reports did not construct or condone a view of Spring-heeled Jack as a heroic rogue defying the forces of authority. As we shall see shortly, theirs was essentially a conservative appropriation of the legend. Rather it was in the penny serials from the late 1860s that this image was promoted and cemented. The opening scene of the 1867–68 serial, *Spring-heeled Jack, The Terror of London*, depicts a braggart of a policeman whose supposed courage Spring-heeled Jack swiftly and publicly exposes as mere bluff. Numerous critics of such literature took offence at the brutal 'heroics' of Spring-heeled Jack and the humiliation and beatings inflicted upon police officers.[62]

This raises the awkward issue as to how one should interpret vicarious associations with Spring-heeled Jack's actions. On the one hand they seem to

---

[59] For popular reception of the police and ongoing anti-police sentiment see Emsley, *Crime and Society in England*, pp. 221–52; Archer, 'Men Behaving Badly', pp. 47–8; Taylor, *Crime, Policing and Punishment*, pp. 82–7; and Philips and Storch, *Policing Provincial England*. James Lea's investigation into the Alsop attack suggested the police were unintentionally influential in the conduct of Spring-heeled Jack's crimes. It had been Spring-heeled Jack's authoritative claim that he was a policeman that had duped Jane Alsop into fetching him a candle at the start of the encounter. Later, when responding to the family's call for help, three men had passed 'a tall man wrapped in a large cloak, who said as they came up, that a policeman was wanted at Mr Alsop's'. They passed on without further hesitation but Lea was convinced this cloaked figure was Spring-heeled Jack, clearly knowing whose house it was, and using the police once again as a way of diverting any suspicions about his presence in the street. In such ways Spring-heeled Jack appropriated the authority of the police to his own purposes. See *The Times*, 23rd February 1838.

[60] See Storch, 'Plague of Blue Locusts', and also Inwood, 'Policing London's Morals'.

[61] See Emsley, *Crime and Society in England*, p. 84.

[62] See Anon., *Spring-heeled Jack* (1867), pp. 2–3. For examples of press criticisms of Spring-heeled Jack stories see *Pall Mall Gazette*, 21st July 1890, p. 3, and *Quarterly Review*, July 1890, pp. 150–3.

sustain the struggle for older, customary behaviours by imaginatively providing a powerful liberation from a restrictive society. Yet on the other these models of imagined behaviour can be seen as being part of the system of constraint. Whilst drawing a degree of moral condemnation, Spring-heeled Jack's penny literature arguably sated or nullified any real urges to violence or rebellion. Although the imagination was being given the freedom to indulge in all manner of bloody and anarchic behaviours, the ultimate bodily response from the individual was passivity and tacit consent. In this way the radical potential within a plebeian adoption of Spring-heeled Jack could actually diffuse real aggression, thereby implicitly serving the needs of authorities and tamers of popular culture. It is not just the case that the available evidence is skewed towards a conservative interpretation of Spring-heeled Jack, although this is certainly true. One can detect a number of ways in which this 'popular' cultural figure served influential hegemonic applications.

Whilst Spring-heeled Jack can be viewed as having originated in an organic oral culture (not necessarily of 'the people' so much as of the locality), the press was certainly willing to use him as a means of forwarding its own agendas. Once in the newspapers Spring-heeled Jack was as much 'their' creation as a product of popular oral culture. Although journalists clearly sneered at the supernatural allusions surrounding this strangely modern folkloric character, they were willing to perpetuate this haze of associations in their reports. In doing so one seems to get an elite interpretation of what popular culture could produce when given free rein, providing predominantly middle-class readers with journalistic perspectives on what 'the people' best responded and related to. As a result they were arguably more successful at forwarding dominant conservative interpretations of Spring-heeled Jack than others were at articulating his more radical aspects. Firstly, through presumably selected accounts the press consistently and persuasively presented Spring-heeled Jack as a threatening menace. Newspapers tacitly emphasised the randomness of his attacks, encouraging all Londoners in early 1838 to share the press' concern with safety in the streets. Furthermore, they manipulated their readership by predominantly highlighting attacks against women, most often lower-class women. As indicated above, this placed emphasis on the inappropriateness and potential risks of female movements about the street at night. The press presentation of Spring-heeled Jack's 'performed' violence echoed customary practices such as charivari, although the customary sanction that such rituals had enforced no longer derived from the local community but the newspapers themselves.[63] In this way the respectable metropolitan press had effectively appropriated a controlling and regulating element of popular

---

[63] For more on charivari see Underdown, 'But the Shows of Their Street'. For parallels in France in the 1830s see Wiese Forbes, *Satiric Decade*.

customary culture and propagated its essence via an increasingly influential media. Rather than the local community's use of charivari promoting or reinforcing moral or sexual regulation, the developing nineteenth-century press now enacted a more remote but similar function over an amorphous imagined community of readers.

Secondly, as one of the key means by which notions of a controlled masculinity were propagated, the respectable press also seized upon Spring-heeled Jack as a personification of the boisterous masculine 'other' that it sought to discredit.[64] He was frequently described as being both brutish and animalistic, but also cowardly and 'unmanly'. In 1841 the *Bristol Mercury* condemned 'the freaks of the unmanly ruffian who ... has been ... annoying and frightening females', his unmanliness defined by the way he terrified and assaulted women and children before cowardly running away.[65] This was particularly noted during his appearances in the King's Road, Camden, in the same year. Describing him as a 'brute', *The Era* reported that 'on the appearance of any male ... [he] darts into a doorway and hides'.[66] Such behaviours were presented as being in marked contrast to the reform of manners in which 'the law-abiding ... woman-respecting Englishman ... was emerging as a cultural ideal, and, increasingly, arch[e]type'.[67] Spring-heeled Jack's function in this formulation was to be presented as a symbol of inappropriate, uncouth masculinity that employed unrestrained physical violence to serve its own needs.

Finally, by drawing upon popular melodramatic narratives, the press, where possible, emphasised Spring-heeled Jack's monstrosity by contrasting him with the heroic figure of the policeman. Whether it was intended or not, press coverage of Spring-heeled Jack encouraged the view of the metropolis as under attack. In these particularly heightened circumstances the unpopular agents of popular cultural constraint were promoted by the authorities as defenders of ordinary people. Following Spring-heeled Jack's appearances in Richmond in late 1837, newspapers credited the effectiveness of the local police in causing him to 'quit the green lanes of that fashionable resort' for neighbouring localities. When he

[64] On male violence in this period see Emsley, *Hard Men*; Wiener, *Men of Blood*; Archer, 'Men Behaving Badly'; Spierenburg, *Men and Violence*; Lees, *Carnal Knowledge*; Newburn and Stanko, *Just Boys Doing Business*; and Stanko, *Everyday Violence*.
[65] *Bristol Mercury*, 13th February 1841.
[66] *The Era*, 11th April 1841. See also *Daily News*, 22nd August 1882. One occasionally finds rare inversions of these gendered expectations in the 1838 attacks. A retrospective article from 1884 claimed Spring-heeled Jack frightened a blacksmith in Uxbridge to such an extent 'as to force him to keep his bed in consequence of the shock he sustained'. By contrast, when he appeared before 'a valorous laundress' in Hammersmith in the guise of 'an immense baboon, six feet high, with enormous eyes', the 'courageous woman ... flew at him with such fury that he was glad to give up the contest'. See *All the Year Round*, 9th August 1884, p. 346.
[67] Wiener, *Men of Blood*, p. 31.

moved on to Kingston 'the police of that borough soon rendered his visits most dangerous to his own safety, and he in consequence crossed the [Thames]'.[68] In these encounters the police may not have been effective enough to catch him, but they at least asserted sufficient pressure to curb his actions and push him away from a certain area, thus contributing to his migratory appearances.[69] In these conservative appropriations of Spring-heeled Jack the press used his scares to ingratiate the police to their readers.

Compared with Spring-heeled Jack, police officers were depicted as embodying a new masculinity that alloyed courage with discipline and self-control in the service of the community.[70] When a number of frightened women and children informed Constable Markham that Spring-heeled Jack had been seen in Kentish Town, it was reported that the police officer was 'determined on capturing him and putting an end to his career'.[71] He 'drew his staff and, screwing his courage to the sticking point, waited for the monster'. When the Spring-heeled Jack imitator appeared from a lane and headed towards a group of children, Markham single-handedly tackled him, 'seizing him by the collar, dragged him to a butcher's shop, by the light of which he discovered he wore a mask, embellished at the mouth with blue glazed paper'.[72] He then conducted the hoaxer to the station house. Given the presence of what was frequently referred to as a 'monster', the bold 'hero' protecting helpless females (who, as we have seen, were frequently compelled to participate in the construction of their role as victim) contributed to the essential trinity of any gothic melodrama. The difference was that these stories were played out spontaneously in the streets and lanes of early-Victorian London. Despite the prevailing of law and order over chaos in Markham's account, Spring-heeled Jack reports could rarely guarantee the desired triumph

---

[68] *Morning Chronicle*, 10th January 1838.

[69] The 1839 Rural Constabulary Act and the 1856 County and Borough Police Act meant developing police forces accompanied Spring-heeled Jack's migration into the provinces. See Taylor, *Crime, Policing and Punishment*, pp. 80–1. In 1868 the *Manchester Times* directly credited the development of police forces for causing Spring-heeled Jack's supposed disappearance, declaring 'the new police were too many for him'. See *Manchester Times*, 1st August 1868. For similar expressions see *London Society*, February 1863, pp. 152–3.

[70] A different portrayal of masculinity was adopted by Captain Finch in the 1847 Teignmouth case. Given that female victims had been 'rather roughly handled', Finch cited his supposed infirmity and 'advanced state of life' as a way of discrediting Miss Morgan's servant's conviction that she could clearly identify him as the man who had twice assaulted her in January of that year. In his defence Dr Withers, a local medical practitioner, stated that the accused was 'labouring under an internal disease, and any excitement or bodily exertion might cause instantaneous death'. As such, Finch invoked a non-masculine, non-threatening fragility that reconstructed him in similar terms used to describe Spring-heeled Jack's female victims. See *Daily News*, 29th March 1847, and *Lady's Newspaper*, 3rd April 1847, p. 321.

[71] *The Examiner*, 25th March 1838.

[72] *Morning Post*, 20th March 1838.

of good over evil that audiences craved from their appreciation of stage plays and serialised novels.

Spring-heeled Jack never became respectable in the popular imagination. His ethnographic accounts remained fixed to portrayals of a frightening, predatory character.[73] Even after his heroic reinvention in cheap literature he retained some rough edges in his use of violence and ruthless pursuit of his victims, in one case to the point where a corrupt clerk committed suicide to escape the torment.[74] As a certain romanticism crept in to reflective accounts he was still remembered as a rogue, albeit one who targeted the rich or the immoral. As suggested in this chapter, a persistent association with viciousness and illegality may also have been due to the fact that he served a useful function in authorities' construction of customary and masculine 'otherness', embodying qualities that were no longer deemed to have any place in 'modern' society. Paradoxically, it was in this role as the perennial outsider that he was incorporated into Victorian culture. For all his great dexterity, Spring-heeled Jack was destined to be a figure always out of step with the age in which he lived.

Authoritative voices in early-Victorian society seem to have been more successful in co-opting Spring-heeled Jack into serving conservative and possibly reforming agendas than those who may have wished to appropriate him as an icon of imagined rebelliousness. Yet whilst authorities certainly spoke with a louder voice, they clearly lacked a singular one. Both the magistracy and the press were implicitly involved in granting the legend a degree of credibility (though not necessarily with an acceptance of its supposedly supernatural dimensions). By entertaining testimony from the likes of Jane Alsop and Lucy Scales, by conducting investigations, and through dealing with various imitators in London, Brentford and Teignmouth in the 1840s, the magistracy was clearly embroiled in the development of Spring-heeled Jack's evolving legend. Yet as was seen above, magistrates appear to have demonstrated far greater restraint than the press when it came to incidences involving Spring-heeled Jack's name.[75] Judicial treatment of Spring-heeled Jack's imitators suggests that he was rarely

---

[73] Spring-heeled Jack was not wholly immune to a shift in behaviours. Accounts increasingly told of how he made startling appearances that continued to shock people, but he no longer attempted to physically harm his 'victims'. He demonstrated such inconsistent behaviours in Neath in November 1898 that one newspaper declared his actions to be 'very strange and unaccountable'. See *Western Mail*, 15th November 1898.

[74] See Anon., *Spring-Heeled Jack* (2008 reprint), p. 96.

[75] Katrina Navickas has highlighted how magistrates had similarly given credibility to the imaginary General Ludd by accepting and responding to the premise that such a figure might actually exist. See Navickas, 'The Search for "General Ludd"', pp. 284–5 and 293. Like the press and the police, the magistracy was at the forefront of contemporary efforts to reform popular cultures, especially as what had previously been viewed as customary practices became illegal. See Bushaway, *By Rite*, pp. 207–79.

regarded as a true criminal, more often as a foolish prankster in need of a stiff reprimand.

If not always a criminal, he was always a rebel who tacitly refuted the period's dominant discourse towards a taming of both popular cultures and masculinities. Lacking the allure (and safe temporal distance) of the reimagined eighteenth-century highwaymen he nevertheless shared something of their romanticised individuality by similarly asserting his free will to mischief and violence through bold action and cunning. Yet plebeian communities could not actively couple Spring-heeled Jack's anti-authoritarian performances to their own grudges in the same way they had with a leader figure like Captain Swing, not least because the press portrayal of Spring-heeled Jack as a threat to all seemed to have proven so convincingly persuasive to such a broad metropolitan audience.[76] Beyond this lies the difficult interpretative issue of plebeian silences. Any counter-hegemonic potential within folkloric thought and imagining was essentially implied, never stated. Whilst its persistence was itself a cause for uncertainty and unease, its challenge to dominant hegemonies and reforming cultures never extended far beyond the fact of its coexistence.

Finally, whilst radical appropriations of Spring-heeled Jack may have appeared weak and muted, hegemonic conservative applications were by no means secure. If his penny dreadful incarnations pandered to vicarious fantasies of violence and anti-authoritarianism, his numerous imitators served as a reminder that these fantasies could spill over into acting out in the real world. The channelling of these dark and tumultuous desires into vicarious fantasies contained within cheap literature or even newspaper reports could be read as another victory for the taming of a formerly boisterous popular culture. Rather than ritualised customary enactment, most people seemed content to internalise such urges and have them sated through commercial entertainments. Yet ultimately the inability to corrode these instincts or their popularity suggests this was a compromise at best. Internalisation did not equate to genuine reform, merely to a turning away from the external. An urge to Spring-heeled Jackery may have been left to reside in the imaginations of untold thousands.

---

[76] The struggle for interpretations of Spring-heeled Jack is considered in more detail in Chapter 7.

4

Spring-heeled Jack and Victorian Society

As with gender, issues of social class were intricately woven into the development and operation of Spring-heeled Jack's legend. This chapter firstly examines the way anti-aristocratic feelings informed both 'official' and popular interpretations of his suspected identity. At the same time the swirl of popular supernatural rumour that surrounded his name enabled the lower classes to be conceived and presented as a superstitious 'other' compared to the respectable bourgeoisie. Following from this, it then examines how social position informed the credibility (or not) of witnesses and victims and argues that it was only when middle-class witnesses spoke out that Spring-heeled Jack gained credibility. Thirdly, it uses the literary recreation of Spring-heeled Jack as a heroic and dashing aristocrat in the 1860s–70s to reflect on shifting class perceptions later in the century. These various considerations will be used to argue that Spring-heeled Jack provided an unusual lens through which differing elements of the social strata could view themselves and others, being a site for cross-class allegiances, as well as a means of reiterating bourgeois hegemonic ideals and of reinforcing social divisions.

Spring-heeled Jack and Perceptions of the Social 'Other'

There appears no evidence to suggest that Spring-heeled Jack was perceived to have held a grudge against any particular social group, for he attacked domestic servants, laundresses, craftsmen and the daughters of respectable business-men with equal impunity. Yet contemporaries were very quick to suspect that if Spring-heeled Jack was not a supernatural being then he was most likely a predatory aristocrat or gang of 'gentlemen' engaged in a malicious prank. These assumptions reflected a contemporary prejudice against the aristocracy by both the middling and labouring classes.[1] The emerging, dynamic middle classes who were simultaneously promoters and advertisements for their ideals of self-

---

[1] This chapter only obliquely touches upon the historiographical debate about when we can refer to the middle and working classes as emerging as self-conscious formulations. For interesting reflections on this see Cannadine, *Class in Britain*; Wahrman, *Imagining the Middle Class*; and Joyce, *Visions of the People*.

help, self-discipline, progress and competition were naturally opposed to what they viewed as aristocratic idleness, moral corruption and economic profligacy. Perceived as parasitic upon their urban and agrarian rents, the aristocracy shifted between country and city, especially for the London 'Season', with an air of extravagance that jarred with bourgeois notions of restraint and careful accumulation. Developing in the post-Napoleonic War period, a growing emphasis on urban etiquette and civility encouraged the portrayal of the young aristocratic man about town, the 'Regency "Corinthian"', as a latter-day rake, one whose life was filled with little more than 'dandyish display, indulgence in flesh and horseflesh, gambling, drinking bouts and brawling with … night watchmen'.[2] Contemporary works such as Pierce Egan's *Life in London* (1820–21) reinforced a view that London was a pleasure palace of debauchery and vice for wealthy young men. By the late 1820s what would be retrospectively recognised as a (proto-)Victorian sensibility of self-control and public deportment ensured there was mounting disapproval of behaviours that the middling sort associated with both 'plebeian workplace culture and Regency bucks'.[3]

It was not only the middle classes that disapproved. As indicated in Chapter 2, an anti-aristocratic tone informed much popular theatrical melodrama in this period.[4] Whilst the idea of the callous aristocrat preying on vulnerable women could be traced back to the likes of the Earl of Rochester and other seventeenth-century rakes, it was perhaps promoted less by observed realities than the demented aristocrats of late-eighteenth-century gothic novels and their cheap, plagiarised chapbook versions. Such stereotypes were perpetuated in the 1830s by illegal radical newspapers which reported on sex and violence amongst the highborn 'to illustrate aristocratic decadence'.[5] Spring-heeled Jack's aristocratic associations were formed in the immediate period after the crushed expectations of the 1832 Reform Act, when lower-class political activists still bore resentment towards the privileged aristocratic politicians who had been the authors of their disillusionment.

This anti-aristocratic tone was best captured by G. W. M. Reynolds' radical journalism and fiction, the latter achieving greater popularity than Dickens' works in the 1840s.[6] His serialised urban gothic epics, *The Mysteries of London* (1844–48) and *The Mysteries of the Court of London* (1848–56), may have followed the initial appearance of Spring-heeled Jack, but they spoke directly to the persistent and popular anti-aristocratic ethos in which he had emerged.

---

[2] Robinson, *Imagining London*, p. 17.

[3] Ibid. See Egan, *Life in London* (1821), and also Arnold, *City of Sin*; Linnane, *Lives of the English Rakes*; Peakman, *Lascivious Bodies*; Murray, *High Society in the Regency Period*; and Mason, *Making of Victorian Sexuality*.

[4] See John, *Dickens's Villains*, and Ledger, *Dickens and the Popular Radical Imagination*.

[5] Clark, *Women's Silence*, p. 112.

[6] Punter, *Literature of Terror*, vol. 1, p. 145.

The *Mysteries* have been described as 'fictional running indictments of the corruption of the British aristocracy'.[7] Possessing all the sadism and pornography that the gothic genre had long associated with a depraved aristocracy, these works demonised the upper classes into corrupt, vampiric monsters which fed upon the brutal exploitation of the poor.[8] In tone it was a continuation of that which had underpinned some of Spring-heeled Jack's more biting press reports of January 1838. As the *Penny Satirist* had joked, Spring-heeled Jack was a ghost sent 'to warn the sinful inhabitants of this land of the coming judgments of the Devil, for their awful selfishness and grasping greediness, by which they suck the blood of the poor, and fasten upon the produce of their industry with their savage claws'.[9]

Middle- and lower-class critics of the aristocracy found common allegiance in the popular notion that Spring-heeled Jack's activities in 1837–38 were the result of a wager by privileged 'gentlemen'. This strand of the legend was present from the first press reports on contemporary oral rumours. On 28th December 1837 the *Morning Chronicle* had claimed that the antics of 'Steel Jack' were part of 'a wager … to play off these freaks for a number of nights in nine different parishes without being apprehended'.[10] Reports in early-mid January 1838 stated 'some individuals … of … the higher ranks of life' had made a wager to appear in 'many of the villages near London in three different disguises – a ghost, a bear, and a devil'. Initially, the wager was said to involve a dare to simply 'enter gentlemen's gardens for the purpose of alarming the inmates of the house'. This had inadvertently led to seven ladies being robbed of their wits, if rumour was to be believed.[11] Aided by press exaggeration, the villainous intent of the gentleman's wager was quickly intensified. What had been unintended consequences were swiftly presented as the explicit purpose of a cruel bet, the aim not to simply trespass and frighten but to actually scare to death. As *The Examiner* reported on 14th January, the bet was of 'an even more grave nature' than previously expected, for 'if it be true [it] amounts to murder … the bet is that the monster

---

[7]   Ibid., p. 160.

[8]   For more on Reynolds' dichotomous social view of 'corrupt aristocrats and vicious criminals' see Mighall, *Geography of Victorian Gothic Fiction*, p. 55.

[9]   *Penny Satirist*, 20th January 1838, p. 2. This article also highlighted rumours of 'a wager between some wealthy scamps of aristocracy'.

[10]   *Morning Chronicle*, 28th December 1837.

[11]   *The Times*, 9th January 1838, p. 4.

shall kill six women in some given time'.[12] These attacks by a member or members of the gentry upon common folk could obviously be read as an explicit acting out of the rich preying upon the poor. Seemingly beyond the reach of the law and merely viewing the lower orders as the playthings of their callous sports and cruel wagers, the monstrous appearance adopted by these 'gentlemen' served as a reflection of the inhumanity which lurked beneath their frightening disguises.

If the idea of a gentleman's wager and prank appeared a little far-fetched it was at least a relatively more palatable explanation for Spring-heeled Jack's appearances for those who were unwilling to entertain the notion that a super-natural entity was stalking the metropolitan hinterlands. It enabled middle-class commentators to articulate their own sense of moral superiority by highlight-ing the inappropriate behaviours of these cruel 'gentlemen' (the press using the term with obvious lack of sincerity). Several newspapers carried accounts that gave credence to the rumour that the suburban ghost was actually a man of some means. Amidst the flurry of accounts received by John Cowen in the wake of his first announcement, *The Examiner* reprinted a claim that 'some individ-ual ('gentleman' he has been designated) drives about with a livery servant in a cab, and, throwing off a cloak, appears in these frightful forms'.[13] Similarly, 'A Resident of Paddington Green' had seen a figure dressed in white near his home. When chased the 'ghost' had leapt into a waiting cabriolet to escape his pursuers.[14] There was an unintended but potentially radical consequence to framing Spring-heeled Jack as an aristocrat. In the name of self-defence it tacitly gave the common man licence to set upon suspected wealthy individuals, revoking the usual social barriers and expected deferential relationship between the lower and upper classes.

Once the press ran with the idea of a gentleman's wager, Henry de La Poer Beresford, the third Marquis of Waterford, was swiftly appropriated into the evolving legend. The barely veiled assertions that he was the metropolitan Spring-heeled Jack of 1838 appear to have been a lazy supposition founded upon Waterford's public renown for drunkenness, vandalism and a propen-sity for violence. Waterford had accrued this damning reputation several years prior to the Spring-heeled Jack appearances, making him an easy target for press

---

[12] *The Examiner*, 14th January 1838, p. 27. The wager element remained a familiar component in Spring-heeled Jack's narrative template throughout the nineteenth century. It reappeared in Spring-heeled Jack's supposed manifestations in Sheffield in 1873 and Liverpool in 1887. In the latter the *Liverpool Citizen* claimed a person of some obvious wealth had 'a bet of a thousand pounds to one hundred' that those who wanted to take up the wager could not appear as Spring-heeled Jack 'without being caught and exposed'. See *Liverpool Citizen*, 29th October 1887, and also *Sheffield and Rotherham Independent*, 23rd May 1873, and the *Sheffield Times*, 31st May 1873.

[13] *The Examiner*, 14th January 1838, p. 27.

[14] *Morning Herald*, 16th January 1838.

condemnation of aristocratic male rowdiness. *The Examiner* had been particularly dogged in bringing reports of the Marquis' wayward activities to public attention.[15] Yet the paucity of evidence connecting him to Spring-heeled Jack meant that even this obvious opponent of the Marquis had to refer to the gentleman's wager as being the work of 'some persons of the Waterford class' who were entertaining themselves 'at the expense of decency and humanity', rather than the pranks of the man himself.[16]

His most outrageous activities had taken place at Melton Mowbray in April 1837. *The Examiner's* description of this incident as an 'unprovoked and wanton outrage' was exactly the terminology newspapers used to describe many of Spring-heeled Jack's attacks in early 1838.[17] Under the heading 'Aristocratic Sport at Melton', *The Examiner* reported how men of 'rank and fashion' had gathered to watch the Croxton Park Races. At three o'clock in the morning of Thursday 13th April the town had been awoken by Waterford leading a gang of 'gentlemen' in an assault upon the town constables. These unruly aristocratic thugs then proceeded to paint some house doors and an inn sign red, smashed a window and committed other sundry acts of vandalism. When the constables and the watch managed to apprehend one of the culprits and place him in the watch house, Waterford and some companions went to his rescue, threatening the gaolers with murder if the prisoner was not released. Fearing for their lives, the constables meekly complied. The next day special constables were sworn in but the rioting was repeated, this time not with paint but with the use of 'noise, oaths, and blackguard language like unto it has seldom been heard at any place,

---

[15]   When Waterford was found drunk in White Hart Street, Drury Lane, early one morning in May 1836, the newspaper made sure to mention that he had been 'surrounded by thieves and prostitutes'. See *The Examiner*, 22nd May 1836, p. 331.

[16]   *The Examiner*, 14th January 1838, p. 27.

[17]   *The Examiner*, 16th April 1837, p. 252.

and never before in the streets of Melton'.[18] Waterford escaped the town but a warrant was issued for his arrest.

His subsequent court case was passed up from the local magistrates to the Quarter Sessions, to the Leicester Assizes. Whilst this was indicative of the seriousness of the offence, particularly that of prison-breaking, it also hinted at a reluctance on the part of the judiciary to tackle the unruly behaviour of a marquis who, like many of the landed gentry, was himself a magistrate. *The Examiner* was convinced that these judicial manoeuvres afforded Waterford's legal representatives time to negotiate a more lenient settlement.[19] The paper's suspicions appear to have been justified, for when the case concluded in August 1838 Waterford and his companions were acquitted of the charge of rioting and convicted of the lesser charge of common assault. They were fined a hundred pounds; a rather paltry sum for such men of wealth.[20] Clearly disgusted by the outcome, *The Examiner* claimed it was evidence of one law for the rich, another for the poor. It noted that if 'poor ruffians' were inclined to mimic Waterford's assault on constables, his destruction of property, his attack on a local gaol and the freeing of a prisoner, 'they would soon learn the peculiar privileges of the aristocracy, and that what are high crimes in the poor are but … the sowing of wild oats in the rich'. It added that 'had men in working jackets indulged in the same frolics, as we see them termed, they would have been sent to the tread-mill

---

[18] Ibid. Waterford and his companions subsequently conducted another vandalising spree in Windsor in June 1837, breaking knockers from doors and throwing them through the windows of the houses. Some of them then attacked a constable who tried to stop them. Several members of the group also disfigured the statue of Henry VI at Eton College. Following publication of these activities in the *Morning Post*, Waterford claimed it was all lies. See *The Examiner*, 18th June 1837, pp. 387 and 394. It is worth noting that the *Morning Chronicle*'s early report on 'Steel Jack' in December 1837 was entitled 'Effects of Aristocratic Example'. It began by highlighting pranks that were rumoured to be the work of 'certain parties who have recently figured before the public in an unenviable character'. Its account of their destroying a statue, lighting firecrackers attached to the door knocker of a house on Royal Hill, Greenwich, and attempting to remove a pub sign all echoed Waterford's activities. Even if Waterford's gang was not directly responsible, the article's title implied that wayward aristocrats had set a bad example that others were now following. The article's shift onto the appearance of Steel Jack implicitly linked these acts of vandalism in Greenwich to the Lewisham scares, thereby prompting associations between aristocratic 'larks' and the character who would become Spring-heeled Jack. See 'Effects of Aristocratic Example', *Morning Chronicle*, 28th December 1837.

[19] See *The Examiner*, 18th June 1837, p. 387, and 16th July 1837, p. 461.

[20] *The Examiner* calculated that a fine of a hundred pounds for Waterford and his companions was 'about equivalent in effect to a fine of sixpence on a day labourer'. See 'Law for the Rich', *The Examiner*, 5th August 1838, p. 482.

for six months.'[21] The paper held out hope that Waterford would at least lose his right to act as a magistrate, having so disturbed the peace and flagrantly defied and humiliated the law enforcers at Melton.[22]

Despite the lack of any direct ties to the Spring-heeled Jack appearances, the association with Waterford only grew over time, particularly after his death in a riding accident in 1859. In an 1884 summary of the 1838 scare *All the Year Round* mentioned the Marquis of Waterford, although it admitted that 'not a shadow of proof could be ever adduced in support of this theory'. All it could do was reiterate that there had been a general belief that the scare was the result of 'several persons' from 'high families'.[23] Perhaps for want of a more plausible explanation, by the twentieth century the unsubstantiated assertions had started to harden into 'facts'.[24]

Yet if Spring-heeled Jack was used to berate a morally corrupt aristocracy he was also employed by the predominantly middle-class press to shape perceptions of the lower classes. Spring-heeled Jack spoke to fears about the veneer of modern society. As one contemporary writer put it, 'We look along the surface of society, and behold it illuminated by brilliant and beautiful lights; but if we venture to penetrate into its depths, we discover a whole universe of errors, wild fancies, fables, and fantastical creations, springing up perpetually out of a bottomless gulf of darkness.'[25] As with press reports on the persistence of popular belief in witchcraft, fortune telling, supernatural folklore and superstition, the recording of popular rumour and speculation surrounding Spring-heeled Jack was another way of simultaneously constructing and reinforcing that dark gulf between the social classes.[26] In this context, Spring-heeled Jack embodied a

[21] Ibid., p. 482. This was a popular theme for *The Examiner* where Waterford was concerned. See *The Examiner*, 8th July 1838. See also 'Law for the Rich', *The Examiner*, 9th December 1838. Similar sentiments were made in a fictional story about Spring-heeled Jack in 1888. When the hoaxer is caught and unmasked he is revealed to be the eldest son of the local baronet and lord of the manor. The story ends: 'It is to be hoped that Spring-heeled Jack's social position did not save him from the punishment he richly deserved.' See 'The Biter Bit', *Young Folks Paper*, 25th August 1888.

[22] *The Examiner* had to wait five years before it could report that moral justice had been restored. In November 1843 the paper noted that Waterford, having settled down to a life of respectability on his country estate in Tipperary, was now suffering vandalism on his own property. With barely concealed delight it added, 'If we remember rightly, the Marquis set a brilliant example of this sort of feat at Melton Mowbray some few years ago.' See *The Examiner*, 25th November 1843, p. 738.

[23] *All the Year Round*, 9th August 1884, p. 346.

[24] See Brewer, *Reader's Handbook*, p. 1038, and *Daily Mirror*, 5th January 1954, p. 9. This rather dated idea formed the central revelation in Haining, *Legend and Bizarre Crimes*.

[25] Augustus St John, *Education of the People*, p. 23.

[26] For more on this see Bell, *Magical Imagination*, Chapter 3.

disturbing creation dredged up from the murky depths of the popular imagination and articulated by its collective propensity for the supernatural.

As the mouthpiece of the educated middle classes, the respectable press, led, in circulation terms at least, by *The Times*, was quick to articulate differences of interpretation between plebeian explanations and the views respectable individuals were expected to embrace. This distinction was evident from early January 1838. In response to the stream of letters that followed in the wake of his first announcement, the Lord Mayor stated that 'it was evident that considerable terror had been excited by the appearance of some man or men in the outlets of the metropolis, in disguise, and that a great deal of mischief might arise from a pantomimic display at night'. This 'official' interpretation was followed by his dismissal of more fanciful notions as he announced that it was 'quite impossible that there could be any foundation for the report that the ghost performed the feats of a devil upon earth, by clawing and tearing the flesh and clothes off poor people'.[27] Yet newspaper accounts continued to carry reports, often from respected gentlemen, that 'the servant girls about Kensington, and Hammersmith, and Ealing, told dreadful stories of the ghost or devil'.[28] Such accounts reiterated that at the lower levels of society the mysterious attacker was neither viewed nor accepted as a disguised gentleman but as something supernatural.

The Spring-heeled Jack scares allowed middle-class journalists to draw correlations between a host of negative traits associated with the lower classes. As a later commentator wrote, superstition 'will always be found in company with ignorance' which tended to be found 'in ... the hovels of the poor'.[29] This writer claimed domestic servants adored supernatural interpretations of nocturnal noises in their employers' residence, asserting that 'such tales constitute the food on which their minds exist; and they are angry with anyone who should snatch them from a dark and "fearful joy," and place them in the light of reason ... to them truth is an insipid thing'. He went so far as to claim that 'Life would lose all its charm' for them if they were deprived of their belief in the supernatural.[30] By comparison, when newspapers referred to Spring-heeled Jack as a 'ghost', they tended to bound the word within quotation marks, though it should be noted that this was not done consistently across all publications or even within the same article. The use of quotation marks suggested an ironic distancing from the apparent credulity of the masses whose collective ignorance and superstition rendered them resistant to the period's emphasis on reason and intellect. To

---

[27] *Morning Chronicle*, 11th January 1838.
[28] *The Times*, 9th January 1838, p. 4.
[29] Ollier, 'Few Passages on Dreams', p. 504.
[30] Ibid., p. 507.

drive the point home one of the *Morning Herald*'s first reports on the suburban ghost was entitled 'Credulity and Superstition; or a Tale of Diablerie'.[31]

Through these approaches the press implicitly differentiated their readership from the popular mindset upon which they reported. As such, the 'popular' was not simply what people actually did or believed; it was also a construction of journalistic discourse that was layered over such activities. Negatively associated with the lower classes, it implied a propensity towards unreasoned, sensational-ised interpretations of phenomena and collectively irrational responses to them.[32] The way in which people were liable to interpret Spring-heeled Jack scares became one means by which they could perceive their own social standing and their relationship to a supposedly rational, enlightened modernity. Therefore, whilst being initially generated by popular rumours, middle-class journalistic interpretations of Spring-heeled Jack were far from detached reflections on a popular cultural phenomenon; they were intricately implicated in the legend's construction, interpretation and dynamics.[33]

Spring-heeled Jack's negative inferences upon the nature of the upper and lower classes suggest he was a cultural device which was best managed by the middle classes for their own ends. He served to articulate issues and anxieties surrounding social division and control. Press reports do not seem to have presented Spring-heeled as a 'folk devil' in the sociological sense of a demonised scapegoat deemed threatening to dominant hegemonic values.[34] He was too often at the geographical and cultural margins to be considered a real threat. Far from a simple hysterical panic, Spring-heeled Jack offered educated elites an opportunity to publicly promote their epistemological understanding of the world, one that increasingly denounced traditional supernatural views in favour of rational, scientific or at least pseudo-scientific interpretations.[35]

Class and the Credibility of Accounts

Given these crude and somewhat vague perceptions of 'class' differences, it is not surprising to find that the social standing of Spring-heeled Jack's witnesses and victims informed the credibility of their accounts. Based on a perception of the lower classes as mired in superstitious ignorance, the press implicitly distrusted

---

[31] *Morning Herald*, 10th January 1838.
[32] For contemporary concerns about the masses see Mackay, *Extraordinary Popular Delusions*. See also Melville Logan, 'Popularity of Popular Delusions'.
[33] These issues will be explored in more depth in Chapter 7.
[34] See Cohen, *Folk Devils and Moral Panics*, and Goode and Ben-Yehuda, *Moral Panics*.
[35] See McCorristine, *Spectres of the Self*, and Bown, Burdett and Thurschwell, *Victorian Supernatural*.

testimony from the likes of domestic servants and treated such cases with a reflexive scepticism. Cowen, the Lord Mayor of the City of London, similarly dismissed the welter of plebeian accounts as the result of 'the greatest exaggerations' and stated that he withheld his belief in statements regarding both the nature of the attacker and the 'ghost' having frightened so many women to death. When he referred to an account from an 'authority which he could not question', an incident involving an attack on the servant 'of a gentleman who resided near his house at Forest Hill', he seemed to allude to the information having derived from this respectable neighbour rather than a trusted domestic servant of his own.[36]

This continued throughout the century. David Clarke has illustrated something similar in the 'Park Ghost' Spring-heeled Jack scare in Sheffield in May 1873. Whilst initial rumours of a ghost haunting the area around the Cholera Monument came from female, working-class sources, they were prone to being dismissed as mere tittle-tattle. It was only when the ghost shifted its activities to the nearby Norfolk Road that police became more responsive. Once its middle-class residents were willing to give credence to the rumours, the stories became more credible, spreading across the city and nightly attracting crowds of people hoping to catch sight of the ghost.[37]

Nowhere was this issue of middle-class respectability bolstering the legend of Spring-heeled Jack more apparent than in the two most publicised attacks in February 1838. The assault on Jane Alsop, the daughter of 'a gentleman of considerable property', led to widespread press coverage, a magistrate's investigation and the questioning of suspects.[38] The attack a week later on Lucy Scales, the sister of a 'respectable butcher', met with a more cursory response from both media and magistrates.[39] Lea, the magistrate's investigator, appears to have been a very able detective, but he largely conducted his inquiries into the Scales attack off the back of his attempts to solve the Alsop case. The Alsop case was newsworthy for a number of reasons. Prior to the Alsop family's appearance before the Lambeth Street magistrates the press was inclined to dismiss the actions of Spring-heeled Jack as 'more the effect of imagination than reality'. It was the 'authentic particulars' of the attack 'on a respectable young lady', an identifiable individual, which raised Spring-heeled Jack above the morass of rumour and 'remove[d] all doubt on the subject'.[40] The emphasis on the Alsops' respectability was a particularly important distinction. They risked considerable social

---

36   *The Examiner*, 14th January 1838, p. 27.
37   Clarke, 'Unmasking Spring-heeled Jack', p. 37.
38   See *Morning Chronicle*, 22nd February 1838; 'Gross Outrage on a Young Lady', *John Bull*, 25th February 1838; and 'The Ghost Again', *Bell's Life in London*, 25th February 1838.
39   *Morning Chronicle*, 8th March 1838. See also *Morning Post*, 7th March 1838.
40   *The Times*, 22nd February 1838, p. 6.

embarrassment by bringing news of the assault before the magistrates, especially when it was entwined with the name of Spring-heeled Jack, a character being derided in the respectable press as a superstitious nonsense. The fact that Mr Alsop and his three daughters were all prepared to give a similar account added to their credibility as reliable witnesses. Although he would later question Jane's interpretation of her assailant's appearance, Lea's report into the incident stated that he 'was perfectly satisfied of the truth of the statement of Miss Alsop as to the violence inflicted upon her by the person she described; indeed, the whole family, all of whom had seen him, agreed precisely in the description.'[41]

There seems a certain irony to the fact that it took an attack by what Lea claimed to be a drunken imitator and the subsequent testimony of a respectable family to actually make Spring-heeled Jack a more credible threat.[42] As Lea put it, 'The character [of Spring-heeled Jack] was now assumed by many thoughtless young men, who considered it a good lark.'[43] Yet at the same time the Alsops' testimony supported the predominant journalistic interpretation that Spring-heeled Jack was nothing but a vicious prankster. For all her claims about fire-breathing and claws, Jane Alsop's assailant was not the supernatural creature of rumour but clearly a disguised man who had first appeared at their gate in such a manner as to convince her that he was a policeman. The Alsops' account and its press coverage made the threat real whilst countering wilder popular interpretations of what Spring-heeled Jack was. This was also true in the case of the key suspects. Rather than arresting a violent aristocrat spurred on by a gentleman's wager, the investigation identified far less sensational culprits in Mr Payne and Mr Millbank, a couple of drunken craftsmen. The aristocratic predator appears to have been a speculative fantasy drawn from popular prejudices shaped by melodrama and the radical press. When it came to the mundane nature of having to solve the crime, expectation and experience directed the investigators towards the lower classes rather than the upper.[44]

The Teignmouth case of 29th March 1847 represented the most explicit articulation of social differences in a Spring-heeled Jack encounter. It was this

---

[41] *The Times*, 23rd February 1838, p. 7.

[42] During this hearing Mr Guard, one of the policemen investigating the attack, announced he had been contacted by 'a gentleman ... who holds a situation in the Bank of England' and was a neighbour of the Alsops. This gentleman had claimed 'he would be able to produce the parties implicated in the outrage in a day or two'. Guard's willingness to introduce this rather vague assertion into the proceedings seemed at least implicitly informed by the man's respected position as much as any particular knowledge or insight he had to offer. See *Morning Chronicle*, 28th February 1838, p. 7.

[43] *The Times*, 23rd February 1838, p. 7.

[44] See *The Times*, 2nd March 1838, p. 7. The only time an imitator from a relatively distinguished social background was caught and punished was in the Guernsey case in 1891. See *Daily News*, 16th September 1891, and *Birmingham Daily Post*, 19th September 1891.

class dynamic that made the trial (and Spring-heeled Jack's name) briefly news-worthy once again. As with all cases that came before the magistrates, this was another incident of an imitator assuming Spring-heeled Jack's mantle. As the *Hampshire Telegraph* wrongly reported, the accused was 'charged ... with playing the disgraceful character of "Spring-heeled Jack"'.[45] Imitating Spring-heeled Jack was not in itself a crime. Whilst described in the *Lady's Newspaper* as 'a "Spring-heeled Jack" investigation', this was actually an assault trial. The suspect, Captain Finch, a respected, sixty-year-old ex-military officer, was said to have molested several women during the previous winter, and one, a domestic servant, had brought an accusation of assault against him. At the opening of proceedings the complainant's representative, Mr Tucker, underlined the social differentiation, his client being the servant of a local lady who 'belonged to the humblest rank', whilst 'the defendant, Captain Finch, had been considered highly respectable'. Tucker firmly appreciated his dilemma: 'Should he not succeed in establish-ing the charge, the effect of the girl's evidence might prejudice her through life; should he succeed, the moral character of one who had hitherto moved as a gentleman would be blasted.'[46] Class was clearly an underlying factor in the trial, but for both the accused and the victim it was closely entwined with, and expressed in terms of, moral standing and public reputation rather than crude socio-economic distinctions.

The defendant, described only as 'the servant of Miss Morgan', had been assaulted twice at night in January by 'a man disguised in a skin coat' and wearing a horned mask. She had identified Finch as her assailant and a witness supported her claim by testifying that he had seen Finch earlier the same night by the Teignmouth Bridge in a similar disguise. For his part, Finch drew upon a number of respectable witnesses to aid his defence. His physician, Dr Withers, testified to Finch's poor health, whilst two majors and a captain testified that they knew Finch well, and had never known him to be outside after four o'clock in the afternoon. One of these individuals, Major Stevenson, had even visited Finch on the day of one of the assaults. The case lasted several hours, and Mr Kelson, one of the magistrates, expressed the 'great difficulty and responsibility' they faced. He noted that the 'evidence of so many gentlemen as to the general character and high standing of Captain Finch ... was of material import', but the accused lacked a demonstrable alibi. By contrast, the court was inclined to value the servant girl's claims about his identity, she 'having seen him with and without the disguise'. The magistrate admitted it was his 'painful duty' to find against Finch, for he was himself 'a brother officer' and appreciated the damage such a

---

[45] *Hampshire Telegraph*, 10th April 1847, p. 1.
[46] *Lady's Newspaper*, 3rd April 1847, p. 321. See also *Daily News*, 29th March 1847.

decision would do to Finch's reputation. His five pounds fine was something of a triviality compared to his ruined social respectability.[47]

Given this appealing narrative of the honest poor woman triumphing against the vicious man who had attempted to hide behind his respectability, infirmity and monstrous disguise, it is not surprising that the Chartist newspaper, the *Northern Star*, reported on it. It gave a précised account of the case and repeated that the magistrates had 'expressed pain at finding an old soldier guilty of such an assault, but there was no material refutation to [the] complainant's evidence.' It also noted that the servant had 'thanked the bench for their impartiality'.[48] In an inversion of the newsworthiness of the Alsop case, what drew the press to this courtroom drama was the fact that the magistrates, despite an acute appreciation of the class dimensions, ultimately sided with the domestic servant over the respected officer.[49]

Remaking Spring-heeled Jack as Aristocratic Hero

The decade of Spring-heeled Jack's emergence and development, 1838–48, was a crucible of social tensions marked by the consequences of parliamentary reform, responses to the New Poor Law, the hopes and failures of Owenite trade unionism, the mass demonstrations and overt class rhetoric of Chartism, and the bitterness of work relations and riots in the 'hungry forties'.[50] By comparison, the second half of the nineteenth century experienced a relative decline in such bombastic class antagonism. The anti-aristocratic ethos that had informed early theories about Spring-heeled Jack also became more muted as the developing working classes increasingly viewed the middle, not the upper, classes as their paternalistic protectors or their most immediate social adversary. That said, one's claims about the dampening of class tensions in Spring-heeled Jack encounters in the second half of the century are necessarily limited by the fact that later accounts tend to be sketchier and lacking in the telling details of reports from

---

[47] *Lady's Newspaper*, 3rd April 1847, p. 321.

[48] *Northern Star*, 3rd April 1847, p. 6. A shorter account in *Bell's Life in London*, 4th April 1847, p. 3, wrongly gave the servant's name as Morgan, her employer's name.

[49] The assault on Mrs Ann Amsinck by James Painter in Kilburn, London, in March 1838 offers an interesting social inversion to this case. Amsinck, described as 'a most respectable married lady', demonstrated feisty resistance to Painter who had dressed up as a ghost to scare her. When Painter fled, Amsinck pursued him into his employer's house nearby and, according to Painter, hit him in the face. Amsinck's actions seem to have been at least partly motivated by a respectable woman taking offence at the insolence of a young footman. In this case the class dimension seemed to have counteracted the more familiar dynamic of male 'Spring-heeled Jack' impersonators intimidating female victims. See 'Capture of Spring-heeled Jack', *Morning Post*, 4th April 1838.

[50] See Vernon, *Politics and the People*, and Royle, *Revolutionary Britannia*.

the 1830s and 1840s. Yet Spring-heeled Jack's reimagining as a heroic aristocratic figure in the penny serials of the late 1860s and 1870s suggests there was a perceptual shift taking place, at least within the imaginary space of cheap fiction.

Published by the Newsagents Publishing Company, the anonymously authored *Spring-heel'd Jack: The Terror of London* ran between 1864 and 1867. Rather than the villainous creature of 1838, he was reimagined as a costumed gentleman of means who took it upon himself to protect the poor and weak. This shift was evident from the first issue. The front cover depicted a man dressed in rather archaic black clothes and cloak, wearing a white face mask and knee-high leather riding boots. The back cover's promotional blurb declared, 'Whereas, a little over a quarter of a century ago, a person known to the police as Spring-Heeled Jack did frighten and cause the death of several persons, the daring deeds and startling adventures of this wonderful man will be published in weekly numbers.'[51] The anonymous author spun out a number of subplots into which Spring-heeled Jack intermittently intervened. In one storyline he saves a lower-class woman from Ralph Grasper, her clerk husband's employer, who sought to blackmail her into surrendering herself to him. In another he threatens to take a bullying, drunken landlord to hell if he does not become a dutiful husband and abstain from alcohol.

One could read this new Spring-heeled Jack as an advocate of sobriety and moral reform, a mouthpiece for contemporary bourgeois platitudes about morality and self-control. Yet his aristocratic background and his disdain for the law made him an awkward character for bourgeois appropriation. As the hero notes in a moment of self-reflection, 'I know, as well as anyone, that this conduct ill becomes a gentleman, but … it is part of my nature to frighten people half out of their wits.'[52] Yet his propensity for violence, something seized upon as part of a bourgeois moral panic about the influence of such literature on working-class youths, was exactly what appealed to his predominantly plebeian readership. The vicarious enacting of violence against authority figures, the defence of the honest poor against the corrupt rich, and the valuing of popular justice over the law had long informed popular ballads, songs, melodrama and even the predominantly nocturnal activities of the blacken-faced saboteurs of General Ludd and Captain Swing.

In the conclusion to the episodic storyline Spring-heeled Jack fights with the blackmailer Ralph Grasper on the roof of a house, and Grasper falls to his death. As Spring-heeled Jack leaves the house he is seized by a passing watchman and

---

[51] Anon., *Spring-Heel'd Jack* (1867). Literary transitions had also been witnessed in the 'penny bloods' of the 1840s. The aristocratic vampire Sir Francis Varney gradually evolved into a more sympathetic character as his serial progressed. See Rymer, *Varney the Vampyre*.

[52] Anon., *Spring-Heel'd Jack* (1867), p. 307.

his mask slips. In a blatant plot contrivance the watchman recognises him, having worked as a servant of the hero's family in his youth. The man shouts, 'Spring-heeled Jack! … The Mar', before Spring-heeled Jack punches him and escapes.[53] Presumably the 'Mar' would have become 'Marquis', alluding back to the earlier associations with Waterford. In an abrupt ending Spring-heeled Jack returns to his hotel, gathers his valuables and escapes to the coast in a post-chaise, pursued by the police. Just as they think they have captured him on an outcrop of rocks, he takes a daring leap into the sea and escapes on a ship bound for Spain.

The aristocratic background alluded to through this series became even more central to a later penny series of the same name from 1878 to 1879. First published in the *Boy's Standard*, this story continued with the theme of Spring-heeled Jack as a heroic masked avenger. Whilst the earlier series had emphasised that the protagonist was a wholly different person to the one who terrorised London in 1838, this later series was founded on the conceit that it was based on Spring-heeled Jack's journal or confession, one which offers a sympathetic re-reading of his actions in early 1838 (incorrectly stated throughout this storyline as having occurred in early 1837). In this series Spring-heeled Jack is identified from the beginning as Jack Dacre, the son of a baronet and heir to Dacre Hall in Sussex. Jack's father, Sidney, had been a younger son of a baronet and had gone to India to make a fortune. When Sidney's father and older brothers die he returns to claim the title, but he and his wife are drowned in a shipwreck off the English coast. There are only two survivors, Jack and Ned Chump, the faithful old sailor who rescued him. Being a child, Jack is disinherited by Michael Dacre, his father's first cousin who claims the baronetcy and the hall. With rather contrived plotting, the only person who had witnessed the marriage of Jack's parents in India was Alfred Morgan, a clerk to whom Jack's father had entrusted his Indian plantations. With proof of Jack's parents' marriage having been lost in the shipwreck, the villainous Morgan agrees to withhold knowledge of the marriage if Michael Dacre will give him the plantations. Michael, formerly the estate's steward, agrees so as to keep his title. He then hires an assassin to kill Jack, but the youth escapes by leaping from Dacre Hall's tower into the moat. This daring act leads Michael to refer to Jack as 'Master Spring-Heels', a name he subsequently adopts as his alter ego.[54]

With Ned as his loyal lower-class retainer, Jack starts a campaign to harass Michael, adopting the moral purpose of traditional ghosts to haunt the guilty. His plan is to prevent Michael from collecting the rents from his various tenants in London and in southern England by stealing them in the guise of Spring-heeled Jack. Pandering to his predominantly plebeian readership, the

---

[53] Ibid., p. 318.
[54] Anon., *Spring-Heeled Jack* (2008 reprint), p. 24.

anonymous author draws a clear moralised distinction between Ned Chump and Jack Dacre. Having 'the sailor's natural respect for honesty', Ned dislikes the idea of theft. By comparison, Jack 'had been brought up under the shadow of the East India Company' and believed 'pillage and robbery seemed to be the right of the well-born'. Acculturated into this world view by his father's associates, 'his moral sense was entirely warped'.[55] They go to Southampton to construct the spring-heeled boots, and Jack then fashions a disguise in the vein of 'the theatrical Mephistopheles', the devilish apparel intended to 'strike terror into the guilty breast of his cousin.'[56]

Jack's own issues of disinheritance and the evil manipulations of (older) relatives are echoed in his first adventure as Spring-heeled Jack. Confronting one of the Dacre tenants at a Dorking farm, he discovers that the wicked farmer had hidden his brother's will upon his death so that his niece would not obtain the farm, and it would pass to him. Somewhat melodramatically, the girl is chained up in a room in the farmhouse, and whilst the appearance of Spring-heeled Jack is sufficient to unhinge the farmer's mind, the girl is not frightened by him. The farmer's deception is revealed when Jack leaves the girl and the will at the doorstep of a local Justice of the Peace. Jack takes the farmer's money and leaves a receipt for Michael signed 'Spring-heeled Jack'. He continues this campaign by pursuing Michael to London and stealing rents there too. It is these activities, aimed at persecuting the deceitful Michael and Alfred Morgan, which serve as an explanation for Spring-heeled Jack's metropolitan appearances in 1838. In a later episode Jack has fallen in love with the daughter of a baronet and general and becomes involved in yet another plot revolving around inheritance. The general's wife (the girl's stepmother) and a servant attempt to murder the daughter, for she is destined to inherit her father's fortune unless she dies before him. As such, the issue of rightful inheritance, devious elder usurpers, and the importance of wills and legal documentation to prove the truth form leitmotifs throughout the story. Again, Spring-heeled Jack's devilish appearance is used to extract a confession from the guilty, and, having saved the girl, he departs. In a final confrontation at Dacre Hall he takes Morgan's papers and escapes, leaving the man so tormented by the constant harassment that the villainous clerk hangs himself. With written proof of his parents' marriage and therefore his rightful inheritance, Jack exposes Michael's fraud, and the usurper is forced to leave the country. Jack is then able to reveal that he was the demonic figure who saved the general's daughter, and the story concludes with their happy marriage.

[55] Ibid., p. 30.
[56] Ibid., p. 33.

The question that arises from these serials is why did the aristocratic Spring-heeled Jack shift from predatory villain to champion of the weak in this period, at least in penny fiction?

Of course, the transition from historical criminal to (literary) folk hero was not new. Spring-heeled Jack followed a trajectory previously traced by more plebeian characters such as Dick Turpin and Jack Sheppard. Such cultural metamorphosis was undoubtedly aided by temporal distancing. By the late 1860s Victorians were a generation removed from the original scare of 1837–38, and Spring-heeled Jack, becoming malleable in the collective memory, was more prone to being transformed from a historical to a legendary figure. By the 1860s he had lost many of his most vicious aspects, transforming from a clawed, fire-breathing monster to a mischievous prankster. Yet this in itself does not explain why the Spring-heeled Jack of penny fiction was remade as a favourable aristocratic hero, especially after the negative associations with predatory 'gentlemen' in 1838.

There are a number of influences upon this transformation. One involves changing plebeian perceptions of the upper and middle classes. The 1832 Reform Act may have marked an important symbolic change for the middle classes, but it hardly confirmed the start of a 'bourgeois century'. As contemporaries such as William Cobden observed, the English remained 'a servile, aristocracy-loving, lord-ridden people'.[57] The period between 1850 and 1880 witnessed a protracted incorporating of the wealthiest sections of the upper middle classes into a governing elite rather than the relinquishing of control to bourgeois impostors.[58] Yet regardless of these historical realities, the popular perception was of an increasingly assertive and intrusive middle class and a concurrent growing remoteness on the part of the upper classes. The middle classes' efforts to improve Victorian society encroached upon working-class lives as they led attempts to reform and rationalise disreputable aspects of popular culture and custom such as blood sports, bare-knuckle boxing, gambling and drinking, activities that the Regency gentry had previously patronised and indulged in too.[59] The ending or modification of many of these activities meant from the mid century regular contact between the upper and lower classes declined. This was furthered by the fact that the Victorian aristocracy were not invested in reform efforts or philanthropy to the same degree as the middle classes.

Compared with daily encounters with an authoritative middle class (in the form of employers, educators, magistrates, philanthropists and administrators

---

[57] See Bedarida, *Social History of England*, p. 41.
[58] See Royle, *Modern Britain*, pp. 116–17.
[59] See Beaven, *Leisure, Citizenship and Working-Class Men*; Huggins, *Victorians and Sport*; Golby and Purdue, *Civilisation of the Crowd*; Holt, *Sport and the British*, pp. 12–73; and Bushaway, *By Rite*.

of the Poor Law), this general remoteness of the aristocracy from most people's quotidian experiences enabled them to be appropriated as romanticised figures of fantasy. This was enhanced by minor aristocrats such as marquis and baronets no longer being associated with metropolitan Regency rowdiness but, having retreated to their country estates, with an imagined rural idyll, as Britain evolved into an increasingly urbanised society. Whereas mid-century urban social inves- tigation seemed to encourage tensions between the middle and working classes, generating fears about moral and public health threats on the one hand, the restrictive supervision and control of labouring peoples' lives on the other, the aristocracy were able to undergo a popular fictional re-visioning into a protective and paternalistic role.[60] This fantasy seemed to find its most symbolic depiction in the striving of a masked aristocratic avenger intent on righting wrongs. The protagonists of the Spring-heeled Jack serials were appealingly anachronistic heroes in what was perceived (and portrayed) as an increasingly bourgeois age. Unlike the systematic and structural changes and regulation that various levels of Victorian governance were gradually introducing, Spring-heeled Jack, as an aristocratic vigilante, dealt with issues in a personal and dynamic way, correct- ing individual injustices with his daring and, if needs be, his fists.[61] This same spirited individualism informed the attraction of penny dreadful highwaymen, their disregard for the law and its enforcers having a vicarious appeal to indi- vidual agency in a society marked by increasing restriction and restraint. By comparison with such dashing aristocratic heroes, the conniving villains were often colourless characters who hid behind the law or a gloss of social respect- ability, people like the white-collar administrator Alfred Morgan or the corrupt employer Ralph Grasper.

The stories also appeared to be responsive to current events. The issues of deception and fraud surrounding the inheritance of a baronetcy in Spring- heeled Jack's 1878–79 serial resonated with the sensationalised legal case of the Tichborne claimant. This real story of aristocratic imposture ran for almost a decade. In 1865 Arthur Orton, a London-born butcher living in New South Wales, Australia, claimed to be Roger Tichborne, the heir to the Tichborne baronetcy and fortune, who had disappeared at sea in 1854. Managing to convince some people (including Roger's own mother) but not others, the affair

---

[60] The idea of the socially concerned young aristocrat (and the issue of rightful inheritance) was also found in more respectable novels of the period such as Benjamin Disraeli's *Sybil, or The Two Nations* (1845).

[61] In this context Spring-heeled Jack served as a predecessor to other masked avengers and proto- superhero aristocrats with a penchant for disguise, most obviously Baroness Emmuska Orczy's *The Scarlet Pimpernel* (first performed as a play in 1903); Marcel Allain and Pierre Souvestre's more morally ambiguous *Fantomas* (1911); Johnston McCulley's *Zorro* (1919); Lee Falk's *The Phantom* (1936); and Bob Kane's *Batman* (1939).

eventually evolved into two lengthy trials that lasted between 1871 and 1874. Orton's claim was firstly contested and, having lost the case, he then had to stand trial for perjury. The extensive press interest suggests the popular imagination was taken by the aristocratic intrigue and the juxtaposition between the worlds of the lower and upper classes, the latter perhaps serving as further evidence of their perceived remoteness from one another.[62]

Alongside these broader historical developments there were influences derived from the literary format in which these stories appeared. Spring-heeled Jack's literary transformation was arguably the result of efforts to bring the character into line with conventions that cynical publishers knew to be popular with young readers. The most popular penny dreadfuls tended to be those 'which invested with knightly qualities the knave of the *Newgate Calendar*'.[63] It is worth noting that in both serials the aristocratic protagonist could not be simply presented as a normal baronet or marquis. To make a connection with a predominantly plebeian readership it required the aristocrat, at least temporarily, to be rendered an honourable knave. Spring-heeled Jack's 1878 serial certainly reflected what E. S. Turner termed the 'one basic plot running through the Gothic thrillers', a scenario that became 'the basic plot of the nineteenth century ... that of the young and rightful heir deprived of his birthright by evil-scheming relatives or guardians'.[64]

The value of such a device to penny dreadful hacks was obvious. In terms of plot mechanics it created adversity and drama for the hero, gave him a villain- ous adversary, and yet always offered a convenient *deus ex machina* at the end, the restoration of a rightful inheritance guaranteeing a neat and upbeat conclu- sion to a story that may suddenly face cancellation when sales dipped too low. In being denied his potential power and position the nobleman was laid low, thereby obtaining some awareness of the victimisation and hardship that existed for the poor and powerless. His disinherited state made him a kindred victim of the corruption that oppressed the lower orders and provided him with the necessary motivation to become that familiar penny dreadful protagonist, the roguish hero. His willingness to oppose injustices, even if it made him an outlaw, also made him truly noble in moral, not just social, terms. As both a baronet- in-waiting and a roguish highwayman figure, the literary Spring-heeled Jack of the 1860s and 1870s encapsulated an intriguing hybridity of high and low, the respectable and the rough. What made Jack Dacre such an appealing fictional hero was a boldness, forged from innate aristocratic arrogance and self-belief, which would not permit him to be crushed by misfortunes. It is hard to believe

---

[62] See McWilliam, *Tichborne Claimant*.
[63] Turner, *Boys will be Boys*, p. 46.
[64] Ibid., p. 18.

that this positive message of determination and individual agency did not speak to the daily circumstances of many plebeian readers' lives.

Bourgeois critics appear to have been deaf to such appeals. For them the very format in which Spring-heeled Jack's literary adventures were published was embroiled in issues of class perception. The reinvented Spring-heeled Jack found himself in the company of fictionalised highwaymen and street arabs, penny dreadful characters who symbolised all that was wrong with the reading tastes of the lower classes and the dangerous desires such stories supposedly stirred within them. As the journalist and self-proclaimed amateur social investigator James Greenwood put it, works such as *Spring-heeled Jack*, *Tyburn Dick* and *The Black Knight of the Road* all contained a 'poison' which served as 'open encouragers of boy highwaymen' by exciting youthful minds to mimic such 'daring exploits'.[65] Spring-heeled Jack's inclination towards violence, his breaking into private properties and taunting or brawling with law enforcers seemed to embody the basest instincts of the 'mob'. Bourgeois commentators may have attempted to use penny dreadfuls that glorified the outlaw as a site for reinforcing socio-cultural divides, but the moral panics that flared up with regard to such literature in the late 1860s and early 1890s (given his popularity as a penny dreadful character, Spring-heeled Jack found himself implicated in both) also spoke of fears that those boundaries were too permeable.[66] As Greenwood put it, this 'pen poison finds customers at heights above its natural low and foul waterline ... How otherwise is it accountable that at least a quarter of a million of these penny numbers are sold weekly?'[67] Such cross-cultural transferences and communications between 'high' and 'low' resulted in an apparently undesirable expansion of the 'popular'. In this context the literary appeal of Spring-heeled Jack, one of the most colourful characters in a penny dreadful gallery of rogues, threatened an insidious undermining of notions of an impervious bourgeois respectability.

Spring-heeled Jack provided an unusual cultural phenomenon through which different elements of early-Victorian society could imagine and articulate a sense of social self and otherness. This discourse rarely used the language of 'class'. As seen throughout this chapter, social distinctions were more frequently expressed through crude and highly moralised judgements formulated around dichotomies of wealth/greed and poverty/ignorance. Although used to indicate distinctions, even divisions between classes, Spring-heeled Jack more frequently served as an imaginative site upon which social groups could potentially align themselves against a third element. Such formulations were contextually contingent and therefore frequently contradictory. The mercurial depictions and interpretations

---

[65] See Greenwood, *Wilds of London*, p. 89. See also *St James Magazine*, April 1869.
[66] For more on this see Springhall, *Youth, Popular Culture and Moral Panics*, pp. 71–97.
[67] See Greenwood, *Seven Curses of London*, pp. 91–2.

of Spring-heeled Jack can be treated as an example of the monstrous hybridity one gets when different classes communicate, or fail to communicate, through a common trope.

Emerging in a period of heightened social tensions, one can see hegemonic and counter-hegemonic urges within Spring-heeled Jack. Popular culture and, more nebulously, popular mentalities were embattled on a number of fronts, witnessing campaigns that sought to moderate, modify and regulate customary practices and to reform popular thought. This in turn was part of a broader trend towards increasing societal constraint, the slow maturing of the controlling, institutionalised Victorian society of the factory, workhouse, asylum, prison and school.[68] In such circumstances it would perhaps be tempting to read Spring-heeled Jack as a symbol of vicarious resistance to constraint. On whatever register one wished to place him Spring-heeled Jack personified anti-authoritarianism. He was opposed to religious authority as a demon, scientific authority as a contemporary spectre, and legal authority as a malicious criminal. The spontaneity of his manifestations and the impromptu ghost hunts inspired by them easily circumvented the increasingly systematic constraints that granted social elites a sense of order and control, at least until crowds started to congregate on consecutive nights and the police were then able to anticipate their gathering. This seemed to be bolstered by his obvious allusion to popular ideas of both ghosts and the devil in a period when traditional notions of the supernatural were being rejected. Both of these supernatural tropes had long been used to express and imaginatively right the injustices against the poor in songs, ballads and stories.[69] Equally, if we are to place any faith in the rumours about an aristocratic wager, then Spring-heeled Jack could be read as resistance by a group of young aristocrats against a bourgeois reform of manners.[70] Their actions, suggestive of an appropriation of the mischievous, knockabout protest customary culture of disguise and assault, made them genuine lords of misrule.

Yet such an interpretation does not tally with contemporary accounts and ultimately rings false. Spring-heeled Jack caused disruption but he rarely provided a carnivalesque release of plebeian tensions. Even when he was not attacking plebeian communities, most of his victims tended to be drawn from the lower echelons of Victorian society. For all his later literary recreations, in 'real' encounters Spring-heeled Jack was never perceived as a champion of the people.

---

[68] See Wiener, *Reconstructing the Criminal*; Foucault, *Madness and Civilization* and *Discipline and Punish*; and Goodlad, 'Beyond the Panopticon'.

[69] See Bell, *Magical Imagination*, pp. 192–226, and Handley, *Visions of an Unseen World*.

[70] The promotion of public and civil conduct in Victorian cities did not end the idea of the callous aristocratic libertine. It found renewed expression as one of the many theories put forward to account for Jack the Ripper's nature and identity in 1888. See Frayling, 'The House that Jack Built', pp. 13–16.

He was more often constructed as the threatening outsider who encouraged the delineating and reinforcement of communal norms and boundaries. At the same time his individuality, assertiveness and energy formed a distorted reflection of the hallmark qualities that became the modernising, Victorian bourgeois ideal. These very qualities set Spring-heeled Jack at odds with the increasingly intrusive, restrictive and coercive forces of the society over which they were gaining governance. As with monstrosity in the early-modern period, Spring-heeled Jack could be read as a sign of moral wrongness and rebellion against the accepted order, but his more successful, and certainly more dominant, interpretation tended to be that of the external danger that served as a means of encouraging greater conformity.

5

Spring-heeled Jack and London

When the Lord Mayor of the City of London was informed of Spring-heeled Jack's appearances around the metropolis in January 1838 his characteristically detached response was that such a figure 'was not calculated for the meridian of London'.[1] A few days later a magistrate and barrister echoed this sentiment when he declared that 'this visitation in the nineteenth century, so near the metropolis … [is] too absurd for belief'.[2] Whilst such bizarre and superstitious accounts may have been expected to find fertile soil in rural communities, they seemingly had no place in London, at least as it was perceived by the metropolitan elite. Yet it was Spring-heeled Jack's initial terrorising of the metropolitan region that granted him such notoriety, publicity and lasting potency in the popular imagination. In part that power derived from the sustained anxiety Spring-heeled Jack supposedly generated in the capital in 1838. In 1863 George Augustus Sala claimed London had been 'thrown into periodic spasms of terror' by Spring-heeled Jack's activities, whilst a later article claimed 'the inhabitants of London and its suburbs [had been] kept in a constant state of terror' by his antics.[3]

Looking in from the safety of the provinces the threat appeared exaggerated. Whilst the metropolitan press alluded to widespread fear and apprehension, the *Ipswich Journal* merely recorded that London's magistrates had heard 'a great many complaints … respecting a "Ghost" or monster, who has for some time past been annoying the inhabitants of the suburbs'.[4] Mere annoyance does not tally with talk of terror and people being frightened witless. Yet amidst the swirl of rumours and claims London seems to have become transformed into a crucible of fear in which a resilient legend was forged. Rather than simply being just another urban ghost, his ambiguous nature and incongruous, migratory appearances in and around one of nineteenth-century Europe's most self-consciously modern capitals generated a powerful sense of discordance that went a considerable way to individualising him. Until the early 1840s London seemed to anchor

---

[1] *The Times*, 9ᵗʰ January 1838, p. 4.
[2] *The Times*, 11ᵗʰ January 1838, p. 7.
[3] See Augustus Sala, 'Shows', p. 276, and *All the Year Round*, 9ᵗʰ August 1884, p. 345.
[4] *Ipswich Journal*, 3ʳᵈ March 1838

his migratory instincts so that the capital that had been his cradle became both his playground and hunting ground. Once he began to roam further afield, and with the safety afforded by the passing of time, Londoners began to appropriate him as their own. With a melodramatic flourish plays and penny serials from the 1860s added the epithet 'The Terror of London' to his name. In 1838 suburban communities had been only too happy to move Spring-heeled Jack on to neighbouring districts, but a retrospective piece in *All the Year Round* in 1884 noted how it had become 'difficult to assign the exact locality which gave birth to this extraordinary freak, either side of the Thames claiming the distinction'.[5]

As seen in Chapter 2, Spring-heeled Jack was by no means unique in being a 'ghost' in the metropolis, for London was undoubtedly as haunted as anywhere else in Victorian England. The Hammersmith Ghost, the St Giles Ghost and the Bermondsey Ghost were perhaps only the better known of the mass of phantoms that informed nineteenth-century London's rich folklore.[6] Yet Spring-heeled Jack's ambiguous ontology prevented him from simply being viewed as just another ghost. Ghosts were essentially passive visual spectacles which resonated with a sense of the modern city as an urban phantasmagoria. Spring-heeled Jack was tangible and active, reaching out to scratch, maul and even breathe fire. Even as a ghost, he did not operate as popular cultural expectations would dictate. Although he was originally named the 'Peckham Ghost' by one letter writer to the Lord Mayor, subsequent press revelations of Spring-heeled Jack's wide-ranging migration around the capital seem to have prevented the moniker sticking, necessitating a title that was not linked to one specific place as the aforementioned ghosts were.[7] Ghosts were expected to haunt a single location, not flit across the length and breadth of the capital. Even if he can be said to have haunted a particular type of place it tended to be the emerging suburbs rather than the older parts of the capital.

As such, he seemed well suited to the perversely contradictory and complex mystery of the metropolis itself. London was both the centre of Britain's economic, political and imperial power and at the same time harboured some of the worst examples of nineteenth-century urban depravity and criminality. For all its visual spectacle and sheer physical scale London was defined by an unknowability derived from what has been described as 'its alterity, its multiplicities, its excesses, its heterogeneities'.[8] Such qualities made the city a powerful locus for the projection of fantasies, imaginings that have exerted influence over

5   *All the Year Round*, 9th August 1884, p. 346.
6   See Roud, *London Lore*; Clayton, *Folklore of London*; Sutherland, *Ghosts of London*; Williams, *Religious Belief and Popular Culture in Southwark*; and, although dated, O'Donnell, *Ghosts of London*.
7   See *The Times*, 11th January 1838, p. 7.
8   Wolfreys, *Writing London*, p. 4.

contemporaries and historians alike. Treating Spring-heeled Jack as an example of what Steve Pile refers to as 'urban marginalia', an aspect of the supernatural that becomes central to divulging the 'desires and fears of cities', this chapter seeks to gain an appreciation of how early-Victorian London was conceived and experienced by its inhabitants.[9] Importantly, metropolitan accounts of Spring-heeled Jack between 1838 and 1841 suggest that he both operated within and challenged the constructed falsity of many of those fantasies.

Nicholas Freeman has recently suggested various ways in which Victorian London was conceived through a literary and artistic 'language of London' which developed between the death of Dickens in 1870 and the outbreak of the First World War.[10] Yet the capital had obviously not been mute prior to this. Freeman recognises Dickens as having been among the most verbose of its early-Victorian articulators, and he was in turn part of a longer tradition that went back to the early-modern period via the likes of Thomas De Quincey, William Blake, Henry Fielding, William Hogarth and Daniel Defoe. Adapting Freeman's notion of a language of urban life, Spring-heeled Jack will be considered as a piece of urban syntax, a symbolic way of connecting and relating the quotidian and imaginary cities of London living at the start of the Victorian period. Firstly, it briefly sets Spring-heeled Jack's appearances in the context of evolving perceptions of London's typography and the perceived nature of the modern city, examining how geographical conceptualisations of the capital were notably more amorphous and fluid in the early 1840s than they were by the late 1880s. Secondly, as a gauge for reading the fears and desires that Londoners projected onto their city (or it projected onto them?) it considers Spring-heeled Jack's relationship to a contemporary urban gothic sensibility. Finally, it explores Spring-heeled Jack's function in suburban London, an aspect of metropolitan life that has generally remained eclipsed by focus on the capital's political, economic and social functions.

Perceptions of Early Victorian London

Spring-heeled Jack appeared in a period before the intensification of the typographical divides that have come to shape our perceptions of Victorian London and offers us a markedly different sense of contemporary understandings of the metropolis. His press accounts depict a London before the prevalence of the dichotomous overworld/underworld conceptualisation was promoted in the writings of social investigators from the 1840s onwards. Intrinsically associated

---

[9]   Pile, *Real Cities*, p. 22.
[10] Freeman, *Conceiving the City*, p. 4.

with notions of 'below' were the ideas of hidden threat and the potential for destabilising the civilised social order that existed 'above'. Between the 1840s and 1880s these typographical conceptualisations underwent a shift, the horizontal perception of 'above' and 'below' being reformulated into a spatial east-west split, the dangers and negativity associated with 'below' being transplanted and supposedly ghettoised in the East End.[11]

In the early-Victorian period this evolving typography of an east-west axis lacked the sharp demarcation that it would come to acquire through Gustave Doré's striking etchings in *London: A Pilgrimage* (1871), W. T. Stead's exposé of East End child prostitution in 1885, and the Whitechapel murders three years later.[12] The London of the late 1830s possessed a less simplistic typography with pockets of rich and poor living in closer proximity to one another, distinguished by moralised dichotomies of the 'respectable' and the 'rough' rather than neat spatial segregations.[13] Although there was an obvious and arguably growing appreciation of areas of poverty and crime, the press reports of Spring-heeled Jack's early appearances suggest a London that was either less aware of its internal threats or less in need of having to generate one.[14] The most noticeable typographical distinction in such accounts was not a schizophrenic divide between east and west but between an ambiguous rural periphery and a more solid metropolitan centre that he was disinclined to enter.

Journalistic accounts of the attacks on Jane Alsop in Bow and Lucy Scales in Limehouse, the latter more obviously urban and clearly not as respectable as the former, failed to prompt comment about the east end of the metropolis. The area had not yet come to bear the taint of the demonised or pathologised city within a city, the imagined dark 'other' that was presented to newspaper readers by the time of the Ripper attacks. Press reports on Spring-heeled Jack's encounters and appearance merely listed locations. In marked contrast to reports about

---

[11] For the Victorian topography of the buried city see Flint, *Victorians and the Visual Imagination*, pp. 139–66. Typographical notions of a hidden nether city were not simply replaced by the East/West End dichotomy; they found literary expression in fin-de-siècle works such as George Gissing's *The Nether World* (1889) and Jack London's *The People of the Abyss* (1903).

[12] This was also facilitated by London's grandiose civil engineering schemes of the mid-Victorian period which radically altered the physical cityscape. Streets, landmarks and communities were rearranged or erased, particularly as railway lines cut through poorer districts where land tended to be cheaper. Coupled with London's remarkable expansion in the second half of the nineteenth century, there were a variety of influences upon a reconceptualised imagined geography of the capital by the 1880s. See Robinson, *Imagining London*, p. 47; Nead, *Victorian Babylon*; Halliday, *Making the Metropolis*; Kellett, 'Railway as an Agent of Internal Change'; and Winter, *London's Teeming Streets*.

[13] These notions were clearly evident in the journalism and fiction of Charles Dickens and G. W. M. Reynolds, and, a little later, in Henry Mayhew's journalistic social explorations.

[14] See Joyce, *Capital Offenses*; Marriott, 'Spatiality of the Poor'; Shore, 'Mean Streets'.

the Ripper, press speculation on the nature and actions of Spring-heeled Jack never presented him as the Lamarckian product of a depraved environment, not least because his migratory propensities meant he could never be linked to any one definable locale.[15]

Spring-heeled Jack's migratory appearances sketched out a myriad of locations both north and south of the Thames, in what would become more widely termed the West End and East End by the early 1880s.[16] In doing so he can be read as both a bizarre reflection of contemporary urban explorers and a corrective to their understanding of the capital. Accounts of Spring-heeled Jack's activities provide a fleeting (and unintentional) sketch of different metropolitan localities, but they were mere flashes of illumination in the growing darkness of the ever-expanding, increasingly unknown and incoherent metropolis. This renders Spring-heeled Jack an agent of what Nicholas Freeman has termed 'Impressionist London', a conceptualisation of the capital in which the city is known 'only fleetingly, and from a wholly subjective position'.[17] The *Hampshire Advertiser* captured this sense of ambiguity of purpose and place when it noted that 'the celebrated "Spring-heeled Jack" [was] now practising his vagaries in the vicinity of London'.[18] Given their apparent randomness, even Spring-heeled Jack's developing narrative could not give them an internal coherence or systematic pattern that could be used to mark out a coherent representation of the capital.[19] Rather Spring-heeled Jack became a means of mapping a heterogeneous city through stories, generating small anecdotal vignettes of knowableness that were made all the more memorable by their association with the bizarre and the supernatural.[20] In form, although not in content, they were akin to the accounts provided by Dickens in his *Sketches by Boz* and in the journalistic investigations that eventually evolved into Henry Mayhew's *London Labour and the London Poor*. As with the authorship of the journalistic investigator, Spring-heeled Jack's name and media character were the only things that connected the disparate images of different Londons that arose from their perambulations.

---

[15] For this interpretation of the Ripper see Walkowitz, *City of Dreadful Delight*, p. 195.

[16] See Freeman, *Conceiving the City*, p. 50. For the development of perceptions of the East End during the Victorian period see Perry Curtis, Jr, *Jack the Ripper*, pp. 32–47; McLaughlin, *Writing the Urban Jungle*; and Walkowitz, *City of Dreadful Delight*, pp. 18–39.

[17] Freeman, *Conceiving the City*, pp. 26–7.

[18] *Hampshire Advertiser*, 10th March 1838.

[19] The migratory nature of the legend should not imply that Spring-heeled Jack's actions were purely random or lacked premeditation. When investigating the Alsop assault, Lea presumed Spring-heeled Jack had been in the Bow area for a month prior to the attack and that he knew the area and family fairly well. See *The Times*, 23rd February 1838.

[20] For a concise summary of Spring-heeled Jack's movements around the capital in 1838 see *All the Year Round*, 9th August 1884, pp. 345–50.

If one were to labour the point, it could even be said that his adoption of disguise (if we take this interpretation of his being) to enter regions of London unrecognised preceded the tradition of disguising adopted by Victorian journalists and social investigators such as James Greenwood, and by the wealthy who dressed down to move freely amidst the slums of the East End towards the end of the century.[21] Like the latter, Spring-heeled Jack was engaged in a transgressive, thrill-seeking masquerade, though unlike them he did not seek titillation at the extremes of urban living but rather chose to menace the moderate in the suburbs and villages on the cusp of being subsumed into the metropolitan sprawl. It is this avoidance of London's most notorious rookeries and slums that reiterate that he was obviously not a genuine urban explorer but merely a shadowing, inverted spectre of their early modes and methods.

Spring-heeled Jack's early appearances coincided with more systematic efforts to map, classify and know London beyond the journalistic anecdote. The Statistical Society of London had been founded in 1834, and 1841 marked the development of a more sophisticated, methodical form of population census intent on capturing information. The period's public health scares, particularly cholera, urged the mapping of sanitary conditions in Bethnal Green in 1848, and by 1867 cholera maps of the entire city had been produced.[22] Such efforts to measure and visualise the city encouraged a sense of control over the capital. But these representations of place were static formulations of a lived London.[23] The metropolis, as experienced, was not to be found in this data but in the way it made people feel.

Spring-heeled Jack's encounters wove the fantastical into the most mundane act of Londoners simply moving from place to place. The London revealed by his activities, predominantly a pedestrians' city, was necessarily a slower city than that afforded by transport.[24] As such, it was one in which particular routes and landmarks tended to be more intricately known, being personally mapped and regulated by the familiar passage between home and workplace, shops or places of leisure. Compared with the pedestrians' amble or brisk stroll, Spring-heeled Jack's encounters were frequently defined by their fleeting nature. Whilst he may

---

[21] For more on this see Koven, *Slumming: Sexual and Social Politics*.

[22] Dennis, *Cities in Modernity*, p. 55. This optimism that London could be charted, mapped and known through the accumulation of empirical data grew after the appearance of Spring-heeled Jack but had faded by the end of the century. See Freeman, *Conceiving the City*, p. 143.

[23] See Flint, *Victorians and the Visual Imagination*, pp. 8–10.

[24] For more on this aspect of London life see Nead, *Victorian Babylon*, pp. 74–9. For a more theoretical treatment see also De Certeau, *Practice of Everyday Life*.

have simply walked away after his attack on Lucy Scales, most other accounts told of sudden appearances, swift actions and equally fast escapes.[25]

Spring-heeled Jack's appearances disrupted the familiar rhythms of traversing the city and of daily life, offering an intense, brief glimpse of a different London.[26] Alan Robinson has argued that 'the salient feature of Victorian London was mobility', of people, services and goods, but as a modern industrial city it was also defined by speed, of railways, steam-powered manufacturing and, a little later, the telegraph.[27] As a creature of movement and speed and as a fleeting, incoherent, seemingly phantasmagoric metropolitan experience, Spring-heeled Jack personified the age in which he emerged. One newspaper later described Spring-heeled Jack as having 'burst upon the metropolis' in 1838, and whilst we know his emergence to have actually been more evolutionary, it captures a sense of the impact such a figure had.[28] The *Morning Herald* suspected he was aided by the developing train system. Having been seen around Uxbridge it was believed he returned to central London via the great Western Railway before harassing the neighbourhoods of Hanwell, Brentford, Ealing, Acton, Hammersmith and Kensington.[29] Yet it was rumour that truly facilitated the sheer number of appearances in different metropolitan locations. The apparent ubiquity fostered by this provided one of the strongest claims to his possessing supernatural powers, whilst also encouraging the sense of a city under siege and suffering a blitzkrieg of the uncanny.

The Urban Gothic

Spring-heeled Jack generated a powerful confluence between the fantastical and the mundane in the urban environment.[30] This metropolitan landscape of emotion, desires, anxieties and fantasies was perhaps best captured by a contemporary urban gothic sensibility, and Spring-heeled Jack both drew from and

---

[25] As with the height of his leaping, we have to consider that accounts of his speed were also prone to being exaggerated in retelling. When chased by men in Bow in early 1838 Spring-heeled Jack escaped 'by the most extraordinary agility, and ... a thorough knowledge of the locality'. By the 1880s he was apparently capable of outrunning a pursuing horse and cart. See *The Times*, 23rd February 1838, p. 7, and *Northern Echo*, 1st August 1884.

[26] See Amin and Thrift, *Cities*, pp. 16–19. See also Highmore, *Cityscapes*, pp. 140–61.

[27] Robinson, *Imagining London*, p. 45.

[28] *Bradford Observer*, 4th November 1875, p. 8.

[29] *Morning Herald*, 10th January 1838.

[30] For a call to examine the historical urban landscape from this conjoined perspective see Parsons, *Streetwalking the Metropolis*, p. 1.

fed the vitality of such a perception.[31] Spring-heeled Jack spoke to the fears and fantasies of early-Victorian Londoners, reactions which were encouraged by the nature of the modernising metropolis itself. Its growth from the start of the nineteenth century led to the emergence of 'a new sort of social life' in which everyday life involved an increasing number of 'random encounters with strangers' and the potential for 'sudden eruptions of violence'.[32] These seemingly contradictory spatial fears, the vastness of the unknown city and the possible proximity to danger, were entwined in a sense of the urban uncanny. Associating this sense of unease with both the vulnerable exposure of agoraphobia and the suffocating confines of claustrophobia, Anthony Vidler has argued that the urban uncanny fosters a psychological 'distancing from reality forced by reality'.[33] This does not arise from an inherent quality within a particular urban space, but a psychological and physical interaction with it, one which collapses boundaries between the real and imagined.

A predisposition towards such interactions was the influence of the nocturnal urban environment upon the mind. It seems little coincidence that the vast majority of Spring-heeled Jack's metropolitan appearances and attacks occurred at night, when familiar streets had become distorted by darkness or the eerie glow of the gaslights that had been installed in most of the capital's streets by the early 1840s.[34] Like all urban phantoms Spring-heeled Jack spoke to these 'uncanny effects of city life'.[35] Yet unlike more commonplace phantoms the rich theorising surrounding spectrality cannot be simply applied to a figure who was only sometimes understood to be a ghost and at others a demon, goblin or just a disguised man.[36] Such a being did not merely speak to the persistence of supernatural fears but a very tangible sense of threat in darkened streets. That he was a genuine cause of widespread panic is in little doubt, but how far one can tease apart the physical threat from more supernatural allusions is nigh on impossible to gauge. Rather it was the alloying of these two fears (at least in popular interpretations) within Spring-heeled Jack that made him such a potent menace.

[31]   These distinctions are akin to De Certeau's notions of 'place' as mapped and static, and 'space' as actualised and lived. See De Certeau, *Practice of Everyday Life*, p. 117.

[32]   Plotz, *The Crowd*, p. 1.

[33]   Vidler, *Architectural Uncanny*, p. 6.

[34]   More steady electrical illumination did not become widespread until the late 1870s. For the nature of street lighting see Nead, *Victorian Babylon*, pp. 104–6. For more on darkness as stimulus towards supernatural interpretations see Nashe, *Unfortunate Traveller*, pp. 208–50; Lamb, 'Witches and other Night-Fears', pp. 90–6; and Ekirch, *At Day's Close*, especially pp. 3–30.

[35]   Pile, *Real Cities*, p. 163.

[36]   For more on hauntological theory see Pilar Blanco and Peeren, *Popular Ghosts*; Gordon, *Ghostly Matters*; Pile, *Real Cities*, pp. 131–64; and Derrida, *Spectres of Marx*.

Whilst Spring-heeled Jack can be read as a manifestation of immediate environmental uncertainties, he was part of larger imaginings of the metropolis. Nineteenth-century London was not just passively ripe for fantasising; its size, complexity and nature seemed to actively encourage an urge towards perceiving it in fantasised terms. Spring-heeled Jack resonated with a number of conceptions of contemporary London, particularly the idea of the capital as a modern Babylon, even more so as a dark gothic labyrinth. Urged by an evangelicalism and a more muted popular millenarianism that pulsed beneath the surface of early-Victorian society, contemporaries were inclined to view London as a moral reflection upon man, likening it positively to a new Jerusalem, and more negatively (and more frequently) to an immoral Babylon. With the exception of the *Penny Satirist* the press studiously avoided any connection between Spring-heeled Jack as a punisher of sin in a wicked city, presumably unwilling to fan the panic and also unwilling to give credence to supernatural interpretations of his being. Journalistic interpretations presented a secular interpretation of a human prankster, though, as will be seen in Chapter 7, this did not exclude some dalliance with supernatural tropes. Their reports on popular rumours that Spring-heeled Jack was a devil or demon were certainly conducive to, if not necessarily directly influenced by, the biblical rhetoric used to describe nineteenth-century London.[37] However, as with many of these perceptions of London, Spring-heeled Jack demonstrates a contemporary playing with biblical imagery, his appearances in suburban neighbourhoods being far removed from Babylonian notions of excess and sinfulness.

If this rhetoric was a little too grandiose, the idea of London as a labyrinth had more immediate hold on Londoners' imagination. Whilst having literary precedents in Henry Fielding's *An Enquiry into the Causes of the Late Increase in Robbers* (1750) and Thomas De Quincey's *Confessions of an English Opium Eater* (1821), as an imaginative conceit it developed as the city grew in size and complexity during the nineteenth century. In the years preceding Spring-heeled Jack's emergence, Dickens' journalism and fiction were already (re-) constructing London as 'a powerful mythic locale'. His imagining of the city did not merely inform perceptions of London but influenced and even 'supplanted the actual city in the public (and, in some ways, historical) imagination', creating what Freeman has termed a 'Dickensian simulacrum' of the metropolis.[38] His fictions were neither wholly separate from nor simply imposed on a real city but frequently came to shape understandings and expectations as to how that quotidian city should be read. For all his political and sociological asides, G. W. M.

---

[37] See Dennis, *Cities in Modernity*, pp. 46–51.
[38] Freeman, *Conceiving the City*, pp. 20–1.

Reynolds' hugely popular urban gothic melodrama, *Mysteries of London* (1844–48), appears to have been built on fantasised Dickensian foundations.[39]

These attempts by Dickens and Reynolds to locate earlier gothic tropes into a recognisably modern London created a frisson with readers, and Spring-heeled Jack proved that they had force beyond the written page. In both gothic fictions and 'real' accounts of Spring-heeled Jack's appearances that powerful thrill came from removing the temporal and geographical distance that had defined earlier literary works. Rather than the wildernesses and ruins of Catholic Spain or Italy, the modern British capital now 'provided the loci for mystery and terror … the dark alleyways of cities were the gloomy forests and subterranean labyrinths'.[40] Gothic tropes that had grown hackneyed and formulaic by the 1830s were given renewed vitality when the edifice in which people were incarcerated was no longer some foreign aristocratic castle but Jacob's Island in *Oliver Twist*, or the slums near Smithfield Market in the *Mysteries of London*. The city-as-edifice worked in the same way as the gothic castle had, its spatial threats derived from its simultaneous expansiveness and its 'tomb-like claustrophobia'.[41] The imagined gothic city was both familiar and defamiliarised, with one foot in a recognisable reality and the other in a place born of fears of the unknown.[42] Its depiction of labyrinthine streets and alleys spoke to the fragmentary and incomprehensible nature of the growing metropolis, its size and complexity ensuring that its inhabitants' knowledge and understanding of their own city was always subjective and limited.

As such, Spring-heeled Jack evolved in a city that had already been fantasised and exoticised into something more than tangible bricks and mortar. In the context of these imagined Londons Spring-heeled Jack, as a ghost, devil, man-beast or vicious predatory aristocrat, was not merely at home but represented an embarrassment of gothic riches. With all these interpretations in

---

[39] See ibid, pp. 160–3, and also Mighall, *Geography of Victorian Gothic Fiction*. The notion of a dark, labyrinthine city was reiterated throughout the rest of the century, in penny dreadful fictions such as *The Wild Boys of London*, in Conan Doyle's Sherlock Holmes stories and Arthur Machen's metropolitan-based tales, including *The Three Imposters*. For the continuation of these fantasising instincts in the twentieth century see Wasson, *Urban Gothic*.

[40] Botting, *Gothic*, p. 123. See also Punter and Byron, *The Gothic*, pp. 26–31, and Mighall, *Geography of Victorian Gothic Fiction*, pp. 27–77.

[41] Punter and Byron, *The Gothic*, p. 262.

[42] In the decades following Spring-heeled Jack's initial appearances the monstrous arguably became *the* conceptual lens for investigators driven by curiosity but beset by fear as they probed the capital's chthonic secrets. Driven by evangelicalism and utilitarianism, the collated data tended to be interpreted through lenses of morality and pathology which naturally fed a fear of 'darkest London'. The term is derived from John Law's *In Darkest London* (1891) and Arthur Osbourne Montgomery Jay's *Life in Darkest London: A Hint to General Booth* (1891), both of which were metropolitan responses to William Booth's *In Darkest England and the Way Out* (1890).

simultaneous circulation Spring-heeled Jack became a concentrated node of urban gothic monstrosity, a cultural cipher that had multiple types of fearful 'otherness' imprinted upon or enfolded within it. Descriptions of Spring-heeled Jack in 1838 sometimes conflated the diabolical and bestial with the figure clad in armour, at other times shifted between them. These qualities of hybridity and metamorphosis are part of the cultural power of monsters in general and in this case in particular, for they 'exceed and disrupt those systems of classification through which cultures organise experience'.[43] Such excessiveness and transformative energy certainly granted Spring-heeled Jack the imaginative force to tower above London's mere ghosts in 1838.

From the perspective of the educated elite Spring-heeled Jack carried the stigma of being a haunting vestige of past superstitions. When confronted with the Spring-heeled Jack phenomenon the first interpretations that ordinary Londoners reached for were not men in disguise but supernatural folkloric tropes such as demons, ghosts and bestial hybrids, expressions of a familiar and traditional popular cultural semiotics of 'otherness'. For journalists writing for a respectable middle-class readership, Spring-heeled Jack was presented as an anachronistic expression of old superstitions that had suddenly erupted and found widespread resurgence in the modern city. Jarring with London's perceived image as a centre of modernity and civilisation, the incomprehensibility of this was even more pronounced. Whilst the press dismissed Spring-heeled Jack's accounts as exemplars of popular credulity, these superstitious inclinations were used to articulate fear of popular ignorance, itself an expression of wider unease about the lack of influence over the urban masses.[44] Worse yet, Spring-heeled Jack did not merely represent a revival of old superstitions in the modern city; stimulated by the modernity of that city he represented an updating of such ideas to operate within its amorphous sprawl and less personal and tightly bound social relations. Spring-heeled Jack did not express traditional concerns so much as new urban anxieties. He was not some revenant returned from the past but a haunting figure derived from the present.

Despite his obvious gothic trappings Spring-heeled Jack tells a different story to the one reflected in Victorian gothic fiction, exposing such readings of London as indulgent fantasising. The idea of civilisation having failed to reach certain parts of the city facilitated the gothic idea of lingering 'anachronistic vestiges', gaps in which supernatural beliefs could be retained.[45] The unknown and supposedly untouched left voids in one's knowledge of the city which the individual

---

[43] Punter and Byron, *The Gothic*, p. 264. See also Warner, *Fantastic Metamorphosis, Other Worlds*; Cavallaro, *Gothic Vision*, pp. 190–8; Lunger Knoppers and Landes, *Monstrous Bodies/Political Monstrosities*; and Huet, *Monstrous Imagination*.

[44] See for example *Morning Chronicle*, 10th January 1838.

[45] Mighall, *Geography of Victorian Gothic Fiction*, p. 49.

and collective imaginations filled with the possibility of sinister threats, even supernatural occurrences. Yet whilst powerfully evocative, Spring-heeled Jack does not easily fit into this depiction. In urban gothic tales it was the environment that harboured mysteries and dangers, yet it was Spring-heeled Jack, the migratory predator, who embodied these qualities within himself as an individual, rather than the tame suburban environment in which he appeared. Linked to this was the fact that it was people, not the locale, that were the target of his flash hauntings or assaults.

The labyrinthine London was never present in testimony about Spring-heeled Jack delivered before magistrates or recorded by journalists. This may have been a London portrayed by investigative journalists and fiction writers, but most of its inhabitants experienced it in a more humdrum manner. Whilst Spring-heeled Jack embodied the notion of the solitary monster, he tended to draw attention to the stagey nature of such formulations. In appearance and actions his monstrosity was something of a performance, possessing a stylistic flamboyance lacking in the average metropolitan mugger (although the violent consequences of that theatricality could be genuine enough). As Peter Ackroyd has put it, "'Spring-heeled Jack' became a true London myth because he was so fantastic and artificial a monster'.[46] Spring-heeled Jack serves to expose the artifice of metropolitan gothic literature. Readers were content to play with their fears of the unknown metropolis, to titillate themselves with imagined dangers and desires and to participate in a controlled 'troubling of the quotidian'.[47] Their response was wholly different when that gothic monster lacked the comforting distance and boundaries afforded by the literature which promoted such ideas. The urban gothic's dark appeal abruptly vanished when Spring-heeled Jack appeared to violate the perceived divide between the imaginary and the real. Suddenly the ersatz threat and fear constructed in a fantasised space was replaced by more powerful genuine feelings rooted in the mundane. Spring-heeled Jack was not confined to some imagined city of dreadful night or by the comforting constraints of narrative expectation.[48] In appearing to be a physical materialisation of the monstrous, alluding to folkloric entities yet credible enough to be picked up by the respected metropolitan press, Spring-heeled Jack conflated the quotidian and imaginary to challenge urban epistemologies in a way that contemporary gothic literature could not.

Whilst highlighting the artifice of contemporary gothic perceptions, Spring-heeled Jack also becomes ensnared in a web of scholarly fantasies associated

---

[46]   Ackroyd, *London*, p. 502. Ackroyd rightly uses Spring-heeled Jack to illustrate a persistent urban belief in the supernatural but he is over-reliant on Haining's flawed work for information.

[47]   Punter and Byron, *The Gothic*, p. 286.

[48]   See Thomson, *City of Dreadful Night*, and Mighall, *Geography of Victorian Gothic Fiction*, p. 35.

with the modernising nineteenth-century metropolis. Despite allusions to accomplices in several accounts, the abiding image of Spring-heeled Jack was as a peripatetic loner. As such, he serves as a symbol of urban alienation, a being whose monstrous appearance (or disguise) represented the dehumanised urban dweller. Such a view would mark him as a herald to late-nineteenth- and early-twentieth-century sociological perceptions of life in advanced capitalist urban societies. Yet one needs to sound a note of caution before running away with the idea of Spring-heeled Jack as some monstrous patron saint of the urban dispossessed. Even if he did resonate with a contemporary sense of dislocation within the developing urban environment, we have to be wary about blurring sociological paradigms with historical realities. Urban dwellers could choose to adopt such a perceptual stance, but loneliness and disconnection were not necessarily intrinsic states even within the largest nineteenth-century cities.[49] Nor does Spring-heeled Jack conform to the modern city as a dreamlike phantasmagoria, a constant spectacle of new sights and experiences. Rather he reached out to grab and cut his victims, imprinting his existence not solely upon their senses but on their flesh too. His earliest encounters were bruising corporeal engagements which could not be ignored by the supposedly blasé attitude of Georg Simmel's 'metropolitan man'.[50]

Spring-heeled Jack also has some affinity with the flâneur, a privileged observer and cultural product of the modern metropolis.[51] In line with a long literary tradition that now provides the canonical works for a history of London's psycho-geography, he was a metropolitan urban wanderer. Like the flâneur, Spring-heeled Jack haunted sites of urban transference (streets) and was inclined towards London's more respectable areas rather than its poorer districts. Yet he differs sharply in his unwillingness to simply partake in what Lynda Nead has referred to as the 'ocular freedom' that stemmed from the (masculine) visual culture of the metropolis.[52] In transgressing from looking to touching (and worse) he broke a key taboo of urban life. That said, others have noted that the city was 'a hunting ground' for flâneurs.[53] This more purposeful formulation is certainly more appropriate to Spring-heeled Jack's metropolitan activities in the late 1830s and 1840s. Jack's assertive movements, his leaping over

[49] See for example Simmel, 'The Stranger'; Park, 'The City'; and Wirth, 'Urbanism as a Way of Life'. For subsequent responses and challenges to these views see Tonkiss, Space, the City and Social Theory, pp. 17–29.

[50] See Simmel, 'Metropolis and Mental Life', and Pile, Real Cities, pp. 19–21.

[51] Walter Benjamin located this urban social type as emerging in Paris during the reign of Louis-Philippe, the exact period in which Spring-heeled Jack originated. For this and a contesting of Benjamin's dating see Ferguson, 'Flâneur On and Off the Streets'.

[52] Nead, Victorian Babylon, p. 66. See also Tester, The Flâneur.

[53] Frisby, Cityscapes of Modernity, p. 43.

walls, intruding into gardens and churchyards, transgressed numerous public and private boundaries. In this he was more in the vein of Michel de Certeau's heroic pedestrians, mapping his own city and his own 'spatial stories' through his erratic perambulation and thereby defying the official ordering of metropolitan space.[54] Abandoning the flâneur's anonymity, his theatricality, notoriety and media exposure publicly marked the places he passed through, causing them to become part of his narrative mapping of the capital.

Spring-heeled Jack and Suburban Cultures

As his initial moniker indicates, Spring-heeled Jack, the 'suburban ghost', haunted London's developing suburban environment. Generally tending towards its urban-rural fringe he preyed on the 'neighbouring villages within three or four miles of London' and 'made the suburbs his hunting-ground'.[55] Unlike traditional ghosts he did not haunt one particular locale but prowled freely and widely about the outskirts of the metropolis. Yet in doing so he conformed to the liminal nature of ghosts by existing in a borderland that was neither wholly rural nor urban.[56] His unstable transformations from phantasmal white bull to armoured ghost, anthropomorphic beast to fire-breathing demon were indicative of influences bleeding in from both sides of this fluid boundary. Spring-heeled Jack's activities encourage us to turn from familiar impressions of civic, industrial or poverty-stricken London to examine how notions of supernatural urban folklore were incorporated into its newer cultural environs.

Although London's suburban development dated back to the eighteenth century, it witnessed a marked increase in scale and extent in the period in which Spring-heeled Jack first appeared.[57] In the 1830s London's suburbs were still emerging in a rather organic fashion and still tended to be the refuge of the wealthy. South London suburbs such as Clapham, Balham, Streatham and Tooting were still 'scattered villages around which many very large houses had sprung into being', a consequence of wealthy merchants seeking escape to 'the rustic suburbs'.[58] Indicative of their unplanned nature, the growth of Clapham in

---

[54] For more on this see De Certeau, *Practice of Everyday Life*, and also Pile and Keith, *Geographies of Resistance*.

[55] See *The Times*, 9th January 1938, p. 4, and *All the Year Round*, 9th August 1884, p. 348.

[56] Elizabeth McKellar has emphasised how nineteenth-century London's heterogeneous landscape requires us to rethink our over-simplistic urban/rural dichotomies. See McKellar, 'Peripheral Visions', p. 45.

[57] The term 'suburbia' did not become widespread until the 1890s. See Dennis, *Cities in Modernity*, p. 179.

[58] Villiers, *Stand and Deliver*, p. 239.

south London had initially been spurred by the congregating of similar-minded evangelical families from the turn of the nineteenth century. The growth of the north London suburbs of Kensington and St John's Wood, both of which received visits from Spring-heeled Jack in late December and early January 1838, had resulted from the development of suburban omnibus routes in the 1830s.[59] This changed from the mid century when architects and speculative builders began to construct suburban districts to a more orderly and systematic design to accommodate London's rapidly increasing population.[60] The influx of white-collar clerks and artisans made established suburbs less appealing and resulted in an ongoing process in which inner suburbs such as Camden Town declined in status as the more desirable, wealthier suburbs pushed ever further out from the centre.[61] Once the pace of suburban development began to accelerate the suburbs acquired their familiar image of dull regimentation, a perception reiterated by a body of jaded late-nineteenth-century literature.[62]

Spring-heeled Jack's appearances in the nascent suburbia of the late 1830s help us penetrate these later derogatory associations and see contemporaries' seemingly contradictory sense of suburban life in the 1830s and 1840s. Press reports promoted an appealing image of the suburbs as peaceful havens that were remote from the noise and bustle of the capital. In January 1838 the *Morning Herald* referred to Spring-heeled Jack's appearance in 'the quiet and retired villages of Ham and Petersham, where in the image of a diabolical imp he nightly reigned supreme'.[63] When he appeared in Lewisham and Blackheath in early January 1838 it was reported that women and children in 'these peaceful districts' were so fearful that they 'durst not stir out of their houses after dark'.[64] An 'inhabitant of Stockwell' referred to Spring-heeled Jack as 'some person who makes it his delight to frighten the peaceable inhabitants of the suburbs', whilst the Lord Mayor commented on the terror his antics had created in a 'retired and peaceful neighbourhood' in 'the outlets of the metropolis'.[65]

Yet the peaceful fringes of the metropolis were also presented as solitary and isolated. In March 1838 *The Watchman* used the rather strange expression of Spring-heeled Jack having appeared 'in the lonely parts of the metropolis'.[66] The encounter at the Alsop house in Bearbinder Lane, Bow, had emphasised

[59] See Robinson, *Imagining London*, pp. 45–6.
[60] See Dennis, *Cities in Modernity*, pp. 179–205, and Robinson, *Imagining London*, p. 47.
[61] See 'The Formation of London Suburbs', *The Times*, 25th June 1904.
[62] See Hapgood, *Margins of Desire*; Hayden, *Building Suburbia*; Miele, 'From Aristocratic Ideal to Middle-class Idyll'; and Silverstone, *Visions of Suburbia*.
[63] *Morning Herald*, 10th January 1838.
[64] *Morning Chronicle*, 11th January 1838.
[65] *The Times*, 11th January 1838, p. 7.
[66] *The Watchman*, 7th March 1838.

the essentially remote and rural locale in which the Alsops' house was situated. *The Times* described it as 'a considerable distance from any other, and in very lonely spot' which 'afforded ample opportunity for the ghost … to play off his pranks with impunity'.[67] When he appeared in Tottenham and Edmonton for three weeks in October 1841 he haunted 'the byways and lanes' rather than the thoroughfares.[68] This emphasis on urban loneliness was undoubtedly enhanced by Spring-heeled Jack's propensity for nocturnal attacks and the avoidance of areas most likely to have a police presence. Yet it also seemed to play to the spatial fears that informed a sense of the urban uncanny. As Spring-heeled Jack's haunting of the quiet back roads of the capital's outer districts show, the price of a quiet, semi-rural existence was a gnawing sense of isolation, exposure and vulnerability, especially after dark. This media impression of solitary pedestrians inhabiting a lonely modern metropolis is offset by a closer reading of Spring-heeled Jack's reported encounters, many of which took place when his victims were accompanied by family, friends or other companions.[69]

These seemingly contradictory experiences of suburban space were echoed in a number of juxtapositions that defined the suburban dweller. The Victorian suburbs may have appeared a retreat from modern urban life into a semi-rural existence, but they were actually defined by new lifestyles, reliance upon new technologies (in terms of transport and utilities), and a modern desire to escape the metropolitan bustle.[70] Living in the suburbs was an expression of assertiveness and defensiveness. On the one hand the suburban villa or semi-detached house was a sign of social distinction and of possessing sufficient means to escape the metropolitan squalor. These distinctions were carried into suburban communities, with internal differences being marked by house design or even how one travelled to and from the city. Yet on the other hand it represented the seeking of distance, the need for a refuge from the scale and heterogeneous nature of the modern metropolis. By comparison the suburbs were manageable in size and inclined towards milder degrees of differentiation between more homogeneous peoples. Suburban living also tended to be defined by both privacy and a muted neighbourly competitiveness, with these internal-external tensions fostering an intensified awareness of both 'self' and 'other'. Richard Dennis has described suburbs as 'communities of conflict (resisting "others") and competition (keeping up appearances) as much as neighbourly harmony'.[71] This was compounded by the fact that its inhabitants resided in one place but worked elsewhere. Such a

---

[67] *The Times*, 23rd February 1838, p. 7.

[68] *Freeman's Journal*, 26th October 1841. See also Villiers, *Stand and Deliver*, p. 238.

[69] For examples see accounts of his 1838 appearances at Kensington Palace, Bow, Limehouse and Blackheath in *All the Year Round*, 9th August 1884, pp. 346–8.

[70] See Dennis, *Cities in Modernity*, pp. 182–3.

[71] Ibid., p. 223.

lifestyle seemed to suggest suburban dwellers appeared to have less emotional investment in notions of a collective community. At best its inhabitants were a clustering of like-minded people who shared a view of their homes as a retreat from the bustle, pollution and dangers of the capital.

As an intrusive symbol of 'otherness' Spring-heeled Jack served two contradictory functions within suburban communities. His encounters spoke to doubts about the feasibility of being able to successfully escape the darker aspects of metropolitan life, especially its (perceived increase in) criminal threats to one's property and person. Thomas Lott, writing to the Lord Mayor to confirm the rumours, declared that Spring-heeled Jack was 'some determined thief who visits houses in the absence of the head of the families, and who seeks by this method of at once paralyzing the energies of the servants to obtain and escape with his booty on easy terms'.[72] A sense of the urban uncanny was almost indigenous to aspirational suburban dwellers, for it arose from the 'fundamental insecurity … of a newly established class, not quite at home in its own home'.[73] Spring-heeled Jack's intrusion into residential suburbs transformed the known into the uncertain, the *heimlich* or homely into *unheimlich* or uncanny.[74] In rendering the familiar strangely unfamiliar and exposing suburbanites to hitherto unrecognised dangers (or at least the threat of such dangers) he temporarily displaced local communities from their usual urban rhythms. His appearance disrupted illusions of suburban seclusion, fracturing attempts to collectively construct a fiction of the suburbs as essentially separate from the rest of the city.

Yet it was Spring-heeled Jack's intrusive presence which served as a means of temporarily generating or awakening a dormant sense of community in localities that did not have a deep-rooted sense of themselves as communities. Suburban communities may have been spatially more dispersed, especially on the metropolitan fringe in the 1830s and 1840s, but Spring-heeled Jack demonstrates that rumour operated as effectively here as it did in more concentrated inner-city neighbourhoods. Narrated accounts and rumour generated a sense of common threat to an imagined community by some outside intruder. Rather than some remote danger, reports indicated that Spring-heeled Jack could appear on the very threshold of one's property, even going so far as to summon members of the household by knocking on doors and ringing bells. Press accounts about the servant girl who lost her mind when she opened the door to 'no less dreadful figure than a spectre', and the mauling received by Jane Alsop on her own doorstep

---

[72] *Morning Chronicle*, 11ᵗʰ January 1838.
[73] Vidler, *Architectural Uncanny*, pp. 3–4.
[74] For more on *unheimlich* see Freud, *The Uncanny*, pp. 121–62, and Royle, *The Uncanny*.

reiterated the immediacy of the menace.[75] When he appeared in Tottenham Spring-heeled Jack even knocked the door to the Burnetts' household wide open before terrifying the inhabitants by walking around on the roof (according to the family).[76]

The response of suburban communities was mixed. Those who deemed to address the Lord Mayor or write to *The Times* suggested it fell to the head of individual suburban households to tackle the threat posed by Spring-heeled Jack. Thomas Lott claimed he was going to move his family from his 'town residence' to Hornsey, where 'some scoundrel had been alarming the neighbourhood in these disguises'. Yet with an emphasis on suburban private property he stated that 'if I catch Mr Ghost on any part of my premises I shall administer that to his substantial part that, if ever he reappears, it shall only be ... as a ghost in fact'. Lott added, 'Other heads of families in my neighbourhood having expressed the same determination, I trust the ghost will soon be laid.'[77]

Yet whilst this may have reflected the attitude of the heads of wealthy households, other accounts suggest that plebeian suburban dwellers were quick to come to the aid of Spring-heeled Jack's victims or band together to hunt for him. When the Alsops had shouted for the police from their upper-storey windows it was actually people in the John Bull public house some little way off that had heard and responded.[78] Walking near the Alsop residence, James Smith, a coach wheelwright, later testified that he had heard a female scream 'and believing it to be someone attacked or in distress, he quickened his pace to render what assistance he could'. He met up with Richardson, a shoemaker, and it was these two men who had first come to the family's assistance. When Smith reached the gate of the Alsop residence the family had 'asked if we were the police, and we replied that we were not, but we expected that ... the police, would come up shortly'.[79] The same was supposedly true when an elderly woman encountered Spring-heeled Jack near Clapham churchyard. An eager throng of locals were so keen to hunt her attacker that they quickly obliterated the strange footprints that he had left in the soil.[80] Reports of groups of local men arming themselves and turning out at night to patrol their communities became a familiar part of Spring-heeled

---

[75] See *The Times*, 9th January 1838, p. 4, and 22nd February 1838, p. 6. It is tempting to read these disruptive doorstep pranks as indicative of tensions arising from an outward migration from the city to the suburbs, particularly on the part of disgruntled locals who were witnessing the encroachment of the metropolitan population. However, there is no indication in the available data that the targeted victims were new arrivals or in any way figures of local resentment.

[76] See *Freeman's Journal*, 26th October 1841.

[77] *Morning Chronicle*, 11th January 1838.

[78] *The Times*, 23rd February 1838.

[79] *The Times*, 2nd March 1838.

[80] Villiers, *Stand and Deliver*, p. 245.

Jack accounts. These informal, collective efforts gave the lie to a later assertion that 'it is curiously illustrative of the law-abiding habits of Englishmen that no attempt was made to organise a Vigilance Committee and shoot the ghost on sight'.[81] Whilst not armed with guns, these communal vigilantes could have easily committed acts of grievous violence. Therefore, Spring-heeled Jack's appearances suggest that whilst communal bonds of mutuality may have been more attenuated in suburban London than inner-city neighbourhoods at the start of the Victorian period, they could be swiftly created and drawn upon in times of need.

Spring-heeled Jack was an expression of the incomprehensibility of the modern metropolis at the start of the Victorian age. His visibility about the capital failed to offer insight, coherence or control, for unlike traditional ghosts which were spatially 'fixed' Spring-heeled Jack's migratory 'hauntings' did not imbue one particular site with supernatural significance; rather they sketched out the parameters of London in an impressionistic, spectral manner of their own. Accounts of his appearances in the press and oral rumour were fragmentary, reiterating the difficulties of imagining a coherent city. At the same time they highlight the contemporary urge to impose incorporating or ordering motifs upon the capital, most obviously in terms of biblical associations with Babylon or typographical notions of civilisation 'above' and a netherworld 'below'. Spring-heeled Jack embodied the epistemological uncertainties that arose from the blurring of the quotidian and subjectively experienced city, being uncontrollable and unknowable, both brutally physical and seemingly phantasmal. In this way he resonated with the power of both the seen and unseen, a tension that Kate Flint has claimed was embroiled in Victorian notions of the modern city.[82] He made London known to its residents in a way formal means of cognitive ordering – maps, plans or statistical data-collecting – could not, giving contemporaries (and us) access to the imaginary and emotional typography of the capital.[83]

The idea of the city as a text, especially as a palimpsest, has become a cliché and in this case is not wholly accurate.[84] It was not a case of Spring-heeled Jack simply scrawling an imagined, fantasised London over the hard text of its physical spaces, for in accounts of his activities the mundane and the mysterious bled into one another. Nor did he merely iterate the fantasised dangers of traversing the streets of a city that was always constructed from one's circumscribed knowledge and comprehension of one's surroundings. Importantly, Spring-heeled Jack demonstrates seemingly contradictory tensions in serving to

81 *Daily News*, 22nd August 1882.
82 See Flint, *Victorians and the Visual Imagination*, p. 140.
83 For more on this see Pile, *Real Cities*, p. 2. See also Donald, *Imagining the Modern City*.
84 See Barthes, 'Semiology and the Urban', and Donald, 'Metropolis: The City as Text'.

articulate a fantasised early-Victorian London whilst acting as a corrective to many aspects of the urban imaginary. On the one hand he strongly appealed to contemporary notions of urban fears as expressed in the urban gothic, being the haunting spectre or man-monster in the modern labyrinth. Yet on the other his overt theatricality, the idea that he was just a man in disguise, and the genuine fear prompted by such a character having stepped beyond the safe bounds of a literary or theatrical fiction exposed those fantasising instincts as a highly self-conscious piece of artifice. Similarly, fantasies of typographical ordering between London's 'respectable' and 'rough' elements were challenged when Spring-heeled Jack, rumoured to be a gentleman prankster, avoided the capital's assumed sites of criminality and poverty to create havoc in the suburban outskirts. In doing so he also punctured the collective fantasy of an evolving suburbia, revealing its conscious fictionalisation as a locale safely detached from the problems of the metropolitan centre.

The years 1838 to 1841 were formative in the making of Spring-heeled Jack's legend. If he had stayed in Barnes he would have been merely another rural ghost consigned to becoming a brief footnote in local folklore. Yet his movement around the capital and his consequent impact on both Londoners' imaginations and the metropolitan media operated like a cultural dynamo, generating suffi-cient energy and influence to launch him out into the provinces too. Following this initial energising Spring-heeled Jack was subsequently recharged through local cultural generators, or what I will term cultural-spatial nodes. It is to a more in-depth study of these that we must turn to next.

Part III

Cultural Dynamism

6

Cultural Nodes: Localities

Following the London scares of early 1838 Spring-heeled Jack was swiftly appropriated by numerous localities beyond the metropolis. In March 1838 the *Hampshire Advertiser* claimed a local criminal was as hard to catch as Spring-heeled Jack.[1] The following month the *Brighton Gazette* recorded that Spring-heeled Jack had 'found his way to the Sussex coast'.[2] By June the *Bristol Mercury* reported that Spring-heeled Jack was appearing 'in most of the boroughs, villages and cities in England'.[3] Unlike Jack the Ripper's enduring connection with Whitechapel, an association which branded his legend into the psychic geography of the district, Spring-heeled Jack's migratory nature created a more diffused legend across a broader range of specific localities.[4] In examining this migratory impulse within Spring-heeled Jack's legend this chapter engages with the nature of cultural transferences and interactions in Victorian England.

This chapter explores the importance of differing cultural localities as sites or spatial nodes of popular cultural generation, arguing that localised spaces and places were amongst the key 'engines' that provided the operational dynamics for popular cultures in general and the generation and perpetuation of Spring-heeled Jack's legend in particular. It was in specific localities that incidents, influences and beliefs became connected and embodied in the identifiable 'Spring-heeled Jack' signifier, informing how and why his accounts were formed, operated and received in different places at different times. This chapter adopts the view of cultural spaces as an integral part of those narratives.[5] As such, it seeks to explore

---

[1]   *Hampshire Advertiser*, 10th March 1838.
[2]   Quoted in *The Times*, 14th April 1838.
[3]   *Bristol Mercury*, 2nd June 1838.
[4]   Whilst Spring-heeled Jack was not anchored to one place his migratory propensities did not necessarily weaken his impact on the local collective memory. At least one London street was long associated with him. See *Newcastle Courant*, 13th May 1881, p. 6.
[5]   For more on this see Gunnell, *Legends and Landscape*, p. 14. For the difficulties in defining the 'local' as a historical unit see Sheeran, 'Discourses in Local History'. For its importance to an understanding of popular cultural operation see Wood, *Politics of Social Conflict*, pp. 26–37. Rather than attempting to offer a generic definition of 'locality' this chapter focuses on the specificity of particular 'places' and 'spaces'.

the interaction between the Spring-heeled Jack 'text' and the context in which it operated. Through a focus on localised cultures this chapter seeks to soften rigid dichotomies such as urban/rural and metropolitan/provincial. As indicated in the previous chapter, the 'metropolitan' was far from a singular, homogeneous concept, and such falsehoods are only compounded when one tries to set them into dichotomous formulations against their provincial 'other'.[6] This is not to suggest that these cultural distinctions did not exist, merely that an oppositional conceptualisation is more prone to obscuring than revealing historical realities and cultural transferences.

The chapter begins with an examination of how cultural localities acquired and reworked Spring-heeled Jack through a combination of resident and migratory factors. Of particular importance here was the fluid, metamorphic quality of the legend and the way it could be shaped to the physical and cultural environment in which it operated. Secondly, it considers the differing communal responses that were provoked by Spring-heeled Jack's appearances, with reactions often being influenced by the anxieties and attitudes within the specific locality in which they occurred. The chapter then explores how Spring-heeled Jack was enveloped into the marking (and making?) of local places, with his spatial 'performances' potentially having both conservative and radical dimensions. Given his origin around London, it will be argued that his appropriation into other localities illustrates they possessed degrees of vitality and agency that have been persistently underestimated by our inclinations towards thinking in terms of metropolitan cultural impositions on the provinces. Through these various considerations this chapter seeks to probe the issue of how and why Spring-heeled Jack served different functions in different places and how this linked to his durability across much of the Victorian period.

Generating Localised Accounts: Resident Factors

Spring-heeled Jack's erratic movements around the country and his adoption into different cultural localities were shaped by the interaction between pre-existing resident or receptive factors within those localities and by external factors that served to enable his migration. The local environment was itself the key resident factor in the reception of Spring-heeled Jack. Whether rural or urban, the nature and influence of the local landscape played upon the imagination, generating both mundane and speculative concerns arising from their respective environments. These concerns took different forms in different locales.

---

[6] See Royle, *Modern Britain*, p. 239.

Augustus Jessop nicely summarised the fears that arose from living and working in a rural environment:

> When a man has to walk two or three miles from his work, 'in the hush of the moonless night,' weary, wet, and hungry through lonely by-paths ... it would be strange indeed if he did not meet with scares as the years go by. If his imagination be never so dull, the old traditions, handed down from ages past it may be, come in to help him. He thinks it would be impious to doubt that disembodied spirits still hover about the scenes of their earthly pilgrimage.[7]

Highlighting the isolation involved in many rural occupations, Jessop claimed rural labourers had a 'tendency to people the solitudes with phantoms, and give them form and substance', an instinct informed by their 'absorbing faith in the unseen world'. He noted that whilst they may have little faith in God he had never encountered a rural dweller 'who did not believe in the devil and his angels'.[8] Writing in 1901 a later commentator stated that 'the wide and brooding darkness' of the countryside at night and 'the absolute loneliness of the fields and roads ... tend largely to the fostering of superstition' among rural workers.[9] The rural environment seemingly encouraged an agoraphobic sense of vulnerability and exposure to open space, whilst the deep, unbroken darkness of night formed a large, black canvas onto which the imagination could imprint supernatural entities derived from both oral and literary cultures.

Importantly, both writers believed such fears were unknown in well-lit cities where policemen patrolled the streets and one was never privy to an unsettling solitude. This was not wholly accurate. As seen in the last chapter, unease arising from solitude and isolation featured in many of Spring-heeled Jack's urban and suburban attacks. Writing about the London scares of 1838 Elizabeth Villiers noted that the capital's 'lonely ways were filled with perils, and cautious folk seldom ventured abroad after dark without sufficient escort'.[10] That said, urban anxiety was more likely to derive from the claustrophobia of living so close to one another. As a lawless, amoral fiend who attacked without apparent motive or provocation Spring-heeled Jack embodied all the most feared traits of the urban stranger, that figure of threat sketched out in the works of the early urban sociologist Georg Simmel. Such a character was not usually individualised, for his menace resided in his anonymity, the fear being that amidst the myriad unknowns one passed in the modernising city one could not know who may

---

[7] Jessop 'Superstition in Arcady', p. 737.

[8] Ibid., pp. 738–9 and 743. In 1830 Robert Forby noted that a 'belief in supernatural appearances ... is often closely connected with the natural features and formation of the country in which it prevails'. See Forby, *Vocabulary of East Anglia*, vol. 2, pp. 385–6.

[9] Thelwell, 'Power of Darkness', pp. 291–2.

[10] Villiers, *Stand and Deliver*, pp. 239–40.

intend harm. At best urban dwellers could resort to visual indicators of potential threat, often relying upon associations linked to gender, age, class, demeanour and dress.[11] Spring-heeled Jack did not neatly conform to this sociological model. His appearance and actions individualised and deliberately exposed him, although his disguise confounded any attempt to read most of the signs by which other strangers were assessed. Fears of danger from strangers were not grounded in the quotidian urban environment but arose from one's interpretation of and psychological response to such a locality. These fears were culturally constructed, being the product of learned perceptions derived from oral and print media which informed one's interpretation of the local environment.[12]

Even if different environments encouraged psychologically different forms of unease, a common way to imaginatively express these fears was in terms of supernatural tropes. The pre-existence of vibrant supernatural mentalities was a second key resident factor that enabled Spring-heeled Jack's ease of adoption into localities. Whether appearing in city, town or village, his erratic perambulations suggest locals possessed a 'framework of local beliefs, legend, knowledge … and explanation' for interpreting and understanding their locality.[13] People continued to draw upon the familiarity of these local idioms, narrative tropes and beliefs in the construction of Spring-heeled Jack's accounts. For example, Spring-heeled Jack was predominantly portrayed as an outdoor ghost, most likely to be encountered in the 'wilds' of nature or the urban street rather than in the 'civilised' (and civilising) domestic interior. Such phantoms traditionally tended to be of a more violent disposition. Jacqueline Simpson has noted how accounts of 'outdoor haunting … are often so macabre that they are almost grotesque', especially compared to domestic ghosts which tend to possess 'a far more restrained and dignified manner'.[14] As such, Spring-heeled Jack's inclination towards scaring and even assaulting people in streets or lanes was very much in keeping with expectations of ghosts when encountered outside.

Regardless of their urban or rural natures, when Spring-heeled Jack entered different localities he became entangled in the cultural webs of their long, imaginative traditions of mapping, interpreting and understanding the locality through legendary associations and supernatural tropes.[15] The operation of Spring-heeled Jack's legend was not solely nor simply determined by local typography but by the body of pre-existing stories within that locality that could be reworked to

---

[11] See Simmel, 'The Stranger'.

[12] Engle Merry, 'Urban Danger', p. 68.

[13] Bushaway, 'Tacit, Unsuspected, but still Implicit Faith', p. 190.

[14] Simpson, 'Ghostly View of England's Past', p. 27.

[15] See Gunnell, 'Legends and Landscape in the Nordic Countries', p. 308. For a recent illustration of the way in which this could apply to London as much as rural communities see Roud, *London Lore*, pp. 68–9, 132–3, 184–5, 254–5 and 310–11.

accommodate his encounters. Spring-heeled Jack's appearances marked him as a 'new' creation of a locality but also one that resonated with recognisable elements within its collective folklore, making him a new variant on local predecessors and peers. As one commentator put it, 'Nearly every winter the gossips seem to have some new ghost story ... [and] some of the older and simpler folk will generally try to connect it with some half-forgotten legend which is worth preserving'. Rather than stemming from older tales Spring-heeled Jack was linked back to them, working in reverse to the expected 'forward' transmission of oral tales down through the generations.[16] Absorbed into the popular imagination from the press and, later, penny dreadful serials, Spring-heeled Jack was co-opted and associated with local phantoms, pre-existing haunted sites, and communal histories of the supernatural or the macabre. Predominantly rural Norfolk had several insubstantial 'black figures' associated with lonely country lanes, one of which would supposedly spring out of an oak tree on unsuspecting passers-by in the village of Little Melton, near Norwich. Similarly, Hampshire folklore suggested a case of a leaping figure being known around Aldershot prior to Spring-heeled Jack's appearance at the army camp in 1877.[17] Given that the jumping motif was already present in both cases, the alloying of local and imported elements enabled the conflating of Spring-heeled Jack with pre-existent tales, the result being the generation of a localised oicotype of the legend.[18]

Therefore, despite his individualised traits, Spring-heeled Jack conformed to generic legend-telling traditions, his story being articulated within a framework which involved familiar narrative strategies and performance techniques. Even his migratory nature did not necessarily distinguish him amongst local folkloric characters. Various parts of England were plagued by Jack o' Lanterns, Will-o'-the-Wisp figures who were said to pursue people at night, and by phantom black dogs with fiery or saucer-like eyes.[19] Although his supernatural qualities were questionable, his common appropriation into familiar supernatural folkloric genres invoked narrative principles that governed locals' interpretations of his activities. Contemporary accounts from those who had grown up in rural communities suggest the landscape in and around their villages and townships

---

[16] James, *Bogie Tales of East Anglia*, p. 47. See also Gunnell, 'Legends and Landscape in the Nordic Countries', p. 311.

[17] See *Norfolk and Norwich Notes and Queries*, 31st December 1904, pp. 105–6, and Boase, *Folklore of Hampshire*, p. 16.

[18] For the concept of oicotypes and oicotypification see Dundes, *International Folkloristics*, pp. 137–51.

[19] See Simpson and Roud, *Dictionary of English Folklore*, pp. 16–17, 25 and 326, and L'Estrange, *Eastern Counties Collectanea*, pp. 2–3.

swarmed with supernatural entities, tales and interpretations.[20] Nor were cities wholly devoid of such phenomena either. As one critic put it in 1858, whilst it was 'commonly imagined that superstition avoids great cities, and locates itself amid woods and streams in the depths of the country' even a passing knowledge of Londoners would dispel such misconceptions.[21]

Of course, when it comes to Spring-heeled Jack's operation in different localities we frequently operate through the lens of contemporary bias. Our dependence on Victorian journalists, folklorists and antiquarians naturally encourages us to mimic their turning a blind eye to the urban and to follow their gaze out of the cities to look upon rural communities as vestiges of a fading culture.[22] It suited contemporaries to present rural communities as the traditional, superstitious 'other' against which a progressive 'modern' urban identity could be formed. Simon Dentith has claimed that this sense of environmental and cultural division 'entered intimately into people's sense of themselves and of the communities in which they lived'.[23] However, Spring-heeled Jack disrupted such neat formulations by running amok in large cities, small towns and rural villages. His highly publicised appearances in and around London in 1838 robbed metropolitan dwellers of their easy resort to reflexive urban/rural or metropolitan/provincial dichotomies.

As if to reiterate the falsity of such rigid divisions, many of Spring-heeled Jack's earlier attacks in and around London had occurred in its more 'rural' spaces,

---

[20] See for example Bamford, *Autobiography of Samuel Bamford*, vol. 1, pp. 27–35; Lovett, *Life and Struggles of William Lovett*, p. 8; and Clare, *The Shepherd's Calendar*, pp. 10, 33–4 and 73. See also Handley, *Visions of an Unseen World*, pp. 177–209, and Vincent, *Literacy and Popular Culture*, pp. 157–60.

[21] Augustus St John, *Education of the People*, p. 32. See also Williams, *Religious Belief and Popular Culture*, pp. 54–86.

[22] Rural folklore was taken to be the remnants of a former world view and mindset that predated recent urban and industrial expansion. These remnants were perceived as 'survivals', cultural fossils from a former age that were being swiftly eroded by modern 'progress'. It was this sense of a rapidly depreciating source of access to previous mentalities that prompted many folklorists to their researches. See Bennett, 'Geologists and Folklorists' and 'Folklore Studies and the English Rural Myth', and also Boyes, 'Cultural Survival Theory'. Given these notions, Spring-heeled Jack would not even have registered as a valid example of 'folklore'. He represented an example of new or at least newly reformulated folklore at a time when it was meant to be dying out. Both his contemporaneousness and questionable validity as a genuine supernatural entity appears to have caused his omission from nineteenth-century folkloric studies.

[23] Dentith, *Society and Cultural Forms*, p. 101. These divisions were reinforced by nineteenth-century commentators on rural England. See for example William Cobbett, *Rural Rides* (1830), Sir James Caird, *English Agriculture in 1850–1851* (1851), and H. Rider Haggard's *Rural England* (1902). It was also reinforced through literary and artistic portrayals of urban and rural cultures. See Ebbatson, *Imaginary England*; Sayer, *Women of the Fields*; and Williams, *Country and the City*, especially pp. 153–232.

particularly at its suburban fringes and around its expansive 'open' areas such as Clapham and Blackheath Commons. It would be inappropriate to simply view this as a case of provincial (largely rural) migrants moving into the capital and bringing their local superstitions with them.[24] The legend neither moved with nor retained such rigidity. This rural-urban transition would have arguably taken time to percolate into urban culture, whereas accounts of Spring-heeled Jack's activities in 1837–38 moved swiftly from rural fringe to metropolitan centre in a few short months. The more realistic proposal remains that the legend's transmission to (and from) London's streets was aided by a pre-existing, fertile urban instinct for a belief in ghosts.[25] The fact that Spring-heeled Jack migrated *from* the capital to the rest of the country denied urban dwellers the comforting perception that cities were somehow isolated from such credulity. It was the very centre of urban modernity in Britain that had bequeathed this supposedly supernatural visitant to the provinces, inculcating superstitious Londoners in the legend's initial dynamism.

Spring-heeled Jack's local receptivity was aided by the anxieties generated by a given environment and the way a region's pre-existing folkloric traditions would inform the familiar assumptions of storytellers and listeners, thereby influencing the narrative contours accounts of his appearances would take. It was this strong localising of the legend that enabled later provincial accounts to speak of Spring-heeled Jack, or sometimes *a* Spring-heeled Jack (suggesting that people believed there was more than one) without ever seeming to make a direct connection with the character that had terrorised London in 1838. As a Manchester newspaper noted, 'Although Spring-heeled Jack had his activities recorded in cities and towns all over the country and, what's strange, all at the same time, local people were quite sure that he spent most of his time in Ashton [Manchester].'[26] Despite the name being well known throughout the country, each local manifestation tended to be presented as existing in isolation to others, commonly claimed as a local phenomenon rather than as a roving figure from elsewhere.[27] Yet whilst local specificity was undoubtedly important

---

[24] For this rural to urban transfer see Davidoff and Hall, *Family Fortunes*, p. 25; Hollen Lees, *Exiles of Erin*, pp. 164–97; and Hoggart, *Uses of Literacy*, pp. 24–5. For contemporary migration patterns see MacRaild and Martin, *Labour in British Society*, pp. 62–85, and Pooley and Turnbull, *Migration and Mobility in Britain*.

[25] See Davies, *The Haunted*, pp. 60–2.

[26] *Gorton and Openshaw Reporter*, 27th December 1957.

[27] This raises questions about nineteenth-century metropolitan cultural dominance over provincial regions. As suggested in the previous chapter, a metropolitan culture was not as homogeneous as contemporary assumptions sometimes suggest. Nor, as Rosemary Sweet has indicated, did provincial towns necessarily aspire to mimic metropolitan cultures. See Sweet, *The English Town, 1680–1840*, pp. 257–66.

to the generation of these narratives, one has to remain wary of turning it into an overly determining structural factor that encourages an underestimation of external influences. The very randomness of Spring-heeled Jack's appearances seem to reiterate that whilst local contextual factors could enable his adoption, they could never wholly determine it.

Generating Localised Accounts: Migratory Factors

The key factor that granted Spring-heeled Jack the ability to migrate from place to place was the malleability of the narrative components that formed his legend. Unlike the Ripper whose image and mythos gradually solidified from numerous competing rumours and interpretations, Spring-heeled Jack never quite obtained this level of coherence in the popular imagination.[28] Like most local legends, Spring-heeled Jack's lacked a definitive version though much of its narrative content clearly derived from the London accounts of 1838. Despite the metropolitan press' initial role in disseminating these narrative elements, the provincial press very swiftly started to print occurrences in other regions. These newspapers established narrative patterns of expectation, providing previously formulated scenarios from elsewhere which localised incidences could adapt to their own pre-existing body of folkloric narratives. As such, Spring-heeled Jack's migratory wanderings were less an interaction between the 'national' and 'local' or the 'metropolitan' and the 'provincial' than between a host of localities which were largely fuelled by the intercourse between print fiction and oral rumour surrounding 'real' encounters.

The nucleus of Spring-heeled Jack's legend was formed around a memorable name and an associated athleticism. Revolving around this was a host of 'satellite' narrative tropes, amongst the most frequent of which were the following: surprise leaping attacks; the appearance and/or assault in lonely lanes; the targeting of women; the impact on victims including loss of wits, being frightened to death or scared to leave their homes; claws and fire-breathing; laughing, speaking or silence; the imperviousness to attack; the wager; the dim-witted or gentleman prankster; the morphology and hybridisation of being ghost, beast-man or demon; and the armed vigilantism of local men and youths. In turn these encompassed a number of narrative aspects: Spring-heeled Jack's physical appearance and actions, the locality of encounters, his supposed motivations and uncertain ontology, and local responses. Some later cases, such as Sheffield in 1873 and the mimic in the Clyde herring port in late 1937, were particularly rich

---

[28]   See Oldridge, 'Casting the Spell of Terror'.

examples which embodied many of these tropes.[29] In May 1873 the *Sheffield and Rotherham Independent* claimed that Spring-heeled Jack's appearances were the result of a bet that a man could frighten people in the locality between Easter and Whitsun without being caught, an assertion that gained some credibility when he failed to make any more appearances after the Whitsun holidays. Suggesting insight into the details of this wager, the local newspaper claimed the 'ghost' was supposedly 'a young fellow of weak intellect' who was set to win fifty pounds if he succeeded.[30]

Yet not all of these elements had to be included for a mysterious figure to acquire the 'Spring-heeled Jack' moniker. Some accounts were constructed from very few tropes. In early October 1838 the mere fact that three men had been caught dressed as women and were subsequently involved in a brawl with police officers was enough for *The Standard* to report it under the heading 'The Spring-heeled Jack Nuisance'. When a 'Spring-heeled Jack' appeared in Surrey in August 1882 the *Daily News* reported that it was the actions of an 'imbecile' with 'a sheet and a lantern'. Perhaps given the weakness of the imitation the newspaper actively compared his foolish behaviour as akin to 'the original Spring-heeled Jack' which had terrified the inhabitants of Kensington 'some forty odd years ago.'[31]

Although Spring-heeled Jack frequently underwent recontextualising to fit into a local environment, a point best illustrated by the shifts between his phantasmal and bestial portrayals, there was not usually a wholesale appropriation into a local context. Rather the local environment (both typographical and cultural) was influential in shaping a hierarchy of central and peripheral tropes in any particular account, a process that informed the encouraging or discouraging of certain signifying elements over others. What was typically retained was an amalgamation of locally existing folkloric 'texts' and external, migratory narrative tropes derived from print media. This mercurial trait had been present from the very beginning. As accounts moved ever closer to London from their largely rural origins in Barnes in autumn 1837 Spring-heeled Jack had transformed from a phantasmal bull to a white bear, to something increasingly anthropomorphic. Whereas rural locales possessed long folkloric traditions of phantasmal animals, these could not be so easily accommodated in the modern metropolis. By anthropomorphising Spring-heeled Jack into a steel-armoured ghost he became, relatively speaking, more credible.[32] As the attack on Jane Alsop in February 1838 indicated, he continued to evolve, adopting a more demonic countenance

---

[29] See *Daily Mirror*, 6th December 1937.
[30] *Sheffield and Rotherham Independent*, 23rd May 1873.
[31] See 'Worship Street: The Spring-heeled Jack Nuisance', *The Standard*, 2nd October 1838, and *Daily News*, 22nd August 1882, p. 4.
[32] See *Morning Herald*, 10th January 1838.

with eyes like 'red balls of fire' and sharp claws.[33] Similarly, when he ventured out into the provinces his image shifted again. The account in the *Brighton Gazette* in 1838 was typical in recording that by the time he had reached the Sussex coast he had, according to one witness, reverted to 'the shape of a bear' or some animal that walked on all fours.[34] When he appeared in predominantly rural Lincolnshire in 1877 eyewitnesses similarly described a figure 'dressed in a sheep skin, or something of the kind, with a long white tail to it'.[35]

These migratory transformations impacted on the narrative possibilities available in accounts of Spring-heeled Jack. Whilst metropolitan victims had made much of the harm done by a demonic figure's metal claws and fire-breathing, in the provinces these disappeared as he took on more bestial associations.[36] As time passed he also became less vicious. Increasingly, people were no longer physically assaulted or grappled. Rather Spring-heeled Jack adopted a baffling strategy of leaping up to women at night, terrifying them with a maniacal laugh, then leaping away, leaving them shocked but unmolested. Despite his obvious physicality when attacking Londoners in the late 1830s and early 1840s, provincial accounts were also more inclined to depict him as a ghost. This seems to have derived less from an identifiable 'rural' mentality informed by supernatural folklore than a more general inclination in the popular imagination to frighten oneself with ghosts when feeling isolated. The sentries at remote posts on the Aldershot army base in 1877 referred to a 'ghost' when they were harassed by an unknown entity, and it appears to have been a familiar trope in such circumstances.[37]

Therefore, localised Spring-heeled Jack encounters did not simply recreate a rigid template narrative that had been constructed in 1837–38 and was simply incorporated in its entirety from outside the region. Instead, informed by localised factors they adopted some of the transferable tropes within that formulation (most obviously the name), adapted others and completely neglected

---

[33]   *The Times*, 22nd February 1838. See also *The Times*, 23rd February 1838, and *The Examiner*, 4th March 1838.

[34]   See *The Times*, 14th April 1838.

[35]   *Illustrated Police News*, 3rd November 1877. David Hopkin has raised the important question of whether narrative variation of a legend in a particular locality represented genuine differences derived from geographical location or the influence of more personal attributes of storytellers such as their gender, occupation or individual character. With a few remarkable exceptions the available evidence on specific Spring-heeled Jack encounters tends to be either sketchy or condensed. Furthermore, they were frequently filtered through the educated condescension of contemporary journalists or antiquarians, thus depriving us of many of the clues by which we could pursue Hopkin's interesting query. See Hopkin, 'Legendary Places', p. 67.

[36]   The only exception I have found was the attack on a woman in Whitby in 1838. See *Leeds Mercury*, 19th May 1838.

[37]   See *The Times*, *North Wales Chronicle* and the *Preston Guardian*, all from 28th April 1877.

the rest. This operation of the legend in different localities can be seen as a form of what folklorists term 'troping'. This involves 'the manipulation and remodeling within different cultural environments of a familiar or recognizable character'. Yet whilst it has been claimed that 'such figures carry with them a potentially enormous amount of "tropic baggage"', this was not necessarily the case with Spring-heeled Jack.[38] To stretch the metaphor, he could be assimilated into localities with a minimum of unpacking, bringing merely the tropic equivalent of a toothbrush – his name.

This was key to the legend's second migratory factor, namely the retrospective application of Spring-heeled Jack's name to frightening or strange encounters. This was the hook that helped attach the rather fluid collection of narrative tropes outlined above to a localised incident through its single most consistent aspect. Frequently, Spring-heeled Jack was not identified at the time but in hindsight, the corpus of his legend being constructed through a backward rather than a forward-looking perspective. With reference to oral testimony from his grandparents in Sheffield, David Clarke has noted how accounts of 'ghosts, agile prowlers and mystery assailants, sometimes – but not always – linked in the popular imagination with the activities of Spring-heeled Jack'.[39] By the 1880s, the period Clarke refers to, Spring-heeled Jack had certainly become an established, individualised trope which provided an explanatory function in such cases. (Of course, this retrospective application does not explain why such associations were only made sometimes and not others.) When Elliott O'Donnell's nurse gave an account of her encounter with Spring-heeled Jack in Herefordshire in the 1880s she described how something had bounded over a hedge, scared her and leapt away again. It was her aunt who later told her that it must have been Spring-heeled Jack since he 'had recently been terrifying country folk by bounding over walls and haystacks at night'.[40] Appropriating the name of Spring-heeled Jack in this way retrospectively imposed form and shape onto a localised incident involving shock, evasion and a lingering sense of puzzlement. As mysterious as Spring-heeled Jack remained, the mere idea of him was enough to suggest comprehension, his familiar narrative filling in some of the blanks left by such a baffling experience and providing a more specific formulation by alluding to a recognised character rather than a mere ghost. This was perhaps most pertinent in the growing urban localities where physical expansion equated to a relative contraction in one's known space. If one was to be confronted with a stranger then better that it was a 'known' stranger such as Spring-heeled Jack. In this simple function, the superficial comprehension of strange encounters, one

---

[38] Mack, *Wonderful and Surprising History of Sweeney Todd*, p. 96.
[39] Clarke, 'Unmasking Spring-heeled Jack', p. 33.
[40] O'Donnell, *Haunted Britain*, p. 75.

can see something of his enduring appeal and persistence throughout much of the nineteenth century.

Localised Functions

All legends that are repeated and survive do so because they necessarily serve a communal purpose. As both cultural product and practice a legend symbolically articulates 'the collective experiences and values of the group to whose tradition it belongs'.[41] Whilst frequently seeking to entertain, it is also a mode through which to 'inform, explain, warn or educate' others.[42] The incorporation of localised incidences or figures into the Spring-heeled Jack mythos served a number of local functions, at least until it waned towards the end of the century.

Firstly, as with the period's craze for spiritualism, Spring-heeled Jack can be read as another contemporary reformulation of 'traditional' supernatural beliefs.[43] He may have remained grounded in local ethnographic ghost lore rather than being located in the more pseudo-scientific discourses surrounding séances, and his name clearly resonated with all the other Jacks of oral folklore (and chapbook literature), but he possessed aspects that were notably new. Whereas Jack, the owner of the seven league boots, had worn magical footwear, folklorists such as William Gerish pointed to Spring-heeled Jack's spring heels, presumed to be mechanical devices, as evidence of his relative modernity.[44] Through the aid of mechanisation Spring-heeled Jack could perform feats that had previously been confined to magical folklore. As such, he encapsulated the supposed disenchantment that derived from industrial modernisation and yet also alluded to the compensatory search for re-enchantment that was to be found in contemporary magical shows which similarly employed mechanisations to create abnormal feats and illusions. Like these entertainments, he also afforded a seemingly contradictory connected-but-distanced engagement with older supernatural ideas.[45] Spring-heeled Jack could allow one to speak freely of ghosts but, if needed, there was always the option of adopting an ironic distance from such matters by dismissing him as a mere human prankster. When Spring-heeled Jack visited Norwich in the early 1850s a local street ballad recorded that he was believed to have either risen out of the ground as a portent of death or

---

[41] Tangherlini, *Interpreting Legend*, p. 22.

[42] Simpson, 'Local Legend', p. 25.

[43] For more on nineteenth-century spiritualism see Melechi, *Servants of the Supernatural*; Lamont, 'Spiritualism and a mid-Victorian Crisis of Evidence'; and Pearsall, *The Table-Rappers*.

[44] See *Norfolk and Norwich Notes and Queries*, 5th November 1898, p. 411.

[45] See Landy and Saler, *Re-enchantment of the World*; During, *Modern Enchantments*; and Cook, *Arts of Deception*.

descended from the heavens. It concluded that 'many more tales of this ghost were told that were strongly believed by young and by old'.[46] This miasma of speculation certainly indicates an openness to belief in something more than the terrestrially mundane. Recounting this event in 1880, Mark Knights noted how the 'circumstantial stories' of Spring-heeled Jack had given elderly Norwich dwellers 'abundant opportunity for gossip of a conjectural nature'. Spring-heeled Jack, a consciously modern legend, enabled speculation about ideas that in their older, unreconstituted folkloric form would have jarred with the rationalising rhetoric of the period.[47]

More importantly, Spring-heeled Jack's appearances and encounters were spatial occurrences that were appropriated into localised mappings of both place and community. The specificity of place was important to the formulation and reception of Spring-heeled Jack accounts, but it was also important to their credibility. This served to root his accounts in the mundane world, as real events in known sites, whilst the association with the fantastical simultaneously imbued that location with a sense of difference.[48] The power of these incidents arose from the spatial dissonance derived from this mundane-in-the-fantastical and fantastical-in-the-mundane. In most accounts Spring-heeled Jack was encountered on roads, both a common, tangible location for memorable incidences and the natural routes along which his legend would be transmitted. Yet urban and rural environments tended to accommodate their hauntings in different localities, and Spring-heeled Jack was very much in keeping with these local expectations. In towns and cities he was typically associated with particular buildings or sites. When visiting Norwich in the early 1850s he was said to originate from 'the waste of the brickground between the line of railway – then being made – and Southwell Road'.[49] In London in 1882 he loitered 'in a lonely spot in Woodpecker Lane, between New Cross and Rotherhithe', whilst in Darlington two years later he was seen in Neasham Road and Rise Carr. In Ashton, Manchester, the 'entrance to Parson's Yard by the side of the Boar's Head, and Wicker Gate in Scotland Street, were two of his vantage points'.[50]

Spring-heeled Jack's most frequent urban spatial association after streets was with churchyards. As liminal sites between the dead and living, they provided a potent blend of the sacred, the macabre and possibly the supernatural. Spring-

---

[46] Norfolk Heritage Centre, 'Pranks of the Ghost'.

[47] Knights, *Norfolk Stories*, p. 7. For the relationship between the supernatural and rhetorical modernity see Bell, *Magical Imagination*, pp.117–56.

[48] A similar technique was repeatedly used in contemporary street ballads and broadsides related to fictional ghosts. See for example Hindley, *Curiosities of Street Literature*, p. 138.

[49] Knights, *Norfolk Stories*, p. 8.

[50] See *Daily News*, 22nd August 1882; *North-Eastern Daily Gazette*, 28th January 1884; and *Gorton and Openshaw Reporter*, 27th December 1957.

heeled Jack's association with graveyards tapped into older folkloric superstitions that tended to focus around such places. Even if they were not viewed as wholly sacred they at least possessed a sense of spatial 'otherness' compared to the rest of the locality. In the early 1830s in particular urban churchyards had become linked with bodysnatching in the popular imagination, and more than one graveyard 'ghost' had turned out to be a person protecting the corpse of a family member from theft.[51] Elizabeth Villiers gave an account of Spring-heeled Jack from 1838 in which an elderly woman was attacked outside Clapham churchyard. Her two sons who had left her alone to retrieve an item she had left at a friend's passed 'a solitary pedestrian', a tall, slim man sporting dark clothes and a fashionable cape. Shortly after, they heard their mother scream and raced back to find her holding onto the churchyard railings and claiming 'a black object had leapt past her, clearing the railings in a bound to disappear into the shadows' of the graveyard. The implication was that it had been the solitary pedestrian.[52] When Spring-heeled Jack had appeared in Tottenham in October 1841 he had escaped a pursuing policeman by fleeing into a nearby churchyard. In Wrexham in 1886 he created 'the utmost excitement and alarm ... in the district lying between the Wrexham cemetery and Exlusham', whilst in Chirk, Denbighshire in 1887 it was reported that 'he performs his antics in the churchyard'.[53] Spring-heeled Jack clearly conformed to popular expectations that ghosts were likely to be encountered in these most imaginatively engaging of heterotopian sites.[54]

In the countryside ghosts were more inclined to loiter on lonely roads, near bridges or by unusual typographical or man-made features, particularly gibbets.[55] Legends tended to cluster at a communities' perceived boundaries, formulating around locations which emphasised the uncertain, liminal fringes where a known 'owned' place met and merged with the unknown and the unowned. Typically, these were located at 'crossroads ... hilltops, gates, stiles, patches of no-man's-land', whilst the most haunted roads in a locality tended to be those

---

[51] Such was the case of the St Giles' Church 'ghost' in London in 1834. See Davies, *The Haunted*, pp. 60–1.

[52] Villiers, *Stand and Deliver*, p. 245.

[53] See *Freeman's Journal*, 26th October 1841; *Cheshire Observer*, 16th January 1886, p. 2; and *Leicester Chronicle*, 24th December 1887, p. 4.

[54] For more on Foucault's notion of 'heterotopia' see Tonkiss, *Space, the City and Social Theory*, pp. 132–5.

[55] Gibbets remained 'a significant part of the English landscape' until the mid 1850s. The practice of gibbeting criminals and leaving their corpses to rot denied them a Christian burial and helped contribute to fears of haunting. Gibbets were often located at 'parish boundaries that traversed common land', again reinforcing a sense of supernatural possibilities in liminal spaces. See Davies, *The Haunted*, p. 53.

that ran along or crossed over parish boundaries.[56] As in urban centres, Spring-heeled Jack's rural accounts tended to highlight specific locations. Prior to the arrest of Richard Bradford, the butcher who had dressed as a woman to bait Spring-heeled Jack in February 1845, local rumour indicated that he had been seen in Boston Lane, a road between Brentford and Hanwell. In Warwickshire in the 1880s Spring-heeled Jack had been 'a terror in lonely country districts', for he was in the habit of concealing himself 'behind hedges abutting on the highway near churchyards'. In the vicinity of Neath in 1898 Spring-heeled Jack had terrorised servant girls on Cimla Hill before moving into the more heavily populated town.[57]

The association with these communal markers eased Spring-heeled Jack's incorporation into local memory. A haunted space was an intensified space, one that became easier to remember, even memorialise. As personal encounter or, more often, related story, Spring-heeled Jack performed this transformative act, articulating a sense of emotionalised space by infusing it with fearful con-notations. Like all ghost stories, accounts of his actions enlivened and altered localised spaces by imprinting the aura of the encounter upon it. In doing so specific locations became signifiers which triggered memories and stories of the intrusion. Indulging in ideas of ghosts, demons or even vicious human pranksters all represented a willingness to mark space. Such accounts served to construct what the social theorist Henri Lefebvre referred to as 'representational space', that is space which is subjectively imbued with alternative, often subver-sive readings to more official spatial orderings such as formal maps. As such, Spring-heeled Jack's legend reflected an appropriation of physical space in the local imagination, one which created an altered reading and understanding of local typography.[58]

Spring-heeled Jack's localised spatial functions were shared by numerous local accounts of ghosts, fairies and other supernatural entities. Yet he also differed from them too. The folklorist Timothy Tangherlini has nicely defined a legend as 'a traditional, (mono)episodic ... localized and historicized narrative of past events told as believable'.[59] Spring-heeled Jack's legend largely conformed to the mono-episodic, localised parts of this but obviously diverged from the tradi-tional and, in some cases, the historicised aspects. Local legends tended to attach

---

[56] See Simpson, 'Local Legend', p. 28, and Davies, *The Haunted*, p. 46. The likelihood of roadside hauntings was enhanced by the practice of burying suicides at crossroads. Believed to be among the restless dead, their burial at crossroads was supposed to disorientate spirits if they returned. The practice was ended in 1823.

[57] See *Age and Argus*, 8th February 1845, p. 3; *Notes and Queries*, 10th Series, 18th May 1907, p. 395; and *Western Mail*, 15th November 1898, p. 6. See also *Ipswich Journal*, 14th March 1885.

[58] See Lefebvre, *Production of Space*, p. 39. See also Dennis, *Cities in Modernity*, pp. 104–5.

[59] Tangherlini, *Interpreting Legend*, p. 22.

themselves to unusual features in the environment, either natural or architectural, the existence of which usually served as post hoc verification for the tale.[60] This generally required an elapse of time in which the local community could collectively forget the original function of an object before rereading it in terms of its legendary associations.[61] Spring-heeled Jack's contemporaneousness did not allow his legend to operate in this way. Even within oral cultures he was presented more as current news than remote legend, a narrative approach which negated the structuring format of older local legends which were related as having been experienced by previous generations. In what would become recognised as a more modern urban folkloric formulation, his encounters had to be presented as having happened to a friend of a friend.[62] Whilst this association with a living, peripheral acquaintance brought the threat closer than the temporal distance of historical legends, it was never so near as to have been directly experienced by the teller or listener themselves. Devoid of the comforting safety of the past, this narrowed space between the contemporary locality and self generated a more thrilling frisson and perhaps a heightened cathartic release from the fear expressed in the account.

As a contemporary menace Spring-heeled Jack could not perform the usual ghostly task of linking memory, place and identity. A sense of locality both existed in and was composed of local narratives and memories. Whilst ghosts evoked a temporal dissonance, existing in the present but firmly anchored to some past time or event in the history of the community, Spring-heeled Jack did not. Created in the present he had no such purchase on the past, especially in terms of the specific locality he happened to be passing through. Even if locals accepted their indigenous ghosts as aspects of their community and their past, Spring-heeled Jack always came from outside those communities. Nor did he ever linger long enough to put down roots so as to contribute to a local community's historical sense of itself. At best he was a fleeting, if memorable, visitor. Only when he was perceived as a hoaxer, and the hoaxer was revealed, did the link to the local community manifest itself. In these cases the prankster who had temporarily placed himself outside the community by his actions was reintegrated, albeit grudgingly. During the interregnum between the scares and the revelation of the assailant being one of their own, the rest of the community had been encouraged to draw together, usually to form patrols of men and boys against the perceived threat. As such, accounts of Spring-heeled Jack became a means of temporarily reinvigorating communal bonds built around stories

---

[60]   See Simpson, 'Local Legend', pp. 27–9.
[61]   Clarke suggests this happened to Spring-heeled Jack in retrospect in Sheffield. See Clarke, 'Unmasking Spring-heeled Jack', pp. 42–3.
[62]   For a modern compendium of such tales see Brunvand, *Too Good to be True*.

which reinforced identification with both specific localities and one another. In cases where pranksters were captured there was often an understandable anger directed towards the individual, who was frequently portrayed as a weak-minded fool who could have caused real harm, but their actions were never presented as a betrayal of the community from within. Such was the case in rural Warwickshire in the 1880s. Spring-heeled Jack's terrorising of women in the locality had led to a communal hunt which resulted in the capture of a local coal merchant's son who had dressed up in ghostly mask and a long white sheet. Taking the hoax further than most, he had supposedly fitted springs to his shoes.[63] Lambasting his foolishness, his captors still implicitly viewed him as one of their community.

Spring-heeled Jack's contemporaneousness was complicated from the 1860s onwards by the fact that contemporary accounts continued to be generated whilst coexisting with a developing emphasis on his earlier, now 'historical', narratives.[64] As with seemingly isolated localised encounters there was a remarkable degree of disconnection between these contemporary and 'historical' narratives. That this development began when it did can plausibly be put down to the fact that these retrospective interpretations derived from the first generation of early Victorians who had grown up in the legend's heyday. Whilst his contemporary accounts continued to fulfil the various functions indicated in this and previous chapters, his incorporation into nostalgic reflections served a more conventional purpose. Just as Spring-heeled Jack helped mark a specific place, so he also became a signifier through which to reconnect with a remembered (or imagined) past. In these cases Spring-heeled Jack was usually invoked as a colourful bogeyman from a superstitious childhood from which individual writers had subsequently evolved.[65] In this context his value as a symbolic marker had less to do with the history of a locality and more to do with personal histories of intellectual and psychological development.

Spatial Performances

The dramaturgy of Spring-heeled Jack's manifestations went beyond mere mapping of a locality. As localised performances they were a means by which a

---

[63] See William Jaggard's contribution to *Notes and Queries*, 10th Series, 18th May 1907, p. 395.

[64] For examples of this trend towards retrospective articles on Spring-heeled Jack from the 1860s see *London Society*, February 1863, pp. 152–3; *Temple Bar*, May 1863, p. 276; *Leeds Mercury*, 26th September 1865, p. 3; *Manchester Times*, 1st August 1868; and *Bradford Observer*, 4th November 1875, p. 8.

[65] See Vincent, *Literacy and Popular Culture*, pp. 156–60, and Rose, *Intellectual Life of the British Working Classes*, pp. 58–91.

cipher could be imbued with social purpose and cultural meaning. When reports circulated that Spring-heeled Jack had been seen in Chapelfield in Norwich in the early 1850s, one Norwich ballad claimed that every night for a week the streets of the city were thronged with hundreds of people eager to catch sight of him.[66] Later, in Birmingham 'many thousands of people assembled in High Street and the Bull Ring to see Spring-heeled Jack leap from the roof of the market hall against the spire of St Martin's Church, and for a fortnight afterwards pursued this ubiquitous spectre all over the town'.[67] Referring to an appearance of Spring-heeled Jack in late-nineteenth-century Portsmouth, F. J. Proctor recounted how he had stood 'awestruck among a crowd watching the leaps of the spook over tombs on a starry midnight'.[68] Safe in the crowded, gaslit streets, confrontation with and hunts for Spring-heeled Jack could be transformed into a cheap, shared, impromptu entertainment for sensation-hungry urban consumers.[69] This was especially true after the 1840s when Spring-heeled Jack appeared to lose much of his initial viciousness and replaced it with a greater emphasis on merely surprising pedestrians and taunting pursuers. Unlike traditional local legends Spring-heeled Jack afforded urban communities the opportunity to not merely recount stories but actively participate in a current narrative as his hunters.

These hunts for Spring-heeled Jack, like other urban ghost hunts, provided an opportunity for local communities to publicly and visibly assert themselves in 'their' space. When police tried to move on crowds that had gathered to see 'Spring-heeled Jack' near the Cholera Monument in Sheffield in May 1873, scuffles broke out. Rumours of Spring-heeled Jack being in the locality were not just a powerful way of drawing urban crowds; in seeking to see or even capture this famously elusive figure the crowds were granted a purpose that meant they were at least temporarily less willing to tolerate the efforts of police to control *their* streets in Victorian England.[70] In these circumstances, sensationalism overrode obedience.

Spring-heeled Jack's apparent ability to provoke crowds to rush through the streets in pursuit of rumoured sightings can be read as what Michel De Certeau termed a spatial 'tactic', one that was often employed in tacit opposition to more official spatial orderings and understandings of a locality. In their movements Spring-heeled Jack's pursuers generated 'their own spatial meanings, producing

[66] See Norfolk Heritage Centre, 'Pranks of the Ghost'.
[67] *Birmingham Daily Post*, 12th January 1888.
[68] Proctor, *Reminiscences of Old Portsmouth*, p. 27.
[69] See Davies, *The Haunted*, pp. 90–4.
[70] Clarke, 'Unmasking Spring-heeled Jack', p. 38. A similar occurrence took place with regard to the Bermondsey ghost in 1868. See Davies, *The Haunted*, pp. 61–2.

urban space in … idiomatic ways'.[71] In these chases the city was no longer an ordered plan of mundane streets, monitored and controlled by developing police forces. Rather it was transformed into a terrain in which the mysterious, perhaps even the supernatural, was being sought and hunted. Most of the spatial tactics outlined by De Certeau are temporary, private disruptions to ordered space. However, Spring-heeled Jack's notoriety, and particularly his allusions to the supernatural, meant such public disruptions were more likely to be logged in the collective memory and imagination, in effect prolonging the disruptive tactic and the escape it continued to offer from formal spatial orderings. In such circumstances Spring-heeled Jack could become implicated in the struggle for the interpretation of local spaces.

The nineteenth-century popular imagination was familiar with thinking and expressing protest through imaginary figures. This included notable migratory, regional characters such as the elusive Ned Ludd and Captain Swing. Katrina Navickas' recent work on the mythology of General Ludd suggests particularly strong parallels with the operation of Spring-heeled Jack's legend. Both operated at the neighbourhood level yet witnessed a pan-regional appropriation of a collective figure, the migration of which was aided by oral rumour and, over longer distances, newspaper reports. Navickas claims Ludd represented a popular radical desire for a leader, and, unable to procure one locally in the face of official repression, people invented an imaginary one.[72] Whilst Spring-heeled Jack was certainly not a radical leader of men, his vicarious freedom in an increasingly disciplined and controlled society clearly inspired numerous hoaxers to follow his idiosyncratic activities. Through donning a disguise to mimic or evoke Spring-heeled Jack they presumably found something appealingly liberating or empowering. How far this was linked to protest against social restraint and how much it derived from their own psychological deviancy is open to question. Yet almost regardless of whether he was real or a hoaxer Spring-heeled Jack offered a guerrilla enactment of the carnivalesque, a spatial disruption that temporarily confounded contemporary efforts to reformulate urban space as a site of regulation, surveillance and therefore (self-) restriction.[73]

These parallels with other imagined figures merely illustrate the similarities in their cultural operation; it is not suggested that Spring-heeled Jack was a popular

---

[71] Tonkiss, *Space, the City and Social Theory*, p. 138. See also De Certeau, *Practice of Everyday Life*, p. 31.

[72] See Navickas, 'Search for "General Ludd"', especially pp. 283–4 and 294–5. See also Jones, 'Finding Captain Swing', pp. 429–58, and Polletta, *It Was Like a Fever*.

[73] For the increasing restraints on urban popular cultures see Springhall, *Youth, Popular Culture and Moral Panics*; Golby and Purdue, *Civilisation of the Crowd*, especially pp. 144–202; and Inwood, 'Policing London's Morals'. For the rural context and nineteenth-century resentments see Reay, *Last Rising of the Agricultural Labourers* and *Rural England*, and also Lee, *Unquiet Country*.

liberator. As illustrated in Chapter 3, it is equally easy to read Spring-heeled Jack as an agent of restriction rather than a radical force, one which asserted control over certain spaces and sections of the community through the use of fear. Through him local communities could also articulate their moral norms, particularly that it was wrong to harm the more vulnerable members of that community, and that property and boundaries should be respected. Like more modern urban folktales some accounts of Spring-heeled Jack even emphasised the punishment of possible sexual impropriety by the young. As F. J. Proctor recounted, Spring-heeled Jack was said to 'jump over hedges to frighten courting couples spooning in the fields of Landport', spaces that were in the process of being incorporated into the urban expansion of Portsmouth.[74] As with many local legends it is more appropriate to recognise that Spring-heeled Jack could both 'depict …and, at the same time, contest the social order'.[75]

In terms of both scale and density nineteenth-century urban development arguably stimulated rather than negated a desire for some form of communal bonds. At the same time it also offered new ways of encouraging a sense of community, amongst which we can include emerging modern urban folklore. As such, Spring-heeled Jack became another strand in the weaving of temporary communities, a notion expressed in their participation in the street theatre that surrounded his hunts and, more generally, through the exchange of shared narratives surrounding a common figure. Based around shared stories rather than kinship these looser knowledge or narrated community nevertheless possessed what Fran Tonkiss has referred to as 'affective and voluntary bonds' amongst 'fictional kinship groups'.[76] Although such communities were differently constructed and constituted, one should not assume their bonds were automatically weak, for they still demanded an imaginative investment on the part of their more diffused members.

Rural dwellers' responses to Spring-heeled Jack appear to have been slightly different to those of urban communities, although we have to be wary of contemporary biases that sought to present dichotomies between rural believers and sceptical urbanites who viewed Spring-heeled Jack as a 'lark'. Accounts suggest he remained a source of genuine dread in the countryside, providing a new name for old fears born from solitude and darkness. When rural communities gathered against Spring-heeled Jack there was little sense of it being an ad hoc entertainment and more the need to repel the threat to a besieged community. In 1886 the comic paper *Fun* described 'Spring-heeled Jacks' as 'terrible inflictions in quiet, peaceful districts'. Recounting how a 'supposed S. H. J. appeared in the

---

[74]   Proctor, *Reminiscences of Old Portsmouth*, p. 27.
[75]   Siikala, 'Reproducing Social Worlds', p. 59.
[76]   Tonkiss, *Space, the City and Social Theory*, p. 24.

neighbourhood of Manchester recently', it described a figure 'scantily attired in white [who] bounded wildly through the suburban streets at night' before racing 'across country, after dusk, at an astounding rate'. The account was accompanied by the familiar tropic elements of women suffering fits and becoming hysterical, frightened boys, and 'countrymen [who] rolled into wet ditches, paralyzed with fear'. Faced with this threatening 'apparition', 'the suburban populace rose to a man, and armed with horsewhips, toasting-forks, broom-handles, pokers, brickbats, and flat-irons, they chased the supposed Jack, uttering horrible cries of vengeance'. The punchline to the piece was that locals had mistaken a cross-country runner who liked training at night for Spring-heeled Jack, illustrating again that the combination of a mysterious figure and athletic ability was all that was often required to incorporate a local incident into the legend.[77] Whilst the nature of the publication would suggest much of this was heightened for comedic effect, the resort to collective vigilantism in supposedly peaceful neighbourhoods was far from unique.[78]

In their use of Spring-heeled Jack's performances rural communities alluded to a more muted form of spatial assertion. In at least one northern community Spring-heeled Jack was associated with local moors, sites which frequently had lingering legendary associations but also possessed contemporary symbolic links to social and political agitation.[79] The *Wakefield Examiner* reported that when 'a ghost called "Spring-heeled Jack"' had been driven from the town he had reappeared on the nearby East Moor at night.[80] A number of rural reports also claimed Spring-heeled Jack escaped pursuers by crossing into fields, thereby transgressing private boundaries. Like ghosts that passed through walls, one could read Spring-heeled Jack's unhindered movement across fields as collectively imagined incursions into private property, in effect asserting a communal negation of the recognition of such boundaries. However, given that many of these accounts came from later in the century, it would perhaps be stretching credibility to suggest this derived from a lingering resentment at enclosures.[81] Even if such associations could be found it would be unwise to simply suggest a direct causal link between local tensions and the appearance of Spring-heeled Jack in the region. His erratic movements are themselves indicative of the fact that his behaviour was rarely that transparent. As much as this apparent

[77] 'Knicknacks', *Fun*, 3rd March 1886, p. 98.
[78] See for example Varden, 'Traditions, Superstitions and Folklore', p. 86.
[79] See Navickas, 'Moors, Fields, and Popular Protest', pp. 93–111. In the same year Spring-heeled Jack terrorised London the Chartists held one of their first great mass meetings at Kersall Moor near Manchester in September 1838.
[80] *Manchester Times*, 10th May 1850.
[81] See for example *Bristol Mercury*, 31st October 1878, p. 6, and *Northern Echo*, 1st August 1884, p. 4.

randomness jars against the historian's desire to impose patterns and understanding on the functioning of past cultural practices, it has to be accepted that a satisfactory explanation as to why he appeared exactly when and where he did remains elusive.

Spring-heeled Jack's legend was undoubtedly informed by the nature of the communities and local environments he passed through, but these contextual factors should not be understood as (overly) determining cultural structures. Rather than being simply appropriated into a static, pre-existing, localised mental landscape of supernatural folklore, he altered and added to it, being able to mark his passing by possessing a greater degree of individuality than more generic spectres. At the same time communities' sense of having pushed the threat of Spring-heeled Jack elsewhere enabled them to reassert their agency over 'their' local space. In these ways he served a similar function as the idea of *heimat* in German history, that is 'the negotiation of locality, place, and tradition in the face of historical change'.[82] Grounded in the relationship between local landscape and community, *heimat* was frequently dependent upon a sense of collective insiders in conflict with an external 'other'. As with migratory accounts of Spring-heeled Jack this typically led to the expulsion of the threat whilst also serving to rouse the community to an appreciation of external influences beyond their locality.[83] Generally, those influences were treated in terms of modern 'progress' coming into conflict with local tradition, a simplistic distinction somewhat complicated here. Spring-heeled Jack embodied both 'modern' urban legend traits and associations with local communities' 'traditional' narrative tropes. He was also simultaneously a transregional and local entity. Through localised appropriations, he demonstrated communities' ability to reconfigure a 'national' figure via their local context.

This was clearly demonstrated during his appearance in Sheffield in 1873, when locals living around the Park district of the city came to refer to him as the 'Sheffield Spring-heeled Jack'. This sense of local appropriation seems to have persisted in the area, for in a newspaper report on Sheffield's winter fair in 1876 one of the attractions was 'Wombwell's celebrated menagerie'. Amongst its recent additions was 'a hobgoblinscope … in which the principal attraction is Spring-heeled Jack of Rotherham'. In the context of a localised awareness of Spring-heeled Jack it is interesting to note that the newspaper added, 'Perhaps the inhabitants of Rotherham may have heard of the marvelous flights of this gentleman, but his name is as yet unknown to fame so far as we are aware.'[84]

[82]   Moltke, 'Heimat and History', p. 87.
[83]   Ibid., pp. 93–4.
[84]   Clarke, 'Unmasking Spring-heeled Jack', p. 34, and *Sheffield and Rotherham Independent*, 28th November 1876.

Spring-heeled Jack was not a colonising metropolitan figure in the provinces, nor did he simply represent the adoption of a national character. Although the metropolitan press had given the legend some early semblance of coherence via the idea of the wager, when Spring-heeled Jack moved into the provinces he once again became the mercurial creation of local speculation and rumour from which he had first emerged in late 1837. As a result of his localisation his 'narrative' became noticeably more fractured and diverse after he left the capital in 1838. Importantly, whilst the provincial press formed a web of stories about Spring-heeled Jack, they were not always reporting on accounts in their own locality. Regional newspapers frequently picked up and reported on Spring-heeled Jack's activities in other parts of the country. In some cases regional newspapers even felt obliged to print a denouncement of other papers' claims of Spring-heeled Jack rumours in their localities. In November 1878 the *Essex Standard* stated that 'the rumours relative to the appearance of the Aldershot "Spring-heeled Jack" at Colchester ... are without the slightest foundation', a claim somewhat undermined by his subsequent capture on the Colchester army base the following month.[85] This local appropriation of a widely known folkloric character allows us to appreciate Spring-heeled Jack as just one amongst numerous cultural products and practices by which people could increasingly feel a sense of shared belonging to an imagined 'national' community in this period. Yet significantly in the context of this chapter their principal point of contact with this broader, more amorphous 'national' conceptualisation was always via their own locality and the sense of identity and agency it engendered.[86]

This was most evident when local communities employed Spring-heeled Jack as a means of expressing local pride. Following the attack on a woman in Whitby in 1838 the *Leeds Mercury* used the incident to express confidence that local law enforcement agencies would prove more effective than the metropolitan police in capturing Spring-heeled Jack.[87] When a Spring-heeled Jack figure appeared in Richmond in 1884 it was claimed by the *York Herald* that locals who 'firmly believe in ghosts' took him to be 'the uneasy spirit ... of one of the warriors slain long ago in one of the many gallant struggles fought in this neighbourhood'.[88] In these functions Spring-heeled Jack illustrates how external influences, perceived

[85] This statement by the *Essex Standard* was also reprinted in other newspapers. See the *Bury and Norwich Post*, 12th November 1878, p. 7.

[86] See Anderson, *Imagined Communities,* and also Brake, Bell and Finkelstein, *Nineteenth-Century Media,* especially pp. 295–325. A sense of Spring-heeled Jack as a national or at least a nationwide figure only really came from retrospective newspaper articles that reflected back on his activities and thereby highlighted his apparent ubiquity. See for example *All the Year Round,* 9th August 1884.

[87] *Leeds Mercury,* 19th May 1838. For more on this function see Simpson, 'Local Legend', p. 32.

[88] *York Herald,* 2nd August 1884, p. 3.

as intrusions, were not so much expelled as incorporated as a means of glorifying the locality. If locals did not go so far as to make Spring-heeled Jack part of their community, they at least made him of use to that community.

One only really gains a sense of Spring-heeled Jack as a national rather than a local folkloric entity via the agglomeration of accounts in the growing number of provincial and metropolitan newspapers and journals. The quasi-omnipotent perspective granted by sifting through this accumulated evidence is more likely the preserve of the historian than the contemporary (localised) newspaper reader.[89] Spring-heeled Jack was undoubtedly a known and reasonably familiar trope, but at a national level he was little more than a catchy moniker linked to mystery and athleticism. It was in his local applications that these sketchy associations were granted greater focus, solidity and function. As such, Spring-heeled Jack serves to illustrate the persistent importance of locality in our understanding and interpretation of Victorian popular cultures.

The operation of his legend reveals localities to be powerful nodes of cultural dynamism, exchange and negotiation. The cultural 'energies' at work in localities derived from the reciprocity between 'inside' and 'outside' forces. Spring-heeled Jack illustrates how cultural practices could alter local space. Appropriated from outside the locality via stories of encounters, the narrative alchemy of those accounts helped transform known space into an enchanted place, reinforcing it by making it known again, and in a new way. At the same time local space influenced practices. Localities may have shared common tropes such as Spring-heeled Jack, but they did not occupy homogeneous cultural worlds. Spring-heeled Jack was constantly reinvented as he traversed the country, shifting back and forth between the bestial, the demonic and the human. This ongoing adoption and adaptation of the legend into local cultures can be read as an organic, largely unconscious expression of regional identity and empowerment based on particular geographical locations and their localised folklore. Localities always appropriated rather than expropriated Spring-heeled Jack because no single place, not even London, could serve as an identifiable 'owner' from which to take him from.

If the ideological purpose of legends is to illustrate how local communities are rooted and ordered in time and place, then the interaction between Spring-heeled Jack's stories and the locality in which they occurred helped create narrative landmarks. These formed a means by which communal identities

---

[89] Unlike Scotland and emergent nineteenth-century nations such as Germany, England was not compelled to draw its local legends into national collections as evidence of a pre-existing national 'folk' identity. English folkloric endeavours tended to favour the regional study. See Ashton, 'Beyond Survivalism', pp. 19–23.

could be drawn from and projected onto their local sense of place.[90] This process also helped reiterate an understanding of communal insiders and threatening outsiders. As such, Spring-heeled Jack's narratives both shaped and reflected how local spaces were perceived, conceptualised, and experienced. Importantly, whilst this powerful interactive relationship informed a sense of place and identity for locals, it was also instrumental as one of the cultural generators that sustained Spring-heeled Jack's migratory legend. It was his repeated enchanting of the mundane, the power to transform a sense of place, that gave his legend purpose and durability.

---

[90] This is not to suggest that localities would have had a homogeneous interpretation of Spring-heeled Jack accounts. These would have obviously been open to local contestation, a point most clearly indicated in the press reports surrounding his diverse appearances in London in early 1838.

7

Cultural Modes: Oral, Literary and Visual

Spring-heeled Jack's grammar of the fantastical was transmitted and translated across a variety of cultural modes, causing him to become an ever-shifting reproduction and reconstruction of himself. Whilst this led to alterations in Spring-heeled Jack's actions and appearances, even his very nature, these developments should not be viewed as elaborations upon or degenerations of a 'pure' ur-story. Rather all versions, with their resonances and disparities from one another, were incorporated into the legend.[1] Writing in 1869 James Greenwood suggested a scale of influence in regard to three popular cultural modes of the period. Whilst cheap literature was prone to stirring the imagination, the impact of visual images was both more immediate and accessible. More powerful yet was the appeal of the penny gaff theatre in which penny serials were staged and visual images given animation by actors.[2] This chapter begins by examining the ways in which Spring-heeled Jack found expression in this range of oral, literary, visual and theatrical modes. Rather than engaging with Greenwood's suggested hierarchy, the main focus will be on the fluidity with which Spring-heeled Jack moved between these modes and what this suggests about the cultural transference and symbiosis between them in this period.

Whilst exploring linkages it will also be argued that the circuit between these cultural modes was faulty, at least in the case of Spring-heeled Jack. This will be illustrated through the ambiguity that arose from his shifting back and forth between corporeal and phantasmal representations, so that he often possessed coexisting but seemingly contradictory conceptualisations in the popular imagination. Such contradictions suggest that information about Spring-heeled Jack's ontology did not transfer simply between oral and literary accounts and visual depictions. Taken as indicative of the persistence of a strong nineteenth-century oral culture, it will demonstrate the ways in which oral narratives clearly failed to follow the shifts that Spring-heeled Jack's depictions underwent in literary

---

[1] For interesting reflections on the infeasibility of a singular 'basic story' and the dynamics which foster multiple narrative versions of a tale see Hernstein Smith, 'Narrative Versions, Narrative Theories', pp. 139 and 141.

[2] Nead, *Victorian Babylon*, p. 156.

form. As with all folkloric tales, old and new, Spring-heeled Jack's was inherently unstable and fluid, for there was no 'basic' single story from which others derived or departed. Rather there was only a mass of stories which responded to or resonated with previous formations.[3]

Finally, these coexisting narratives will be used to consider the struggle for interpretation of Spring-heeled Jack. In doing so this chapter seeks to probe broader issues about where the ownership of popular cultural tropes was located, who the instigators and facilitators who shaped and governed the popular imagination were, and whether these agencies shifted during the Victorian period. Underlying this chapter is the question of whether Spring-heeled Jack was ultimately part of a culture 'of' or 'for' the people.[4] Given his fluidity across multiple cultural modes, the idea of being a product generated from 'within' or 'outside' a popular culture will necessarily be contested. In the case of Spring-heeled Jack one sees both interaction and disconnection between 'plebeian' constructions and the interpretative impositions of social superiors. Spring-heeled Jack's convoluted fusing of cultures 'of' and 'for' the people will be shown to raise difficult questions about how we should conceive the porous boundaries that normally derive from such a neat dichotomy. By focusing on cultural modes this chapter continues to probe the issue of where cultural 'energy' comes from. Rather than the nodal power of cultural localities, it considers the various arcs of transmission that generate cultural dynamism.

Cultural Modes

Oral
Oral cultures retained their tenacity in nineteenth-century cities and villages alike. Despite the changes being wrought by urbanisation, urban communities, like their rural counterparts, tended to be clearly defined by spatial boundaries and landmarks so that the 'horizons of the working class areas of the industrial cities were often ... confined essentially to the immediate neighbourhood'.[5] In such circumstances oral folklore still possessed considerable strength, and even with the rise of an increasingly literate population oral gossip remained the natural mode of communication in all plebeian communities. This was demonstrated by Spring-heeled Jack's animation in a vibrant, oral urban folklore. By operating in what has come to be identified as the classic mode of (later) urban legends, namely as having happened to a friend of a friend, his accounts were

---

[3] For a good example of this see Roalfe Cox, *Cinderella*.
[4] Bailey, 'Conspiracies of Meaning', p. 140.
[5] Dentith, *Society and Cultural Forms*, p. 58.

close enough to have credibility amongst the looser communal relationships of growing cities but detached enough not to require proof. When journalists tried to track down witnesses or victims their efforts were continually frustrated. As the *Morning Herald* stated in January 1838, 'Although the stories were in everybody's mouth, no person who had actually seen the ghost could be found.' When the reporter located named victims 'they immediately denied all knowledge of it, but directed him to other persons whom they had heard had been ill treated, but with them he met with no better success'.[6] Likewise, in Norwich in the early 1850s 'everyone had heard someone else say he or she had seen this Spring-Heeled Jack'.[7]

The power and fluidity of oral storytelling was indicated in a story featuring Spring-heeled Jack in the *Essex Standard* in 1889. The men gathered in a pub were quite happy to listen to a supernatural story by 'Old Silas' even though they had heard it 'a dozen times' because in each telling there were always new variations on the same tale. However, illustrating the way that such tales were not received in a homogeneous fashion, Old Silas' new rendition causes a brief argument about ghosts, with another character declaring, 'Ghosts is all tommyrot … I never seed no ghosts, and more wouldn't nobody else if they didn't get boozing'.[8] If the pub was a predominantly homosocial environment in which oral tales were passed on, then women tended to have their own narrative networks. In an article about night noises and ghost stories in 1844 Charles Ollier drew upon familiar gender stereotypes by declaring female domestic servants and particularly 'the gossips in the kitchen' were 'very industrious and very effectual propagators of wonderful stories'. He added that some servant girls 'have been known to make startling noises in the dead of night, purely to give birth to an awful story; and … in an incredibly short space of time they themselves believe the very marvels they invent'.[9]

Given that provincial newspapers either ignored or reported incidences some time after they had happened, the large urban crowds that sought to catch sight of Spring-heeled Jack were less likely constituted as a result of printed news and more probably from the vitality of neighborhood rumour. This was particularly the case with Spring-heeled Jack, for his bizarre appearance and actions fed into a 'public taste for the marvellous'.[10] Illustrative of both points, Spring-heeled Jack's appearance in Norwich does not appear to have been reported by the local press. However, as a contemporary local street ballad claimed, this had not stopped the city's streets being thronged with hundreds of people every night for a week, all

---

6   *Morning Herald*, 10th January 1838.
7   Knights, *Norfolk Stories*, p. 8.
8   *Essex Standard*, 28th December 1889, p. 2.
9   Ollier, 'Few Passages on Dreams', pp. 507–8.
10 *All the Year Round*, 9th August 1884, p. 349.

keen to see him. Capturing his mercurial depiction in local rumour it stated:

> Some say he was black and some say he was white,
> Some said he was short and some said he was tall,
> But many amongst them saw nothing at all.
> Some learned old women were heard for to say,
> That they certainly see him descend from the sky,
> While others declar[e]d it was a sign of some death
> As they actually see him rise out of the earth.[11]

Popular speculation about Spring-heeled Jack was incredibly rich. From 1838 onwards he was described through supernatural associations as a ghost, a demon, even the devil himself. A report in the *Daily Telegraph* from 1875 indicated that whilst opinion remained diverse, there was 'a certain consensus of tradition to the effect that he was a tall, thin, lithe man, usually clad in a macintosh overcoat and a low-crowned "billycock" hat'. Yet consensus over appearance did not restrict speculation over his identity or abilities:

> Some people believed him to be a harlequin, clown, or other acrobat, with a morbid taste for annoying and frightening innocent and timid females. Others recognised in him a well-known Marquis whose madcap freaks had at the time acquired an unenviable notoriety. Others again were of the opinion that he was a certain Royal Duke of immense wealth and with somewhat eccentric proclivities.[12]

Beyond these familiar ideas of an aristocratic prankster, the explanation to which the press was willing to grant most credence, was a wilder tumult of speculation. According to Elizabeth Villiers, after an attack on a carriage in Streatham in early 1838 'alarms came so thick and fast the scoffers were silenced … It seemed everyone who lived near … Clapham, Wandsworth, Tooting and Streatham … had some strange tale to tell.' She declared (without justification) that 'rather unaccountably, public opinion veered from thinking him a new form of highwayman and declared he was an inventor experimenting with a form of flying machine'.[13]

As indicated in the previous chapter, his memorable name was central to his widespread application and operated in a similar way to the popularity of catch phrases. Charles Mackay recognised this contemporary urban trend as a popular folly. In London phrases such as 'What a shocking bad hat!' had their vogue, and the capital proved to be 'peculiarly fertile in this sort of phrases, which spring up suddenly, no one knows exactly in what spot, and pervade the whole population

---

[11] Norfolk Heritage Centre, 'Pranks of the Ghost'.
[12] *Bradford Observer*, 4th November 1875, p. 8.
[13] Villiers, *Stand and Deliver*, pp. 244 and 247.

in a few hours, no one knows how'.[14] In a similar fashion Spring-heeled Jack's name formed a useful shorthand which signalled a host of other associations, most notably mystery and elusiveness, but also allusions to the supernatural and hoaxing. The application of the moniker in conversation drew listeners into a known frame of reference so that 'the knowledge that was knowingness [helped] complete its circuitry'.[15]

Literary

Despite having identifiable origins in oral accounts, Spring-heeled Jack's transformation into a more widely known figure was aided by his transference into various literary modes, firstly in the metropolitan and provincial press, and later in penny serials and numerous fictional tales in comics and magazines. One of the key facilitating factors aiding this transmission between cultural modes was the development of popular literacy in the nineteenth century. Several historians have echoed contemporary claims that the acquisition of plebeian reading skills was driven less by a desire to acquire 'useful knowledge' than to stimulate the imagination.[16] In a fictional tale from 1894 it was suggested that a lower-class youth, having obtained the ability to read, used it 'to cram what little intelligence he had with stories of pirates and robber kings, with secret murders and the doings of Spring-heeled Jack and other worthies of the blood-and-thunder literature which now covers the length and breadth of the land'.[17]

Whilst the metropolitan press may not have been accessed by the capital's lower orders in the late 1830s and early 1840s, it was undoubtedly instrumental in helping generate, shape and transmit the emerging Spring-heeled Jack legend.[18] This was done in a number of ways. Alongside oral rumour one has to credit the press promotion of Spring-heeled Jack accounts as encouraging

[14] Mackay, *Extraordinary Popular Delusions*, pp. 620–1. See also pp. 619–31, and Bailey, 'Conspiracies of Meaning', pp. 146–8. Spring-heeled Jack's name seems to have operated in a similar manner to what are now termed memes. See Blackmore, *Meme Machine*.

[15] Bailey, 'Conspiracies of Meaning', p. 148.

[16] Royle, *Modern Britain*, p. 355. See also Vincent, *Literacy and Popular Culture*, p. 196; Brantlinger, *Reading Lesson*; and McAleer, *Popular Reading and Publishing*, pp. 14–15. Royle suggests considerable regional variations in literacy levels in 1839. In London male literacy was as high as 88.4%, and female literacy 76.1%. In northern England the comparative rates were 79.4% and 57.7%, and in the south-east 67.4% and 60.0% respectively. See Royle, *Modern Britain*, p. 351.

[17] See *Manchester Times*, 12th October 1894 (supplement). See also *The Speaker*, 26th July 1890.

[18] For the late-eighteenth-century development of a metropolitan and provincial network of urban printers, booksellers, bookbinders, stationers and newspapers see Brewer, *Pleasures of the Imagination*, pp. 138–9, and Wilson, 'Citizenship, Empire, and Modernity', pp. 72-4. For the development of the Victorian press and sensationalist journalism see Rubery, 'Journalism'; Williams, *Get Me a Murder a Day!*, pp. 14–64; Maunder and Moore, *Victorian Crime*; and Boyle, *Black Swine in the Sewers*.

imitators. Whilst both were potent forces of dissemination, it was the press that tended to distribute an awareness of the character up to levels of urban society which may not have normally accessed local gossip. A contributor to *Bentley's Miscellany* in 1839 emphasised that he had found out about Spring-heeled Jack being shot at in Regent's Park via the newspapers.[19] In doing so it facilitated the legend's shift from local to metropolitan and, ultimately, to a (diffused) nation-wide phenomenon. As such, whilst oral and print cultures were both important in circulating the legend, their interaction meant the extended reach of the press enabled Spring-heeled Jack to leap beyond a local, oral context.

Beyond this obvious operation of the printed media, the press was more complicit in the development of the legend. Firstly, it was often newspapers that imposed the 'Spring-heeled Jack' moniker on local 'ghosts' to give incidences a name and shape. Whilst possessing something of Spring-heeled Jack's agility, the 'Peckham Ghost' of 1872 was not initially linked to his legend. Rather it was the *Illustrated Police News'* reflections on the earlier Spring-heeled Jack scares in the capital that encouraged the association.[20] Secondly, the reprinting and summarising of Spring-heeled Jack articles from the metropolitan press in provincial newspapers served to encourage subtle alterations more frequently associated with oral transmission. For example, there were notable slippages in the reporting of the attack on Jane Alsop. On 22nd February the *Morning Chronicle* reported Mr Alsop's assertion that his daughter's attacker had had accomplices, for her assailant had left his discarded cloak when he fled, and yet 'there must have been some person with him to pick it up' for it could not be found. What had been speculation reported in one paper had hardened into 'fact' by 1st March when the *Bradford Observer* stated that Jane Alsop's attacker had 'left his cloak behind him which someone else picked up and ran off with'.[21] Similarly, in January 1838 the *Morning Herald* had referred to accounts of Spring-heeled Jack wearing 'large claw gloves', but accounts of the attack on Jane Alsop simply referring to the damage caused by 'his claws'.[22] These shifts, whilst not large, were significant in shaping a public sense of who or what Spring-heeled Jack was. The alterations derived not so much from gaps between oral and printed accounts as the subtle transformations that arose from one newspaper summarising accounts in another.

[19] *Bentley's Miscellany*, 6th July 1839, p. 345.
[20] *Illustrated Police News*, 28th December 1872. The link between the Peckham Ghost and Spring-heeled Jack was subsequently reiterated in a poem that appeared in *Fun*, 4th January 1873. The press operated in a similar manner with regard to Spring-heeled Jack's appearance in Everton in 1904. See *News of the World*, 25th September 1904.
[21] See *The Times*, 22nd February 1838, p. 6, and *Bradford Observer*, 1st March 1838, p. 4.
[22] See *Morning Herald*, 10th January 1838, and *Morning Chronicle*, 22nd February 1838.

Furthermore, despite efforts to assert a dispassionate, logical overview above the clamour of oral rumour the press was equally prone to exaggeration. In January 1838 the metropolitan press had swiftly increased the number of intended victims in the asserted 'death' wager that supposed pranksters were engaged in. Somewhat less menacing were the exaggerated claims about the size of the wager that had encouraged his appearances in Sheffield in 1873, with one local newspaper citing fifty pounds, another raising it to a hundred pounds.[23] The press could also encourage the exaggeration of minor aspects of reports into more solid features of the legend. In 1865 the *Leeds Mercury* claimed that Spring-heeled Jack's reason for attacking girls had been to cut their hair. This effectively extrapolated a generalised motive from what appears to have been a single case in Bristol in the early 1840s.[24] In doing so the actions of one hair fetishist were presented as an explanatory model for Spring-heeled Jack's renowned inclination for attacking women. Therefore, press reportage clearly shared something of the slippages and mercurial qualities of oral accounts of Spring-heeled Jack; where he possessed fluidity within oral culture he had a more subtle viscosity in print culture.

Finally, the press gave Spring-heeled Jack a voice. In oral accounts he rarely spoke. Yet just as publication of the infamous 'Dear Boss' letters gave Jack the Ripper a multitude of ranting voices, so the press occasionally gave voice to Spring-heeled Jack and his victims. On such occasions journalists came to play all parts in the narrative as they recreated the encounter. In adding this dimension the printed media often used Spring-heeled Jack as a glove puppet through which to articulate their own agendas. In January 1838 the *Penny Satirist* printed a humorous account of a hunt for Spring-heeled Jack by two men, both of whom take a large dose of opium before setting out. In Kensington Gardens the two men doze on a bench but one is roused by Spring-heeled Jack singing in a tree above them. The song was presented in the first person, thereby encouraging identification with the monster rather than his hunters. It begins:

> I came from Pandemonium,
> If they lay me I'll go back;
> Meanwhile around the town I'll jump
> Spring-heeled Jack.[25]

---

[23] For an example of this exaggeration compare *The Examiner*, 14th January 1838, p. 27, and *The Sun*, 20th January 1838. For the Sheffield case see the *Sheffield and Rotherham Independent*, 23rd May 1873, and the *Sheffield Times*, 31st May 1873.

[24] *Leeds Mercury*, 26th September 1865, p. 3.

[25] See *Penny Satirist*, 27th January 1838, p. 2. This appears to have been the start of a trend in literary accounts for Spring-heeled Jack to speak in doggerel rhyme. See for example *Gorton and Openshaw Reporter*, 27th December 1957.

The song comically summarises many of the theories about Spring-heeled Jack that were awash in London in early 1838 before picking on the *Penny Satirist's* favoured targets. It suggests people believed him to be 'a Marquis, a-larking for a boast', but it then implicates the Bishop of London, claiming he had donned the demonic disguise to test 'if people's minds have yet got rid of superstition'. This becomes the theme for the rest of the song with subsequent stanzas stating:

> With all the scientific skill
> And learning of the age,
> It's pleasing to see how safely still
> A ghost can walk the stage.

> I'll back to Pandemonium,
> And bring a legion here;
> For I see that spite of gas and steam,
> The coast's still clear.

> The ghostly fathers of the church
> Are getting out of date,
> I'll bring another ghostly tribe
> To pension on the State.

In this comical sketch Spring-heeled Jack is presented as 'a huge green figure, very luminous and transparent'. How far such a phantasmal vision was informed by the opium is left unstated.[26]

A later song was incorporated into a fictional ghost story in the *Essex Standard* in 1889. It similarly begins in the first person:

> Oh, jolly is the night when the stars are shining bright,
> And the moon is hid from sight beneath the sea,
> Then I'm out upon the track,
> For my name is Spring-heel Jack,
> And I love the winter darkness for a spree.

> From roof to roof I leap, when the people are asleep,
> And down the walls I creep without a sound,
> And I bound along the street,
> Frightening everyone I meet,
> Till they talk of me in all the country round.

The song concludes by advising:

> Then if you are afraid, lest by Jack you be waylaid,
> It is better that you stayed here drinking beer,
> So we'll drink the night away

---

[26] *Penny Satirist*, 27th January 1838, p. 2.

And go home by light of day
So that wicked Spring-heel Jack we need not fear.[27]

The song reiterates and arguably exaggerates Spring-heeled Jack's uncanny abilities. Yet in the vein of many street ballads it typically ends with humorous relief from any genuine sense of threat, emphasising the sanctuary of the pub in which the song was sung.

Spring-heeled Jack had parallel lives as a 'real' person in press reports and as a fictional character in penny dreadfuls. The mid-century fusion of developments in printing technologies with increasing plebeian literacy rates created a huge growth in popular fiction, with the urban population 'offering a seemingly ever-expanding captive market for stories that effectively evoked the gothic flavour of city life'.[28] Despite their flaws – cardboard characterisation, overblown or trite dialogue, rambling, episodic plots – penny dreadful stories such as Spring-heeled Jack's were often vivid and fast paced. Unlike the penny bloods of the 1840s which had been aimed at adults, penny dreadfuls of the 1860s onwards were targeted at (predominantly male) juveniles. Whilst having to account for a degree of hyperbole, James Greenwood claimed 'tens and hundreds of thousands of boys ... purchase ... the pernicious trash'. Worse yet was his realisation that penny fiction was sold 'in quiet suburban neighbourhoods, far removed from the stews of London', even reaching into 'serene and peaceful semi-country towns'.[29] As such, Spring-heeled Jack's name and a particular fictionalisation of his activities became known to a broad range of youths from across the labouring and middle classes.[30]

Colin Henry Hazlewood's *Spring-heel'd Jack, The Terror of London: A Romance of the Nineteenth Century* (1867) was a key transitional text, for whilst alluding to supernatural tropes such as ghosts and demons, the titular character was actually a man in a costume with spring-powered boots. Implicitly aligning with press interpretation of a non-supernatural character this became the fundamental basis for all subsequent Spring-heeled Jack serials. One detects Edwin J. Brett's influence and knowledge of the cheap literature market in his Newsagents Publishing Company's desire to reinvent Spring-heeled Jack as a misunderstood

---

[27] 'Old Balls's Ghost', *Essex Standard*, 28th December 1889, p. 2.
[28] Maunder and Moore, *Victorian Crime*, p. 45.
[29] Greenwood, *Seven Curses of London*, pp. 88 and 92. For details of the penny dreadful trade see Springhall, *Youth, Popular Culture, and Moral Panics*.
[30] See *Belfast News Letter*, 26th October 1869, for commentary on the popularity of Spring-heeled Jack's penny serial. Although such material was less likely to reach the upper classes Spring-heeled Jack was not unknown to them. Numerous race horses and even a particularly swift hare at the Barlow Hounds hunt were named 'Spring-heeled Jack'. See *Derby Mercury*, 28th January 1874, p. 2.

hero rather than a villain. Revitalised and recreated as a costumed vigilante, Spring-heeled Jack's concern for justice but disdain for the law equated him with the likes of Robin Hood. By toning down the supernatural associations he came to resonate with the popular roguish hero so beloved of penny dreadful hacks and their readers.[31]

In 1878–79 the *Boy's Standard* ran a serial which was also entitled *Spring-heeled: The Terror of London*.[32] Whilst the story contained violence and scares, it was more focused on intrigue than gore. Contained within a framing device which claimed the story was a summary of a diary belonging to the original Spring-heeled Jack, it proposed an interesting reinterpretation of the 1838 scare. However, given the limitation and expectations of penny dreadful fiction it offered little sense of its protagonist's interiority and fell back on external action and clunky exposition, its disinherited young nobleman protagonist being a duplicate of many such cheap fictional heroes. Yet it was in these literary fictions that Spring-heeled Jack's famed leaping became exaggerated from accounts of notable athleticism in the late 1830s and 1840s to his supposed superhuman ability to leap over stage coaches and spring up to second-storey windows. Whilst earlier reports had referred to his speed and agility, they had never described the abnormal leaps later attributed to him in penny fiction. As such, the popular image of Spring-heeled Jack as some superhuman leaper was more the product of penny serial fictions than oral rumours.

In 1890 Alfred Burrage (writing under the penname of 'Charlton Lea') produced a Spring-heeled Jack serial published by Charles Fox that was considerably lengthier than his 1878–79 adventures. He penned another Spring-heeled Jack series in 1904 for the Aldine Publishing Company. Aldine was known for its 'libraries', serials about familiar figures such as Jack Sheppard, Dick Turpin, Claude Duval and Robin Hood, all characters who had shared Spring-heeled Jack's transmission back and forth between oral folklore and literary portrayals. Echoing the tales of military Spring-heeled Jacks from the army base pranks of 1877 and 1878, the protagonist of this final serial was a disgraced army officer.[33]

---

[31] Even Spring-heeled Jack's name fitted neatly with the protagonists of other series such as *Moonlight Jack, Gentleman Jack* and *Sixteen-String Jack*.

[32] George Augustus Sala has been associated with the authorship of this serial although this is questionable. Having already obtained financial compensation in 1871 from an author who had claimed that Sala had penned *Sweeney Todd*, he seems to have been attempting to publicly distance himself from the penny fiction trade in which he had initially found work. See Turner, *Boys will be Boys*, pp. 32–3.

[33] See ibid., pp. 65 and 98. Indicative of a long tradition of symbiosis between popular oral and literary cultures, knowledge of folkloric heroes had been kept alive by chapbooks and street ballads as much as by oral folktales. For an example relating to Tom Hickathrift, the Norfolk Giant, see Wood, 'Pedlar of Swaffham', pp. 170–5.

These details hint at the way literary fictions both contribute to and reflect aspects of oral and newspaper accounts, a relationship that will be considered in more detail later in this chapter.

Visual

A final, powerful form of dissemination came via visual images and theatrical portrayals of Spring-heeled Jack. Victorian society has been said to have been marked by a 'frenzy of the visible'. The development of the advertising industry and illustrated newspapers in the second half of the nineteenth century certainly serves as a reminder that accompanying the rise of a popular literate culture was a mass culture of consumption steeped in and driven by the visual. What was increasingly appreciated in the Victorian period was the subjectivity of the viewer compared with early-modern views of vision as a passive and unproblematic camera obscura.[34] This idea had a powerful influence on the Victorians' understanding of ghosts and apparition theories and was amply demonstrated through the diverse range of images associated with Spring-heeled Jack.

Early newspaper depictions were little more than crude sketches alluding to some of the most prominent rumours in circulation at the time.[35] Developments in print technology meant that whilst his penny dreadful serial of 1867 still used black and white illustrations they were increasingly executed with evolving sophistication. Even within the same penny dreadful or newspaper Spring-heeled Jack could be portrayed in different ways. The 1867–68 series started by depicting him as a cloaked, darkly clothed masked man with riding boots, but then he evolved into a Mephistopheles-type character with horns, claw-like fingers, a pointed beard and headwear that altered between a feathered cap and a top hat.[36] The *Illustrated Police News'* 1872 depiction of the Peckham Ghost as a long-eared figure in white was markedly different to the ethereal entities portrayed in its April 1877 feature on the Aldershot Ghost. By contrast, its illustration of Spring-heeled Jack's supposed appearance in Lincolnshire in November of the same year suggested something more solid, dark and bestial.[37] When he returned to Aldershot in 1878 the comic paper *Funny Folks* portrayed him as a

---

[34] See Flint, *Victorians and the Visual Imagination*, pp. 3 and 21. See also Pick, 'Stories of the Eye', and Levin, *Modernity and the Hegemony of Vision*. For Victorian advertising see Church, 'Advertising Consumer Goods in Nineteenth-Century Britain', and Naremore and Brantlinger, *Modernity and Mass Culture*.

[35] See *Penny Satirist*, 10th March 1838, p. 1.

[36] See *Spring-heeled Jack* (1867), pp. 17, 49, 81 and 209. For illustrations of Spring-heeled Jack as a bestial hybrid replete with horns, a mane, bat-like wings, claws, fangs and hooves see Anglo, *Penny Dreadfuls*, pp. 68–73.

[37] See *Illustrated Police News*, 28th December 1872, 28th April 1877, and 3rd November 1877. See Dennis, *Cities in Modernity*, p. 85, and Anderson, *Printed Image*, for the influence of mass-produced printed images in this period.

thin, inhuman creature with an oversized head and large eyes, wearing a black bodysuit and possessing small, bat-like wings.[38] Visual images had to attempt the unenviable task of trying to fix Spring-heeled Jack's mercurial descriptions to the page. Unlike the literary influences that bled into oral accounts, these visual depictions do not seem to have had much impact on subsequent descriptions. Here the sense of division between the 'real' and fictional seemed stronger, as if the pictures were recognised as mere artists' impressions of something that people wanted to remain mysterious and never wholly seen.

The disseminating of Spring-heeled Jack into Victorian cultural life via the theatre was, in many ways, the natural evolution from his 1838 metropolitan scares. Before he ever set foot upon the stage there was already a highly theatrical element to his 'real' encounters. In both appearance and manner Spring-heeled Jack offered a performance intended to seize the attention. His costume, fire-breathing and agility were all imbued with elements of conscious display, whilst his pursuers and perhaps even his victims became incorporated into a piece of impromptu, melodramatic street theatre.[39] Early on, in January 1838, the Lord Mayor had referred to Spring-heeled Jack's 'pantomime disguise', and the following month a journalist described the suburban ghost's activities as a 'masquerade'.[40] Provincial accounts of Spring-heeled Jack were somewhat diminished in comparison with his metropolitan appearances, not least because he lost those theatrical aspects which had played most powerfully to the popular imagination: the fire-breathing and the claws.

Whilst Spring-heeled Jack may have appealed to the sensational content of penny gaff productions, the developing music hall industry of the second half of the century was less open to his supernatural allusions. Certainly by the late nineteenth century music hall's predominant focus was on the prosaic and a celebration of the everyday. Whilst the earlier penny gaffs had entertained ghosts, the comic grotesques of some music hall acts were still firmly rooted in the mundane.[41] Promoting questions about who promoted Spring-heeled Jack and for whom, it was not the predominantly plebeian penny gaffs or the mass entertainment of the music halls that provided a stage for Spring-heeled Jack but the more respectable theatres.[42] In August 1848 the Theatre Royal, Hull

---

[38] *Funny Folks*, 26th October 1878. This precipitated a shift towards more vampiric depictions that will be discussed further in the next chapter.

[39] See Epstein Nord, 'City as Theatre'.

[40] See *Morning Chronicle*, 11th January 1838, and *The Times*, 23rd February 1838, p. 7.

[41] See Bailey, 'Conspiracies of Meaning', pp. 139–40.

[42] This is not to say that Spring-heeled Jack had not been taken up in more plebeian entertainments. As early as April 1838 the street entertainments outside London's Pavilion Theatre had included a Spring-heeled Jack attraction, described as 'kvite as large as life' and available for viewing 'for the small charge of von hapenny'. See *The Standard*, 17th April 1838.

staged 'a new comic ballet' entitled *Spring-heeled Jack*, though such performances seem to have remained a rarity before the 1860s.[43] At the end of June 1863 the Grecian Theatre, London, staged *Spring-Heeled Jack; or. The Felon's Wrongs*.[44] This then toured the provincial theatres in the mid 1860s and was staged at the New Adelphi Theatre, Birmingham in March 1864. Indicative of its presumed appeal, it was the headlining piece at the reopening of Northampton's newly refurbished Theatre Royal on Saturday 28th October 1865. The theatre was reportedly crowded, although this seemed to be due to the reopening of the building rather than the play itself.[45] A more successful four-act play, *Spring-Heel'd Jack; The Terror of London*, was created by W. Travers in 1868. First staged at the Marylebone Theatre at the start of June, by early August this 'sensational drama' had moved to the Britannia Theatre, and subsequently moved to the Royal Colosseum in May 1869. Given that this was based on the penny serial that had started running slightly earlier, this theatrical depiction would have presented Spring-heeled Jack as a roguish hero. However, in a play with an identical title that premiered at the Victoria Theatre, London, in June 1880 Spring-heeled Jack appears to have slipped back to his wicked ways. In its enticing advertisement for the play *The Era* promised, 'The daring exploits and evil deeds of this midnight marauder are most graphically illustrated in this powerful drama.'[46] As such, his theatrical depictions were no more fixed than any other mode, and whilst they did reflect the influence of the penny dreadfuls, they did not remain beholden to them.

Cultural Transference

Throughout the Victorian period Spring-heeled Jack shuttled back and forth between, and found articulation through, a number of cultural modes. In these

---

[43] See the *Hull Packet*, 4th August 1848, p. 4. Peter Haining mentioned an 1840 Spring-heeled Jack play by James T. Haines. A search of numerous metropolitan and provincial newspapers between 1838 and 1841 reveals Haines to have been a prolific playwright during this period, but there does not appear to be a single press advertisement or critic's review for a production related to Spring-heeled Jack. See Haining, *Legend and Bizarre Crimes*, p. 114.

[44] See *Reynolds's Newspaper*, 28th June 1863, p. 4, and also Anglo, *Penny Dreadfuls*, p. 71.

[45] For Birmingham see *The Era*, 27th March 1864. For the Northampton performances see *The Era*, 29th October and 5th November 1865. Having been top of the bill on opening night the play was swiftly relegated to the concluding performance on the Monday. During the rest of that first week attendance at the theatre was said to be moderate. As such, one may suppose the large numbers that attended on the opening night were there for that event rather than the play itself.

[46] See *The Era*, 31st May 1868; *The Standard*, 22nd August and 8th September 1868; *The Era*, 3rd January 1869; and *Liverpool Mercury*, 10th May 1869, p. 1. For the 1880 play see *The Era*, 6th and 20th June 1880.

transmissions, particularly their connections and divergences, Spring-heeled Jack indicates the porosity between and inherent lack of purity within such modes.[47] Oral recollections were likely to be bastardised reiterations of half-remembered written accounts or elements of plays and should certainly not be thought of as a more 'authentic' form. Regardless of whether it was an oral or literary account or a theatrical performance, all shared the fundamental function of wishing to generate a thrill of artificial terror for consumption by their differently constituted audiences.[48] There were other recognisable similarities across cultural modes. Oral accounts of Spring-heeled Jack were notably mono-episodic, and this was echoed in press accounts and even penny serials, both of which tended to string together varying numbers of singular incidences to inform an article or a more meandering fictional narrative.

An identifiable synergy appears to have existed between Spring-heeled Jack's oral, literary and theatrical modes. Originating in the hubbub of local south London gossip in 1837, he moved fluidly into a metropolitan (and beyond) print culture following press reports of the Lord Mayor's announcement on the attacks in January 1838. This literary existence was swiftly extended by pamphlets that contributed to his evolving legend.[49] Oral rumour and the freshness of memories relating to the London scare may have been sufficient to generate new accounts into the 1840s, but the continuing willingness of the provincial press to shadow the organic evolution of Spring-heeled Jack's migratory legend undoubtedly helped too. Even though press reports were quick to criticise the actions of suspected hoaxers and the credulity of people who believed in them, a news-hungry print media was itself implicated in the process; acting as a vehicle by which Spring-heeled Jack was transmitted, circulated and even validated, the press simultaneously propagated what it sought to critique.[50] As seen in the previous chapter, once promoted through the press Spring-heeled Jack found himself co-opted into a broad range of contexts which further extenuated his existence in local oral cultures. In the Black Country in the mid nineteenth century he was said to have been seen on the roofs of pubs and churches, these associations being informed by local clergymen who used his name as a warning

---

[47] For more on this see Wood, 'Pedlar of Swaffham', p. 175; Fox and Woolf , Spoken Word; Hall, Cultures of Print, p. 57; and Vincent, Literacy and Popular Culture, especially pp. 196–227.

[48] See Clery, 'Pleasures of Terror', pp. 164–81, and Carroll, Philosophy of Horror, pp. 159–95.

[49] See such anonymous works as Apprehension and Examination of Spring-Heel'd Jack, Authentic Particulars of the Awful Appearance of Spring-Heeled Jack, and The Surprising Exploits of Spring-heel Jack. The British Library formerly held examples of these works but they have subsequently been lost. For some indication of their content see All the Year Round, 9th August 1884, and Dash's forthcoming Spring-heeled Jack: Sources and Interpretations, pp. 319-22.

[50] For the common reader's inclination towards belief of the written word see Rose, Intellectual Life of the British Working Class, p. 97.

against the dangers of alcohol.[51] Following a notable decline in reports in the 1850s and early 1860s, the appearance of the two metropolitan plays in 1863 and 1868, and particularly the latter's associated penny serial publication seemed to have led to a flurry of appearances in the 1870s. Although initially referred to only as ghosts, Spring-heeled Jack's name became associated with the 'Peckham Ghost' in 1872, the 'Park Ghost' in Sheffield in 1873, the 'Aldershot Ghost' in 1877 and 1878, and the disturbances at the Colchester army base later that year. In turn these renewed oral rumours seemed to stimulate further fictional tales, in particular the 1878–79 series, *Spring-Heel'd Jack, The Terror of London*. It seems more than coincidental that 1904 saw both the publication of Alfred Burrage's *The Spring-heeled Jack Library* and Spring-heeled Jack's late 'sighting' in Everton.

Many of Spring-heeled Jack's cultural energies ran along tried and tested contours of modal transmission and symbiosis, although his unusual contemporaneous folkloric existence represented new dimensions that needed to be incorporated into these existing operations. Eager to feed their audience's fascination with violent crime, penny gaff managers had often staged lurid improvisations around contemporary press reports such as the murder of Maria Marten in 1827 (this became a penny gaff favourite, *The Murder in the Red Barn*) and the dismemberment of the corpse in the Edgware murder of 1836.[52] Given this it is unlikely that an entrepreneurially minded gaff proprietor would have missed the opportunity presented by press reports of Spring-heeled Jack, especially in 1838. Spring-heeled Jack was well placed to appeal to the gaff audience, for accounts of his attacks possessed all the necessary ingredients of sensational crime, allusions to the supernatural, damsels in distress and challenges to authority. However, such was the ephemeral nature of penny gaff promotional material that it has not been possible to locate hard evidence of productions linked to Spring-heeled Jack. Despite this there are more indirect suggestions that such productions had taken place. Victorian puppet shows often adapted the most popular melodramas from penny gaffs. Amongst the perennial favourites were stories about Dick Turpin, Jack Sheppard and Sweeney Todd, and, according to Robert Mack, from around 1860 they were joined by performances of *Spring-heeled Jack*.[53] The relatively late date suggests it may have taken

---

[51] See www.bbc.co.uk/legacies/myths_legends/england/black_country/article_2.shtml.

[52] Reciprocity between 'popular' literary fictions and melodramatic plays had also been established by the time of Spring-heeled Jack's first appearances. Given the popularity of Newgate fictions in the 1830s, one of the most popular penny gaff productions had been the adaptations of William Harrison Ainsworth's *Jack Sheppard* (1839). See Springhall, *Youth, Popular Culture and Moral Panics*, pp. 23–4. For Spring-heeled Jack this cultural transference continued into the mid twentieth century. Todd Slaughter's film, *The Curse of the Wraydons* (1946) was an adaptation of an earlier Spring-heeled Jack play. See Haining, *Legend and Bizarre Crimes*, p. 115.

[53] See Mack, *Wonderful and Surprising History of Sweeney Todd*, p. 252.

some time for Spring-heeled Jack to be transmitted from penny gaff to puppet show. Yet once this was achieved it is plausible that, compared to the relatively limited audiences for Spring-heeled Jack's penny serials and theatrical plays, the itinerant puppet show that wound its way around the provinces from small town to village and from fair to fete became one of the most ubiquitous cultural modes by which his name and legend were promoted.[54]

By the 1850s penny fictions were also becoming another popular source for theatrical productions. Juvenile readers who had 'had their appetites whetted by reading in "penny dreadfuls" about ... Spring Heeled Jack or Jack Sheppard could see them brought to life, playing to crowded houses nightly, on the penny gaff stage'.[55] This was most clearly seen in operation in 1868 when Spring-heeled Jack was simultaneously the protagonist of a popular penny serial and also treading the boards at the Marylebone Theatre. In this case the penny serial clearly came first. When promoting the play *The Era* announced that whilst it was 'written expressly for [the Marylebone] Theatre by W. Travers', it had been 'taken from the popular work, now publishing, entitled Spring-heeled Jack; or The Terror of London'. Blatantly cashing in on the popularity of the serial, the play did not even bother to change the title, although it offered its own theatrical appeal to a popular engagement with Spring-heeled Jack via its use of 'extraordinary effects [and] spectral illusions'. A later advertisement relating to its move to the Britannia Theatre claimed it was 'founded on the exploits of the notorious Spring-Heeled Jack', suggesting the play not only drew from penny fiction but was also attempting to tap into his folkloric incarnations in the memory of Londoners.[56] This was made more explicit in the 1880 play. Here advertisements emphasised the links with Spring-heeled Jack's real existence beyond the stage by promoting it as

---

[54] Earlier, in the 1850s, Spring-heeled Jack had proved himself capable of appropriating existing puppet figures into his own legend. Henry Mayhew noted how the character of the devil in London's Punch and Judy shows had been popularly renamed 'Spring-heeled Jack'. See Mayhew, *London Labour and the London Poor*, vol. 3, p. 52.

[55] Springhall, *Youth, Popular Culture and Moral Panics*, p. 24. Colin Henry Hazlewood, the (unnamed) author of the 1867-68 Spring-heeled Jack penny serial, was also the resident playwright at the Britannia Theatre. He had personally performed this transference between penny dreadful and the stage with one of his own earlier works. In 1865 Hazlewood penned *The Confederate's Daughter or the Tyrant of New Orleans*, which began publication in May 1865. It seemed to have been popular enough to encourage Hazlewood to turn it into a play of the same name. This was first performed at the Britannia Theatre from August 1865. The penny serial must have made an impression on its readership for when Hazlewood penned *Spring-heeled Jack; The Terror of London* he did not mention himself by name but presented it as being 'by the author of the Confederate's Daughter'. For the penny serial see *Reynolds's Newspaper*, 7th and 14th May 1865. For the play see *The Era*, 6th August 1865, and *The Standard*, 7th August 1865, p. 4.

[56] *The Era*, 31st May 1868, p. 8, and 30th August 1868, p. 8. See also *The Orchestra*, 13th June 1868. For more on Victorian stage ghosts see Davies, *The Haunted*, pp. 232–40, and North, 'Illusory Bodies'. For an association with Spring-heeled Jack see *The Standard*, 1st October 1864, p. 4.

'an extraordinary and startling drama, founded on the doings of a miscreant, the particulars of which will be found in the history of Hammersmith'.[57]

Of course, Spring-heeled Jack was not unique in moving between different cultural modes of expression, nor even in transgressing the boundaries between fiction and reality. Like Jack Sheppard and Dick Turpin he had his origins in historical reality but accumulated a larger, more legendary existence by moving into fiction. At the same time contemporary literary characters like Ally Sloper and Sherlock Holmes journeyed in the opposite direction, beginning as fictions but acquiring sufficient 'weight' as to be thought of as real individuals by some.[58] In the 1840s Sweeney Todd had also shifted easily between theatrical play and cheap literary fiction, whilst from the mid-century period notorious real-life criminals began to migrate from press accounts into literary fictions, resulting in a subsequent conflating of reality and fantasy.[59] Yet unlike many of these characters, Spring-heeled Jack's cultural existence was predicated upon a dynamic contradiction of containment and liberation. As a literary and theatrical character he was both safely contained and remote, but as a roaming, contemporary folkloric figure he was free and potentially near. The lack of direct connection between these coexisting literary and oral accounts complicates Michael Saler's views on popular engagement with Sherlock Holmes and the ironic imagination. Largely dismissing the credulous minority who believed Holmes to be real, Saler's notion of the ironic imagination suggests a willing and knowing engagement in a fantasy of Holmes' reality.[60] Spring-heeled Jack did not necessarily accommodate this playful indulgence. None of his victims ever claimed to have been attacked by a penny dreadful character; such fictions merely coexisted with a 'real' assailant. There was also an edge to Spring-heeled Jack that Holmes lacked. The former was clearly capable of leaping back and forth between reality and fiction, to the point where an ironic, knowing stance was confronted by the categorical uncertainty of both the 'real' and the 'fictional'.

Whilst the above suggests the existence of a circuit between Spring-heeled Jack's modal transferences, it had notable faults. This derives not so much from the difficulty of trying to map a direct causal link between Spring-heeled Jack's propagation in one cultural mode and subsequent responses by others (such an idea implicitly assumes cultural transference operates in a linear fashion), but rather from the fact that despite those transmissions his cultural expressions

---

[57] *The Era*, 6th June 1880.
[58] For these claims see Bailey, *Popular Culture and Performance*, p. 47, and Saler, 'Clap if You Believe', p. 601.
[59] See Emsley, *Crime and Society in England*, pp. 82–4. For the conflating of scepticism and supernatural belief in Victorian ghost and detective stories see Ascari, *Counter-History of Crime Fiction*, pp. 55–65.
[60] See Saler, 'Clap if You Believe', p. 606.

were marked by their disconnection and even isolation from one another. There was always a plethora of Spring-heeled Jacks differently imagined, his multiple modes of cultural transmission tending to fracture rather than consolidate him. Mass print media helped make Spring-heeled Jack widely known, but in disseminating him across the country its depictions were often made impersonal and remote through locating him elsewhere. As seen in the last chapter, this was a marked contrast to his existence in oral culture which usually localised him into the vicinity.

Spring-heeled Jack showed the interaction between oral, print and visual cultures to be rather messy and haphazard. Whilst a symbiotic relationship may have existed between his oral and literary expressions, they did not necessarily duplicate depictions or interpretations. Whether he was mauling or rescuing women his literary portrayals and press reports implicitly promoted his physicality, whereas oral accounts tended to promote phantasmal interpretations. In the 1870s when he was believed to trouble the 'lonely, dark roads' of rural Norfolk he was described as 'a man, some eight or nine feet high, habited in a long, black cloak, who would suddenly and noiselessly appear at the side of … a wayfarer, peer closely into his victim's face, and, with a diabolical laugh or yell, disappear as suddenly as he came'. This solid, physical depiction was much closer to the appearance and nature of the London Spring-heeled Jack of 1838. Yet it was also suggested that mere rumours of his appearance in the vicinity caused locals to 'be afraid to venture out into the lanes after dark, fearful that they might see the apparition'.[61] Given this ontological uncertainty, Elliott O'Donnell concluded his account of Spring-heeled Jack with the declaration that 'all attempts to … prove if he were spirit or human being failed'.[62] To complicate things further his corporeal and phantasmal natures could even be evoked within the same account. In an incident in Eye in Suffolk in 1842 he initially possessed physicality as he was successfully captured and held in the police station house. Yet rumour supposed that he then 'converted into a spirit, and so managed to make his escape'.[63] Similarly, soldiers at the Aldershot army camp in 1877 claimed the 'ghost' appeared impervious to their shots but also possessed sufficient physical form to slap them in the face.[64]

This constant shifting between the phantasmal and corporeal not only denoted incomprehension on the part of Spring-heeled Jack's witnesses and victims, but also indicates that the transmission of information between cultural modes was frequently obfuscated. Essential details as to Spring-heeled Jack's

---

[61] *Norfolk and Norwich Notes and Queries*, 29th October 1898, pp. 409-10, and 5th November 1898, p. 411.

[62] O'Donnell, *Haunted Britain*, p. 76.

[63] *Ipswich Journal*, 2nd April 1842.

[64] See *Illustrated Police News*, 8th September 1877.

nature remained unfixed or got lost between literary accounts, oral retelling and pictorial impressions. These gaps and shifts were partly the result of the nature of how oral cultures operated and how journalists were summarising and responding to fragmentary snippets of information. Degrees of selectivity, adaptation and elaboration had long formed part of the persistent strength of oral folklore and, given the evidence of this legend, continued to do so until the end of the Victorian period. Complicating any simple distinctions between the ghost of oral folklore and the disguised man of penny literature, an account from 1904 declared, 'Some people denied [Spring-heeled Jack's] existence and put him down as a mere phantom of popular story.'[65] Hoaxers also complicated such neat divisions. Their actions and their capture obviously gave greater veracity to interpretations of Spring-heeled Jack as a physical being. Yet the strength of oral folklore, and the persistent belief in the existence of supernatural entities generally meant that, rather than dispelling the legend, hoaxes were accommodated. When a human hoaxer was revealed people did not automatically assume that all previous appearances had been hoaxes too. Rather they believed the prankster was merely taking advantage of the fear created by a genuinely supernatural being. As such, the legend persisted and was even augmented by hoaxers' continual allusions to a 'Spring-heeled Jack' character. Such was the ontological ambiguity engendered by these inconsistencies that one perplexed Edwardian inquirer to *Notes and Queries* asked an even larger question: 'Was Spring-heeled Jack a real or an imaginary being?'[66]

Spring-heeled Jack's penny dreadful reinterpretation from 1867 to 1868 arguably tamed him, for despite his opposition to the law and a certain sadistic mischievousness that got the better of him on occasion, he now possessed an inherent goodness. Yet regardless of the literary makeover from a supernatural fiend to a champion of justice, provincial folkloric manifestations remained firmly fixed to his original depiction as a malevolent entity. This seems to indicate the tenacity of his character as it existed in oral culture, suggesting it was not simply the nattering handmaiden of shifting literary portrayals.[67] Whilst differing and sometimes contradictory interpretations coexisted within the popular imagination without apparent conflict, Spring-heeled Jack being simultaneously a hero and villain, physical and phantasmal, he tended to be more one than the other depending on the particular cultural mode through which he was accessed and became known. Even if his literary depictions were more inclined to circulate in urban areas, press reports indicate that urban dwellers were not necessarily more

---

[65] See *Norfolk and Norwich Notes and Queries*, 31st December 1904, p. 106.

[66] *Notes and Queries*, 10th Series, 30th March 1907, p. 256.

[67] For differences between oral folktales and literary stories see Propp, *Theory and History of Folklore*, especially Chapter 2.

disposed towards the literary interpretation of Spring-heeled Jack as a disguised man. As evidenced throughout this study, many conformed to the ethnographic notions of him being a ghost. The apparent disconnection between literary and oral accounts hints at an inherent flaw in the 'circuit' of his cultural transmission, for his markedly different depictions coexisted without directly interacting. Spring-heeled Jack's legend certainly possessed momentum, but it never really obtained internal unity. His ability to move between cultural modes was not necessarily hindered by this. In fact, one could even argue that the cultural dynamism of his legend was positively facilitated by those very qualities of instability and incoherence, allowing him to be appropriated as different things in different contexts.

There were negative consequences to this fluidity. Other imaginary characters of the nineteenth century such as John Bull, Ally Sloper, and (following the highly influential drawings of Sidney Paget) Sherlock Holmes all possessed far greater potency from being instantly recognisable. The lack of a fixed and therefore easily identifiable image arguably hindered the depth to which Spring-heeled Jack could plant himself into the popular consciousness or memory. This seems to reiterate that both his cultural currency and durability were vested more in his semantic than iconic power. This may also go some way to explaining the nature of Spring-heeled Jack's existence in Victorian Britain, for whilst he was clearly a known figure he was for the most part confined to the cultural and spatial margins by more successful or at least more prominent characters. Peter Bailey's work on Ally Sloper has clearly illustrated how this popular character moved from comics into music hall and pantomime, whilst being further popularised through a range of merchandise.[68] By comparison Spring-heeled Jack's public visibility was highly sporadic. His particular appeal was arguably grounded in this need to be seen prowling at the cultural margins, not plastered over everything, for only by remaining elusive could he retain his intriguing mystique. The occasional peaks in public engagement with Spring-heeled Jack indicate that whilst he was clearly able to capture the imagination of a broad cross-class audience, he was not able to retain it with any consistency. The operational dynamic of his legend was marked by a waxing and waning. Whilst revivals were prompted by new plays, penny serials or clusters of rumour, slumps tended to be encouraged by the fatigue of familiarity, a creeping scepticism or, most devastating of all, distraction by more novel sensations, issues that will be addressed in the next chapter.

---

[68] Bailey, *Popular Culture and Performance*, p. 55. Like Spring-heeled Jack, Ally Sloper underwent a reimagining, transforming from a lower-class loiterer and confidence trickster in the 1860s to a swell and comic dandy in his own paper from 1884. He also shared Spring-heeled Jack's migratory nature, although Sloper followed the more comprehensible routes determined by fixtures in the London social calendar and visits to provincial events and resorts. See ibid., pp. 55–8.

The Struggle for Interpretation

Whilst Spring-heeled Jack's legend was defined by the interrelational and even symbiotic modal dynamics examined above, there was also a conflictual dimension to this relationship. At the heart of the struggle for control between differing cultural modes was the issue of where the authority behind his generation, perpetuation and interpretation was located. Although newspaper reports were dependent upon oral rumour, the journalistic need to collate, summarise and construct a coherent overview tended to bring a different interpretative gloss to the diversity of what was being said in rumour or oral testimony. These demands often meant oral accounts were, at best, knapped and more frequently broken apart into fragments or condensed to fit the concerns of the reporter. In doing so oral accounts disseminated in the press were ripped from the local context in which they were told and to which they related, and were then filtered through the (usually condescending or dismissive) interpretations of the journalist. In this way the advancing of a dominant press discourse derived implicitly from the form of printed media and more explicitly from its function.[69]

Printed accounts were composed within framing devices which usually promoted a rationalised view of the Spring-heeled Jack phenomenon. When rumours about Spring-heeled Jack began to circulate around Bury, Suffolk, in December 1878 the *Bury and Norwich Post* 'endeavoured to ascertain the real truth of the matter'. Dismissing the rumours as the product of 'the vague fears of timid persons', the newspaper tracked down a porter at the Suffolk General Hospital, a person described by the newspaper as the 'one source' from which the stories had derived. It used the porter's testimony to reiterate that 'what he saw was a man dressed up, and any sensible person will not be long in coming to the same conclusion'.[70] As this account suggests, there was a considerable imbalance of power between the many voices that were attempting to shape interpretations of Spring-heeled Jack. What an individual or number of individuals supposedly thought they had experienced counted for less than the journalistic interpretation which sought to influence how their readers should understand it. Oral accounts, particularly those provided by the less powerful in Victorian society (the lower classes and young women), were dominated by a journalistic voice that was essentially bourgeois and masculine.

---

[69] The metropolitan press, whilst selling well, was not truly popular in the traditional sense of being of 'the people'. For sales figures for *The Times*, *Lloyd's Illustrated London Newspaper*, *Reynolds's Weekly Newspaper* and the *News of the World* see Ledger, *Dickens and the Popular Radical Imagination*, pp. 142 and 144.

[70] See *Bury and Norwich Post*, 24th December 1878, p. 4.

This was articulated in both the titles and tone of the earliest articles which attempted to dismiss the incidences as nonsense. On 10th January 1838 the *Morning Chronicle*'s article, entitled 'Credulity – The Ghost Story', opened with the following statement: 'Never has credulity and superstition been so strongly exemplified than in the ghost story alluded to by the Lord Mayor.' It noted that the story 'has had a wider range of circulation than any previous tale of the kind on record'. Getting its interpretation in quickly, the newspaper summarised 'some particulars of the alleged pranks of the ghost, imp, or devil, who ... is by many persons believed to be a member of a certain band of aristocrats who, for a wager, has undertaken to personify a supernatural being'. Having provided sketchy details about the numerous places the ghost had been seen around London, the article then sought to make light of the rumours by highlighting an 'amusing circumstance' in which a police inspector on a white horse had been mistaken for the ghost and inadvertently caused a local scare. It concluded by stating its suspicions that 'the Peckham statement' (the letter sent to the Mayor) would turn out to be a concoction of rumours and falsehoods.[71] Typically, the *Penny Satirist* took a more humorous approach. Whilst finding its own comic uses for Spring-heeled Jack, it also mocked the nature of the oral mode by which his name was circulated:

> The ghost is generally about the size of a man, but it takes various forms. Sometimes it has the shape of a bear, sometimes it jumps like a kangaroo, and very frequently it is dressed like one of the knights of Jerusalem, in shining bright armour which gleams ... like phosphorous. We saw a man who told us that, being at Ilford one day, he met a man who told him that he had fallen in with a woman who positively assured him that she knew a girl who had fairly lost her old wits by the sight of the ghost.[72]

If metropolitan newspapers had initially been dismayed at the extent of popular credulity surrounding rumours about Spring-heeled Jack, they gradually altered their tone to a less intrusive editorial voice. Broadsheets turned to collating and publishing written accounts from a diverse range of informants. Rather than a direct connection to oral rumour these sources were printed replications of letters to the Mayor. As such, their content had been processed and shaped by the letter writer, then by the Mayor and his officials who chose to make select letters public, and finally by the journalists who printed them, often in truncated versions.[73] By the time they reached the newspapers' readers they had undergone a triple transference from oral to print cultures. In late February the earlier condemnation of superstitious ignorance transformed into worthy concern about the 'outrages' enacted against Jane Alsop and Lucy Scales, especially when the

---

[71] *Morning Chronicle*, 10th January 1838.
[72] *Penny Satirist*, 20th January 1838, p. 2.
[73] See for example *The Times*, 11th January 1838, and *The Examiner*, 14th January 1838, p. 27.

former's appearance before magistrates seemed to ground the rumours through an identifiable victim and detailed testimony. After mid March and the unsuccessful attempts to charge anyone for the assaults the press interest waned, and Spring-heeled Jack stories were no longer afforded their previous column inches.

Of course, once Spring-heeled Jack's appearances proliferated beyond London he became enveloped in a web of provincial newspapers that extended his existence into the early twentieth century. Yet the disconnection between oral rumour and journalistic reflection persisted in provincial reports too. In 1884 the *North-Eastern Daily Gazette* reported that 'the wildest rumours have been afloat in Darlington regarding some mysterious being who has been playing antics in the ghost line for nearly a week'. As with earlier accounts this suggests how press reports generally trailed oral accounts and that such rumours had to build sufficient intensity or sustainability to become newsworthy. Picking up on the transformative dynamic in Spring-heeled Jack's oral accounts, the newspaper noted, 'From a simple ghost he has developed into a kind of supernatural being. He can stride several yards at a time, leap hedges and walls like a greyhound, and one person actually declares that he has darted across the Tees.' Whilst this had led to the typical response of women and children being afraid to leave their homes at night, the newspaper actively attempted to dispel such fears. It reported that it had made 'some enquiries concerning the "Ghost", and … we can assure all those who are in trepidation on the subject that the wild rumours now afloat have more existence in the imaginations of persons than in real life'. As with the press investigations in January 1838 the paper reported that the 'most difficult thing our representative had to do was to find any person who had really seen the ghost'. Unlike those earlier accounts this newspaper succeeded in finding an eyewitness, a workman called Thomas Nellis. He had given chase to Spring-heeled Jack across a field, but the ghost had outpaced him, aided in Nellis' opinion by 'some mechanical apparatus fixed to his boots' that helped him take huge strides. Yet in one of the most explicit exposures of the press' agenda regarding Spring-heeled Jack the report ended with Nellis' certainty that he had chased a disguised man, not a supernatural entity. Driving the point home, the newspaper stated that 'it is to be hoped that this announcement will dispel the fears of those persons who are in terror of a visit from the Eastburn apparition'. It concluded by reassuring readers that the ghost was soon expected to be in the Darlington police cells.[74]

The press typically sought readers' consent for its interpretations of Spring-heeled Jack through these various methods and stances. By promoting the prankster or gentleman wager narrative, newspapers implicitly limited and

---

[74] '"Spring Heeled Jack" in Darlington', *North-Eastern Daily Gazette*, 28th January 1884.

discredited the viability of other, more supernatural interpretations. Theirs was a discourse that marked the boundaries of the possible. Whilst press reports conceded to the existence of other interpretations, they were contained within a controlled discursive space in which the editorial or journalistic voice had both predominance and the final word. This is typical of the operation of hegemonic discourses which tend to encompass 'the contending forces of subordination, persuasion, consent and resistance'. In such circumstances 'alternative meanings ... even some alternative senses of the world ... can be accommodated and tolerated'.[75]

Despite these attempts to assert a dominant interpretation and an authoritative voice, the hegemonic influence of the press was weakened from within in a number of ways. Firstly, the press was obviously not a collective, singular voice; different publications had different readerships and concerns. Underlying this were the tensions between improving agendas and commercial imperatives, the Victorian press being neither sufficiently public nor private to clearly advance either need.[76] Whilst all tended to be drawn to the mystery of Spring-heeled Jack's motives and the impunity of his actions, the tone of newspapers varied considerably. This lack of consistency was seen in the way the press variously attempted to intensify or slacken the public fear surrounding Spring-heeled Jack. His activities could be sensationalised as 'outrages' or marginalised into mere 'larks'. In early March 1838 *The Watchman* printed a rather matter-of-fact report on Spring-heeled Jack, the account presented as just another piece of police news. Yet just a week later the *Morning Post* wrote of the '"Spring-heeled Jack" mania' that was being stirred by 'the extraordinary and highly reprehensible exploits' of two cloaked men who had appeared before a servant boy in Great Marylebone Street. Given that their arms had been outstretched towards him and that their faces were 'smeared with red ochre or brickdust', the boy had instantly assumed them to be linked to the '"Spring-heeled Jack" family'. The shock had caused him to collapse and long after the men had fled the boy was left insensible.[77] Such reports hardly served to dispel public fears even if they did reiterate the popular journalistic view that the scare was the work of mundane pranksters rather than anything more supernatural. Similarly, when a Spring-heeled Jack imitator terrorised Camden in April 1841 *The Era*'s tone was one of deadly earnest in seeking to warn readers against the dangers posed by this apparent rapist. This contrasted markedly with the *Freeman's Journal* report on a Spring-heeled Jack appearance in Tottenham in October of the same year. Despite this later Spring-

---

[75] Wood, 'Pedlar of Swaffham', p. 168.

[76] For more on the nature of the Victorian press see Jones, *Powers of the Press*.

[77] See *The Watchman*, 7th March 1838, and *Morning Post*, 13th March 1838, p. 7. For media-provoked scares in this period see Bartholomew and Evans, *Panic Attacks*, pp. 1–39.

heeled Jack being linked to throwing fire, the newspaper dismissed the culprit as 'A. Jackass'.[78] The difference in tone indicates the varied way press discourse could influence readers' responses if not their interpretations.

Comic or satirical publications tended to employ Spring-heeled Jack's artifice and absurdity as a means of mocking authority figures. This was seen above, when the *Penny Satirist* used his scare to direct jibes at the Bishop of London in 1838. Following his reappearance at the Aldershot army base in 1878, *Funny Folks* ridiculed the seemingly contradictory orders of the military authorities who had issued soldiers with live ammunition but then had forbidden them from shooting at the 'ghost'.[79] Spring-heeled Jack's theatricality and his increasingly anachronistic character seemingly primed him for ludicrous applications in humorous printed accounts. In being appropriated as a vehicle for satire and comic wit, his threat was diffused by humour, with the result that the distance between 'real' assaults and printed reflections became even greater. As cheap weekly newspapers developed later in the century, there was a marked shift towards commercialised sensationalism which made them less willing to probe at the source of such stories and to print the wildest of speculations.

This unevenness of tone and approach hints at other failings in the formation of a convincing interpretative discourse by the press. The two most detailed testimonies of 1838, those of the Alsop and Scales families, both strongly suggested that whilst Spring-heeled Jack had produced balls of flame, they were not derived from a diabolical capacity to breathe fire. The figure who had approached the Alsop household had had to wait for Jane Alsop to bring him a candle before he could perform his stunt, whilst Lucy Scales' sister had described their assailant as holding a small lantern which he had revealed before puffing his ball of flame. To firm up these points some newspapers reported on James Lea's investigations which had called upon the expertise of an employee of the Pavilion Theatre to provide his professional opinion as to how Spring-heeled Jack may have performed his fire-breathing feats.[80] Yet regardless of this explicit statement of manufactured special effects, popular rumour still entertained the idea of a fire-breathing, supernatural being.[81] Despite press efforts to present and thereby dismiss Spring-heeled Jack as a human prankster, the ambiguity surrounding his nature in popular rumour enabled him to verge on the supernatural in the popular imagination. The press interpretation lacked persuasiveness for some

---

[78] Compare the tone of reports in *The Era*, 11th April 1841, with *Freeman's Journal*, 26th October 1841.

[79] See for example *Penny Satirist*, 27th January and 10th March 1838, and *Funny Folks*, 26th October 1878.

[80] *The Times* 22nd February 1838, and *Morning Post*, 7th March 1838.

[81] See for example *All the Year Round*, 9th August 1884, p. 349.

people, for whilst they may have accepted the journalists' premise, they persisted in indulging more imaginative and therefore more intriguing interpretations.

The press was also prone to undermining its own 'rational' assertions. As with the haze of oral rumour, the press (inadvertently) promoted mixed messages. On 11th January 1838 the *Morning Chronicle* reported the Lord Mayor's comment that whilst people had clearly been terrified by 'some man or men', the accounts had suffered from 'the grossest exaggeration'. Having declared that he gave no credence to reports that the ghost was 'a devil upon earth' he then added that he had it upon unquestionable authority from a neighbour that a servant woman 'had been frightened senseless'. Not only was he presenting his own 'friend-of-a-friend' oral contribution, but when he described the figure who had scared the servant woman as possessing 'a long horn, the emblem of the king of hell himself' he seemed to undermine his own claims about earthbound demons.[82] This was also seen with the appearance of Spring-heeled Jack at the Aldershot army base in 1877. Whilst the *Preston Guardian* suggested the Aldershot Ghost was an eccentric or lunatic, *The Times* advanced the view that it was an army officer engaged in a prank.[83] Such divergences exposed the press' own tendency towards unsubstantiated speculation.

Finally, although newspapers frequently deplored the extent of popular credulity expressed in accounts of Spring-heeled Jack, they were themselves still willing to litter their reportage with supernatural references and allusions.[84] The knowing irony implied by containing the word 'ghost' within quotation marks was weakened by the fact that those leading punctuation marks could appear and disappear within the same article. Even where the use of quotation marks remained consistent it would be wrong to assume that the implication of knowing irony was in any way reflective of those from whom the accounts or rumours had been garnered or whether they necessarily used the term with a similar knowingness. Rather Spring-heeled Jack seemed to articulate conflicting semantic discourses around the word 'ghost', each seeking to dominate inter-pretations of what he was and how he could (or could not) be located within rationalised explanations. Once Spring-heeled Jack migrated to the provinces the supernatural nomenclature of spirits and imps was extended to descriptions of a 'terrible hobgoblin', and even allusions to the diabolical when he supposedly left a cloven hoof print and a whiff of brimstone in his wake. When he appeared at

---

[82] *Morning Chronicle*, 11th January 1838.
[83] See *Preston Guardian*, 28th April 1877, and *The Times*, 28th April 1877, p. 10. David Hopkin's work on French soldiers in the nineteenth century would indicate that this account and the 1878 attacks on sentries in Colchester fitted into a pre-existing folkloric narrative. The familiar story told of how soldiers posted on sentry duty at isolated locations at night encountered a 'monstrous apparition'. See Hopkin, 'Storytelling, Fairytales and Autobiography', pp. 192–3.
[84] *Morning Herald*, 10th January 1838.

Aldershot one newspaper referred to him as an 'evil goblin', another as a ghostly visitant.[85] What was not clearly delineated in most of these later reports was whether these terms represented recorded oral rumour or a mocking journalistic interpretation of such notions.

The attempt by the press in 1838 to make sense of encounters and to retrospectively construct a broader story linking a series of disparate events contributed to Spring-heeled Jack's vitality and power in the collective imagination. Rather than presenting a series of random copycat crimes, the press narrative forged a singular, dangerous individual who appeared superhuman in his ability to move around the city with such speed and prolificacy. At a more fundamental level the wealth of press reports on Spring-heeled Jack's contemporary activities implicitly reiterated that he was not to be thought of as a figure of remote popular folklore but as a modern news item and a potentially immediate threat. In giving him a name the press both fanned and helped manage anxieties by imposing a basic sense of coherence over the diverse clamour of rumour. If this amounted to the press' greatest 'victory' in the interpretative struggle between cultural modes, it proved to be something of a pyrrhic one.

This study of Spring-heeled Jack is overly reliant upon printed sources, especially newspaper reports and commentary. This is less a willing choice than the dictates of circumstances which have failed to bequeath us substantial, alternative forms of evidence. The verbosity of journalists and the vast silences of subaltern groups naturally skew our appreciation of oral-literary interpretations of Spring-heeled Jack. If the dominant power in this struggle appears to be the press it was largely because the printed mode made the greatest assumptions about its own power and authority. The popular perception was perhaps somewhat different. In his or her letter to the Mayor the 'Peckham resident' had asserted that the press had 'the whole history [of Spring-heeled Jack's activities] at their finger ends, but through interested motives are induced to remain silent'. Clearly, some felt the press to be either powerless to print the Spring-heeled Jack story or else complicit in its absence from the newspapers.[86] It is impossible to accurately gauge how widely press interpretations were internalised by readers, although press reports throughout the Victorian period indicate that supernatural interpretations persisted. Even here we need to be wary about taking supernatural

---

[85] See *Bradford Observer*, 13th February 1845, and *Manchester Times*, 18th May 1850. For the Aldershot descriptions see *Hampshire Telegraph*, 9th October 1878, and *Illustrated Police News*, 28th April 1877.

[86] *The Times*, 9th January 1838, p. 4. Interestingly, Mr Hobler, one of the Lord Mayor's staff, directly refuted this two days later when he declared, 'If anything serious had resulted from the tricks which were said to have been already played ... the newspapers, out of which it was almost impossible to keep anything likely to attract curiosity would have been ready enough to take hold of it.' See *Morning Chronicle*, 11th January 1838.

interpretations at face value, for they served newspapers' inclination to conflate biases linking oral culture, 'superstitious' beliefs and the lower classes.[87] Popular culture possessed a strong strain of mockery and the carnivalesque, and Spring-heeled Jack was a parody of the devil as much as alluding to a real one. Whilst oral accounts were willing to employ a diabolical symbolism to describe him, it did not necessarily mean the authors or audience of the account genuinely believed it.

More importantly, the written evidence can only prove under-representative of Spring-heeled Jack's ubiquity and strength in the popular imagination. Rumours of his presence usually required an 'event' for them to coagulate into a newsworthy story. This was seen in a village in east Norfolk in September 1845. Thomas Purdy, a fifty-year-old man suffering from pleurisy, wandered outside his house one night in a delirium and frightened a neighbour who saw him at her window. Her cries of alarm brought a young man called Henry Noble to her aid, and 'thinking that it was a spree of a certain Spring-heeled Jack who had been terrifying the neighbourhood of late' the young man inflicted a severe beating upon Purdy who died the next day.[88] Spring-heeled Jack's association with this tragic occurrence seemed to provide the spurious 'proof' for the rumours that had preceded it, even though it was a case of mistaken identity. Prior to this unfortunate event there appears to have been no written record of Spring-heeled Jack's actions in this area. As such, the scattered incidences which made it into the press or, more rarely, the courts, were most likely a fraction of the amorphous tales that swirled about his name in mid-nineteenth-century oral culture.

Newspapers also mistakenly presented oral rumour as possessing an organic messiness compared with the shaping, constraining framework of journalistic interpretation. This view from 'above' meant they often failed to appreciate that oral rumour was also attempting to frame Spring-heeled Jack within a popular idiom too, most commonly that of the supernatural encounter. In their oral recounting of incidences involving themselves or others people asserted their authorship over a particular interpretative understanding. In doing so they transmitted a diffused tale that was owned by all who heard it and yet was the possession of no one storyteller in particular. In mass gatherings to either see or capture Spring-heeled Jack people became incorporated into both his immediate performance and his unfolding narrative. This found its most extreme form in those numerous mimics who crossed the audience-performer boundary by

---

[87] See for example 'Superstition in the Nineteenth Century', *Hampshire Telegraph*, 28th March 1857; *The Times*, 7th April 1857; and *Manchester Times*, 11th September 1858.
[88] 'Curious Charge of Murder at Yarmouth', *Illustrated London News*, 27th September 1845.

dressing up and enacting their own Spring-heeled Jack fantasies.[89] However, personal oral accounts were relatively few. More often the relationship was between the press as performer and its readers as the audience. In such circumstances Spring-heeled Jack was frequently little more than a site for stimulating interaction and an interpretative struggle between oral and literary modes. In this situation he was both 'inside' and 'outside' that dynamic, being both bound by and a product of a narrative but also existing beyond the story, as an external 'real' generator of potentially more stories. As a product of cultural and interpretative contestations, Spring-heeled Jack's rich elaboration in oral rumour and story can be seen to represent the fecundity and strength of oral cultures. However, as with most folklore, Spring-heeled Jack's articulation in oral culture cannot be read as a conscious counter-hegemonic discourse. At best, as Antonio Gramsci noted, it represented a voice (not *the* voice) of subaltern groups bleeding through into the historical record, one that was fitfully picked up and reshaped from literary elitist perspectives in the press.[90]

Spring-heeled Jack's cultural dynamism derived from the seemingly contradictory ways his various expressions interacted across different cultural modes. On the one hand there was an identifiable if largely unintended synergy and symbiosis between print and oral modes. It was not simply a case of journalistic reflections imposing shape on a morass of oral speculation, although this was certainly attempted. Oral accounts subsequently adopted and adapted elements of these printed interpretations so that Spring-heeled Jack experienced an ongoing transference between oral and literary cultures.[91] However, at the same time there was a struggle between oral and print interactions which was frequently more conflictual and consciously divergent from one another. In this interpretative struggle the mode itself became implicated at the centre of contestation. Oral accounts would lay claim to personal experience as the basis of their validity. The press often used this subjectivity to dismiss such testimony, claiming Spring-heeled Jack's witnesses or victims had misinterpreted what they had experienced, their perceptions having been distorted by fear or shock.

---

[89] *Illustrated Police News*, 17th September 1881. For examples of hoaxers and imitators see *Morning Herald*, 2nd March 1838; *Morning Post*, 20th March and 4th April 1838; *The Examiner*, 25th March and 20th April 1838; *Newcastle Courant*, 14th February 1845; *Daily News*, 29th March 1847; *Ipswich Journal*, 21st December 1878; and *The Bristol Mercury*, 24th January 1885. See also Villiers, *Stand and Deliver*, p. 246.

[90] See Mallon, 'Promise and Dilemma of Subaltern Studies', pp. 1506–7. For Gramsci's views on folklore see Gencarella, 'Constituting Folklore', and Crehan, *Gramsci, Culture and Anthropology*, pp. 105–10.

[91] In the context of ghost stories this interaction was an established tradition. In the eighteenth century 'many printed ghost stories were … designed to flow back into speech, allowing them to be re-animated with physical gestures and persuasive linguistic techniques'. See Handley, *Visions of an Unseen World*, p. 218.

The result was reflex interpretations at best, with victims reaching for ghosts and demons to describe baffling encounters, journalists for pranksters and copycat criminals. Ultimately, the subjectivity of both printed and oral accounts led Spring-heeled Jack to be continually constructed and reconstructed from fragments, opinions, cultural predilections and biases. These both reflected and perpetuated the uncertain ontology at the heart of Spring-heeled Jack's legend. It was this core mystery which served as one of the key engines of that legend, powered as it was by a potent blend of speculation, fantasy, disagreement and the articulation of conflicting mentalities.

In his existence across a range of cultural modes Spring-heeled Jack can be read as an early product of an emerging nineteenth-century mass culture. Indicative of his prototype status within such a culture, he owed debts to older folkloric cultures and newer, more commercial ones alike. The endurance granted to Spring-heeled Jack by the ongoing transition back and forth between oral rumour and public print media (and the more 'elite' spheres of awareness that were thereby accessed as a result) suggests that this 'popular' cultural figure was at least partially dependent upon an element of elitist engagement for his longevity. Whilst plebeian oral accounts continued to feed Spring-heeled Jack's legend at a local level, it was commercial ventures produced by penny dreadful authors and their publishers, and theatre managers and their companies of professional actors who disseminated his name into larger and more socially diverse spheres. These multiple cultural transferences certainly negate any simple sense of plebeian 'ownership' of the legend in 'popular' culture and even serve to trouble the concept of popular culture as a culture *of* the people.

8

The Decline and Demise of
Spring-heeled Jack

Following the brief revival of interest in Spring-heeled Jack at the Aldershot and Colchester army bases in 1877 and 1878, the cultural dynamism that had powered his legend began to ebb, his grip on the popular imagination slackening. The 1880s seemed to mark an important transitional period in his decline as there was a noticeable dip in reported 'real' encounters in this decade compared with earlier years. This was recognised by contemporaries. In December 1887 the *Liverpool Mercury* reported on popular interest in a bright star seen in the south-eastern sky before dawn, noting, 'Now that the "Spring-heel Jack" craze is dying out the "Star of Bethlehem" seems to be the craze of the hour.'[1]

This ebbing was best reflected in 'Spring-Heeled Jack', a poem by St John Hammund that was published in *The Idler* in 1900. Whilst popular legends tend to be resistant to aging, this poem clearly portrayed Spring-heeled Jack as an elderly, fading figure in his twilight years. Dressed in a 'long black coat' and with eyes like 'balls of fire' he is described as being:

> gaunt and weird, with a tangled beard,
> And a mark is on his brow.
> His heels are light and shod in steel,
> His arms are thin and worn,
> He buttons his coat to the height of his throat,
> But the sleeves are short and torn.[2]

An accompanying illustration portrayed a slightly stooped old man with beard and earring, tattered clothes, a black domino mask across his eyes and a black hat upon his head. Indicative of the poem's account that he has stolen the female narrator's baby a year earlier, in his left arm he clutches an infant and in his

---

[1] *Liverpool Mercury*, 12th December 1887, p. 6.
[2] *The Idler*, vol.17, July 1900, pp. 492–3.

right he holds a walking stick, further indication that his previous virility has deteriorated.[3]

The longevity of Spring-heeled Jack's legend was aided by the fact that it was not bound to some rigid narrative template but rather consisted more of a raft of tropes that need not all be present for an account to be incorporated into his mythos. Yet the lack of singularity left the legend open to endless distortion that ultimately caused it to wane. Given that this malleability had served him so well into the late 1870s, this chapter will necessarily explore the cultural shifts that caused such a quality to turn against him. As such, it emphasises temporal dynamics as opposed to spatial ones, arguing that Spring-heeled Jack's gradual decline resulted from a combination of factors that may have had a long germination but became more pronounced in the 1880s and 1890s. Key amongst these was the way his polymorphous cultural expressions ultimately provided multiple sites upon which his legend was weakened. Both the oral and literary cultures that had sustained him for so long began to operate against him, pushing accounts of his appearances far beyond the limits of credibility whilst diffusing those elements that had originally made him a potent figure. At the same time the fin de siècle was also marked by powerful mythopoeic instincts that created fictional and real legends which swiftly captured the popular imagination in a way that Spring-heeled Jack no longer could. Although prefiguring the other nineteenth-century characters who grew beyond their initial literary genesis to circulate as myths in a broader cultural sphere, in a Darwinian struggle with Mr Hyde, Jack the Ripper (as a media construct rather than an actual person), Sherlock Holmes and Count Dracula, Spring-heeled Jack became increasingly marginalised as a popular myth that no longer quite worked. Finally, it will explore how the lynchpin to the legend, his name, became diffused into a variety of cultural expressions, transforming him from a specific individual to a more amorphous type associated with elusiveness, athleticism or deception.

The ease with which Spring-heeled Jack's legend incorporated exaggeration, hoaxers and adaptations had been fundamental to the cultural dynamics which sustained him in the popular imagination. Yet the culture that had spawned him in the 1830s was transforming by the 1880s, and several factors conspired to make people less willing to believe or at least suspend their disbelief. Firstly, this was encouraged by an increase in the number of hoaxers being captured; each revelation of a man in a costume whittled away the mystique that had once surrounded the name. Despite having assaulted a policeman in Clewer,

---

[3] His degeneration continued as he supposedly resorted to mugging Manchester's weavers for food on their way to work in the early twentieth century. Rather than nerve-shredding laughter or eerie silence he now spouted doggerel rhyme. See *Gorton and Openshaw Reporter*, 27th December 1957.

near Windsor, in 1885, when the hoaxer was eventually captured he received nothing worse than a stern reprimand from the magistrate.[4] When another hoaxer appeared in a neighbourhood of Liverpool in December 1887 'attired in a sheet', it was actually the 'Spring-heeled Jack' who was taken by surprise, for 'a band of villagers ... stoned him so successfully that he took to his heels'.[5] Incompetent hoaxers appeared to be more a nuisance than a serious threat by the mid-late 1880s. Whilst Spring-heeled Jack's intentions and motivations remained unfathomable, he was clearly not a 'professional' criminal, and his singular persona ultimately isolated him as an amateur troublemaker, prankster and oddity. Rather than tapping into or drawing upon contemporary fears about a perceived criminal underclass, his notoriety was more akin to that of the unfortunate spectacles of the Victorian freak show, although given that he had occupied the popular imagination for several generations he lacked their novelty.

Of course, the notion that Spring-heeled Jack was a hoaxer had been present from his earliest newspaper accounts in 1838. However, a popular willingness to increasingly accept this interpretation can be located in a second, broader change of attitude towards supernatural narratives. Susan Hoyle has argued that part of the reason why witchcraft beliefs went into decline in the nineteenth century was because people were increasingly swayed by the forensic narrative provided by detectives, lawyers and 'expert' witnesses in court. Hoyle accounts for this shift in terms of changing trends in storytelling. People did not necessarily abandon their former 'credulity' but rather were swayed by a more engaging narrative.[6] Within courts and, more importantly, via journalistic reports on their proceedings, people were influenced in the way they should perceive such ideas, reinforcing which types of narrative were acceptable and authoritative, and which were not.

This factor has to be located within a third even broader contextual issue. The late nineteenth century was marked by its fascination with spiritualism, occultism, psychical ability and paranormal activity. Yet Spring-heeled Jack could find little purchase here. His grounding in plebeian folklore denied him relevance to elitist, scientific efforts to incorporate the supernatural into a re-enchanted materialistic worldview, one which frequently interpreted such phenomena as currently misunderstood or unknown aspects of the natural world. Such approaches arguably encouraged the interpretation of a man in a costume rather than having to grapple with the awkward premise that he was a ghost or demon.

---

[4] *Ipswich Journal*, 24th January 1885.

[5] *Leicester Chronicle*, 24th December 1887, p. 4.

[6] Hoyle, 'Witch and the Detective', pp. 48 and 64. This did not necessitate a clear distinction between rational and 'superstitious' thought. Hoyle indicates how the skill of some detectives encouraged others to assume they possessed supernatural powers of their own. See ibid., p. 63.

Even as a ghost his ontological status was no longer secure. Contemporary scientific discourses about spectres explained them (away) as optical illusions or neurological anomalies. From the 1860s he had had to compete with 'Pepper's Ghost' and other ghost projectors which simultaneously awed theatre audiences even as they helped debunk spirit-rising and the existence of 'real' ghosts. As such, whilst often derived from learned discourses, these 'modern' interpretations percolated down into popular culture through literary fiction and theatrical performances.[7] In the 1880s he was too migratory and too frequently associated with a human hoaxer to be of interest to the Society for Psychical Research's investigations into hauntings. By this period even his earlier diabolical association no longer retained its previous power. Popular folkloric belief in a personified devil may have remained strong, but across differing levels of Victorian culture the devil was more inclined to be treated with irony, parody or mockery, often as a cultural shorthand for something other than himself. Certainly in more elite expressions of culture Burton Russell has claimed that artists' and writers' interest in and use of the devil waned after the mid century, having thoroughly exhausted his potential for both horror and comedy.[8] As such, the limitations to one's avowed credulity was determined in part by broader cultural developments of the period.

Although the above was indicative of cultural shifts that were taking place around him, Spring-heeled Jack suffered from more specific alterations too. Firstly, by the mid-late 1880s he was increasingly becoming a tamed figure of fun. In December 1886 he had suffered the indignity of appearing in *Jack and the Beanstalk*, a pantomime at the Grand Theatre, Birmingham. Featuring in a scene entitled 'The Haunted Garrets of the Roof', Spring-heeled Jack and 'the Birmingham ghosts' were said to have 'a rare old time to themselves'. Given this context of 'tuneful music, "catchy" songs, and plenty of fun', Spring-heeled Jack had apparently lost the frisson of fear he had once been able to muster.[9] This notion of tamed, commercial spectacle continued in February 1888 when the enterprising promoters of a local bazaar at Portmandoe attempted to cash in on a Spring-heeled Jack scare along the North Carnarvonshire coast. A town crier announced, 'Spring-heel Jack had been caught, and would be on exhibition from

---

[7] See Smajic, *Ghost-Seers, Detectives, and Spiritualists*.

[8] See Burton Russell, *Mephistopheles*, pp. 201–2 and 213.

[9] *Birmingham Daily Post*, 25th December 1886. See also *The Era*, 1st, 22nd and 29th January 1887, and *Birmingham Daily Post*, 14th January 1887. A 'Spring-heeled Jack' character also appeared in a performance at the Hippodrome in 1903 in aid of the Fresh Air Fund for children living in slums. See *Daily Express*, 1st July 1903.

five to ten each night.' Not surprisingly, this drew crowds who found themselves watching a performance of 'a young man dressed as Spring-heel Jack'.[10]

This transformation went further in 1899 when he appeared in an *Illustrated Chips* comic strip entitled 'A Wild Nights Adventure with Spring-heeled Jack'. Unlike the tall, athletic gentleman of the past this strip featured a squat, fat hoaxer wearing a fanged mask and bat wings. Aided by an accomplice he frightens children from a common (both features of his earlier narrative), appears at the window of a young couple, and scares some policemen before being set upon by birds and comically crashing into a pond.[11] Such depictions can also be interpreted as part of a broader trend towards the sanitisation of violence and the supernatural in later nineteenth-century popular entertainment. In a similar vein, when Punch and Judy shows moved from street entertainments to the drawing rooms of more respectable audiences, the supernatural and macabre content was toned down. One performer told Henry Mayhew that some of his clients 'won't have no ghost, no coffin, and no devil; and that's what I call spilling the performance entirely'. By 1895 Punch's climactic fight with the devil was frequently replaced by a song.[12] Appearing in pantomime most likely resulted in a similar finale for Spring-heeled Jack.

The absence of 'real' accounts, combined with these increasing associations as a mere hoaxer or figure of fun, seemed to have marked a defining break in the collective memory of Spring-heeled Jack as a real entity by the 1890s. A second key factor in his demise was the retrospective formulations which were projected into this collective amnesia, notions that bore all the expected distortions and elaborations of nostalgia and subsequent historical influences. There was a strong sense of Spring-heeled Jack being banished to the past, vaguely to the 1840s when he was arguably most potent. In doing so he was also reimagined as a figment of childhood lore rather than as a contemporary entity. This nostalgic reflection which gathered pace from the 1870s onwards was used as an indication that the children of the early-Victorian period could now safely reconstruct and look back upon their credulous youth from the perspective of adult maturity. Reflecting on Spring-heeled Jack's appearance in Camden in 1841, in 1896 one journal claimed, 'Middle aged fogies will recollect this "bogie" of their childhood.'[13] Similarly, in a piece about Croydon Fair from 1873, R. H. Horne mentions Spring-heeled Jack as a legend that was 'very popular with all schoolboys of the district'. Horne claims he had avoided pursuit and capture by

[10] Despite this gimmick the local scare still left some workmen 'terror-stricken'. See *Bristol Mercury*, 4th February 1888.
[11] *Illustrated Chips*, 9th September 1899, p. 2.
[12] See Mayhew, *London Labour and the London Poor*, vol. 3, p. 43, and Crone, 'Mr and Mrs Punch', pp. 1071–2.
[13] *Musical Opinion and Music Trade Review*, October 1896, p. 14.

leaping 'clean over high hedges or turnpike gates', a feat attributed to 'his wearing india-rubber boots, the soles and heels of which were full of steel watch-springs, as every boy of us thoroughly believed'.[14] Reminiscing about a childhood in Hastings, in 1899 another writer stated, 'Among the earliest things that I can remember is the name of "Spring-heeled Jack", a mythical Satanic incarnation who … was supposed to amuse himself by leaping over houses in the night.' Having declared that 'his existence was firmly believed in by the more credulous', s/he offered a further elaboration by claiming, 'I can almost identify in my memory the houses upon the roofs of which he was said to have left his footprints in the snow.'[15] As these sort of accounts accumulated so Spring-heeled Jack was gradually manoeuvred from being a contemporary menace to an increasingly remote, historical, folkloric tale.

As indicated in Chapter 6, this process of forgetting and misremembering was aided by the fact that Victorian folklorists ignored him. This was due in part to his initial metropolitan associations, but also his obvious contemporaneousness. Neither aspect endeared him to scholars concerned with exploring predominantly rural folk beliefs as examples of 'traditional' mentalities. Supernatural folkloric tropes, most obviously ghosts, were held up as a foil to modernisation, a symbol of previous credulity, and Spring-heeled Jack's evident modernity implicitly challenged the rhetoric of the 'march of intellect' as propagated by nineteenth-century educators, reformers and would-be social engineers.[16] Only in the Edwardian period, as Spring-heeled Jack underwent a more robust transition from a contemporary figure to one located in the past, did amateur folklorists really start to mention him. This was seen throughout 1907 when contributors to *Notes and Queries* gradually resurrected him again through a series of exchanges. Despite recent events in Everton in 1904, they did not seem to initially remember him, suggesting that his swansong appearance had not obtained earlier levels of public interest. Only gradually, via incidences from the 1880s and 1850s, through his being 'one of the bugbears of the 1840s', did they gradually regress back to 1838. Tellingly, one contributor admitted 'he has grown dim in my recollection'.[17]

---

[14] Horne, 'Great Fairs and Markets of Europe', p. 180.
[15] *Temple Bar*, October 1899, p. 265.
[16] For more on these issues see n. 22 in Chapter 6, and Bell, *Magical Imagination*, pp. 129–49.
[17] *Notes and Queries*, 10th Series, 30th March 1907, p. 256. Spring-heeled Jack's 'resurrection' started earlier at a regional level, indicative of the strength of his many provincial existences. As in later recollections, contributions to *Norfolk and Norwich Notes and Queries* in 1898 suggest nobody recalled the London incidences of 1838 and made little of his literary representations. One contributor acknowledged that Spring-heeled Jack was not a purely local creation but claimed there was 'no telling how or when this surprising personage sprang into existence'. See *Norfolk and Norwich Notes and Queries*, 5th November 1898, p. 411. See also 3rd December 1898, p. 418.

Whilst accounts of attacks in the provinces rarely mention the fact that he had a life as a penny serial character, Thomas Ratcliffe, another contributor, recalled how 'into and past the fifties ... at various spots in the midlands this nimble-heeled gentleman had played his jumping pranks'. He recalled that around the end of the 1840s 'there was issued from a London house a life of "Spring-Heeled Jack". It came out in penny weekly numbers, with high illustrations'. His claim that 'the last issue of this marvel was but four or five years ago' suggests possible confusion between earlier publications and Charlton Lea's brief series of 1904. Beyond these misinterpretations were exaggerations too. Ratcliffe claimed, 'There was a good deal of interest in the why and wherefore of Jack's jumping, and how he managed his marvelous flights through the air.' Flying through the air was a considerable embellishment upon the strides and leaps described in the 1830s and 1840s. Showing how later heroic, literary portrayals of the 1860s and 1870s also influenced his recollections, Ratcliffe stated, '[Spring-heeled Jack's] jumps were intended to frighten evildoers ... He was looked upon as a sort of Robin Hood.'[18] Such comments suggest his 1838 terrorising of London had been forgotten. It was only in December 1907 that Harry Hems, one of the last contributors to the discussion, reintroduced the idea that Spring-heeled Jack had been the Marquis of Waterford.[19]

Thirdly, his demise was aided by the nature and associations of his literary manifestations. Literary attempts to provide backstory, explanation and crudely formulated indications of interiority and motivation drained Spring-heeled Jack of much of the mystery that had surrounded him in his early years. Part of his power had resided in his ambiguity, his unknown nature, something that was necessarily compromised by making him the protagonist of his own penny serials. As a result he became less an object upon which to project fears and desires, his various authors prescribing what readers' responses and relationship to Spring-heeled Jack should be. Whilst his move from villain to roguish penny dreadful hero in the 1860s had publicised his name and garnered a new and broader readership, he had started to conform to the familiar mould of penny dreadful stereotypes, thus weakening his previous individuality. Given the seeming ubiquity of roguish highwaymen and boy criminals called Jack, the only thing that really distinguished him from his rivals was his leaping and a bizarre costume. This very fact only reiterated the idea that he was a man in disguise rather than a supernatural entity.

---

[18] *Notes and Queries*, 10th Series, 8th May 1907, p. 394. For a similar retrospective account of Spring-heeled Jack as a 'Robin Hood' figure who stole from the rich and gave to the poor in 1838 see *Lloyd's Weekly Newspaper*, 25th February 1900.

[19] *Notes and Queries*, 10th Series, 7th December 1907, p. 455. See also *Daily Mirror*, 5th January 1954, p. 9.

Worse yet, becoming bound to the roguish highwayman format hindered his former fluidity of expression as such figures' popularity began to wane. Compared with the emergence of new types of protagonists, particularly boy heroes of British imperialism such as Jack Harkaway, and popular detectives like Sexton Blake, the highwayman suddenly seemed rather archaic. These new character types emerged as part of the backlash against penny dreadfuls, the attack not coming solely from critics on the sidelines but from rival entrepreneurial magazine publishers who sought the opportunity to offer something a little different. Edwin J. Brett, a man familiar with the penny dreadful business from his founding of the Newsagents Publishing Company, set up *Boys of England* in 1866. The aim was to provide 'healthy fiction', an antidote to the 'poison' of penny dreadfuls.[20] Jack Harkaway's first appearance in 1871 signalled a shift in reading tastes, for whilst keeping the literary style, energy and knockabout adventure of the penny dreadfuls, his stories dispensed with the gloom of the urban gothic in favour of sun-drenched foreign lands. Harkaway's creator, the barrister Bracebridge Hemyng, took enthusiastic young readers on adventures around the world, with three generations of Harkaways eventually travelling to America, Australia, China, Greece and, in time for the Boer War, the Transvaal.[21] Brett was followed by Charles Fox's *Boy's Standard* in 1875, and the Religious Tract Society weighed in from 1879 with the *Boy's Own Paper*. Despite their own boisterous nature, these rivals to the penny dreadful were more inclined to receive parental approval.[22]

When Spring-heeled Jack's name reappeared in journals in 1890 it was not linked to his existence as a 'real' individual but his association with the corrupting influence of penny dreadful fiction on juvenile minds. This served to enhance his association as a literary fiction rather than as an ethnographic entity. There had been cycles of moral panic since James Greenwood identified penny fictions as one of London's seven deadly sins in the 1860s, but it was given renewed vigour in a July 1890 article in the *Quarterly Review*. Voicing concern about the use of popular literacy in the wake of the 1870 Education Act, it triggered a debate in which Spring-heeled Jack's penny dreadful serial repeatedly featured. It was feared that reading the violent, trashy stories in which he appeared, and absorbing their anti-authoritarian messages, youths would be inclined toward

---

[20] Turner, *Boys will be Boys*, p. 68.

[21] See ibid., pp. 74–87. See also Anglo, *Penny Dreadfuls*, pp. 68–73.

[22] See Rose, *Intellectual Life of the British Working Classes*, pp. 365–438; Springhall, *Youth, Popular Culture and Moral Panics*, pp. 71–97; and Bratton, 'Of England, Home, and Duty', pp. 73–93.

emulation.[23] The *Quarterly Review* declared *Spring-Heeled Jack, or The Terror of London* (presumably Charlton Lea's 1890 serial), *Sweeney Todd, the Demon Barber of Fleet Street, Turnpike Dick,* and *Jack Sheppard* were representative of a 'literature of rascaldom … [which] has done much to people our prisons, our reformatories, and our Colonies, with scapegraces and ne'er-do-wells'.[24] Sounding a similar note of concern for the reading tastes of 'the common people', the *Pall Mall Gazette* condemned *Spring-heeled Jack* and *Sweeney Todd* as works which 'mingled wickedness and folly'. It described *Spring-Heeled Jack* as 'a tale of highwaymen, murderers, burglars, wicked noblemen, and lovely and persecuted damsels, whose physical charms and voluptuous embraces are dilated upon with exceeding unction'. Like other highwaymen, Spring-heeled Jack was presented as "'dashing," "high-spirited," and "bold"', whilst law enforcers were invariably portrayed as tyrannical oppressors or incompetent fools.[25] Such statements serve to reiterate that Spring-heeled Jack had become one amongst many such flamboyant, two-dimensional penny fiction rogues.

Not all were so willing to indulge the moral panic. With a more reasonable approach the *Daily News* stated, 'One cannot pretend to be surprised that boys in a huge town like this kind of nonsense. What does anyone expect them to like?' Given that these stories had to be set in the city as a known contextual reference for their readers, the adventures were bound to lead to 'infringements of the Law'.[26] *The Speaker* went further, criticising the *Quarterly Review* article as 'tremendously overdone'; whilst agreeing that *Spring-heeled Jack* was undoubtedly 'sad trash' it rejected the notion that such works could be used as an indictment of state education or young readers in general.[27] The *Scots Observer* took issue with the *Quarterly Review*'s claims that such literature corrupted the innocent. With a deterministic view we would now find hard to accept it declared 'thieves are born not made, and it needs something more than the rascally literature of Fleet Street to drive men to [crime]'. It added that stories of roguish outlaws appealed to boys' 'spirit of adventure' rather than serving as an inducement to crime and it was more the tone than the subject matter of penny dreadfuls which made them 'dangerous'. It proposed that if *Spring-heeled Jack* was swapped for

---

[23] An earlier piece in the *Saturday Review*, 20th October 1888, noted 'the lower orders read of "Spring-heeled Jack", and will read of "Jack the Ripper" when he finds his way into penny dreadful in the ordinary course of nature. Then they act, or profess to act, in imitation of their models.' For a fictional story which suggests how penny dreadful tales of Spring-heeled Jack became embroiled in young men's perceptions of the world see Walter Besant's 'Self or Bearer', *All the Year Round*, 1st December 1886, pp. 1–72.

[24] *Quarterly Review*, July 1890, p. 152.

[25] *Pall Mall Gazette*, 21st July 1890, p. 3.

[26] 'Penny Fiction', *Daily News*, 19th July 1890.

[27] *The Speaker*, 26th July 1890, p. 104.

'Captain Charles Johnson's most entertaining *Highwaymen and Pirates* … little harm would be done'.[28] On a similar note, the *Musical World* added that the lower classes 'read "Spring-heeled Jack" and the like simply because they have nothing better within reach'. It was convinced that they would enjoy reading Robert Louis Stevenson, H. Rider Haggard and Rudyard Kipling too but claimed 'they do not get the chance'.[29] Whether this was due to the price of such works, the levels of literacy required or both was not elaborated upon.

The power of Spring-heeled Jack was also dissipated as authors started to use him as a touchstone reference to childhood superstition, often employing him as a warm-up act for their own ghost stories. This frequently implied and encouraged a temporal distancing which relegated Spring-heeled Jack to the past again. Writing his tale of Norwich's phantom horseman in 1880, Mark Knights introduced him by way of the claim that 'most middle-aged Norwich folk will remember' the abundant stories of Spring-heeled Jack from 'their early days'.[30] Similarly, 'Old Balls's Ghost' appeared in the *Essex Standard* in 1889 but was set in Colchester at Christmas 1866. One character recites a song about Spring-heeled Jack, alluding to his rumoured 'supernatural appearance … in Colchester more than once on dark evenings'. Another claims, 'My old woman was a comin' up Barkera Hill the other evening, and she saw him scramblin' up over the Roman wall.' How far this was literary invention or reference to a supposedly real incident is hard to tell. It was not particularly important in this context, for once again these introductory comments merely set the mood for another local ghost story.[31]

Stories that did focus on Spring-heeled Jack commonly reiterated the idea that he was a human hoaxer. 'The Biter Bit', which appeared in *Young Folks Paper* in August 1888, was a story about William Leighton, a seventeen-year-old sailor who returns home to find the locals terrified by Spring-heeled Jack. When he declares his ignorance of who Spring-heeled Jack is his father asks if he remembers the Aldershot Ghost, claiming 'we have got an imitator of that fellow here, at quiet Copsely'. Local girls and women have suffered shocks and are terrified to leave their homes at night. The police and locals seem impotent to stop him. Promoting the familiar idea of the heroic young sailor as the man of action, Leighton dons female attire to bait Spring-heeled Jack into attacking him. When he appears Spring-heeled Jack is described as 'a dark thing' whose

---

[28] *Scots Observer*, 2nd August 1890.

[29] *Musical World*, 2nd August 1890, p. 604. For an article on the difference between Spring-heeled Jack's penny serials and Rider Haggard's 'romances' see *Time*, May 1887.

[30] Knights, *Norfolk Tales*, p. 8.

[31] *Essex Standard*, 28th December 1889, p. 2. This temporal distancing was also evident in Charlton Lea's 1890 serial. The *Quarterly Review* presumed it was rather vaguely situated 'about the middle of the eighteenth century'. See *Quarterly Review*, July 1890, p. 152.

face shone with 'a faint unearthly light'. The sailor uses the phosphorous on Spring-heeled Jack's face to guide him to his attacker's throat, and despite being scratched by his 'horrible claws', Leighton forces Spring-heeled Jack into submission and binds him with ropes. He then removes the man's boots 'which were fitted with a curious arrangement of springs'. When the bear disguise is removed in the presence of a constable and men from a nearby inn Spring-heeled Jack is revealed to be the eldest son of a baronet and the lord of the manor, alluding once again to well-established notions of the perpetrator as an aristocratic prankster.[32]

A later tale in the *Hampshire Telegraph* in December 1897 suggested Spring-heeled Jack was nothing more than a combination of popular superstition, circumstantial influences, and misunderstood occurrences. This story, 'The Haunted Terrace', also invoked a temporal distancing by setting its story in a row of terrace houses in Portsmouth in 1837. One family is gathered to tell ghost stories when they hear 'a wild, unearthly shriek' from the top of the house. Two of the men go to investigate and swiftly return, 'their nerves completely gone', claiming, 'It's devils dancing on the roof!' Further along the row an elderly woman was reading *Pilgrim's Progress* and was unsettled by the book's image of the demonic Apollyon. She also hears screeches and thuds and in her heightened anxiety imagines she is set upon by 'a black form, with fiery eyes' which 'springs at her across the room', causing her to faint. In yet another house a shipwright tells his friend about having seen Spring-heeled Jack a fortnight earlier. One rainy night he had seen him 'jump clean over the ramparts as I came round the corner there from off the High street … it had horns and a loose sort of hairy coat, as it jumped right before my face'. His friend suspects he was drunk but then they too hear a sound upstairs. The shipwright claims Spring-heeled Jack has returned and they both hurriedly leave the house. These noises breed fearful superstitions. The elderly woman interprets it as a divine judgement, whilst one of the women in the first house declares, 'There must be a curse on these houses.' All the inhabitants give a week's notice of their intention to leave, the landlord believing it to be a collective attempt to get the rent reduced. Having set up these unsettling circumstances, the author explains them away by revealing that two boys in one of the middle houses had got up into the joined attics and had raced up and down the length of the terraces, their playing creating the strange sounds that had frightened those below. Rather than suggesting this was a deliberate prank, the author's leg-pulling tale is aimed at mocking the misunderstandings of the superstitious adults.[33]

---

[32] *Young Folks Paper*, 25th August 1888.
[33] *Hampshire Telegraph*, 25th December 1897, p. 12.

A fourth key development was the late-nineteenth-century emergence of competing and more powerful figures in the popular imagination. Of particular note were Mr Hyde, Jack the Ripper and Count Dracula, all figures who could articulate the concerns of the period in a way Spring-heeled Jack was no longer able to. Although Spring-heeled Jack had had earlier literary rivals in *Varney the Vampyre* and *Sweeney Todd*, the safe temporal distancing of their stories meant neither had really encroached on his contemporary existence, even though Todd had stirred debate as to whether he had been a real person.[34] It was Robert Louis Stevenson's *Dr Jekyll and Mr Hyde* (1886) which presented the first great challenge to Spring-heeled Jack's position in the popular imagination, for it offered a more sophisticated expression of many of the notions he had previously evoked. Like Spring-heeled Jack, Edward Hyde was the animalistic urban dweller unfettered from moral responsibilities to pursue his instincts and base desires, preying upon the weak in a metropolitan hunting ground. In Spring-heeled Jack's association with gentlemen pranksters he also combined something of Jekyll and Hyde's duality of the respectable and the monstrous. Whilst Jekyll and Hyde said more about bourgeois hypocrisies than aristocratic callousness, David Punter has noted that, in the popular imagination at least, Stevenson's story has become associated with a 'body of semi-legendary history which unmistakably *is* aristocracy-orientated'.[35]

Yet Edward Hyde had several appealing advantages over Spring-heeled Jack by the 1880s. His pseudo-scientific origin did not have to accommodate the (increasingly weak) supernatural associations that still lingered around Spring-heeled Jack. Stevenson's creation was a fundamentally more interesting conception which embodied the hypocrisies of 'civilised' man and personified the dramatic struggle between his conflicting natures. By comparison Spring-heeled Jack lacked depth and tension, being firmly in control of himself as he chose to don disguise and cause havoc. His power and appeal to the imagination had always resided in his surface, in his shifting but horrific appearance and his bizarre actions, more than his seemingly foolish or unfathomable motives. At the same time Hyde personified contemporary fears about the degenerative effects of the urban environment on city dwellers. Described as being 'pale and dwarfish' and 'troglodytic', he clearly resonated with late-nineteenth-century pseudo-scientific discourse that viewed criminals, and by extension, the urban poor, as

---

[34] For Sweeney Todd's life as a cultural figure see Mack, *Wonderful and Surprising History of Sweeney Todd*.
[35] Punter, *Literature of Terror*, vol. 2, p. 2.

subnormal, degenerate or defective products of heredity or environment.[36] Typically portrayed as tall, lithe and a virile acrobat, Spring-heeled Jack's appearance and activities denied him any contribution to this debate, for even if his supernatural nature was in doubt, his seemingly superhuman athleticism was not. As ever, he was a contrary oddity.

If Spring-heeled Jack's saving grace had been that Edward Hyde was clearly bound to the realm of literary fiction, then this collapsed with the appearance of the next and arguably most powerful figure of the late-nineteenth-century popular imagination. From the autumn of 1888 Spring-heeled Jack became entangled with, and forever eclipsed by, Jack the Ripper. The parallels between the two Jacks are quite remarkable. One can read Spring-heeled Jack as a blueprint for the construction of much of the Ripper mythos. Another interpretation would be that, with no clues as to the Ripper's identity, a sensation-hungry public and press cannibalised elements of former urban folklore.[37] Both were initially granted life by the metropolitan press. Press descriptions of the Ripper stole Spring-heeled Jack's cultural lexicon. In early September 1888 *The Star* described the Ripper in bestial terms and as 'a ghoulish and devilish brute', appropriating allusions to the supernatural that had been previously applied to Spring-heeled Jack.[38]

As with Spring-heeled Jack's emergence in 1838, the Ripper's narrative 'was constructed piecemeal over a period of several weeks', and with no real information about the killer or his motives the press similarly invoked notions of 'a "man monster"... who "goes forth stealthily and takes his victims when and where he ... pleases".[39] In a piece of unfortunate timing a play of *Jekyll and Hyde* had opened at the Lyceum Theatre in August, the very month the murders associated with the Ripper began. In his article 'Murder and More to Follow' in the *Pall Mall Gazette* in September 1888, W. T. Stead offered Stevenson's popular literary creation as a model for the Ripper's dual personality. The idea found purchase and helped spawn assertions that the perpetrator was a mad aristocrat or deranged doctor, contributing to the familiar but unfounded notion of

---

[36] Stevenson, *Dr Jekyll and Mr Hyde*, p. 19. This relationship between the human and bestial became increasingly evident in texts expressing late-nineteenth-century anxieties about evolutionary regression, most obviously H. G. Wells' *The Island of Dr Moreau*. For contemporary concerns about degeneration see Luckin, 'Revisiting the Idea of Degeneration'; Hurley, *Gothic Body*, pp. 65–88; Smith, *Victorian Demons*, pp. 14–44; and Ledger and Luckhurst, *Fin de Siècle*, pp. 1–24. For a contemporary view see Cantlie, *Degeneration Amongst Londoners*.

[37] See Evans and Skinner, *Jack the Ripper*, p. 34, and Perry Curtis, *Jack the Ripper*, p. 144. Perry Curtis' examination of the Ripper and the London press suggests the collective and ongoing formulation of the Ripper mythos was a perfecting of the oral-literary cultural interactions that had already been practised earlier in the century with Spring-heeled Jack.

[38] *The Star*, 5th September 1888.

[39] Walkowitz, *City of Dreadful Delight*, pp. 191 and 196–7.

the gentleman killer.[40] The idea of the cruel aristocrat who preyed on women obviously echoed Spring-heeled Jack's reportage in early 1838, but the violence of the Ripper murders took this to an entirely new level. Ultimately, the two Jacks followed similar narrative trajectories, for neither were ever captured and their true identities remained unknown. In denying the press and public a cathartic resolution they escaped mundane historical realities, becoming enveloped in shadowy cloaks of urban mythology.

Beyond these obvious parallels there were occasional moments of conflation. The image of the Ripper as a devil promoting penny dreadful-style stories in *Punch* in October 1888 clearly resonated with diabolical depictions of Spring-heeled Jack, down to the long feather in his cap.[41] The most explicit link between the two came from one of the many letters sent by someone claiming to be the Ripper to the vigilance committees and press. Dated 4th October 1888 it was headed 'Spring Heel Jack, The Whitechapel Murderer' and signed 'Jack the Ripper'. The brief, rambling note claimed to be from an American who had already murdered six women, and who intended 'to make it a dozen' by killing six policemen in the East End. Whether it was a coincidence of geography or a knowing reference to Spring-heeled Jack's earlier metropolitan activities, it claimed he was residing in Bow cemetery, alluding to both his frequent association with cemeteries and the locality of his most infamous attack on Jane Alsop in February 1838.[42] The name 'Spring Heel Jack' would certainly have borne its own folkloric tradition of violent assault in the minds of older Londoners in 1888. The blurred associations continued beyond the autumn of that year. Reporting on the grisly discovery of a mutilated body devoid of head and legs and attributed to being the ninth Whitechapel murder, in September 1889 the *Daily News* wrote of how the police had 'tramped after this spring-heeled Jack of the shambles' with little effect. It claimed that despite their efforts 'once more the beast has slipped through'.[43] Here the Ripper's association with Spring-heeled Jack seems to derive from the latter's developing application as an expression of elusiveness, a point that will be explored shortly.

Despite these correlations there were noticeable differences between the two Jacks, particularly in the relative power of their narratives. Jack the Ripper swiftly

---

[40] *Pall Mall Gazette*, 8th September 1888. See also Walkowitz, *City of Dreadful Delight*, pp. 206–7.

[41] *Punch*, 13th October 1888.

[42] National Archive, MEPO 3/142, p. 195.

[43] *Daily News*, 11th September 1889, p. 4. This blurring continued into the early twentieth century with the 1920s German expressionist movie *Waxworks*. Werner Krauss played 'Springheel Jack' but was referred to in the English captions as 'Jack the Ripper', suggesting the latter's more potent influence in the popular imagination in Britain. See *Saturday Review of Politics, Literature, Science and Art*, 14th July 1928, p. 47.

came to animate the popular imagination in a truly macabre way that Spring-heeled Jack's comparatively juvenile pranks could not. Unverified accounts of people being frightened to death by Spring-heeled Jack's actions now sounded like mere speculative gossip compared to the very real mutilations that were being perpetrated in the East End of London in 1888. In an era of sensational 'New Journalism', Spring-heeled Jack was no longer sensational enough. His former associations with both crime and the supernatural had become familiar, even moribund, via the glut of murderers and ghosts that populated more sensational press media of the period, the best example being the *Illustrated Police News*.[44] Compared to the gore of the Ripper's murders, Spring-heeled Jack now appeared nothing more than a leaping buffoon. The targeting of prostitutes added sex into the potent sensationalist mixture in a way that had only ever been alluded to in rather coy and discreet ways in Spring-heeled Jack's earlier encounters. Rather than melodramatic accounts of sexual harassment and fainting maidens, the Ripper hinted at a darker, more twisted sexual deviance.

The Ripper was also a more credible urban fiend for his age, his mythos deeply entwined in the nature and conditions of the East End and largely (though not wholly) divested of supernatural vestiges.[45] Despite the sensational rhetoric of the newspapers, the Ripper was always perceived as a human monster and all the more horrifying for it. Spring-heeled Jack had been a product of his time, when notions of the diabolical and the phantasmal had still possessed some credible popular cultural currency. However, by 1888 he had become part of the background scenery, lingering on the margins for so long that his previous sensationalism had ebbed into familiarity, perhaps even acceptance. The failure to capture either Jack meant they both retained a phantasmal presence in London beyond their initial appearances, but the lingering fear of the re-emergence of the Ripper would have been of a wholly different order to a new encounter with Spring-heeled Jack, especially by the late 1880s. Finally, at a functional level, Spring-heeled Jack could not articulate the contemporary issues that were alluded to in the contextual and narrative dimensions of the Ripper phenomenon, or certainly not as effectively. As Perry Curtis has illustrated, the Ripper provided a way of talking about a range of contemporary (and frequently interrelated) fears linked to law and order, moral degeneracy, xenophobic prejudice, anti-Semitism and the need for public health reform in the East End.[46] Migratory, geographically remote, increasingly scarce and viewed as a prankster rather than a killer,

---

[44] For late-Victorian sensational journalism see Maunder and Moore, *Victorian Crime*, and Perry Curtis, *Jack the Ripper*, pp. 48–108.

[45] For the theory that the Ripper killed to make magical candles from human fat see Perry Curtis, *Jack the Ripper*, pp. 235–7. See also Walkowitz, *City of Dreadful Delight*, p. 197.

[46] See Perry Curtis, *Jack the Ripper*, pp. 238–52.

Spring-heeled Jack could no longer tap into these potent cultural concerns of late-nineteenth-century metropolitan life.

That Spring-heeled Jack was swiftly downgraded in the popular imagination compared to Jack the Ripper is suggested by a verbal faux pas in a political speech by a Colonel Morrison. Referring to a Mr Evans as 'the "bogie man" of the Radical party', Morrison likened him to Jack the Ripper in the way Evans 'came forward to frighten weak-nerved electors'. This rather ill-received joke prompted a member of the audience to correct him by calling out 'Spring-heeled Jack', to which the Colonel said, 'Yes, like Spring-heeled Jack.' Morrison had written to the *Liverpool Mercury* accusing a journalist of having printed this crass 'slip of the tongue', but a statement from another audience member noted that the Colonel 'did not in the presence of the audience withdraw the more obnoxious phrase or explain that he had made a mistake'. Clearly, being associated with Spring-heeled Jack was less insulting than being associated with the Ripper.[47]

The Ripper rendered Spring-heeled Jack a pale shadow, further easing his displacement from former reality to folkloric bogeyman. It was not so much that he had been tamed as replaced, complacently abandoned by popular cultures that had constructed new, more effective characters for expressing modern fears. One can include here not only the potent individuals indicated above but also real if highly sensationalised figures such as European anarchists and Irish republicans. The bombing of London's underground railways in 1883 and an explosion at Victoria Station in February 1884 ensured the dynamite of these new bogeymen was suddenly far more spectacular and immediate than Spring-heeled Jack's now remote accounts of mere fire-breathing.[48]

That Spring-heeled Jack was irreparably weakened after the emergence of the Ripper is indicated by the way he was himself refashioned in the late 1890s to resonate with Count Dracula, another figure who quickly seized the late-nineteenth-century popular imagination. Bram Stoker's *Dracula* was an instant hit from its publication in May 1897. Respectable journals such as the *Pall Mall Gazette* may have described it as 'horrid and creepy to the last degree' but also recognised it as 'one of the best things in the supernatural line that we have been lucky enough to hit upon'. Even critical accounts in *Punch* and the *Athenaeum* appreciated its allure, whilst *The Lady* alluded to the hypnotic appeal of the vampire by claiming the book's 'fascination is so great that it is impossible to lay it

---

[47] 'Colonel Morrison and Mr. Edward Evans, Jun.', *Liverpool Mercury*, 31st October 1891.
[48] See Bloom, *Violent London*, pp. 226–54; Butterworth, *World That Never Was*; and Jensen, 'Daggers, Rifles and Dynamite'.

aside'.[49] As with the Ripper, at the fin de siècle vampires became a powerful trope for articulating a host of contemporary anxieties, most notably concerns about sexuality, race, empire, disease and degeneration.[50] Dracula could allude to a rich cultural register of meaning that the increasingly anachronistic Spring-heeled Jack no longer could. Even more than the wild speculation about the identity of the Ripper, the Count explicitly appropriated the predatory aristocrat in the metropolis dimension of Spring-heeled Jack's earlier legend. In comparison with this gothic lord Spring-heeled Jack was a mere jester.

With his weakening individuality in the popular imagination Spring-heeled Jack increasingly became a cultural cipher. From May 1899 the boys' magazine *The Wonder* began running a serial about the Human Bat, the 'story of a vampire known as Spring-heeled Jack'. Advertisements depicted Spring-heeled Jack as a slim, white-faced figure in a black bodysuit, possessing bat-like wings and ears, and described as a 'weird being who flies by night to track down his victims'. The pale-faced, bat-like imagery was similarly evoked in the depiction of Dracula on the first-edition paperback cover of Stoker's novel. By July *The Human Bat* was simply being described as 'The story of Spring-heeled Jack the vampire'.[51] This comic book reinvention represented a last, late pulsing of blood through an aging legend. Yet whilst this incarnation possessed all the vigour of his earlier manifestations, his having to take on the guise of the vampire indicated that in the twilight of the nineteenth century Spring-heeled Jack was essentially living an extenuated, rather undead existence of his own. As such, Spring-heeled Jack proved incapable of being continually reimagined like other gothic monsters of the nineteenth century. Some of these rivals had stolen his cultural clothing and marginalised him through their new appeal, rendering him a proto-myth that later legendary figures subsequently added to and improved upon. Like an evolutionary dead end, Spring-heeled Jack had fallen victim to Edward Hyde as a more effective articulation of the dark man of the psyche in an era that

---

[49] See Ludlam, *Biography of Dracula*, pp. 107–8. A hurriedly produced play in the same month was not successful. This was not an attempt to disseminate the character across multiple cultural forms in the manner of Spring-heeled Jack but merely 'a copyright performance ... purely to protect the plot and dialogue from piracy'. See ibid., p. 109.

[50] George MacDonald's *Lilith* was published in 1895, and 1897 saw not only the publication of Stoker's *Dracula* but also Florence Marryat's *The Blood of the Vampire*. Literary analysis of the vampire has become too extensive to cite. For examples see Smith, *Victorian Demons*, pp. 118–49; Warwick, 'Vampires and the Empire'; key samples in Gelder, *Horror Reader*, pp. 145–86; and Glover, *Vampires, Mummies and Liberals*.

[51] See *Illustrated Chips*, 29th April, 6th, 13th, 27th May, 1st July 1899, and 10th November 1900. This image was also close to the description of Spring-heeled Jack in several London appearances in January 1888. In Kensal Green, Queen's Park, and Kilburn Lane he was said to have worn 'black skin tights' and 'a black skullcap', whilst his pale face was 'presumably chalked'. See *Dundee Courier*, 23rd January 1888.

saw the development of psychopathology. The Ripper replaced his buffoonery with butchery, whilst Dracula swiftly came to serve as both a more powerful and flexible monstrosity for expressing a multitude of contemporary anxieties. For all his past fluidity of cultural expression, Spring-heeled Jack was ultimately unable to be continually appropriated for new interpretations. Whatever cultural function monsters needed to articulate in the fin-de-siècle imagination, it seemed others could increasingly say it better.

This needs to be situated as part of a broader cultural shift. The early Victorians had not only viewed excessive use of the imagination as a threat to mental health, they had also associated belief in imaginary characters with the intellectual and social inferiority of children, women, the lower classes and non-European races.[52] By contrast, Michael Saler has argued that the increasing influence of a polymorphous mass media made the practice of immersing oneself in fantasised worlds, of consciously pretending, a more common and socially acceptable experience by the 1890s. The diversity of mass media representations frequently encouraged a blurring between the boundaries of 'fact' and fiction (or in the Ripper's case, mythologising) in a more potent way than had been the case with Spring-heeled Jack earlier in the century. This fin-de-siècle trend towards a knowing and perhaps even wilful 'indulgence of the imagination' was best seen with regard to Sherlock Holmes. Whether naively or ironically, from the 1890s some people were willing to believe that Sherlock Holmes was a real person.

Spring-heeled Jack could not easily offer himself to what Saler terms the fin de siècle's 'ironic imagination'. He claims it was the 'fantastic nature' of Holmes' eccentric genius which separated him from the mundane world and enabled an effective immersion in an enclosed fantasised world.[53] Whilst Spring-heeled Jack's bizarre actions and demonic or bestial allusions arguably served a similar function, his 'real' encounters were very much part of the mundane world and represented a genuine threat of assault that did not easily lend itself to irony. At the same time his literary existence was comprised of sensationalised stories usually located in the past and encumbered with hackneyed tropes of disinherited heirs and damsels in distress. Holmes' contemporary fictional world generally possessed sufficient verisimilitude to lift him above such crude plot elements, whilst his powerful deductive reasoning ensured he was not mired in the ordinary. This persuasive combination of the marvellous and the mundane enabled Holmes to express fantasies of control (via the power of his intellect) over a recognisably modern world. By contrast Spring-heeled Jack offered randomness, disorder, superstition and incomprehension. As such, by the 1890s

---

[52] Saler, 'Clap if You Believe', pp. 606, 618 and 620.
[53] See ibid., p. 601.

people no longer desired to engage in the pretence of Spring-heeled Jack being real in a way they did with Holmes. Spring-heeled Jack had served an implicitly oppositional function to earlier strictures against the imagination, and this too may have helped sustain him at some level. Yet when imaginary beings became more accepted in the late nineteenth century this rebellious aspect became redundant. Spring-heeled Jack now found himself the wrong type of enchantment. It was not that he could change no further, but that public attitudes changed around (and against) him. He was either a prankster and therefore mundane, or supernatural, something that could no longer be accepted at face value without conflicting with one's sense of expected 'modern' thinking on such matters. By contrast Holmes forced no such compromise, providing a secular way of re-enchanting the urban, the rational and the modern without having to resort to the supernatural. Spring-heeled Jack could offer little, and certainly little that was new to the shifting zeitgeist.

The above were all important influences on the decline of Spring-heeled Jack's legend, but arguably most damaging was the looser application of his name in late-Victorian popular culture. The catchy moniker had been vital in granting coherence to his diverse cultural expressions. A gradual degeneration of his specific individuality, concurrent with a forgetting of the legend's origins, caused him to become unfettered from a specific past as he was increasingly disseminated in late-nineteenth-century argot as a term associated with elusiveness and inexplicability. Following a lecture to the Portsmouth Literary and Scientific Society in 1878, a Dr Ward Cousins had noted that naturalists had been unable to locate an ancestor of the sea serpent. To the amusement of the assembly he suggested that it could be described as 'the "spring-heel Jack" of natural history'.[54] In very different circumstances the disgruntled William Saxton, unable to come to terms with the disconnection between former promises of support and his loss of an 1888 Liverpool School Board election, claimed 'it would be worse than foolish to charge the honourable executive of our city with either dereliction of duty or foul play'. He bitterly supposed the only way he could account for the result was 'that Mr Springheel-Jack had paid a flying visit to Liverpool' in order to sabotage his candidature.[55] As applied in these circumstances, Spring-heeled Jack was being transformed from a singular individual to a mode of explanation which granted a superficial coherence to strange or unexpected occurrences.

The name also became a term popularly applied to anyone possessing unusual speed or agility, especially criminals. The *Oxford English Dictionary* suggests this had started as far back as the 1840s. In January 1853 William Turner, a

---

[54] *Hampshire Telegraph*, 23rd November 1878, p.7. See also De Castre, *Norfolk Folklore Collection*, vol. 3, p. 95.

[55] *Liverpool Mercury*, 19th November 1888, p. 6.

man locally known in Lewisham as 'Spring-heeled Jack', and a person who had troubled the area for a number of years, was charged with robbery. As suggested by the testimony of a police constable at the trial, the name had derived from Turner's ability to elude the police until this incident.[56] This continued throughout the rest of the century and by the 1890s the title had become 'a general Victorian nickname for a street robber who relied on speed ... to escape'. People were said to be fearful of carrying large quantities of money because 'there are so many of these spring-heeled Jacks about'.[57] The association with dexterity and athleticism had caused the name to be given to a race horse as early as May 1838, and a number of equine Spring-heeled Jacks appeared in the sports pages of the Victorian press.[58] Perhaps unsurprisingly, the moniker was also appropriated by several professional acrobats and gymnasts in the late nineteenth century. In 1885 Bravo the gymnast arrived in England, and amongst his many stage names was the title 'Bravo, the Spring-heeled Jack'. Likewise, the acrobat W. Rushton was known as 'Spring-heeled Jack, or the Demon Jumper'.[59] Whilst such appropriations were clearly not new in this period the name was more readily claimed, for it retained a certain currency even as its original possessor was being relegated to the cultural margins. In 1897 the *Strand Magazine* printed a piece on Oswald North, the 'Champion Jumper' and referred to him as 'bounding hither and thither like a veritable Spring-heeled Jack'.[60] This dissemination into general parlance continued into the second half of the twentieth century.[61]

The loss of his name's original, individual application marked a fatal blow to Spring-heeled Jack, for it had been the lynchpin that had long held his legend's diverse and frequently contradictory elements together. One can observe, though not strictly date, a transition (and an accompanying semantic weakening) from 'Spring-heeled Jack' to *a* Spring-heeled Jack, to *a type* of Spring-heeled Jack. Whilst this was certainly not a simple, linear development, the notion

---

[56] See *Reynolds's Newspaper*, 16th January 1853, p. 16. *The Standard* gave his name as John Turner and described an individual who two years earlier had robbed a woman at gunpoint in Lewisham Fields. See 'Spring-heeled Jack', *The Standard*, 17th January 1853. For later examples see *Newcastle Courant*, 5th November 1869, and *Northern Echo*, 7th December 1893. In 1870 a newspaper associated his name with a dangerous lunatic in Birmingham. The man was said to outrace all pursuers and have 'Herculean strength and savage ferocity'. See *Morning Post*, 8th September 1870, p. 2. This continued into the twentieth century. See for example *Daily Mirror*, 11th October 1929, p. 2.
[57] Simpson and Roud, *Dictionary of English Folklore*, p. 340.
[58] See *Bell's Life in London*, 27th May 1838, 25th October and 7th November 1840, 8th August 1847, 27th August 1848, 9th March 1851, 17th September 1854, and 1st October 1881.
[59] See *The Era*, 14th November 1885, p. 22, 15th November 1890, and 31st January 1891.
[60] *Strand Magazine*, November 1897, p. 510. For 'Spring-heeled Jack' as a term for someone possessing notable agility see *Cheshire Observer*, 11th August 1888.
[61] See for example 'The Hospital's Cup', *The Times*, 15th February 1928, p. 7, and 'Runaway Steam-roller', *The Times*, 21st March 1960, p. 14.

of Spring-heeled Jack as a 'type' became more marked in the 1880s and 1890s. The *Northern Echo* reported on rumours of 'a ghost of the "Spring-heeled Jack" type' in Richmond in 1884.[62] A 'Welsh Spring-heel Jack' caused a disturbance in Wrexham and Exlusham in 1886. Possessing great speed and agility, he shocked women, frightened the horses and passengers on a Wrexham tramcar, and leapt a large pool of water to make his escape. As such, this late account had many of the features of earlier encounters. Yet suggestive of his having become a type rather than an individual, he was described as a 'ghost of the orthodox description – very tall, dressed all in white, with a face terrible to look upon'.[63] In an 1889 article reminiscing about the St Giles Ghost in the mid-1870s, the *Licensed Victuallers' Mirror* claimed crowds had gathered at night to catch sight of 'the frolicsome sprite', an entity described as being 'in the "Spring heeled Jack" line'. The implication was that the St Giles Ghost shared Jack's prankster nature whilst also alluding to the strong possibility that it was a hoax.[64] Such developments indicate how Spring-heeled Jack suffered a protracted death by semantics.

By the 1890s Spring-heeled Jack was being abstracted into a generic bogeyman to scare children in Lewes and Worthing in Sussex.'[65] This development was indicated in an 1893 story 'Perlycross' by R. D. Blackmore in *Macmillan's Magazine*. Set in 1835, some village boys tell a nervous man about Spring-heeled Jack to scare him further. Not only does this literary tale actually grant Spring-heeled Jack an existence two years prior to his original appearance, it also indicates his shift towards becoming a folkloric bogeyman. The boys tell the frightened man, 'Springheel Jack ... is coming into [the district] now, with his bloody heart and dark lantern.'[66] These two accruals had not been part of previous accounts. Writing in 1931, F. J. Proctor recalled that even after Spring-

---

[62] *Northern Echo*, 1st August 1884, p. 4. The association arose from the 'ghostly figure' having outraced two men in a pursuing horse-drawn vehicle. The St Margaret's Bay Ghost in Kent in 1904 was described as 'this "Spring-heeled Jack"' on account of his speed and elusiveness. Aided by local fogs the 'ghost' was suspected of having escaped detection by hiding in a cave in nearby cliffs. See *Daily Mirror*, 19th November 1904, p. 3.

[63] *Cheshire Observer*, 16th January 1886, p. 2. There was sometimes ambiguity in the way this was presented to newspaper readers. When he appeared in Neath in 1898 the *Western Mail*'s article title referred to 'A "Spring-Heel Jack" at Neath', suggesting one of many, but it subsequently referred to the fact that '"Spring-heel Jack" ... [has] been occupying the attention of Neath people', suggesting a singular individual. See *Western Mail*, 15th November 1898, p. 6.

[64] *Licensed Victuallers' Mirror*, 22nd January 1889, p. 618. These implications were not fixed. In a story in the *Blackburn Standard* a man was said to have 'haunted Downing Street ... like a Spring-heeled Jack', suggesting persistence rather than athleticism or hoaxing. See *Blackburn Standard*, 15th October 1881, p. 2.

[65] Simpson and Roud, *Dictionary of English Folklore*, pp. 340–1.

[66] *Macmillan's Magazine*, June 1893, p. 88.

heeled Jack had disappeared 'his reputation as a ghost was related for years after as a bedtime story in many an inglenook of Old Portsmouth'.[67] Bogeymen retained power over the minds of the young, but even the application of his name could not prevent him from morphing into the less clearly defined assembly of dark figures of childhood psychology.[68] Given all the earlier speculation about his mortal or phantasmal nature, ultimately Spring-heeled Jack became a ghost of his former self.

Despite this rather ignominious death by diffusion by the start of the Edwardian period, his survival as a cultural trope had depended, at least in part, upon that diffusion. Spring-heeled Jack 'types' have seen repeated resurrections since 1904. In December 1937, exactly a century after his first appearance, Campbeltown, a herring port on the Clyde, suffered a scare by a 'white-clad apparition' who had 'adopted the tactics of the notorious Spring-heeled Jack by attaching mechanisms to his feet, enabling him to leap great heights'. For a fortnight he startled women at night by leaping over garden walls, leaving his victims 'in a half-fainting condition'. In response an 'army of 400 men and youths, armed with cudgels, patrolled the side streets and outlying districts of the town' in an attempt 'to lay the ghost'. As in London a century earlier, his seemingly simultaneous appearance in several parts of the town led people to suspect that several perpetrators were 'involved in the masquerade'.[69] A year later the 'Black Flash' began his terrorising of Provincetown, Cape Cod, Massachusetts. Both cases alluded to a 'type' of Spring-heeled Jack figure and there is little to suggest that he was understood to be *the* Spring-heeled Jack of Victorian fame. These and the various other leaping figures of twentieth-century folklore seem to confirm that Spring-heeled Jack had evolved beyond a specific Victorian monster to become a folkloric oicotype that has migrated, been adopted and adapted around the world.[70]

By way of a coda, it should be noted that the synergistic cultural energies that formerly granted Spring-heeled Jack his dynamism may yet be reviving, causing him to return from his global wanderings. On 14th February 2012 a Spring-heeled Jack-type figure was seen near Stoneleigh, Surrey. A family travelling home by taxi at night saw a 'terrifying apparition' near the Ewell bypass. It crossed the carriageway in front of them and leapt a fifteen-foot roadside bank on the other side. The family consciously likened it to Spring-heeled Jack,

---

[67] Proctor, *Reminiscences of Old Portsmouth*, p. 27. It was as a generic bogeyman that his name was associated with hunts by hundreds of children in the Hutchesontown area of Glasgow in 1935 and 1938. See Hobbs and Cornwell, 'Hunting the Monster with Iron Teeth', pp. 127–8 and 136.

[68] For a superb study of bogeymen see Warner, *No Go the Bogeyman*.

[69] *Daily Mirror*, 6th December 1937.

[70] For more on this international existence see Dash, *Spring-heeled Jack: Sources and Interpretations*, pp. 230–317.

though indicative of his role as a cultural cipher, it was described as a 'dark figure with no features'.[71] Given that the name of Spring-heeled Jack has found recent publicity through Mark Hodder's novel and several episodes of *Luther*, the old operational dynamics of fictional depictions encouraging renewed 'real' sightings have perhaps afforded him a rejuvenated existence in the twenty-first century. Like all good monsters, Spring-heeled Jack may yet resurrect himself from his Edwardian demise as his cultural generators, old and new, begin to pulse with long-dormant energies.

[71]   See 'Terrified Banstead family confronted by "dark figure" on bypass', www.surreycomet.co.uk, 23rd February 2012.

Conclusion

Spring-heeled Jack and Victorian Popular Cultures

This study has attempted to engage with popular culture at a relatively abstract level, trying to bring a degree of joined-up thinking back to a concept that is now more frequently viewed through the fragmented lens of particular subdisciplinary interests and perspectives. It has tried to tether these somewhat amorphous conceptualisations through exploration of a specific historical artefact, the Victorian urban legend of Spring-heeled Jack. Whilst this may obviously make me guilty of the very charge I have just leveled at practices elsewhere, it is my hope that I have been able to indicate the broader reflections upon popular cultures that this intriguing character can facilitate. In this vein, this study has sought to contribute to the fascinating historiography relating to imaginary characters, beings who can cast interesting and unusual reflections upon the nature of the cultures in which they were formed and flourished.[1]

Spring-heeled Jack played a highly unusual role in the Victorian popular imagination, for he represented a 'modern' expression of a number of 'traditional' folkloric tropes and practices. It was this alloying of the 'modern' and the 'traditional' that meant he did not wholly belonged to either and was always out of step with both. He was a secularised ghost but something far different to anything that could be summoned by a spiritualist medium in a Victorian drawing room. Yet like spiritualism, Spring-heeled Jack represented a Victorian repackaging of older, ethnographical beliefs in a 'new' age. He was a mechanically aided early-modern demon running riot in a sprawling imperial city where the din of railways and steam engines, and the glow of gas and electric lighting had supposedly drowned out or banished such entities. If he was understood as a modern enchantment it was not necessarily in the sense that Michael Saler and others have suggested, that is as a disenchanted enchantment that knowingly recognises its own sense of playful or ironic pretence.[2] From his arrival in the dark winter nights of 1837–38 until long after he had migrated from British shores, speculation was rife as to his nature, being and motives. If the vocal

---

[1]   Indicative works within this area were identified in the introduction. See Bailey on Ally Sloper, Mack on Sweeney Todd, Crone on Mr Punch, and Saler on Sherlock Holmes.

[2]   See Saler, 'Clap if You Believe' and 'Modernity and Enchantment'.

dismissals of a human prankster in disguise represented the scab of modern rationality, the expected response from a secular worldview, then Spring-heeled Jack revealed that beneath it coursed the fresh blood of supernatural beliefs and a persistent yearning for mystery. One newspaper in January 1838 placed these very ideas in Spring-heeled Jack's mouth when he sang: 'There's nothing more poetical than mystery, I ween, for truth without is stale as beer that in the sun has been. 'Tis light that makes the Radicals so stale and common place, destroying night, they've spoiled the rest of all the human race.'[3]

As an imaginary, folkloric character his legend made him larger than life, and regardless of whatever naysayers tried to suggest, he thereby offered a broader cultural canvas upon which contemporaries could project their anxieties, fears and desires. In these ways Spring-heeled Jack was able to 'capture not only the mass, but the individual within the mass', this being 'the difficult double mechanism necessary for success'.[4] He spoke to fears about living in cities increasingly populated by strangers, but, at the same time, as the threatening 'other' he offered a focus through which those strangers could unite in a sense of at least temporary community. His flare and compounded allusions to various supernatural entities made him ripe for appropriation by those who sought colourful, imaginative escapism from the drab, mundane and monotonous. His stories and real accounts were means by which people could vicariously live out their fantasies of violence and rebellion, yet he also served as a marker to indicate where the bounds of acceptable social behaviours lay and what actions were beyond the pale. It was arguably this association with the forbidden that actually made Spring-heeled Jack 'all the more appealing as a temporary egress from constraint', for whilst people were taught to fear him they could also come to envy his liberated state.[5] At a deeper level, when faced with the uncertainty of modernisation Spring-heeled Jack's folkloric and supernatural elements emitted reassuring flashes of cultural familiarity. For the multitudes who did not necessarily embrace modernity but rather appeared to have had it thrust upon them, his portrayal looked back to the past, whilst his performance remained rooted in the 'modern'. Steve Pile has recognised this seemingly contradictory tension with regard to haunting, noting that it 'ought to be antithetical to modernity', but instead it appears to be located 'at the heart and soul of modernity'.[6]

Spring-heeled Jack's leaps back and forth between cultural forms via different modes of transmission were not unique even within the nineteenth century, for some degree of cultural synergy was achieved by Dick Turpin, Sweeney Todd

---

[3]   *Penny Satirist*, 27th January 1838, p. 2.

[4]   Bailey, *Popular Culture and Performance*, p. 49.

[5]   Cohen, *Monster Theory*, p. 17.

[6]   Pile, *Real Cities*, p. 136.

and Sherlock Holmes. Spring-heeled Jack, however, had powerful multicultural existences that enabled him to trump many of these imaginary rivals, at least for a time. By the nineteenth century Dick Turpin had acquired an air of romanticised anachronism, whilst Spring-heeled Jack stole much of his bold highwayman image and gave it a modern gloss and his own supernatural embellishment. Sweeney Todd could provoke fear and revulsion, but readers and theatre audiences had the comfort of knowing he was confined to his various fictional forms. Spring-heeled Jack, on the other hand, held out the nagging possibility of waiting for those very same people as they left their homes or theatres and turned out into the dark street. Even when one compares him with Sherlock Holmes, a character which had the resources of fin-de-siècle mass culture to animate him in the popular imagination, Spring-heeled Jack's cultural range appears to remain unprecedented. His ability to be reconfigured for relevance in metropolitan and provincial and urban and rural locales, and across oral and literary cultures made him highly versatile. Like many of those mentioned above, he could be associated with public, commercial entertainment and sensational literature, but none of them coexisted as folkloric bogeymen that were spoken of as real around the privacy of the domestic hearth.

In this unusual metamorphic capacity Spring-heeled Jack's reach arguably exceeded that of some of the mythic figures buried far deeper in the British imagination. Fixed in a timeless period that remained vague but remote, even Robin Hood and King Arthur could not possess his freedom and alacrity. The irony of Spring-heeled Jack is that in being different things in different cultural contexts he was ubiquitous but dispersed. His imaginary rivals proved more enduring because they moved less (culturally speaking), thereby retaining a stronger sense of coherence and identification. Spring-heeled Jack's cultural reach may have been long, but his impact was comparatively shallow. The cultural dynamism that had powered Spring-heeled Jack ultimately exhausted him, not by destroying him so much as eroding the core of what he was and perhaps what he had once meant to the popular imagination.

The legend of Spring-heeled Jack invites a number of functionalist interpretations, none of which are so singularly convincing as to encompass all his various dimensions and permutations. Spring-heeled Jack could be read as a fantasised sex attacker, a product of the developing commercialised culture machine (via press, literature and plays for example) or even a sporadic expression of popular hysteria. Whilst this study has suggested hints of all three, to select one interpretation over the others would prove too reductive. This study may not have definitely captured a sense of the totality of Spring-heeled Jack's legend, but it has at least sought to illustrate its fluid, expansive nature and application. A functionalist reading of Spring-heeled Jack's legend would necessarily require a diminution of those important and, from a historian's point of view, useful qualities. Any singular explanation as to what Spring-heeled Jack meant would necessarily neglect those aspects of the legend that do not fit into a narrowed interpretation. Spring-heeled Jack was a cultural and folkloric trope that was defined by its rich heterogeneity and was therefore bigger than any singular interpretation one may care to cage him in.

As was his elusive, prankster nature, Spring-heeled Jack transgressed bound-aries and blurred the dichotomies they sought to maintain, encouraging the hybridity that is frequently embodied within the monstrous. This study has employed an exploratory and explanatory formulation of 'nodes' and 'modes' to emphasise the fluidity and interchange between different aspects of Victorian popular cultures. This has been predicated upon a view that we need to move away from increasingly fragmenting studies of popular cultures whilst realising that we cannot return to the former homogeneity that the idea once possessed. There are undoubtedly drawbacks to any hint of an overly mechanistic model of cultural 'generators' and 'energies', the most obvious being its inherent emphasis on identified culturally generative elements that possess their own internal coherence whilst clearly being influenced by the interaction of others. Yet I would argue that cultural generators such as urban/rural localities possess suffi-cient coherence to at least be recognisable as identifiable areas of historical study and interest, not least for their influence upon popular cultural practices. These concerns are ultimately something of a distraction from the more important point that 'culture' does not exist 'in' the generators so much as being a product of their interactions. The emphasis in a model of fluid, popular cultural operation should not be on its component parts so much as the way in which it encour-ages or aids an exploration of connectivity (and disconnections in Spring-heeled Jack's case) between popular cultures.

What this study has attempted to demonstrate through one particular artefact is that multiple popular cultures, like machine parts, clearly intermeshed. Within what would have to be defined as this 'soft' machine, parts were adapted or added to incorporate the influences of other cultures (elitist or subcultures for example). In trying to rebuild a fragmented popular cultural view we can identify a field or process that had sources of power or 'generators' (locality, tradition and memory, novelty), modes of transmission (oral, visual and literary) and modes of reception (class, gender, race, age, sexuality and, again, locality). By attempting to recognise cultural heterogeneity whilst rejecting the inclination towards its ongoing disjointed analysis, this study has tended to comply with an emerging historiographical trend towards antinomial interpretations. This is perhaps the logical response to the postmodernist rejection of monolithic notions and seemingly rigid dichotomies. Instead of the 'either/or' approach that accompanied hierarchical and oppositional ideas of dominant cultures 'taming' subordinate ones, we come to engage with a more complex and interesting 'also/and' formulation, one which is sustained by its own internal tensions, even contradictions.[7]

It is not sufficient to simply recognise the existence of what Simon Dentith refers to as 'a multiple and heteroglot popular culture'.[8] Historians must look at how those popular cultures interacted, at the generative webs that were woven between them, rather than considering them as fractured, compartmentalised domains. In this relational approach to popular cultures there was no popular 'centre', no monolithic 'thing' to be dominated, crushed, restricted or whittled away. Rather Spring-heeled Jack reflects a constant dialogue and renegotiation between cultural fields, both 'popular' and 'elite', the complexity of which enabled endless interpretations, subversions and evasions that raise questions about the genuine extent of nineteenth-century, bourgeois cultural hegemony. Edward Royle has argued that efforts to reform popular culture reflected a broader, more diverse 'conflict of cultures between old and new, rural and urban, pagan and Christian, oral and written, uneducated and educated'.[9] Spring-heeled Jack's cultural existence suggests these cultures were more interwoven than opposi-tional, that one cultural domain could not be so easily separated let alone set against another. This encourages one to become more suspicious of interpreta-tions that allude to the taming or suppressing of popular culture; Spring-heeled Jack clearly emphasises the highly adaptive nature of folkloric cultures that were not being eroded by modernity so much as transforming to its dress and enter-tainments. His dynamism was frequently dependent upon synergetic and even symbiotic relationships between cultures that we have tended to view as dichot-omous: the metropolitan and provincial, urban and rural, oral and literary.

Despite modernity's emphasis on the urban and the literary, these particular cultures were not by default the dominant aspect in their respective relationships. Rural cultures were not some passive source of supernatural tales that simply filtered into the growing cities with migrants looking for work. Rural commu-nities proved themselves capable of adapting Spring-heeled Jack to their own cultural milieu, often by reconfiguring him to their pre-existing folklore, espe-cially their local ghosts. A similar dynamic is evident between literary and oral cultures. Oral accounts gave rise to Spring-heeled Jack's first newspaper reports and subsequent penny serials. These were retold through oral transmission as gossip, spreading accounts and knowledge of Spring-heeled Jack well beyond those who could read and beyond those predominantly urban areas where such literature was sold. Yet this modern example of 'supernatural' folklore was not

[7]   See Landy and Saler, *Re-enchantment of the World*, pp. 14–16. These approaches resonate with Jeffrey Jerome Cohen's claim that monsters operate as 'the harbinger of category crisis' when studying cultures. See Cohen, *Monster Theory*, pp. 6–7.

[8]   Dentith, *Society and Cultural Forms*, p. 54.

[9]   Royle, *Modern Britain*, p. 250.

sustained simply by oral accounts but literary ones too, each contributing to the vitality of Spring-heeled Jack's legend for most of the century.

Interaction between these different cultures revealed considerable mutability within Spring-heeled Jack's formulation and his propensity for adaption within differing milieus. The fluid interaction between these popular cultural processes suggests a need for hesitancy when asserting claims about shifting relationships between 'dominant' and 'subordinate' cultural expressions in the nineteenth century. This is especially the case when press reports, penny dreadfuls and local rumour encouraged people to hold seemingly contradictory ideas about whom or what Spring-heeled Jack was. Such a feat generally appears to have been achieved without apparent conflict, for whilst this trope moved freely between different cultural modes there remained a certain disconnection between the frightening Spring-heeled Jack of ethnographic reports and the heroic rogue of penny dreadful serials. Spring-heeled Jack's legend encourages us to be aware of vibrant, overlapping, intersecting popular cultures, but also that those cultures did not involve clear and simple lines of transmission. In moving between literary and oral cultures for example, the Spring-heeled Jack trope was also likely to be altered by spatial and geo-cultural determinants in cities and villages, and by the mentalities they (in)formed, as much as by the differing means by which stories and information were conveyed.

It was this perpetuation through both formal and informal cultural modes that meant Spring-heeled Jack did not easily conform to the developing nationwide culture of the Victorian period. The erratic but nevertheless identifiable south to north migration of Spring-heeled Jack sightings as the century progressed seems inexplicable in an age that saw an emerging mass communication network. In such circumstances, with regional newspapers printing accounts from across the country, with penny serials available in other cities beyond London, with ever-developing railway and telegraph links, one would have expected to find parity between accounts of Spring-heeled Jack's appearances in the north and south, east and west. Whilst the interrelationship and information exchange between metropolitan and provincial newspapers helped shape a gestalt national community, the media was not sufficiently unanimous in its own interpretations to prevent markedly different formulations of Spring-heeled Jacks being generated. The press served as an important device for fostering a shared folkloric trope, but it could not and did not determine how those tropic elements were perceived, adapted and used in different communal cultures.

Finally, the cultural functioning of Spring-heeled Jack's legend in Victorian Britain encourages us to reflect upon the rather thorny issue of what was 'popular' about popular culture in this period. It would suggest there is considerable value in John Springhall's definition of the 'popular' as 'a point of social cohesion' between classes, but one that was simultaneously 'contested, fraught with tension, struggles and negotiations'.[10] In such a formulation there was no single group that formed or defined cultural interpretations; at best there were only temporary and contested assertions by different elements within different contexts. Whilst Peter Burke has defined culture as 'a system of shared meanings, attitudes and values, and the symbolic forms in which they are expressed or embodied' the plethora of Spring-heeled Jacks in the provinces, the conflicting views of him as hero or villain, corporeal or phantasmal, implicitly challenged the shared nature of those cultural meanings.[11]

This study has suggested that the involvement of journalists, magistrates, civic officials and respectable citizens was important to the credibility of Spring-heeled Jack, but their engagement was often as a response to more plebeian claims and assertions. If this legend was an expression of plebeian culture then it was one that many of the metropolitan elite participated in during 1838, including the Mayor of the City of London. Nor can it be conveniently assumed that the consumers of his various penny serials were simply the increasingly literate working classes, for contemporary critics voiced concerns that such literature 'infected' middle-class juveniles too. Even when authorities attempted to appropriate Spring-heeled Jack as the demonised model 'other' by which moral, social and 'civilised' behaviours could be gauged, there was a necessary compromise to bourgeois hegemonic values. By attempting to appropriate Spring-heeled Jack's embodiment of former, riotous customary practices and plebeian supernatural beliefs, they were engaging with inherently subversive ideas that jarred with the rational, 'modern' age which they were attempting to promote. Journalists could make claims to interpretative ownership of the Spring-heeled Jack trope but theirs was but one amongst many, and was not guaranteed greater influence simply on account of the print medium in which it was articulated. The educated elite were deeply implicated in the operation and persistence of Spring-heeled Jack's legend, but their voice and their interpretation were not delivered from a commanding position 'over' popular culture. The 'discourses of the dominant' were not necessarily dominant.[12]

Both Spring-heeled Jack's broad cultural diffusion and interaction suggest that, in his case at least, there was no hand upon the rudder of popular culture, for his legend was neither shaped simply from 'inside' or 'outside' popular culture, nor necessarily even through struggle between the two. To stick to these terms is to linger on a top down/bottom up formulation that does not give due credit to the unpredictable movement engendered by different cultural forms and expressions. Cultural processes of appropriation, adaption, reaction and interpretation

---

[10] Springhall, *Youth, Popular Culture and Moral Panics*, p. 33.

[11] Burke, *Popular Culture in Early Modern Europe*, p. xi.

[12] Hopkin, 'Legendary Places', p. 68.

could no more be controlled by a defensive or assertive plebeian agency than by elitist impositions. Rather these were power plays that had to be enacted upon this ever-shifting sea of cultural interaction. When conceived in this way the question of whether Spring-heeled Jack was ultimately part of a culture 'of' the people or 'for' the people becomes less clearly defined and is, perhaps, even incorrectly proposed. Of course, it is recognised that Spring-heeled Jack's rich cultural transformations and interactions are, if not unique, certainly unusual. How far the popular cultural interpretations that arise from studying this legend can be applied to other cultural artefacts in this period or outside it remains unanswered.

This sense of cultural hybridity and fusion ultimately returns us to Spring-heeled Jack and notions of monstrosity. Spring-heeled Jack both traversed and manifested himself within a range of popular culture. At the same time he was dependent upon an elite input into his legend, for the voice of the respectable and the authoritative granted weight to the idea of his existence and gave him a certain gravitas that lifted him above 'mere' plebeian rumour. In conflating the boundaries that would posit an organic folkloric culture against an unauthentic, commercialised (mass) culture Spring-heeled Jack embodied the monstrous hybridity that resulted from combining the two. In his diverse forms, and in his rich potential for cultural signification, Spring-heeled Jack's monstrous hybridity ultimately serves to reflect the complex nature and contradictory tensions of popular culture itself.

Spring-heeled Jack was always characterised by his elusiveness, and this is in part a product of his cultural hybridity. The plethora of Spring-heeled Jacks in the provinces, the conflicting oral and literary views of him as hero or villain, flesh or phantom, make it hard to pin down such a mercurial being. As Cohen nicely puts it, when working with the monstrous we frequently have to accept that 'obscured glimpses' are the best we can achieve, contenting ourselves that they act as 'signifiers of monstrous passing that stand in for the monstrous body itself'.[13] It would be arrogant to assume that this study has managed to capture Spring-heeled Jack where so many others have failed, for his narrative always demands that he successfully eludes his pursuers. At best it has attempted to sift through the clues left by his passing, and through them gain some insight into the popular imagination and cultures from which he sprang.

---

[13] Cohen, *Monster Theory*, p. 6.

Bibliography

Primary Sources

Manuscripts

De Castre, William, 'Norfolk Folklore Collection', Great Yarmouth Library, L398, vol. 3

'Jack' letter, 4th October 1888, National Archive, MEPO 3/142

Yates, William Holt, 'Essay on Superstition', 1853, Wellcome Institute Library, MS.5100

Ballads

Madden Ballad Collection, Cambridge University Library

'The Devil and Little Mike', vol. 21, no. 295

'The Devil and the Lawyer', vol. 21, no. 405

'The Devil Disguises Himself for Fun', vol. 18, no. 949

'The Devil on His Ramble', vol. 21, no. 180

'The Prophecy', vol. 7, no. 562

Norfolk Heritage Centre

'Menagerie of Wild Animals', *Broadsides and Songs*, C821.04 [OS], p. 47

The Pranks of the Ghost, or, The Chapelfield Humbug', *Norwich Songs, Ballads, Etc.*, vol. 4, Colman 59B [XL], p. 80

Newspapers, Magazines and Journals

Age and Argus

All the Year Round

Belfast News Letter

Bell's Life in London

Bentley's Miscellany

Birmingham Daily Post

Blackburn Standard

Bradford Daily Telegraph

Bradford Observer

Brighton Gazette

Bristol Mercury
Bury and Norwich Post
Camberwell and Peckham Times
Cheshire Observer
Cleave's Penny Gazette of Variety
Daily Mirror
Daily News
Derby Mercury
Dundee Courier and Argus
The Era
Essex Standard
The Examiner
Figaro in London
Freeman's Journal and Daily Commercial Advertiser
Fun
Funny Folks
Glasgow Herald
Gorton and Openshaw Reporter
Greenwich, Woolwich and Deptford Gazette
Hampshire Advertiser
Hampshire Telegraph
Hull Packet and East Riding Times
The Idler
Illustrated Chips
Illustrated London News
Illustrated Police News
Ipswich Express and Essex and Suffolk Mercury
Ipswich Journal
Jackson's Oxford Journal
John Bull
Knicknacks
Lady's Newspaper
Leicester Chronicle
Leeds Mercury
Licensed Victuallers' Mirror
Liverpool Citizen
Liverpool Daily Post
Liverpool Echo
Liverpool Mercury
Lloyd's Weekly London Newspaper
Lloyd's Weekly Newspaper
London Society

Macmillan's Magazine
Manchester Times
Morning Chronicle
Morning Herald
Morning Post
Musical Opinion and Music Trade Review
Musical World
Newcastle Courant
News of the World
Nineteenth Century
Norfolk and Norwich Notes and Queries, 1ˢᵗ Series (1896–99) and 3ʳᵈ Series (1904)
North-Eastern Daily Gazette
North Wales Chronicle
Northern Echo
Northern Star
Notes and Queries, 10ᵗʰ Series (1907)
The Orchestra
Pall Mall Gazette
Penny Satirist
People's Periodical and Family Library
Preston Guardian
Punch
Quarterly Review
Reynolds's Newspaper
St James Magazine
Saint Paul's Magazine
Saturday Review
Scots Observer
Sheffield and Rotherham Independent
Sheffield Daily Telegraph
Sheffield Times
The Speaker
The Standard
The Star
Strand Magazine
The Sun
Surrey and Middlesex Standard
Temple Bar
The Times
Trewman's Exeter Flying Post
Union Jack

The Watchman
Western Mail
West Kent Guardian
York Herald
Young Folks Paper

Single Printed Texts

Ackland, Joseph, 'Elementary Education and the Decay of Literature', *Nineteenth Century*, vol. 35 (March 1894), p. 423

Anon., *The Apprehension and Examination of Spring-Heel'd Jack, who has Appeared as a Ghost, Demon, Bear, Baboon, etc* (London, 1838?)

Anon., *Authentic Particulars of the Awful Appearance of Spring-Heeled Jack* (London, 1838?)

Anon., *Spring-Heel'd Jack, the Terror of London: A Romance of the Nineteenth Century* (London, 1867)

Anon., *The Surprising Exploits of Spring-heel Jack in the Vicinity of London* (London, 1838?)

Augustus Sala, George, *Life and Adventures of George Augustus Sala* (London, 1895)

——, 'Shows', *Temple Bar*, vol. 8 (May 1863), pp. 270-9

Beckett, Arthur, 'Lewes Gunpowder Plot Celebrations', *Sussex County Magazine*, vol. 2 (1928), pp. 487-90

Boulton, Richard, *A Compleat History of Magick, Sorcery, and Witchcraft*, vol. 1 (London, 1716)

Brewer, E. Cobham, *The Reader's Handbook of Famous Names in Fiction, Allusions, References, Proverbs, Plot Stories, and Poems* (London, 1911)

Cantlie, James, *Degeneration Amongst Londoners* (London, 1885)

Fitzgerald, David, 'Robin Goodfellow and Tom Thumb', *Time* (March 1885), pp. 304–14

Forby, Robert, *Vocabulary of East Anglia*, vol. 2 (London, 1830)

Gomme, George Laurence, *Folklore as an Historical Science* (London, 1908)

Greenwood, James, *The Wilds of London* (London, 1874)

Harland, John and T. T. Wilkinson, *Lancashire Folklore* (London, 1867)

Hindley, Charles, *Life and Times of James Catnach: (Late of Seven Dials) Ballad Monger* (London, 1878)

Horne, R. H., 'The Great Fairs and Markets of Europe', *Saint Pauls Magazine*, no. 12 (February 1873), pp. 169–85

James, M. H., *Bogie Tales of East Anglia* (Ipswich, 1891)

Jessop, Augustus, 'Superstition in Arcady', *The Nineteenth Century*, vol. 12 (1882), pp. 733–55

Kay, James Phillip, *The Moral and Physical Condition of the Working Class Employed in the Cotton Manufacture in Manchester* (London, 1832)

Knights, Mark, *Norfolk Stories: The Phantom Horseman, The Lost Village and Our Bells* (Norwich, 1880)

L'Estrange, John (ed.), *The Eastern Counties Collectanea* (Norwich, 1873)

Madders, S. S., *The Orginal Sketch of How They Keep St. Valentine's Eve in Norwich* (Norwich, 1855)

Mayhew, Henry, *London Labour and the London Poor*, vols 1–3 (London, 1861)

McDaniel, Walton B., 'Some Greek, Roman and English Tityretus', *The American Journal of Philology*, vol. 35 (1914), pp. 52–66

O'Donnell, Elliott, *Animal Ghosts: Or, Animal Hauntings and the Hereafter* (London, 1913)

Ollier, Charles, 'A Few Passages on Dreams, Night-Noises and Phantoms', *Ainsworth's Magazine* vol. 5 (June 1844), pp. 504–9

Rider Haggard, H., *Rural England* (London, 1902)

Roalfe Cox, Marian, *Cinderella: Three Hundred and Forty-Five Variants* (London, 1893)

Rymer, J. M., *Varney the Vampyre; or The Feast of Blood* (London, 1846)

Scott, Walter, *Letters on Demonology and Witchcraft* (London, 1830)

Sedley, Charles, *Asmodeus; or, The Devil in London: A Sketch* (London, 1808)

Thelwell, M., 'The Power of Darkness', *The Eastern Counties Magazine*, vol. 1 (1901), pp. 291–6

Varden, John T., 'Traditions, Superstitions and Folklore, Chiefly relating to the Counties of Norfolk and Suffolk', in P. Soman (ed.), *East Anglian Handbook for 1885* (Norwich, 1885), pp. 65–132

Villiers, Elizabeth, *Stand and Deliver: The Romantic Adventures of Certain Gentlemen of the High Toby, Their Times, Their Associates, Friends and Victims* (London, 1928)

Wright, Thomas, *The Great Unwashed* (London, 1868)

Secondary Sources

Printed Texts

Ackroyd, Peter, *London: The Biography* (London, 2000)

Amin, Ash, and Nigel Thrift, *Cities: Reimagining the Urban* (Cambridge, 2002)

Anderson, Benedict, *Imagined Communities: Reflections on the Origin and Spread of Nationalism* (London, 1991)

Anderson, Patricia, *The Printed Image and the Transformation of Popular Culture 1790–1860* (Oxford, 1991)

Anglo, Michael, *Penny Dreadfuls and other Victorian Horrors* (London, 1977)

Anon., *Spring-Heel'd Jack, The Terror of London* (London, 2008 [1879])

Archer, John E., '"Men Behaving Badly"?: Masculinity and the Uses of Violence,

1850–1900', in Shani D'Cruze (ed.), *Everyday Violence in Britain, 1850–1950* (Harlow, 2000), pp. 41–54

Arias, Rosario, and Patricia Pulham (eds), *Haunting and Spectrality in Neo-Victorian Fiction* (Basingstoke, 2009)

Arnold, Catharine, *City of Sin: London and Its Vices* (London, 2011)

Ascari, Maurizio, *A Counter-History of Crime Fiction: Supernatural, Gothic, Sensational* (Basingstoke, 2009)

Ashton, John, 'Beyond Survivalism: Regional Folkloristics in Late-Victorian England', *Folklore*, vol. 108 (1997), pp. 19–23

Asma, Stephen T., *On Monsters: An Unnatural History of Our Worst Fears* (Oxford, 2009)

Augustus St John, James, *The Education of the People* (London, 1970 [1858])

Baer, Marc, *The Theatre and Disorder in Late Georgian London* (Oxford, 1992)

Bailey, Peter, 'Conspiracies of Meaning: Music-Hall and the Knowingness of Popular Culture', *Past and Present*, no. 144 (1994), pp. 138–70

——, *Leisure and Class in Victorian England: Rational Recreation and the Contest for Control, 1830-1885* (London, 1978)

——, *Popular Culture and Performance in the Victorian City* (Cambridge, 1998)

Bakhtin, Mikhail, *Rabelais and His World*, trans. H. Iswolsky (Bloomington, Ind., 1984)

Bamford, Samuel, *The Autobiography of Samuel Bamford, vol. 1, Early Days* (London, 1967)

Barthes, Roland, 'Semiology and the Urban', in N. Leach (ed.), *Rethinking Architecture: A Reader in Cultural Theory* (London, 1997), pp. 166–72

Bartholomew, Robert E., and Hilary Evans, *Panic Attacks: Media Manipulation and Mass Delusion* (Stroud, 2004)

Beaven, Brad, *Leisure, Citizenship and Working-Class Men in Britain, 1850–1945* (Manchester, 2009)

Bedarida, Francois, *A Social History of England 1851–1990*, trans. A. S. Forster (London, 1991)

Bell, Karl '"The Humbugg of the World at an End": The Apocalyptic Imagination and the Uses of Collective Fantasy in Norfolk in 1844', *Social History*, vol. 31 (2006), pp. 454–68

——, *The Magical Imagination: Magic and Modernity in Urban England, 1780–1914* (Cambridge, 2012)

Bennett, Gillian, 'Folklore Studies and the English Rural Myth', *Rural History*, vol. 4 (1993), pp. 77–91

——, 'Geologists and Folklorists: Cultural Evolution and "The Science of Folklore"', *Folklore*, vol. 105 (1994), pp. 25–37

Biersack, Aletta, 'Local Knowledge, Local History: Geertz and Beyond', in Lynn Hunt (ed.), *New Cultural History* (Berkeley, Cal., 1989), pp. 72–96

Billig, Michael, *Laughter and Ridicule: Towards a Social Critique of Humour* (London, 2005)

Blackmore, Susan, *The Meme Machine* (Oxford, 1999)

Bloom, Clive, *Violent London: 2000 Years of Riots, Rebels and Revolts* (Basingstoke, 2010)

Boase, Wendy, *Folklore of Hampshire and the Isle of Wight* (London, 1976)

Bondeson, Jan, *The London Monster: Terror on the Streets in 1790* (Stroud, 2003)

Bonnell, Victoria E., and Lynn Hunt (eds), *Beyond the Cultural Turn* (Berkeley, Cal., 1999)

Booth, Michael, *English Melodrama* (London, 1965)

Bord, Janet, *Footprints in Stone* (Loughborough, 2004)

Botting, Fred, *Gothic* (London, 1996)

Bourdieu, Pierre, *The Field of Cultural Production* (Cambridge, 1993)

Bown, Nicola, *Fairies in Nineteenth-Century Art and Literature* (Cambridge, 2001)

——, Carolyn Burdett and Pamela Thurschwell (eds), *The Victorian Supernatural* (Cambridge, 2004)

Boyes, Georgina, 'Cultural Survival Theory and Traditional Customs', *Folk Life*, vol. 26 (1987–88), pp. 5–9

Boyle, Thomas, *Black Swine in the Sewers of Hampstead* (London, 1990)

Brake, Laurel, Bill Bell and David Finkelstein (eds), *Nineteenth-Century Media and the Construction of Identities* (Basingstoke, 2000)

Brantlinger, Patrick, *The Reading Lesson: The Threat of Mass Literacy in Nineteenth-Century British Fiction* (Bloomington, Ind., 1998)

Bratton, J. S., 'Of England, Home, and Duty: The Image of England in Victorian and Edwardian Juvenile Fiction', in John M. Mackenzie (ed.), *Imperialism and Popular Culture* (Manchester, 1987), pp. 73–93

Brewer, John, *The Pleasures of the Imagination: English Culture in the Eighteenth Century* (London, 1997)

Brooks, Peter, *The Melodramatic Imagination: Balzac, Henry James, Melodrama and the Mode of Excess* (New Haven, Conn., 1976)

Brown, Callum, *Up-helly-aa: Custom, Culture and Community in Shetland* (Manchester, 1999)

Brunvand, Jan Harold, *Too Good to be True: The Colossal Book of Urban Legends* (New York, 1999)

Burke, Peter, 'History and Folklore: A Historiographical Survey', *Folklore*, vol. 115 (2004), pp. 133–7

——, *Popular Culture in Early Modern Europe*, rev. edn (Aldershot, 1994)

——, *What is Cultural History?* (Cambridge, 2004)

Burton Russell, Jeffrey, *Mephistopheles: The Devil in the Modern World* (Ithaca, NY, 1986)

Bushaway, Bob, *By Rite: Custom, Ceremony and Community in England* (London, 1982)

——, '"Tacit, Unsuspected, but still Implicit Faith": Alternative Belief in Nineteenth-Century Rural England', in Tim Harris (ed.), *Popular Culture in England, c.1500–1850* (Basingstoke, 1995), pp. 189–215

——, 'Things said or sung a thousand times": Customary Society and Oral Culture in Rural England, 1700–1900', in Adam Fox and Daniel Woolf (eds), *The Spoken Word: Oral Culture in Britain 1500–1850* (Manchester, 2002), pp. 256–77

Butterworth, Alex, *The World That Never Was: A True Story of Dreamers, Schemers, Anarchists and Secret Agents* (London, 2010)

Cadbury, Deborah, *The Dinosaur Hunters: A True Story of Scientific Rivalry and the Discovery of the Prehistoric World* (London, 2001)

Cahill, Robert Ellis, *New England's Mad and Mysterious Men* (Peabody, Mass., 1984)

Cannadine, David, *Class in Britain* (London, 2000)

Carroll, Noel, *The Philosophy of Horror* (London, 1990)

Carter Wood, J. *Violence and Crime in Nineteenth-Century England: The Shadow of Our Refinement* (London, 2004)

Castle, Terry, *Masquerade and Civilization: The Carnivalesque in Eighteenth-Century Culture and Fiction* (Stanford, Cal., 1986)

Cavallaro, Dani, *The Gothic Vision: Three Centuries of Horror, Terror and Fear* (London, 2002)

Chartier, Roger, *Cultural History: Between Practices and Representations*, trans. L. G. Cochrane (Cambridge, 1993)

——, 'Culture as Appropriation: Popular Cultural Uses in Early Modern France', in Steven Kaplan (ed.), *Understanding Popular Culture: Europe from the Middle Ages to the Nineteenth Century* (Berlin, 1984), pp. 229–53

Church, Roy, 'Advertising Consumer Goods in Nineteenth-Century Britain: Reinterpretations', *Economic History Review*, vol. 53 (2000), pp. 621–45

Clare, John, *The Shepherd's Calendar* (Oxford, 1991 [1827])

Clark, Anna, 'The Politics of Seduction in English Popular Culture, 1748–1848', in Jean Radford (ed.), *The Progress of Romance: The Politics of Popular Fiction* (London, 1986), pp. 47–72

——, *Women's Silence, Men's Violence: Sexual Assault in England 1770–1845* (London, 1987)

Clarke, David, 'Bogeyman or Spaceman? The Legend of Spring-heeled Jack', *Paranormal Magazine*, no. 45 (March 2010), pp. 20–5

——, 'Unmasking Spring-heeled Jack: A Case Study of a 19th-Century Ghost Panic', *Contemporary Legend*, no. 9 (2006), pp. 28–52

Clayton, Antony, *The Folklore of London* (London, 2008)

Clery, E. J., 'The Pleasure of Terror: Paradox in Edmund Burke's Theory of the

Sublime', in Roy Porter and Mulvey Roberts (eds), *Pleasure in the Eighteenth Century* (Basingstoke, 1996), pp. 164–81

——, *The Rise of Supernatural Fiction 1762–1800* (Cambridge, 1995)

Cockburn, James, 'Patterns of Violence in English Society: Homicide in Kent 1560–1985', *Past and Present*, no. 130 (1991), pp. 70–106

Cohen, Jeffrey Jerome (ed.), *Monster Theory: Reading Culture* (Minneapolis, Minn., 1996)

Cohen, Stanley, *Folk Devils and Moral Panics: The Creation of the Mods and Rockers* (London, 2002)

Connell, Philip, and Nigel Leask (eds), *Romanticism and Popular Culture in Britain and Ireland* (Cambridge, 2009)

Cook, James W., *Arts of Deception: Playing with Fraud in the Age of Barnum* (Cambridge, Mass., 2001)

Crehan, Kate, *Gramsci, Culture and Anthropology* (London, 2002)

Crone, Rosalind, 'From Sawney Beane to Sweeney Todd: Murder Machines in the Mid-Nineteenth Century Metropolis', *Cultural and Social History*, vol. 7 (2010), pp. 59–85

——, 'Mr and Mrs Punch in Nineteenth-Century England', *Historical Journal*, vol. 49 (2006), pp. 1055–82

——, *Violent Victorians: Popular Entertainment in Nineteenth-Century London* (Manchester, 2012)

Cunningham, Hugh, *Leisure in the Industrial Revolution, c.1780–1880* (London, 1980)

Darnton, Robert, *The Great Cat Massacre and Other Episodes in French Cultural History* (New York, 1985)

Dash, Mike, 'Spring-heeled Jack: To Victorian Bugaboo from Suburban Ghost', *Fortean Studies*, vol. 3 (London, 1996), pp. 7–125

—— (ed.), *Spring-heeled Jack: Sources and Intepretations* (forthcoming)

Davidoff, Leonore, *Worlds Between: Historical Perspectives on Gender and Class* (Cambridge, 1995)

——, and Catherine Hall, *Family Fortunes: Men and Women of the English Middle Class 1780–1850* (London, 1987)

Davies, Owen, *The Haunted: A Social History of Ghosts* (Basingstoke, 2007)

——, 'Urbanization and the Decline of Witchcraft: An Examination of London', *Journal of Social History*, vol. 30 (1997), pp. 597–617

——, *Witchcraft, Magic and Culture 1736–1951* (Manchester, 1999)

D'Cruze, Shani (ed.), *Crimes of Outrage: Sex, Violence and Victorian Working Women* (London, 1998)

——, *Everyday Violence in Britain, 1850–1950* (Harlow, 2000)

De Certeau, Michael, *The Practice of Everyday Life* (Berkeley, Cal., 1988)

Dennis, Richard, *Cities in Modernity: Representations and Productions of Metropolitan Space, 1840–1930* (Cambridge, 2008)

Dentith, Simon, *Society and Cultural Forms in Nineteenth-Century England* (Basingstoke, 1998)

Derrida, Jacques, *Spectres of Marx: The State of the Debt, the Work of Mourning, and the New International*, trans. Peggy Kamuf (London, 1994)

Diamond, Michael, *Victorian Sensation: Or, the Spectacular, the Shocking and the Scandalous in Nineteenth-Century Britain* (London, 2003)

Disher, Maurice Willson, *Blood and Thunder: Mid-Victorian Melodrama and its Origin* (London, 1949)

Donald, James, *Imagining the Modern City* (New York, 2005)

——, 'Metropolis: The City as Text', in R. Bocock and K. Thompson (eds), *Social and Cultural Forms of Modernity* (Cambridge, 1992), pp. 417–61

Dorson, Richard, *The British Folklorists: A History* (London, 1968)

Dundes, Alan, *International Folkloristics: Classic Contributions by the Founders of Folklore* (Oxford, 1999)

Durbach, Nadja, *The Spectacle of Deformity: Freak Shows and Modern British Culture* (Berkeley, Cal., 2009)

During, Simon, *Modern Enchantments: The Cultural Power of Secular Magic* (Cambridge, Mass., 2002)

Dyall, Valentine, 'Spring-heeled Jack – the Leaping Terror', *Everybody's Magazine*, 20th February 1954, pp. 12–13

Easton, Susan, *Disorder and Discipline: Popular Culture from 1550 to the Present* (Aldershot, 1988)

Ebbatson, Roger, *An Imaginary England: Nation, Landscape and Literature 1840–1920* (Aldershot, 2005)

Ekirch, A. R., *At Day's Close: A History of Nighttime* (London, 2006)

Ellis, Joyce M., *The Georgian Town, 1680–1840* (Basingstoke, 2001)

Emsley, Clive, *Crime and Society in England 1750–1900* (Harlow, 2005)

——, *Hard Men: The English and Violence since 1750* (London, 2005)

——, and L. A. Knafla (eds), *Crime History and Histories of Crime: Studies in the Historiography of Crime and Criminal Justice in Modern Society* (Westport, Conn., 1996)

Engels, Friedrich, *The Condition of the Working Class in England* (London, 1987)

Engle Merry, Sally, 'Urban Danger: Life in a Neighborhood of Strangers', in George Gmelch and Walter P. Zenner (eds), *Urban Life: Readings in Urban Anthropology*, 2nd edn (Prospect Heights, Ill., 1988), pp. 63–72

Epstein Nord, Deborah, 'The City as Theatre: From Georgian to Early Victorian London', *Victorian Studies*, vol. 31 (1987–88), pp. 159–88

Estabrook, Carl B., *Urbane and Rustic England: Cultural Ties and Social Spheres in the Provinces, 1660–1750* (Manchester, 1998)

Evans, George Ewart, *The Pattern Under the Plough* (London, 1971)

Evans, Stewart P., and Keith Skinner, *Jack the Ripper: Letters from Hell* (Stroud, 2004)

Ferguson, Priscilla, 'The Flâneur On and Off the Streets of Paris', in Keith Tester (ed.), *The Flâneur* (London, 1994), pp. 22–42

Fields, Kenneth, *Lancashire Magic and Mystery* (Wilmslow, 1998)

Finucane, R. C., *Ghosts: Appearances of the Dead and Cultural Transformations* (Amherst, NY, 1996)

Fiske, John, *Understanding Popular Culture* (London, 1989)

Flint, Kate, *The Victorians and the Visual Imagination* (Cambridge, 2008)

Foucault, Michel, *Discipline and Punish: The Birth of the Prison*, trans. Alan Sheridan (London, 1991)

——, *Madness and Civilization*, trans. Richard Howard (London, 2001)

Fox, Adam, and Daniel Woolf (eds), *The Spoken Word: Oral Culture in Britain 1500–1850* (Manchester, 2002)

——, *Vampyres, Lord Byron to Count Dracula* (London, 1992)

Frayling, Christopher, 'The House that Jack Built', in Alexandra Warwick and Martin Willis (eds), *Jack the Ripper: Media, Culture, History* (Manchester, 2007), pp. 13–28

Freeman, Nicholas, *Conceiving the City: London, Literature, and Art 1870–1914* (Oxford, 2007)

Freud, Sigmund, *The Uncanny*, trans. David McLintock (London, 2003)

Frisby, David, *Cityscapes of Modernity* (Cambridge, 2001)

Fulford, Timothy (ed.), *Romanticism and Millenarianism* (London, 2002)

Gailey, Alan, 'The Nature of Tradition', *Folklore*, vol. 100 (1989), pp. 143–61

Garland Thomson, Rosemarie, (ed.), *Freakery: Cultural Spectacle of the Extraordinary Body* (New York, 1996)

Garrett, Peter K., *Gothic Reflections: Narrative Force in Nineteenth-Century Fiction* (Ithaca, NY, 2003)

Gaskill, Malcolm, 'Reporting Murder: Fiction in the Archives in Early Modern England', *Social History*, vol. 23 (1998), pp. 1–30

——, 'Witches and Witnesses in Old and New England', in Stuart Clark (ed.), *Language of Witchcraft: Narrative, Ideology and Meaning in Early Modern Culture* (Basingstoke, 2001), pp. 55–80

Gatrell, V. A. C., *The Hanging Tree: Execution and the English People, 1770–1868* (Oxford, 1996)

Geertz, Clifford, *The Interpretation of Cultures: Selected Essays* (New York, 1973)

Gelder, Ken (ed.), *The Horror Reader* (London, 2000)

Gencarella, Stephen Olbrys, 'Constituting Folklore: A Case for Critical Folklore Studies', *Journal of American Folklore*, vol. 122 (2009), pp. 172–96

Glover, David, *Vampires, Mummies and Liberals: Bram Stoker and the Politics of Popular Fiction* (Durham, NC, 1996)

Golby, J. M., and A. W. Purdue, *The Civilisation of the Crowd: Popular Culture in England 1750–1900*, rev. edn (Stroud, 1999)

Golicz, Roman, *Spring-heeled Jack: A Victorian Visitation at Aldershot* (Farnham, 2006)

Goode, Erich, and Nachman Ben-Yehuda, *Moral Panics: The Social Construction of Deviance* (Chichester, 2009)

Goodlad, Lauren M. E., 'Beyond the Panopticon: Victorian Britain and the Critical Imagination', *PMLA*, vol. 118 (2003), pp. 539–56

Goodman, Jordan, 'History and Anthropology', in M. Bentley (ed.), *Companion to Historiography* (London, 1997), pp. 783–804

Gordon, Avery F., *Ghostly Matters: Haunting and the Sociological Imagination* (Minneapolis, Minn., 2008)

Greenwood, James, *The Seven Curses of London* (Oxford, 1981 [1869])

Griffin, Carl J.,'Affecting Violence: Language, Gesture and Performance in Early Nineteenth-Century English Popular Protest', *Historical Geography*, vol. 36 (2008), pp. 139–62

——, 'Swing, Swing Redivivus or Something After Swing? On the Death Throes of a Protest Movement, December 1830-December 1833', *International Review of Social History*, vol. 54 (2009), pp. 459–97

Griffin, Emma, *England's Revelry: A History of Popular Sport and Pastimes, 1660–1830* (Oxford, 2005)

——, 'Popular Culture in Industrialising England: A Historiographical Review', *The Historical Journal*, vol. 45 (2002), pp. 619–35

Gunn, Simon, *History and Cultural Theory* (Harlow, 2006)

Gunnell, Terry,'Legends and Landscape in the Nordic Countries', *Cultural and Social History*, vol. 6 (2009), pp. 305–22

—— (ed.), *Legends and Landscape* (Reykjavik, 2008)

Guthrie, Neil, '"No Truth or Very Little in the Whole Story?" A Reassessment of the Mohock Scare of 1712', *Eighteenth-Century Life*, vol. 20 (1996), pp. 33–56

Hadley, Louisa, *Neo-Victorian Fiction and Historical Narrative: The Victorians and Us* (Basingstoke, 2010)

Haining, Peter, *The Legend and Bizarre Crimes of Spring Heeled Jack*, (London, 1977)

Halberstam, Judith, *Skin Shows: Gothic Horror and the Technology of Monsters* (Durham, NC, 1995)

Hall, David, *Cultures of Print: Essays in the History of the Book* (Amherst, Mass., 1996)

Halliday, Stephen, *Making the Metropolis: Creators of Victoria's London* (Derby, 2003)

Handley, Sasha, *Visions of an Unseen World: Ghostly Beliefs and Ghost Stories in Eighteenth-Century England* (London, 2007)

Hapgood, Lynne, *Margins of Desire: The Suburbs in Fiction and Culture 1880–1925* (Manchester, 2005)

Harris, Jason Marc, *Folklore and the Fantastic in Nineteenth-Century British Fiction* (Aldershot, 2008)

Harris, Tim (ed.), *Popular Culture in England, c.1500–1850* (Basingstoke, 1995)

Harrison, J. F. C., *Early Victorian Britain,* (London, 1988)

——, *The Second Coming: Popular Millenarianism, 1780-1850* (London, 1979)

Hayden, Dolores, *Building Suburbia: Green Fields and Urban Growth, 1820–2000* (New York, 2003)

Heilmann, Ann, and Mark Llewellyn, *Neo-Victorians: The Victorians in the Twenty-First Century, 1999–2009* (Basingstoke, 2010)

Hernstein Smith, Barbara, 'Narrative Versions, Narrative Theories', in Martin Mcquillan (ed.), *The Narrative Reader* (London, 2000), pp. 138–44

Highmore, Ben, *Cityscapes: Cultural Readings in the Material and Symbolic City* (Basingstoke, 2005)

Hilton, Boyd, *A Mad, Bad, and Dangerous People? England 1783–1846* (Oxford, 2008)

Hindley, Charles, *Curiosities of Street Literature* (Welwyn Garden City, 1969)

Hobbs, Sandy, and David Cornwell, 'Hunting the Monster with Iron Teeth', in Gillian Bennett and Paul Smith (eds), *Monsters with Iron Teeth: Perspectives on Contemporary Legend*, vol. 3 (Sheffield, 1988), pp. 115–37

Hodder, Mark, *The Strange Affair of Spring-Heeled Jack* (London, 2010)

Hoggart, Richard, *The Uses of Literacy* (London, 1960)

Hollen Lees, Lynn, *Exiles of Erin: Irish Migrants in Victorian London* (Manchester, 1979)

Hollingsworth, Keith, *The Newgate Novel 1830–1847: Bulwer, Ainsworth, Dickens, and Thackeray* (Detroit, Mich., 1963)

Holt, Richard, *Sport and the British: A Modern History* (Oxford, 1990)

Hopkin, David, 'Legendary Places: Oral History and Folk Geography in Nineteenth-Century Brittany', in Frances Fowle and Richard Thomson (eds), *Soil and Stone: Impressionism, Urbanism, Environment* (Aldershot, 2003), pp. 65–84

——, 'Storytelling, Fairytales and Autobiography: Some Observations on Eighteenth- and Nineteenth-Century French Soldiers' and Sailors' Memoirs', *Social History*, vol. 29 (2004), pp. 186–98

Hoyle, Susan, 'The Witch and the Detective: Mid-Victorian Stories and Beliefs', in Willem de Blecourt and Owen Davies (eds), *Witchcraft Continued: Popular Magic in Modern Europe* (Manchester, 2004), pp. 46–68

Huet, Marie-Helene, *Monstrous Imagination* (Cambridge, Mass., 1993)

Huggins, Mike, *The Victorians and Sport* (London, 2007)

Hunt, Lynn (ed.), *New Cultural History* (Berkeley, Cal., 1989)

Hurley, Kelly, *The Gothic Body: Sexuality, Materialism, and Degeneration at the Fin de Siècle* (Cambridge, 1996)

Hutton, Ronald, 'The English Reformation and the Evidence of Folklore', *Past and Present*, vol. 148 (1995), pp. 89–116

——, *The Rise and Fall of Merry England: The Ritual Year 1400–1700* (Oxford, 1996)

Inwood, Stephen, 'Policing London's Morals: The Metropolitan Police and Popular Culture, 1829–50', *London Journal*, vol. 15 (1990), pp. 129–46

Jensen, Richard, 'Daggers, Rifles and Dynamite: Anarchist Terrorism in Nineteenth-Century Europe', *Terror and Political Violence*, vol. 16 (2004), pp. 116–53

John, Juliet, *Dickens's Villains: Melodrama, Character, Popular Culture* (Oxford, 2003)

—— (ed.), *Cult Criminals: The Newgate Novels 1830–47* (London, 1998)

Jones, Aled, *Powers of the Press: Newspapers, Power and the Public in Nineteenth-Century England* (Aldershot, 1996)

Jones, Joanne, '"She Resisted with all her Might": Sexual Violence Against Women in Late Nineteenth-Century Manchester and the Local Press', in Shani D'Cruze (ed.), *Everyday Violence in Britain, 1850-1950* (Harlow, 2000), pp. 104–18

Jones, Peter, 'Finding Captain Swing: Protest, Parish Relations, and the State of the Public Mind in 1830', *International Review of Social History*, vol. 54 (2009), pp. 429–58

Joyce, Patrick, *Visions of the People: Industrial England and the Question of Class, 1848–1914* (Cambridge, 1993)

Joyce, Simon, *Capital Offenses: Geographies of Class and Crime in Victorian London* (Charlottesville, Va., 2003)

Jung, Carl G., *Four Archetypes* (London, 1998)

Kellett, J. R., 'The Railway as an Agent of Internal Change in Victorian cities', in R. J. Morris and Richard Rodger (eds), *The Victorian City: A Reader in British Urban History 1820–1914* (London, 1993), pp. 181–208

Kelly, Jason M., 'Riots, Revelries, and Rumor: Libertinism and Masculine Association in Enlightenment London', *The Journal of British Studies*, vol. 45 (2006), pp. 759–95

King, Peter, *Crime, Justice and Discretion in England, 1740–1820* (Oxford, 2003)

Koven, Seth, *Slumming: Sexual and Social Politics in Victorian London* (Princeton, N J, 2004)

Kramnick, Jonathan Brody, 'Rochester and the History of Sexuality', *ELH*, vol. 69 (2002), pp. 277–301

Laba, Martin, 'Urban Folklore: A Behavioral Approach', *Western Folklore*, vol. 38 (1979), pp. 158–63

Lamb, Charles, 'Witches and other Night-Fears', in R. Vallance and J. Hampden (eds), *Charles Lamb: Essays* (London, 1963), pp. 90–6

Lamont, Peter, 'Spiritualism and a mid-Victorian Crisis of Evidence', *The Historical Journal*, vol. 47 (2004), pp. 897–920

Landau, Norma, *Law, Crime and English Society, 1660–1830* (Cambridge, 2002)

Landy, Joshua, and Michael Saler (eds), *The Re-enchantment of the World: Secular Magic in a Rational Age* (Stanford, Cal., 2009)

Langford, Paul, *Englishness Identified: Manners and Character, 1650–1850* (Oxford, 2000)

Leach, Robert, *The Punch and Judy Show: History, Tradition and Meaning* (Athens, Ga., 1985)

Ledger, Sally, *Dickens and the Popular Radical Imagination* (Cambridge, 2007)

——, and Roger Luckhurst (eds), *The Fin de Siècle: A Reader in Cultural History, c. 1880–1900* (Oxford, 2000)

Lee, Robert, *Unquiet Country: Voices of the Rural Poor, 1820–1880* (Bollington, 2005)

Lees, Sue, *Carnal Knowledge: Rape on Trial* (London, 1997)

Lefebvre, Henri, *Production of Space* (Oxford, 1991)

Levin, D. M. (ed.), *Modernity and the Hegemony of Vision* (Berkeley, Cal., 1993)

Linebaugh, Peter, *The London Hanged: Crime and Civil Society in the Eighteenth Century* (London, 1991)

Linnane, Fergus, *The Lives of the English Rakes* (London, 2006)

Lovett, William, *Life and Struggles of William Lovett*, preface by R. H. Tawney (London, 1967)

Luckin, Bill, 'Revisiting the Idea of Degeneration in Urban Britain, 1830–1900', *Urban History*, vol. 33 (2006), pp. 234–52

Ludlam, Harry, *A Biography of Dracula: The Life Story of Bram Stoker* (London, 1962)

Lunger Knoppers, Laura, and Joan B. Landes (eds), *Monstrous Bodies/Political Monstrosities in Early Modern Europe* (Ithaca, NY, 2004)

Mack, Robert L., *The Wonderful and Surprising History of Sweeney Todd: The Life and Times of an Urban Legend* (London, 2007)

Mackay, Charles, *Extraordinary Popular Delusions and the Madness of Crowds* (Ware, 1995)

Mackie, Erin, *Rakes, Highwaymen, and Pirates: The Making of the Modern Gentleman in the Eighteenth Century* (Baltimore, Md., 2009)

MacRaild, Donald M., and David E. Martin, *Labour in British Society, 1830–1914* (Basingstoke, 2000)

Malcolmson, Robert W., *Popular Recreations in English Society, 1700–1850* (Cambridge, 1973)

Mallon, F. E., 'The Promise and Dilemma of Subaltern Studies: Perspectives from Latin American History', *American Historical Review*, vol. 99 (1994), pp. 1491–515

Marriott, John, 'The Spatiality of the Poor in Eighteenth-Century London', in Tim Hitchcock and Heather Shore (eds), *The Streets of London: From the Great Fire to the Great Stink* (London, 2003), pp. 119–34

Mason, Michael, *The Making of Victorian Sexuality* (Oxford, 1994)

Maunder, Andrew, and Grace Moore (eds), *Victorian Crime, Madness and Sensation* (Aldershot, 2004)

McAleer, Joseph, *Popular Reading and Publishing in Britain, 1914–1950* (Oxford, 1992)

McCorristine, Shane, *Spectres of the Self: Thinking about Ghosts and Ghost-Seeing in England, 1750–1920* (Cambridge, 2010)

McCreery, Cindy, 'A Moral Panic in Eighteenth-Century London? The "Monster" and the Press', in David Lemmings and Claire Walker (eds), *Moral Panics, the Media and the Law in Early Modern England* (Basingstoke, 2009), pp. 195–220

McKellar, Elizabeth, 'Peripheral Visions: Alternative Aspects and Rural Presences in Mid-Eighteenth-Century London', in Dana Arnold (ed.), *The Metropolis and Its Image: Constructing Identities for London, c.1750–1950* (Oxford, 1999), pp. 29–47

McLaughlin, Joseph, *Writing the Urban Jungle: Reading Empire in London from Doyle to Eliot* (Charlottesville, Va., 2000)

McWilliam, Rohan, *The Tichborne Claimant: A Victorian Sensation* (London, 2007)

Melechi, Antonio, *Servants of the Supernatural: The Night Side of the Victorian Mind* (London, 2008)

Melville Logan, Peter, 'The Popularity of Popular Delusions: Charles Mackay and Victorian Popular Culture', *Cultural Critique*, vol. 54 (2003), pp. 213–41

Miele, C., 'From Aristocratic Ideal to Middle-Class Idyll: 1690–1840', in Andrew Saint (ed.), *London Suburbs* (London, 1999), pp. 31–59

Mighall, Robert, *A Geography of Victorian Gothic Fiction: Mapping History's Nightmares* (Oxford, 2003)

Mitchell, Kate, *History and Cultural Memory in Neo-Victorian Fiction: Victorian Afterimages* (Basingstoke, 2010)

Moltke, Johannes von, 'Heimat and History: "Viehjud Levi"', *New German Critique*, no. 87 (2002), pp. 83–105

Moore, Lucy, *Con Men and Cutpurses: Scenes from the Hogarthian Underworld* (London, 2000)

Morgan, Marjorie, *Manners, Morals and Class in England, 1774–1858* (Manchester, 1994)

Muchembled, Robert, *A History of the Devil From the Middle Ages to the Present* (Cambridge, 2003)

Mullan, John, and Christopher Reid, *Eighteenth-Century Popular Culture: A Selection* (Oxford, 2000)

Murray, Venetia, *High Society in the Regency Period: 1788–1830* (London, 1999)

Naremore, James, and Patrick Brantlinger (eds), *Modernity and Mass Culture* (Bloomington, Ind., 1991)

Nashe, Thomas, *The Unfortunate Traveller and Other Works* (Harmondsworth, 1972)

Nava, Mica, 'Modernity's Disavowal: Women, the City and the Department Store', in Mica Nava and Alan O'Shea (eds), *Modern Times: Reflections on a Century of English Modernity* (London, 1996), pp. 38–76

Navickas, Katrina, 'Moors, Fields, and Popular Protest in South Lancashire and the West Riding of Yorkshire, 1800-1848', *Northern History*, vol. 46 (2009), pp. 93–111

——, 'The Search for "General Ludd": The Mythology of Luddism', *Social History*, vol. 30 (2005), pp. 281–95

Nead, Lynda, *Victorian Babylon: People, Streets and Images in Nineteenth-Century London* (New Haven, Conn., 2000)

Newburn, Tim, and Elizabeth A. Stanko (eds), *Just Boys Doing Business: Men, Masculinities and Crime* (London, 1995)

North, Dan, 'Illusory Bodies: Magical Performance on Stage and Screen', *Early Popular Visual Culture*, vol. 5 (2007), pp. 175–88

O'Donnell, Elliott, *Ghosts of London* (London, 1932)

——, *Haunted Britain* (London, 1948)

Oldridge, Darren, 'Casting the Spell of Terror: The Press and the Early Whitechapel Murders', in Alexandra Warwick and Martin Willis (eds), *Jack the Ripper: Media, Culture, History* (Manchester, 2007), pp. 46–56

Park, Robert E., 'The City: Suggestions for the Investigation of Human Behaviour in the Urban Environment', in R. E. Park, Ernest W. Burgess and R. D. McKenzie (eds), *The City* (Chicago, Ill., 1967), pp. 1–46

Parsons, Deborah L., *Streetwalking the Metropolis: Women, the City and Modernity* (Oxford, 2000)

Peakman, Julie, *Lascivious Bodies: A Sexual History of the Eighteenth Century* (London, 2005)

Pearsall, Ronald, *The Table-Rappers: The Victorians and the Occult* (Stroud, 2004)

Perry Curtis, Jr, L., *Jack the Ripper and the London Press* (New Haven, Conn., 2001)

Pettitt, Thomas, '"Here Comes I, Jack Straw:" English Folk Drama and Social Revolt', *Folklore*, vol. 95 (1984), pp. 3–20

Philips, David, and Robert D. Storch, *Policing Provincial England, 1829–1856: The Politics of Reform* (Leicester, 1999)

Pick, Daniel, 'Stories of the Eye', in Roy Porter (ed.), *Rewriting the Self: Histories from the Renaissance to the Present* (London, 1997), pp. 186–200

Pilar Blanco, Maria del, and Esther Peeren (eds), *Popular Ghosts: The Haunted Space of Everyday Culture* (New York, 2010)

Pile, Steve, *Real Cities: Modernity, Space and the Phantasmagoria of City Life* (London, 2005)

——, and Michael Keith (eds), *Geographies of Resistance* (London, 1997)

Plotz, John, *The Crowd: British Literature and Public Politics* (Berkeley, Cal., 2000)

Polletta, Francesca, *It Was Like a Fever: Storytelling in Protest and Politics* (Chicago, Ill., 2006)

Poole, Robert, *Popular Leisure and the Music Hall in Nineteenth-Century Bolton* (Lancaster, 1982)

Pooley, Colin, and Jean Turnbull, *Migration and Mobility in Britain since the Eighteenth Century* (London, 1995)

Proctor, F. J., *Reminiscences of Old Portsmouth* (Portsmouth, 1931)

Propp, Vladimir, *Theory and History of Folklore* (Minneapolis, Minn., 1984)

Pullman, Philip, *Spring-Heeled Jack, A Story of Bravery and Evil* (London, 1989)

Punter, David, *The Literature of Terror*, vols 1-2 (Harlow, 1996)

——, and Glennis Byron, *The Gothic* (Oxford, 2004)

Rauch, Alan, *Useful Knowledge: The Victorians, Morality and the March of Intellect* (Durham, NC, 2001)

Reay, Barry, *The Last Rising of the Agricultural Labourers: Rural Life and Protest in Nineteenth-Century England* (London, 2010)

——, *Popular Cultures in England, 1550-1750* (Harlow, 1998)

——, *Rural England: Labouring Lives in the Nineteenth Century* (Basingstoke, 2004)

Robbins, Ruth, and Julian Wolfreys (eds), *Victorian Gothic: Literary and Cultural Manifestations in the Nineteenth Century* (Basingstoke, 2000)

Robinson, Alan, *Imagining London, 1770–1900* (Basingstoke, 2004)

Robinson, Sheila, 'Jack Valentine', *FLS News*, no. 45 (February 2005), p. 8

Rogers, Nicholas, *Crowds, Culture, and Politics in Georgian Britain* (Oxford, 1998)

Roper, Lyndal, *Oedipus and the Devil: Witchcraft, Sexuality and Religion, 1500–1700* (London, 1994)

Rose, Jonathan, *The Intellectual Life of the British Working Classes* (New Haven, Conn., 2010)

Roud, Steve, *London Lore: The Legends and Traditions of the World's Most Vibrant City* (London, 2010)

Royle, Edward, *Modern Britain: A Social History 1750–1997*, 2nd edn (London, 2002)

——, *Revolutionary Britannia? Reflections on the Threat of Revolution in Britain, 1789–1848* (Manchester, 2000)

Royle, Nicholas, *The Uncanny* (Manchester, 2003)

Rubery, Matthew, 'Journalism', in Francis O'Gorman (ed.), *The Cambridge Companion to Victorian Culture* (Cambridge, 2010), pp. 177–94

Rude, John, 'Against Innovation? Custom and Resistance in the Workplace, 1700–1850', in Tim Harris (ed.), *Popular Culture in England, c.1500–1850* (Basingstoke, 1995), pp. 168–88

Ryan, Mary, *Women in Public: Between Banners and Ballots, 1825–1880* (Baltimore, Md., 1990)

Rymer, J. M., *Varney the Vampyre; or The Feast of Blood* (London, 2010)

Saler, Michael, '"Clap if You Believe in Sherlock Holmes": Mass Culture and the Re-enchantment of Modernity, c.1890-1940', *The Historical Journal*, vol. 46 (2003), pp. 599–622

——, 'Modernity and Enchantment: A Historiographic Review', *American History Review*, vol. 111 (2006), pp. 692–716

Samuel, Raphael, 'Reading the Signs', *History Workshop Journal*, vol. 32 (1991), pp. 88–109

Sayer, Karen, *Women of the Fields: Representations of Rural Women in the Nineteenth Century* (Manchester, 1995)

Scribner, Bob, 'Is a History of Popular Culture Possible?', *History of European Ideas*, vol. 10 (1989), pp. 175–91

Shankman, Paul, 'The Thick and Thin: On the Interpretive Theoretical Program of Clifford Geertz', *Current Anthropology*, vol. 25 (1984), pp. 261–79

Sharpe, James, *Dick Turpin: The Myth of the English Highwayman* (London, 2005)

——, 'History from Below', in Peter Burke (ed.), *New Perspectives on Historical Writing* (Cambridge, 1991)

Sheeran, George, and Yanina Sheeran, 'Discourses in Local History', *Rethinking History*, vol. 2 (1998), pp. 65–85

Shoemaker, Robert, 'Male Honour', *Social History*, vol. 26 (2001), pp. 190–208

Shore, Heather, 'Mean Streets: Criminality, Immorality and the Street in Early Nineteenth-Century London', in Tim Hitchcock and Heather Shore (eds), *The Streets of London: From the Great Fire to the Great Stink* (London, 2003), pp. 151–64

Siikala, Anna-Leena, 'Reproducing Social Worlds: The Practice and Ideology of Oral Legends', in Terry Gunnell (ed.), *Legends and Landscape* (Reykjavik, 2008), pp. 39–67

Silver, Carole G., *Strange and Secret Peoples: Fairies and Victorian Consciousness* (Oxford, 2000)

Silverstone, Roger (ed.), *Visions of Suburbia* (London, 1997)

Simmel, Georg, 'The Metropolis and Mental Life', in David Frisby and Mike Featherstone (eds), *Simmel on Culture* (London, 1997), pp. 174–85

——, 'The Stranger', in C. Jenks (ed.), *Urban Culture: Critical Concepts in Literary and Cultural Studies*, vol. 3 (London, 2004), pp. 73–7

Simms, Norman, 'Ned Ludd's Mummer's Play', *Folklore*, vol. 89 (1978), pp. 166–78

Simpson, Jacqueline, 'A Ghostly View of England's Past', in Terry Gunnell (ed.), *Legends and Landscape* (Reykjavik, 2008), pp. 25–38

——, 'The Local Legend: A Product of Popular Culture', *Rural History*, vol. 2 (1991), pp. 25–35

——, 'Research Note: "Spring-Heeled Jack"', *FoafTale News*, no. 48 (Jan. 2001)

——, and Steve Roud, *A Dictionary of English Folklore* (Oxford, 2000)

Sindall, Rob, *Street Violence in the Nineteenth Century: Moral Panic or Real Danger?* (Leicester, 1990)

Smajic, Srdjan, *Ghost-Seers, Detectives, and Spiritualists: Theories of Vision in Victorian Literature and Science* (Cambridge, 2010)

Smith, Alan W., 'Jack Valentine in Norfolk', *FLS News*, no. 44 (November 2004), p. 8

Smith, Andrew, *The Ghost Story 1840–1920: A Cultural History* (Manchester, 2010)

——, *Victorian Demons: Medicine, Masculinity and the Gothic at the Fin-de-Siecle* (Manchester, 2004)

Smith, Greg T., 'Violent Crime and the Public Weal in England, 1700-1900', in Richard McMahon (ed.), *Crime, Law and Popular Culture in Europe, 1500-1900* (Cullompton, 2008), pp. 190–218

Spierenburg, P. (ed.), *Men and Violence: Gender, Honor, and Rituals in Modern Europe and America* ([Columbus, Oh.], 1998)

Spraggs, Gillian, *Outlaws and Highwaymen: The Cult of the Robber in England from the Middle Ages to the Nineteenth Century* (London, 2001)

Springhall, John, *Youth, Popular Culture and Moral Panics: Penny Gaffs to Gangsta-Rap, 1830-1996* (Basingstoke, 1998)

Stanko, Elizabeth A., *Everyday Violence: How Women and Men Experience Sexual and Physical Danger* (London, 1990)

Statt, Daniel, 'The Case of the Mohocks: Rake Violence in Augustan London', *Victorian Studies*, vol. 20 (1995), pp. 179–99

Steinberg, Marc W., 'The Riding of the Black Lad and other Working-Class Ritualistic Actions: Towards a Spatialized and Gendered Analysis of Nineteenth-Century Repertoires', in Michael P. Hanagan, Leslie Page Moch and Wayne Te Brake (eds), *Challenging Authority: The Historical Study of Contentious Politics* (Minneapolis, Minn., 1998), pp. 17–35

Stephens, John Russell, *The Censorship of English Drama, 1824–1901* (Cambridge, 1980)

Stephens, Walter, *Demon Lovers: Witchcraft, Sex and the Crisis of Belief* (Chicago, Ill., 2003)

Stevenson, Kim, "'Ingenuities of the Female Mind': Legal and Public Perceptions of Sexual Violence in Victorian England, 1850–1890', in Shani D'Cruze (ed.), *Everyday Violence in Britain, 1850-1950* (Harlow, 2000), pp. 89–103

Stevenson, Robert Louis, *Dr Jekyll and Mr Hyde and Weir of Hermiston* (Oxford, 1990)

Storch, Robert D., 'The Plague of Blue Locusts: Police Reform and Popular Disturbances in Northern England, 1840–1857', in Mike Fitzgerald, Gregor McLennan and Jennie Pawson (eds), *Crime and Society: Readings in History and Theory* (London, 1980), pp. 71–94

——, *Popular Culture and Custom in Nineteenth-Century England* (London, 1982)

Storey, John, *Inventing Popular Culture: From Folklore to Globalization* (Oxford, 2003)

Sumpter, Caroline, *The Victorian Press and the Fairy Tale* (Basingstoke, 2008)

Sutherland, Jonathan, *Ghosts of London* (Derby, 2002)

Sweet, Rosemary, *The English Town, 1680–1840: Government, Society and Culture* (Harlow, 1999)

Tangherlini, Timothy R., *Interpreting Legend: Danish Storytellers and Their Repertoires* (New York, 1994)

Taylor, David, *Crime, Policing and Punishment, 1750–1914* (Basingstoke, 1998)

Taylor, George, *Players and Performances in the Victorian Theatre* (Manchester, 1989)

Tester, Keith (ed.), *The Flâneur* (London, 1994)

Thomas, Keith, *Religion and the Decline of Magic* (London, 1997)

Thompson, E. P., *The Making of the English Working Class* (London, 1991)

——, *Customs in Common: Studies in Traditional Popular Culture* (New York, 1993)

Thompson, Stith, *The Folktale* (New York, 1951)

Thomson, James, *The City of Dreadful Night* (Edinburgh, 1993)

Tilly, Charles, *Popular Contention in Great Britain, 1758–1834* (Cambridge, Mass., 1995)

Tonkiss, Fran, *Space, the City and Social Theory* (Cambridge, 2005)

Tromp, Marlene (ed.), *Victorian Freaks: The Social Context of Freakery in Britain*, 2nd edn (Athens, Oh., 2008)

Tropp, Martin, *Images of Fear: How Horror Stories Helped Shape Modern Culture 1818–1918* (Jefferson, NC, 1990)

Turner, E. S., *Boys Will Be Boys* (London, 1975)

Underdown, David, "'But the Shows of their Street": Civic Pageantry and Charivari in a Somerset Town, 1607', *Journal of British Studies*, vol. 50 (2011), pp. 4–23

Vandermeer, Jeff, and S. J. Chambers, *The Steampunk Bible* (New York, 2011)

Vernon, James, *Politics and the People: A Study in English Political Culture, 1815–1867* (Cambridge, 2009)

Vidler, Anthony, *The Architectural Uncanny: Essays in the Modern Unhomely* (Cambridge, Mass., 1992)

Vincent, David, *Bread, Knowledge and Freedom: A Study of Nineteenth-Century Working Class Autobiography* (London, 1981)

——, *Literacy and Popular Culture: England 1750–1914* (Cambridge, 1989)

Vyner, J., 'The Mystery of Springheel Jack', *Flying Saucer Review*, vol. 7, no. 3, (May 1961), pp. 3–6

Wahrman, Dror, *Imagining the Middle Class* (Cambridge, 1995)

Walkowitz, Judith, 'Narratives of Sexual Danger', in Alexandra Warwick and Martin Willis (eds), *Jack the Ripper: Media, Culture, History* (Manchester, 2007), pp. 179–96

——, *City of Dreadful Delight: Narratives of Sexual Danger in Late-Victorian London* (London, 1992)

Warner, Marina, *Fantastic Metamorphosis, Other Worlds* (Oxford, 2002)

——, *No Go the Bogeyman: Scaring, Lulling and Making Mock* (London, 2000)

Warwick, Alexandra, 'Vampires and Empire: Fear and Fictions of the 1890s', in Sally Ledger and Scott McCracken (eds), *Cultural Politics at the Fin de Siècle* (Cambridge, 1995), pp. 202-20

——, and Martin Willis (eds), *Jack the Ripper: Media, Culture, History* (Manchester, 2007)

Wasson, Sara, *Urban Gothic of the Second World War: Dark London* (Basingstoke, 2010)

Waters, Ronald K.G., 'Signs of the Times: Clifford Geertz and Historians', *Social Research*, vol. 47 (1980), pp. 537–56

Wells, Roger, 'English Society and Revolutionary Politics in the 1790s: The case for Insurrection', in Mark Philp (ed.), *The French Revolution and British Popular Politics* (Cambridge, 2004), pp. 198–226

Westwood, Jennifer, and Jacqueline Simpson, *The Lore of the Land: A Guide to England's Legends from Spring-Heeled Jack to the Witches of Warboys* (London, 2006)

Whittington-Egan, Richard, *Liverpool Colonnade* (Manchester, 1976)

Wiener, Martin J., 'Alice Arden to Bill Sykes: Changing Nightmares of Intimate Violence in England, 1558-1869', *Journal of British Studies*, vol. 40 (2001), pp. 184–212

——, *Men of Blood: Violence, Manliness and Criminal Justice in Victorian England* (Cambridge, 2004)

——, *Reconstructing the Criminal: Culture, Law, and Policy in England, 1830–1914* (Cambridge, 1990)

Wiese Forbes, Amy, *The Satiric Decade: Satire and the Rise of Republican Political Culture in France 1830–1840* (Lanham, Md., 2010)

Williams, David, *Deformed Discourse: The Function of the Monster in Mediaeval Thought and Literature* (Exeter, 1999)

Williams, Kevin, *Get Me a Murder a Day! A History of Media and Communication in Britain*, rev. edn (London, 2010)

Williams, Raymond, *The Country and the City* (New York, 1975)

——, *Culture and Society 1780–1950* (London, 1958)

——, *Key Words: A Vocabulary of Culture and Society* (London, 1988)

Williams, S. C., *Religious Belief and Popular Culture in Southwark, c.1880–1939* (Oxford, 1999)

Williams, Wes, *Monsters and Their Meanings in Early Modern Culture: Mighty Magic* (Oxford, 2011)

Willis, Deborah, *Malevolent Nurture: Witch-Hunting and Maternal Power in Early Modern England* (Ithaca, NY, 1995)

Wilson, Ben, *The Making of Victorian Values: Decency and Dissent in Britain, 1789–1837* (London, 2007)

Wilson, Dudley, *Signs and Portents: Monstrous Births from the Middle Ages to the Enlightenment* (London, 1993)

Wilson, Kathleen, 'Citizenship, Empire, and Modernity in the English Provinces, c.1720–1790', *Eighteenth-Century Studies*, vol. 29 (1995), pp. 69–96

Wilson, Stephen, 'Popular Culture? What do you Mean?', *History of European Ideas*, vol. 11 (1989), pp. 515–19

Winter, James, *London's Teeming Streets 1830–1914* (London, 1993)

Wirth, Louis, 'Urbanism as a Way of Life', in Philip Kasinitz (ed.), *Metropolis: Centre and Symbol of Our Time* (Basingstoke, 1995), pp. 58–82

Wolffe, J. 'Judging the Nation: Early Nineteenth-Century British Evangelicals and Divine Retribution', in Kate Cooper and Jeremy Gregory (eds), *Studies in Church History 40: Retribution, Repentance, and Reconciliation* (Woodbridge, 2004), pp. 292–6

Wolfreys, Julian, *Writing London*, vol. 2, *Materiality, Memory, Spectrality* (Basingstoke, 2004)

Wood, Andy, 'The Pedlar of Swaffham, the Fenland Giant and the Sardinian Communist: Usable Pasts and the Politics of Folklore in England, c.1600–1830', in Fiona Williamson (ed.), *Locating Agency: Space, Power and Popular Politics* (Newcastle, 2010), pp. 161–92

——, *The Politics of Social Conflict: The Peak Country, 1520–1770* (Cambridge, 1999)

Wood, Marcus, *Radical Satire and Print Culture, 1790–1822* (Oxford, 1994)

Wright, Thomas, *Some Habits and Customs of the Working Classes* (New York, 1967)

Yeo, Eileen, and Stephen Yeo (eds), *Popular Culture and Class Conflict, 1590–1914: Explorations in the History of Labour and Leisure* (Brighton, 1981)

Zipes, Jack, *Victorian Fairy Tales: The Revolt of the Fairies and Elves* (London, 1989)

Websites

www.bbc.co.uk/legacies/myths_legends/england/black_country/article_2.shtml

www.oldbaileyonline.org/

www.surreycomet.co.uk

Index